PC Overclocking, Optimization, & Tuning

Second Edition

V. Rudometov
E. Rudometov

D1445359

PC: Overclocking, Optimization,
& Tuning,
Second Edition

Copyright (c) 2002 by A-LIST, LLC

A-LIST, LLC
295 East Swedesford Rd.
PMB #285
Wayne, PA 19087
702-977-5377 (FAX)
mail@alistpublishing.com
http://www.alistpublishing.com

This book is printed on acid-free paper.

PC: Overclocking, Optimization, & Tuning, Second Edition
By V. Rudometov, E. Rudometov
    ISBN: 1-931769-05-2

Printed in the United States of America

02 03 7 6 5 4 3 2 1

A-LIST, LLC titles are distributed by Independent Publishers Group and are available for site license or bulk purchase by institutions, user groups, corporations, etc.

Book Editor: Jessica Mroz

CONTENTS

Chapter 1

Introduction

Traditionally, the performance of a computer is usually estimated by its processor. It is generally accepted that it is exactly this unquestionably important element that determines the basic functional capabilities, class, price, and prestige of a modern PC. The 8086, 8088, 286, 386, 486, Pentium, Pentium Pro, Pentium MMX, Pentium II, Celeron, and Pentium III processors are the basic landmarks that separate one generation of computers from another. Processors from AMD, VIA (Cyrix), IBM, and certain other manufacturers also have a huge influence on the development of the computer industry. Experienced users, however, are aware of the fact that other PC components are of no less importance and cannot be neglected. These components include the hard drives, the motherboard and its chipset, the 2D/3D video adapter, monitor, the CD-ROM and DVD-ROM drives, the sound card, the high-performance network adapter for computers participating in a local area network (LAN), and the high-speed modem for computers connected to the Internet. This list could go on and on. Its size depends on the tasks you are going to be solving using the PC, which will determine the computer's requirements for functioning and its technical characteristics. At the same time, of course, performance remains one of the most important parameters.

Both the performance and the functional capabilities of the PC depend to a great extent on the parameters of its individual components, their compatibility, and their coordination. Selecting a computer according to the technical specification is not sufficient. If you really want to get the most out of your PC, you'll need to optimize its setup and configuration. Like any complex device, a modern computer requires proper maintenance and servicing. If these requirements are neglected, your modern, powerful, and expensive computer will be inferior to its optimally tuned predecessors, which by the way are much less expensive.

You should optimize your PC whenever you change the tasks it's intended to perform, and also after upgrading its hardware or software configuration. By specifying appropriate settings and running special utilities, it is possible to compensate (to a certain extent) for the natural degradation of electronic components due to their prolonged usage. To achieve a high level of performance, it is recommended that you update device drivers and BIOS code from time to time. Maintenance procedures, such as defragmentation and scanning the hard drive(s) for errors should be performed on a regular basis. If you neglect these operations, then, in a best-case scenario, this may slow down your system. In a worst-case scenario, this may result in the loss of data. You must also periodically check the latest news related to bug fixes, updates, and service packs released for operating systems and office programs. Compressing the hard drive using programs like DriveSpace or Compression Agent may significantly increase the drive space available to the user. What's more, in certain situations it might even speed up data access, and therefore increase the operating speed of most programs.

However, it's worth noting that even a very carefully optimized and tuned PC, which undergoes maintenance procedures on a regular basis, cannot always meet the ever-growing requirements. Sooner or later, every user will run into the problem of insufficient performance. When standard performance reserves have been completely used up due to the comprehensive optimization, you will have to take more radical steps. Some users solve the problem by buying a new computer, while others upgrade the existing one. Both solutions will cost money, often a very considerable sum. Notice that users often need to replace or upgrade even relatively new computers that are in good operating condition, bought only a year or two ago (or even less)!

You should, however, note that besides hardware and software optimization and upgrade, there is another method of prolonging the life cycle of obsolete computer equipment that is still in good operating condition. This method often gives new life to those computers that already cannot be called modern. This method is known as *overclocking*. The idea of this method is that certain elements and components of the computer can be forced to run at speeds faster than the ones they were rated to operate at. Generally, this increases the operating frequency of the overclocked equipment, thus increasing overall system performance. But, you should realize that this decreases system reliability. Also, you must be ready to accept the fact that overclocking shortens the operating life of the equipment. However, in many cases this is justifiable and does not represent much of a problem.

Indeed, due to the constant improvement of computer technology, the period of time which hardware components can be expediently used is constantly shrinking. As soon as modern, better-quality, and higher-performance components appear on the market, it becomes economically unreasonable to keep using their aged prototypes. And this happens in spite of advanced production technology, increased reliability, and prolonged trouble-free service life of the PC hardware. At present, the operating life of processors, video adapters, and hard drives is usually no more than 2—3 years. This is an average value. However, many users try to replace these generally serviceable components with newer and higher-performance ones even before it becomes really necessary. At the same time, modern hardware components have such a high reliability level that they are guaranteed to operate for more than 10 years. Nonetheless, newer, more advanced, and higher-performance devices generally appear on the market every few months. For this reason, you can allow a little bit of loss of reliability and reserve (for example, from 10 to 5 years), since the period that you'll actually be able to use these elements is relatively short and you really don't need your hardware to last for such a long time. There is always a small chance of system crashes and hang-ups even in a correctly overclocked computer. However, if overclocking was done correctly, a system crash is a rare event, and even if it happens, the results in most cases are not fatal. Of course, you shouldn't use overclocking modes for server components, or, for example, in systems that control mission-critical and potentially dangerous operations (like nuclear power plants, missile launching stations, etc.) or in situations where a life is at stake (operating rooms, etc.). Errors in such systems are not so harmless or allowable.

It should be emphasized that recently, overclocking has become popular even among those who have a completely new PC. Such users, with the aim of further increasing the performance of their system, often ask technical specialists to have overclocking modes set for their processors as soon as they purchase an absolutely new PC. More experienced users often perform the operation themselves at home, choosing the optimal mode while strictly controlling and thoroughly testing hardware components at every step of the overclocking procedure.

The user's natural desire to constantly improve the architecture of his or her computer is not the only reason that overclocking is now so popular. Rather, the main idea of overclocking is usually to save money. Indeed, this procedure, which is by the way applicable not only to processors, allows you to attain a relatively high performance for a relatively low price. The CPU performance gain can reach 20—30%. If you decide to use more extreme and therefore riskier modes, you can gain up to 50%, and possibly more. You can apply similar methods to increase the performance of other components, such as the RAM, the video adapter, and even the hard drive. Doing this immediately places the computer into a higher category. Often overclocked components that were at a lower performance level to start with can now compete with their more powerful and more expensive successors. What's also important is that this is done without spending practically any money. The money you save on the processor alone can be in the hundreds of dollars. And, the insignificant decrease of reliability and stability that comes along with overclocking can be minimized by taking a few measures and following certain recommendations.

Despite the main reason of overclocking computer components obviously is saving money, you really shouldn't look at this method of increasing your PC's performance from that angle alone. Relatively often, even the newest hardware components whose performance is already very high are used in overclocking modes as well. Doing this allows us to take advantage of the latent capabilities of PC components. Overclocking such components increases their performance and improves functional capabilities even further. So, regardless of the fact that the frequency of 500 MHz for processors with the traditional architecture was achieved relatively recently, and has already been, of course, surpassed, certain overclocking enthusiasts have been able to reach heights in the area of 1000 MHz with such processors. It's often the case that such actions are accompanied by corresponding measures that will also increase the performance of the other subsystems included in a modern computer.

The popularization of experience in overclocking elements affects the financial interests of the hardware manufacturers. They, for understandable reasons, do not want to lose any part of their profits. Besides, overclocking methods are also often used by the so-called remarkers, who intentionally change the marking on computer elements — processors or memory modules for example — and pass them off as products of a higher performance, and thus more expensive than they actually are. Some companies, generally smaller ones, go even further. They release devices — for instance video adapters, motherboards, or even entire computers — whose elements have already been overclocked, and, obviously, keep this a secret from the potential customer.

Taking into consideration the opportunity for forgery and in order to defend their commercial interests, most well known manufacturers have included various improvements in their products that inhibit fabrication of fake components and limit the performance-increasing possibilities that come from using overclocking modes.

Nonetheless, note that despite all the desperate efforts of certain processor manufacturers, who do their best to prevent their products from being overclocked, the popularity of overclocking is growing at a rapid rate. Overclocking is further promoted by the release of certain motherboards and chipsets, and even some software, intended to simplify experiments with overclocking. You can easily find a wide range of products on the computer market that are intended for cooling computer components. All this makes setting the appropriate modes, setting the parameters, and testing much simpler.

Not only enthusiastic individuals but also many serious companies have dedicated their efforts to the investigation of overclocking modes and the development of recommendations for their use. Sometimes, such investigations are performed even with support provided by hardware manufacturers. An example of cooperation in this field is the collaboration between Kryotech and AMD. As a result of their investigations, an AMD processor under experimental conditions of extreme overclocking was able to reach 1 GHz long before the release of processors rated to run at such a frequency.

This rather high interest that a number of computer companies seem to be taking in overclocking is relatively easily explained. These types of studies aid in improving the technology, enhancing the architecture, and increasing the performance of hardware components. Furthermore, these investigations serve as a source of statistics on errors and faults, which then allows the manufacturers to develop efficient and reliable hardware and software. After all, the ability of hardware components to retain stability and reliability in overclocking modes serves as an excellent promotion for their respective manufacturers. Certain manufacturers welcome this research, because they use the experience and technology gained from the leading firms that investigate overclocking problems in order to release high-performance hardware. Compaq, for example, offers a platform for high-performance servers based on the technology developed by Kryotech, which provided extreme cooling for AMD Athlon processors overclocked to frequencies 1.5—2 times higher than normal.

As the community of overclocking enthusiasts expands, the number of specialized Web sites related to overclocking problems grows accordingly. These sites are intended to make overclocking even more popular. Generally, materials published there discuss various aspects of the problems that may arise, and give corresponding recommendations.

The materials presented in this book provide an attempt to develop a systematic approach to the overclocking problem and to formulate general and specific recommendations on setting the overclocking parameters for the most important hardware components.

Chapter 2

BIOS Setup

ROM BIOS from, say, Award, has an embedded setup program, which allows you to change the basic configuration of the system. This information is permanently stored in CMOS RAM, so its contents will not be lost after turning the PC off. You can enter the Setup mode by pressing a certain key or combination of keys when you restart or reboot the computer. Usually the <Delete> key is used for this purpose.

The system configuration is modified by setting the values of the appropriate parameters in BIOS Setup and then saving them in CMOS RAM. This procedure is known as *BIOS Setup*.

Most often, the overall performance of the entire computer system depends on the BIOS settings. In many cases, changing parameters in BIOS Setup provides a real possibility of significant improvement of the computer performance. This is particularly true for the parameters that deal with memory.

Generally, default settings ensure the stable operation of the entire system. However, these settings do not guarantee maximum performance. To achieve this, you'll need to try to select settings at which the computer will function at maximum performance and at the same time remain stable. In order to attain maximum performance by means of BIOS Setup, it is necessary to experiment with the settings that define time delays when accessing RAM (**BIOS Memory Timing** menu), internal, and/or external cache memory. It's also advisable to give some attention to the parameters that determine the modes of the video adapter and hard drive.

Managing RAM

Choosing the parameters, you can almost always assume that the less delay, the better. At the same time, settings that are too low may lead to the unreliable operation of the memory, and thus make the whole system unstable. In such a case, simply load the default settings (**BIOS Setup Defaults** menu) and the system will return to its original state. By changing the parameters associated with memory time delays in BIOS Setup, it is impossible to harm the computer. If the system is not working correctly, or if it completely refuses to work, you can simply return to the original settings.

A more detailed explanation of each of the parameters can be found in the manual for the motherboard, or in the appropriate technical literature. Here, you'll find a few examples of how to adjust them with the aim of increasing the RAM operating frequency.

Most frequently, all of the necessary parameters that control the work of the RAM are found in the BIOS Setup menu called **Advanced Chipset Setup.** The items on this menu are listed below. You can usually change the values using $<+>$ and $<->$ or $<$PgUp$>$ and $<$PgDn$>$ keys. **Enabled/Disabled** refers to enabling or disabling the corresponding option.

❏ **Auto Configuration**

All parameters will be set automatically.

In order to be able to set the parameters manually, it is recommended that you disable this option. If this option is enabled, most parameters will be set automatically.

❏ **DRAM Read Timing**

The number of cycles while accessing the memory.

This parameter can take on the values x111, x222, x333, and x444. The less the number of cycles, the better. To achieve maximum performance, you must assign this parameter the lowest possible value. However, make sure that the system is stable at the modified settings. The possible (and recommended) values are: EDO RAM — x222 and x333, FPM RAM — x333 and x444, SDRAM — x111 and x222.

❏ **DRAM Write Timing**

It is recommended that you change this parameter in a way similar to the one used to modify the previous one.

❏ **RAS to CAS Delay**

Try to set the lowest possible value for this parameter. Notice, however, that not every RAM module will be able to work with the lowest setting. Because of this, it is recommended to test your system after changing this setting.

❏ **DRAM Leadoff Timing**

The value of this parameter depends not only on the type of the memory installed in your system, but also on the chipset at the motherboard. For read operations, Intel Triton FX chipset normally does not allow you to set DRAM timing cycles less than 7-x-x-x, while TX or HX chipsets require that this value be no less than 5-x-x-x. For write operations, these parameters should be set to the values no less than 5-x-x-x (FX) and 4-x-x-x (TX and HX).

At a value of 5, the system will be able to work if using 50 nsec EDO RAM or 10 nsec SDRAM. As always, it's worth trying to set the lowest possible value.

❑ **Turbo Lead Leadoff**

❑ **Turbo Read Pipelining**

❑ **Speculative Lead Off**

You should try to enable these parameters, and then test the system's usability and performance. Certain types of RAM can produce a significant growth in performance if these parameters are turned on.

Cache Memory

The parameters that control the work of the cache memory are generally found in the BIOS Setup menu under **BIOS Features Setup**, the items in which are explained in more detail below. Usually you can modify the values using the <+> and <–> or the <PgUp> and <PgDn> keys. **Enabled/Disabled** will enable or disable the option.

❑ **CPU Internal Cache/CPU External Cache**

Internal/external CPU cache. This parameter allows the external/internal processor cache to work (or disables it). Disabling CPU Internal Cache/CPU External Cache will significantly slow down the whole system. However, this may be necessary if you are using any legacy hardware or software.

❑ **CPU L 1 Cache /CPU L 2 Cache**

The processor cache of the first/second level. This parameter enables or disables usage of the first/second level CPU cache for the following processors: Pentium Pro, Pentium II, Pentium III, Celeron, AMD-K6-III, and so on. Disabling this option will slow down your system significantly. However, this may be necessary if you are using legacy adapters or legacy software.

❑ **CPU L 2 Cache ECC Checking**

Uses ECC for the 2nd level cache memory. This parameter enables or disables the level 2 cache memory ECC for those processors built on the architecture using it.

Video Subsystem and Hard Drive

The parameters that control the functioning of the video subsystem, the hard drive, and the system BIOS are usually located in the BIOS Setup menu under **BIOS Features Setup** and **Chipset Features Setup,** whose items are described below. Usually you can modify the values using the <+> and <–> or the <PgUp> and <PgDn> keys. **Enabled/Disabled** will enable or disable the option.

❏ **Video BIOS Shadow**

A "shadow" copy of the video ROM.

This parameter enables or disables creation of a "shadow" copy of the video BIOS in the RAM. When this setting is enabled, the contents of video BIOS will be copied into the RAM, and RAM will actually be used when formally accessing video BIOS. This allows a gain in performance, because working with RAM is obviously much faster than working with ROM.

❏ **Video BIOS Cacheable**

This parameter enables or disables caching the video BIOS. Caching increases the speed of the video output.

❏ **System BIOS Shadow**

This parameter enables or disables creation of a copy of the System BIOS in the RAM. When enabled, a copy of the system BIOS will be created in RAM, and all actual work will be done using this copy (while formally working with the system BIOS). The performance increase is due to the fact that RAM access is much faster than ROM access.

❏ **System BIOS cacheable**

This parameter enables or disables caching the system BIOS. Caching increases the speed at which the system BIOS commands are executed.

❏ **AGB Aperture Size (MB)**

This parameter specifies the size of RAM allocated to AGP video adapters. The parameter ranges from 4 to 256 MB. Memory is allocated dynamically, within the limits set by the values specified. The remaining part of the allocated memory can be used by the operating system.

❏ **AGP/CLK**

This parameter sets the AGP clock frequency, which depends on the divider value and operative frequence of the CPU bus (FSB). When setting this parameter, you'll have two options: 1 (1/1, i.e., AGP clock frequency is the same as CPU clock) or 2/3 (i. e., AGP is at 2/3 of the CPU external clock).

❏ **IDE HDD Block Mode**

Enabling this option will set a block data transfer mode for the hard drive, which will transfer data in blocks. This increases the speed of data exchange and, accordingly, boosts the performance of the disk subsystem.

Chapter 3

Optimizing Hard Drives

B oth the functional capabilities and the performance of any computer are to a large extent determined by the hard drives installed in the system. Working productivity depends not only on the technical parameters of the hard disks, but also on their functional modes and data organization.

Increasing the Speed

Ordering the files is an effective method of increasing the speed of the hard drive. As you use your computer, you are constantly saving, deleting, and editing files, thus changing their size. The repetition of these actions causes a good number of files to become fragmented and scattered arbitrarily around the disk. This process of file fragmentation takes place because new files that you save on the hard drive are physically stored using the free space created by the deletion of other files. Also, the files often become fragmented as you edit them, thus increasing their size. While accessing files that are stored in fragments throughout the hard drive, the read/write head of the hard drive must mechanically shift and reposition itself many times. This takes up a significantly longer amount of time than finding and reading an unfragmented (contiguous) file.

The operation of the hard drive is often complicated by electronic or mechanical malfunctions, or by errors in the file system. As a result, damaged and lost areas appear, known as *bad clusters* and *lost clusters*. The presence of such areas leads to the degradation of the hard drive performance, decreases the amount of available space, and degrades the storage reliability. Bad clusters can appear as a result of a mechanic impact on the physical surface of the hard drive (such as vibrations, banging, etc.) or can be caused by certain viruses. Lost clusters generally develop as a result of errors caused by improper opening and closing files. They can be caused by hardware malfunctions or by errors and bugs in the programs or the operating systems (and in complex systems there are always errors), by incorrectly exiting a program, by turning the power supply off without closing the operating system, and so on. Sometimes you'll be able to get rid of bad clusters by reformatting the hard drive (logical drive). Fighting lost clusters and other errors in the file system can be done with the help of special programs such as ScanDisk, which is included in, for example, Windows 95, Windows 98, and Windows 2000.

Running ScanDisk under Windows 95 is illustrated in Figs. 3.1 and 3.2, which show fragments of the screen.

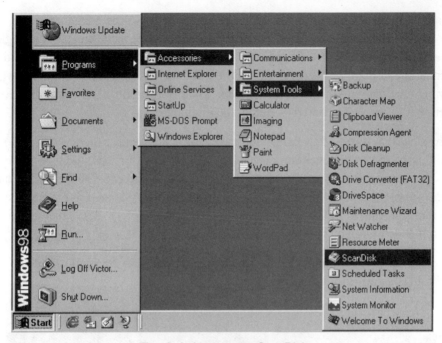

Fig. 3.1. How to run ScanDisk

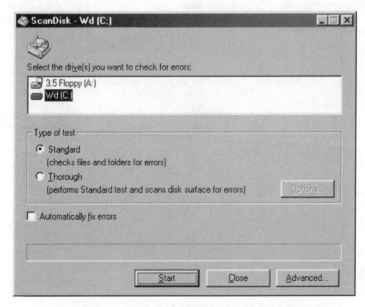

Fig. 3.2. A dialog box in the ScanDisk program

It's advised that you occasionally run the scan not only in the **Standard** mode, but also in the **Thorough** mode, which tests the entire accessible area of the logical drive. This gives you the opportunity to perform a more thorough scan and to exclude the use of problem areas of the hard drive that don't show up when running the scan in the **Standard** mode. To ensure control of the scan, avoid running it in the **Correct Errors Automatically** mode.

Increasing the speed at which fragmented files are read can be done after a preliminary disk defragmentation. It's advised to run this operation periodically with the help of special software such as *defrag.exe* in the MS-DOS 6.xx package, or *speedisk.exe* in Norton Utilities. In Windows 9x systems there is a special program for this — Disk Defragmenter. Note that before defragmentation it's recommended that you run ScanDisk.

The procedure of running Disk Defragmenter in Windows 95 is illustrated by the screenshots shown in Figs. 3.3—3.6.

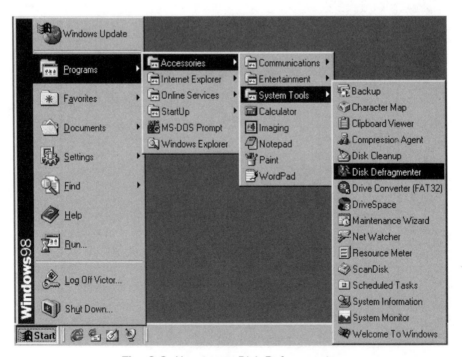

Fig. 3.3. How to run Disk Defragmenter

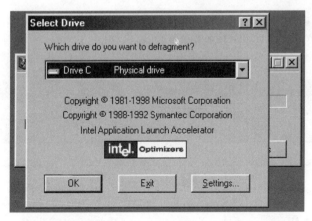

Fig. 3.4. Choosing the logical drive to defragment

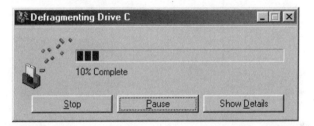

Fig. 3.5. The defragmentation process of the chosen disk

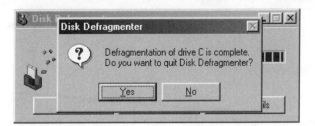

Fig. 3.6. Dialog box upon completion of defragmentation

Windows NT and Windows 2000 also have built-in programs for scanning hard disks for errors, repairing the errors found in the course of scanning, and defragmenting.

To start the built-in Windows NT/2000/XP tool for scanning disks, proceed as follows:

1. Open the My Computer folder.

2. Right-click the disk you are going to scan for errors and select the **Properties** command from the right-click menu (Fig. 3.7).

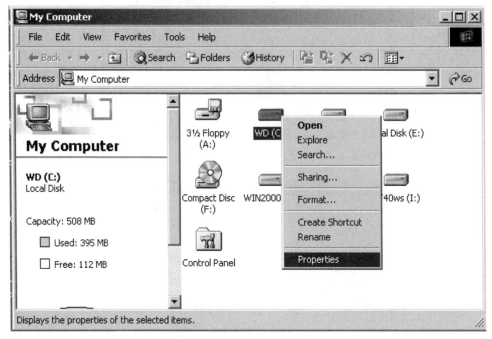

Fig. 3.7. Selecting the **Properties** command from the right-click menu

3. The **Properties** window will open. Go to the **Tools** tab (Fig. 3.8).

4. To scan disk immediately, click the **Check Now** button.

5. A dialog will open (Figs. 3.9 and 3.10). To start the program, click the **Start** button. If necessary, set the **Scan for and attempt recovery of bad sectors** checkbox. The program will then make an attempt to recover bad sectors.

Note that the problem of fragmentation is characteristic not only for Windows 9.*x*, but also for Windows NT 4.0 and Windows 2000. There is a generally accepted opinion, according to which the NTFS file system is implemented in such a way that files stored on NTFS disks become fragmented almost never. However, the fragmentation problem exists even for NTFS, although it is not as pressing when compared to the similar problems with FAT16 and FAT32.

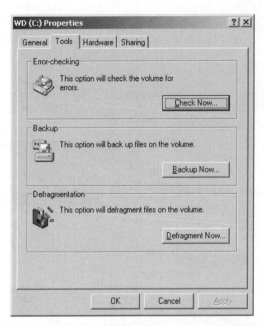

Fig. 3.8. To check the selected disk for errors, click the **Check Now** button

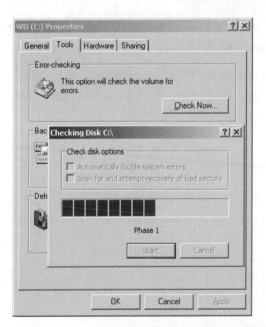

Fig. 3.9. Disk scanning in progress (Windows 2000)

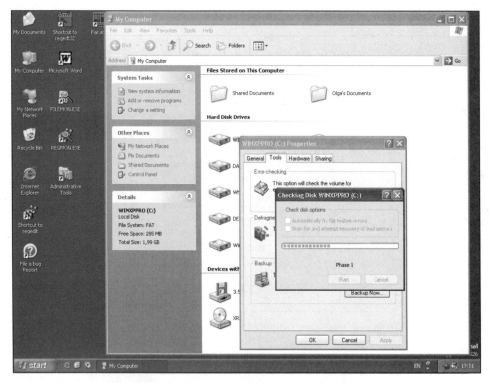

Fig. 3.10. Disk scanning in progress (Windows XP)

Unfortunately, Windows NT 4.0 has no built-in defragmentation utility. Therefore, Windows NT 4.0 users must run third party defragmentation utilities developed specially for this operating system. The most popular program of this type is Norton Speed Disk utility. For example, Norton Speed Disk v. 5.1 is suitable for defragmenting NTFS-formatted drives. An example illustrating the use of this program is presented in Fig. 3.11. The following advantages are characteristic for this program:

❑ MFT optimization

❑ The capability of placing any file at the start or at the end of a *(or* the *if this is only done with one partition)* partition; the capability to place any file after all other files

❑ The capability of folder and swap file defragmentation (for NTFS drives only)

❑ Scheduling functionality

❑ Simultaneous defragmentation of several partition

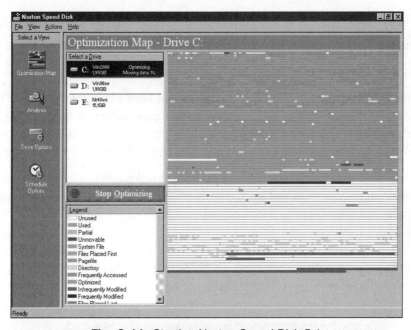

Fig. 3.11. Starting Norton Speed Disk 5.1

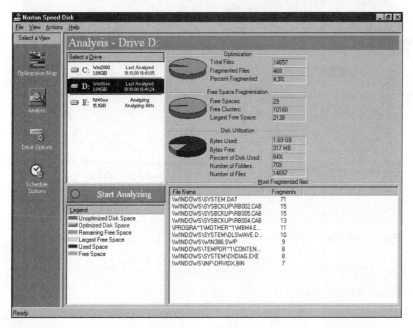

Fig. 3.12. Data on the fragmentation provided by Norton Speed Disk 5.1

❑ Disk diagnostics and error correction using the built-in error-checking tool

❑ Detailed reports on disk fragmentation and on the defragmentation results

❑ Fragmentation analysis (Fig. 3.12)

It should be noted that Norton Speed Disk is not the only defragmentation utility developed for Windows NT. There are other defragmentation tools on the software market, specially developed for Windows NT and Windows 2000. These include such programs as Diskeeper, O&O Defrag (Fig. 3.13), Contig, PerfectDisk, etc.

Windows 2000 and Windows XP, in contrast to Windows NT, have a built-in defragmentation utility created on the basis of the well-known Diskeeper program. This utility has user-friendly interface and characteristics similar to that of Norton Speed Disk. However, the Diskeeper utility uses API calls and this can't be considered an optimum solution, especially for an NTFS file system. There is a generally accepted point of view, which holds that the Norton Speed Disk utility, based on different principles, is more efficient and reliable.

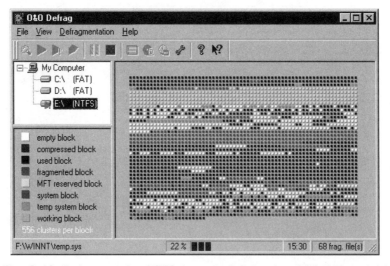

Fig. 3.13. Defragmenting NTFS-formatted disk using O&O Defrag 1.21

Fig. 3.14 shows the procedure of starting the Windows 2000 built-in defragmentation tool.

Fig. 3.15 illustrates the procedure of starting the Windows XP built-in defragmentation tool.

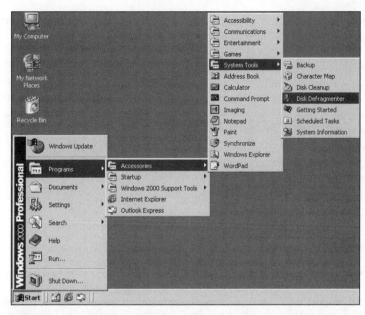

Fig. 3.14. Starting the Windows 2000 built-in defragmentation utility

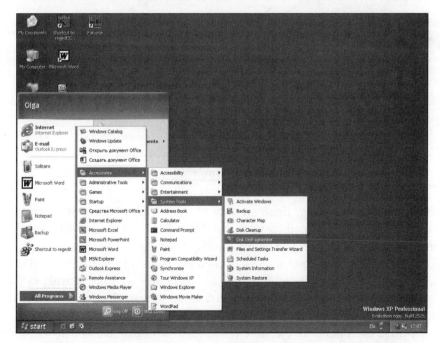

Fig. 3.15. Starting the Windows XP built-in defragmentation utility

Examples illustrating the use of the Windows 2000 built-in defragmentation utility are presented in Figs. 3.16—3.18.

An example illustrating the use of the Windows XP built-in defragmentation utility is presented in Fig. 3.19.

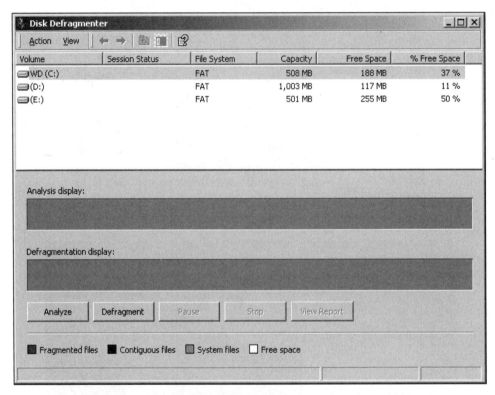

Fig. 3.16. The **Disk Defragmenter** window (Windows 2000)

Besides file defragmentation, there are other ways of speeding up your hard drives by taking their working principles into consideration. For instance, file access time depends on the file physical location on the hard disk. The files to which you would like to provide the fastest access should be placed at the starting cylinders of the hard disk. The further away programs and data are from the starting cylinders, the longer it will take to access them (3 to 5 times longer). You can achieve this if you load the files to the hard disk in a predefined order. The first files loaded onto the hard drive are placed at the start of the data-storage area, which will provide the fastest access time.

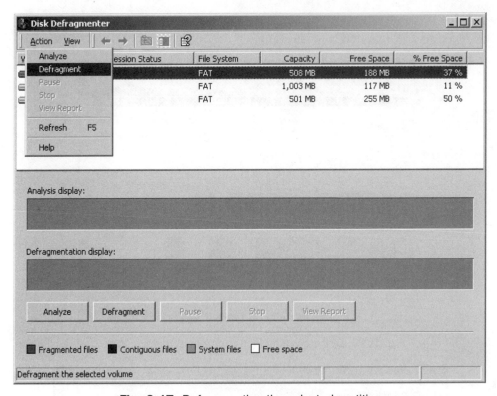

Fig. 3.17. Defragmenting the selected partition

Sometimes, it is possible to improve the computer performance by means of regrouping certain files, which should speed up the hard drive. To rearrange the files on a hard drive already filled with data, you'll need special utilities. For example, you can rearrange MS-DOS/Windows 3.*xx* files using the speedisk.exe defragmentation utility included with Norton Utilities. To do so, launch this program, choose the commands **Directory Order**, **File Sort**, and **Files to Place First** from the **Configure** menu, and set the necessary parameters. Besides file defragmentation, these settings will rearrange the files stored on the disk, thus providing a faster access time for the most frequently accessed files.

Newer hard drives use different ways of hardware/software management that guarantee high-speed reading and writing of data. This is maintained by the appropriate hardware/software facilities of the computer, including software and hardware caching methods, block transfer mode, etc. Generally, you set the appropriate options using BIOS Setup. There are also several software tools available that can accomplish similar tasks. Often a modern operating system will be endowed with these built-in capabilities.

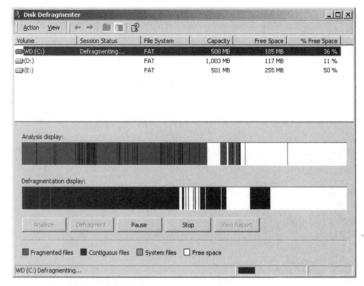

Fig. 3.18. Defragmentation in progress (Windows 2000)

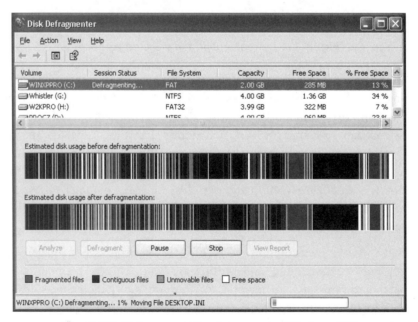

Fig. 3.19. Defragmentation in progress (Windows XP)

Hard drive manufacturers are constantly improving the construction and technical parameters of their products. Besides development of new models, they continue to provide support for the older ones. Web sites of the largest hard drive manufacturers often provide *new drivers*, both for recently released models and for older ones. In most cases, a new driver will allow you to greatly increase the performance of your hard drive.

There are many software tools, such as accelerator programs, that you can use to increase your hard drive speed. As an example, take the Drive Rocket Date Accelerator v.1.14 program from Ontrack Computer Systems, Inc. This program is often used alongside Disk Manager (also from Ontrack) to manage, for instance, drives from the company Western Digital. Another example of an accelerator program is XStore Pro (busmaster drivers for Windows 9*x*, recommended by Chaintech) from HighPoint Technologies. Depending on the available RAM and system configuration, these tools may allow you to increase the hard disk performance up to 60% and the overall performance of the whole computer system up to 10% as opposed to using standard drivers from Intel/Microsoft. The XStore Pro software optimizes system performance by read ahead caching after seeking with large block sizes on the hard disk. To obtain best results it's recommended that you use it in computers with at least 64 MB RAM.

The functioning of a modern operating system is hard to imagine without such a thing as the virtual memory. The virtual memory allows you to simultaneously run more programs than the physical memory of the computer (the RAM) alone. However, the virtual memory consumes much more disk space, and swapping significantly slows down all the programs. Virtual memory was developed for computers with microprocessors of 80386 or higher, and is the space on the hard drive with which modern systems (from Windows 3.*xx* on) work. This space is used as if it were physical memory (RAM). It is able to function this way thanks to a special file, a swap file, to which information from the RAM is periodically moved (swapped). At the same time, consider the fact that read/write operations using the fastest possible hard drive are more than 10,000 times slower than the same operations using the slowest RAM. Therefore, increasing your RAM is the most effective way of lightening the workload of the hard drive and increasing the overall performance of the computer. This is because the frequency of accessing the virtual memory is diminished, which allows you to decrease the time delays required by the hard drive to process queries from application and system programs.

Increasing the hard disk performance (and also, if necessary, that of the CD-ROM and floppy disks) can be accomplished by introducing a procedure such as *program caching.* There are several tools providing this capability, including built-in programs supplied with MS DOS and Windows 9*x* or third-party tools (such as the ones from Norton Utilities).

Increasing Capacity

One of the ways of increasing the hard drive capacity is *selecting optimal cluster size.* All information stored on the hard drive is presented in the form of files. Disk space for storing these files, in turn, is allocated in so-called *clusters.* Clusters comprise a number of sectors of a predetermined size. The size of a cluster usually ranges from 2 to 32 KB. The size of each cluster depends on the disk partition size.

Every file, depending on its length, takes up one or more clusters. Even if the size of the file is less than that of the cluster, that file will nonetheless take up the entire cluster. For instance, when cluster size is 32 KB, a bat-file of a few dozen bytes will take up all 32 KB of disk space. We can estimate that, on average, every file takes up about half of its last cluster. The remainder of the cluster cannot be assigned for another file. Consequently, on the disk there will be a good number of clusters whose space is not fully used, which means wasted disk space (so-called slack space) and loss in capacity. This loss is approximately equal to the number of files on the disk, multiplied by half of the cluster size. For example, if you have 10,000 files on one disk, and a cluster size of 32 KB, you are wasting about 160 MB [10,000 × (32 KB/2) = 160 MB].

In the case of a logical drive that, for example, takes up all of the space of a Seagate 1.08 GB hard drive that has 1,030 MB of informational space with 20,000 files, the slack space comes to approximately 320 MB, or 31% of the hard drive's capacity. If, however, the cluster size were reduced to 16 KB, the slack space on that same drive with the same number of files would be reduced to 160 MB, which is only 16% of the hard drive's capacity. Partitioning the hard disk into several logical disks decreases both the cluster size and the slack space. This procedure will be explained later on.

The ScanDisk program included with Windows 9*x* displays all information on the logical drive (including number of files and folders, cluster size, logical drive capacity, etc.) after finishing the scan (Fig. 3.20).

Methods of improving disk efficiency by reducing wasted space are:

❑ *Archiving files.* Usually, the first candidates for archiving are large sets of rarely used files.

❑ *Partitioning the hard drive into logical drives* of smaller size.

❑ *Installing and using disk compression utilities:* Stacker, DriveSpace, and so on, which organize their own structure of virtual disks.

❑ *Migrating to other file systems,* such as HPFS/NTFS or FAT32, which organize disk space more efficiently than FAT16.

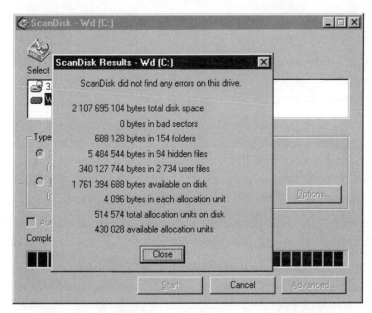

Fig. 3.20. Information appearing after running ScanDisk

The maximum number of clusters allowed for a disk is 65,536. Consequently, the larger the disk, the larger the cluster. Partitioning the hard drive into smaller logical sections — logical drives — can decrease the size of the clusters.

The dependence of cluster size on the size of the disk for the FAT16 file system (under DOS 4.0 and Windows 9*x*) is shown in the table presented below.

Cluster Sizes and the Corresponding Sizes of the Logical Disk (FAT16)

Cluster size	Size of logical disk
2 KB	0–128 MB
4 KB	128–256 MB
8 KB	256–512 MB

continues

Continued

Cluster size	Size of logical disk
16 KB	512 MB–1 GB
32 KB	1–2 GB

Thus, to improve the efficiency of using the hard disk space, it's advised that you divide the large hard disk into several logical disks.

Notice that contrary to popular opinion, partitioning the HDD does not change the performance of the disk subsystem. Rather, it allows you to reduce the slack space by reducing cluster size.

Another method of improving the efficiency of disk space usage is to compress the disk with a special program such as DriveSpace 3. This program implements a special method of data storage that reduces wasted disk space to practically zero. Using the disk compression program DriveSpace 3 allows you to significantly reduce the amount of wasted disk space related to cluster size.

Many users compress their disks with zero compression so as not to waste free space on the disk, and so that they won't notice the performance degradation.

For large disks it is possible to use *FAT32* — a newer file system — which operates using relatively small clusters. However, FAT32 is only supported by relatively new versions of Windows operating systems, namely, Windows 95 OSR2 and later versions.

Developed in 1981, FAT (File Allocation Table) became the first file system for PCs running MS-DOS and earlier Windows versions (Windows 3.1). FAT is very widespread and guarantees a high operating speed. However, up until recently, FAT has not been able to support disks larger than 2 GB.

At present, Windows 9x includes an improved file system of the FAT type called FAT 32, which supports disks up to 2 TB (1 TB $= 1024$ GB $= 1024 \times 1024$ MB $= 1024 \times 1024 \times 1024 =$ KB). Compared with the FAT16, FAT32 uses disk space more efficiently. This is due to the fact that FAT32 uses relatively small clusters.

The table presented below illustrates the dependence of the cluster size on the size of the logical disk formatted for a FAT32 file system (for a PC running Windows 9x).

Cluster Sizes and the Corresponding Sizes of the Logical Disk Sector (FAT32)

Cluster size	Size of logical disk	Operating system
0.5 KB	0–260 MB	Windows 95 OSR2 and newer
4 KB	260 MB–8 GB	Windows 95 OSR2 and newer
8 KB	8–16 GB	Windows 95 OSR2 and newer
16 KB	16–32 GB	Windows 95 OSR2 and newer
32 KB	32 GB–2 TB	Windows 95 OSR2 and newer

The file system FAT32 is completely compatible with all computers and all programs for earlier versions of the MS-DOS and Windows operating systems. However, some problems may arise while using certain disk utilities.

Older versions of disk defragmentation, compression, and management utilities won't work correctly with FAT32-formatted disks. Disk maintenance utilities included with Windows 95 OSR2, such as ScanDisk, Backup, and Disk Defragmenter can fully support disks with FAT32. However, you cannot compress disks with FAT32 using DriveSpace.

FAT32-formatted disks can't be accessed in an original Windows 95 version. Disks that use FAT32 are accessible in Windows 95 OSR2 (Windows 95 4.00.1111), Windows 98, Windows ME, and Windows 2000. However, in Windows OSR2 you can work with FAT32 in MS-DOS mode. Network access is also possible, and the remote computer need not support FAT 32.

Some programs may incorrectly determine the amount of free space on a FAT32 disk if they have not been specifically developed for the new file system. Older programs cannot correctly determine the size of disk partitions larger than 2 GB. Therefore, any information on free or used disk space or on the total disk capacity that is provided by such programs is misleading. Windows 95 version 4.00.950B includes new APIs, which allow you to deal with the given problem.

The task of determining whether the disk is FAT32-formatted is relatively simple. Double-click the **My Computer** icon, right-click the disk you wish to check, then select **Properties** from the menu. In the **General** dialog, the disk type will be displayed in the **Type** field.

After migration to the FAT32 file system, overall performance generally remains the same. However, in some cases you may notice slight performance degradation. When you boot Windows $9x$ in MS-DOS mode or in Windows safe mode, the disks formatted for use may work significantly slower. To solve this problem, you should run the disk-caching program SmartDrive when booting in MS-DOS mode.

To format an existing or newly added disk to use FAT32, use the Fdisk system utility.

This program is intended for creating and deleting partitions on the hard drive. There are two types of partitions — primary and extended. A primary partition is formatted for a particular file system and is assigned a drive letter. An extended partition, on the other hand, can be divided into one or more logical drives. In contrast to primary partitions, an extended partition is not assigned a drive letter. If the partition size is more than 512 MB, Fdisk will prompt you to use the large disk format. Therefore, in the new partitions with sizes exceeding 512 MB, FAT32 will be installed. If FAT32 is not used, the size of newly created partitions will be limited to 2 GB. In order to use all the available disk space of a large hard disk you'll need many logical disks. After the creation of these sections, the computer should be rebooted in order to format the new logical disks.

One of the disadvantages of IDE/EIDE hard drives is their limited capacity. The standard BIOS imposes a limit on the number of cylinders (1024) and sectors (63). Thus, the capacity of the hard disk is limited to 504 MB.

This problem is usually solved using special drivers released to go with each series of hard drives. Consider, for example, the Dynamic Drive Overlay v.6.03 driver released by Ontrack Computer Systems, Inc. This driver is installed using the Disk Manager program from the same company. These tools are used with Western Digital hard drives. Another example is the EZ-DRIVE V2.03S driver from Micro House International, often used with Seagate hard drives.

In order to standardize the installation of larger hard drives, a new method of translating the cylinder, head, and sector specifications of the drive into addresses that can be used by an enhanced BIOS was developed — LBA (Logical Block Addressing). The sector address is translated in the form of a linear, 28-digit sector number, which is transformed for the hard drive into the proper number of cylinders/heads/sectors. To work in LBA mode, it has to be supported by both the hard drive and its driver (or BIOS). When working through BIOS, the hard drive will have 63 sectors, the number of heads equal to a power of 2 — up to 256, and the necessary number of cylinders.

Chapter 4

Compressing the Hard Drive

*U*sage of the specialized tools intended for dynamic compression of the infor-mation stored on the PC's hard drives enables you to use the available disk space more efficiently. In many cases, this allows you to solve the problem of storage space shortage without purchasing additional equipment. The materials pro-vided in this chapter discuss various aspects of selecting and tuning compression tools used in popular operating systems from the Windows family.

Practically all PC users, even beginners, know very well that a PC's resources tend over time to become insufficient to be able to work comfortably, even in cases when they seem to be excessive at first. You are always short on resources! Sooner or later, everyone will encounter this problem.

Obviously, the level of initial redundancy of PC resources and the rate at which they become insufficient depend on initial conditions, such as the cost of pur-chasing the PC, the complexity level of the problems being solved, and the user's experience and competence. Despite the fact that financial investments in your desktop or mobile computer can be rather significant, sooner or later the time will come when you'll be short of resources. When this happens you'll have to face a rather difficult problem, one preventing you from working efficiently and com-fortably.

Certainly, the problem of resource shortage can be solved by upgrading your PC (which is a difficult task in itself) or even by purchasing a new PC. This, however, also involves significant expense, which most users can afford to do at the least a year or two after pervious purchases. The consequences of these new expenses are headaches and a bad mood caused by searching for the optimal solution under conditions of limited financial resources.

However, there is another way of solving the problem, one that may be rather at-tractive to experienced users. The problem of the processor's, memory subsystem's or video adapter's insufficient performance quite often can be solved by careful and cautious overclocking.

Despite the fact that overclocking is generally recognized as a very powerful and efficient method of improving the PC's performance, one must admit that this method is not universal, and can't solve all problems related to resource shortage. This is especially true when dealing with hard disks, which are the most important components of modern PCs. Unfortunately, overclocking won't help you to in-crease the hard disk space; you need to search for other ways of overcoming your disk space problem, at least until you purchase a newer hard drive, which, unfor-tunately, is more expensive.

Dynamic compression of information provides a common workaround for the problem of insufficient disk space. It allows you to increase the disk's free space significantly. What's more important, this can be done without additional financial expenditures on newer and more expensive devices. Furthermore, taking into account the throughput of the interfaces being used (which is normally rather low), information compression, while slightly increasing the processor workload, can in certain cases even increase the overall performance of the system. On the other hand, the built-in reliability mechanisms of the hard drives (implemented both at the software and hardware level), which are currently standard, provide a sufficient level of reliability and safety for storing information.

File Compression in Windows 95/98

The DriveSpace 3 Program

The hard drive can be compressed using a large variety of programs, such as Stacker, DriveSpace, DoubleSpace, etc. However, the only program that provides real capacity increase combined with reliability is the DriveSpace 3 program (Fig. 4.1). It is included with Windows 95 OSR2 and Windows 98 operating systems. To use this program when running Windows 95, you need to install the Microsoft Plus! for Windows 95 software package that includes the program. Note that this program can only compress drives formatted for the FAT 16 file system.

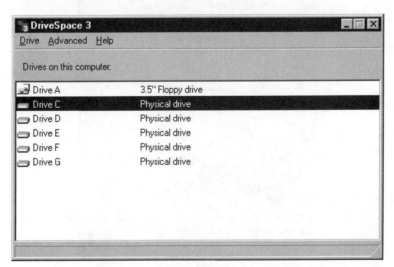

Fig. 4.1. DriveSpace 3 startup window

To load and run this program, proceed as follows:

1. To launch the program, click the **Start** button and select the following commands from the **Start** menu: **Programs** | **Accessories** | **System Tools** | **DriveSpace**.

2. Select the drive you wish to compress.

3. To view the properties of the selected drive, double-click it (Fig. 4.2).

4. Select the **Compress** command from the **Drive** menu. A window will appear with an approximate prognosis on the compression of the selected drive (Fig. 4.3).

5. Click **Start**.

6. Windows will prompt you to create an updated Startup disk (Fig. 4.4). If you already have one, you may choose **No**.

7. In order to create or update the Startup disk, click **Yes**, and then insert the diskette into the drive and click **Create disk**.

8. You will then be prompted to create a backup copy of the drive to be compressed (Fig. 4.5). This procedure is optional. However, it is strongly recommended.

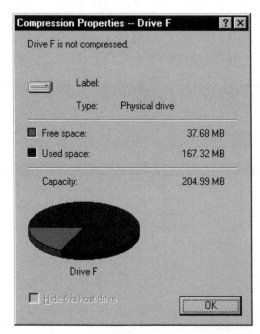

Fig. 4.2. The compression properties of the selected drive

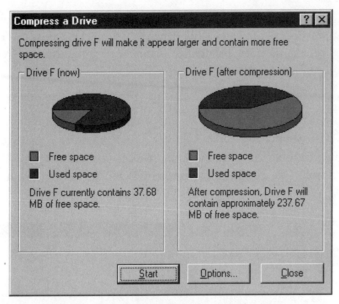

Fig. 4.3. Prognosis on the drive's compression

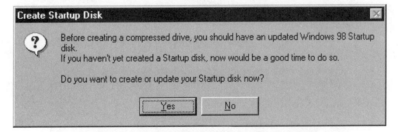

Fig. 4.4. The **Create Startup Disk** window

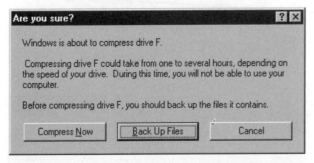

Fig. 4.5. Before actually compressing the drive, the DriveSpace
program requests a confirmation

9. After clicking **Compress now**, the system may prompt you to change the default compression parameters (this depends on the OS version). You can accept the default settings or change them according to your requirements. When you've finished, click **OK**.

10. The disk compression procedure will start (Fig. 4.6). It may take a few hours.

11. After completion of the compression procedure, the program will display the results of compression (Fig. 4.7).

12. Later you'll be able to view the compression properties (Fig. 4.8) any time you need to. The compression properties include compression ratio, free space, etc.

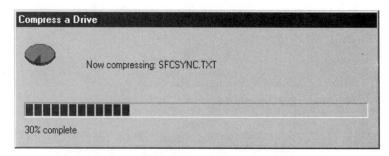

Fig. 4.6. The compression procedure in progress

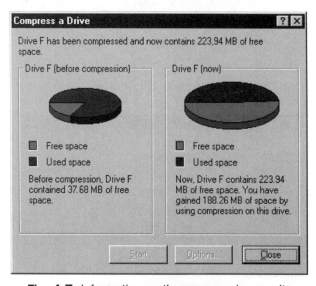

Fig. 4.7. Information on the compression results

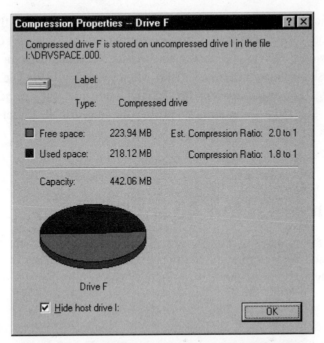

Fig. 4.8. Compression properties of the selected drive

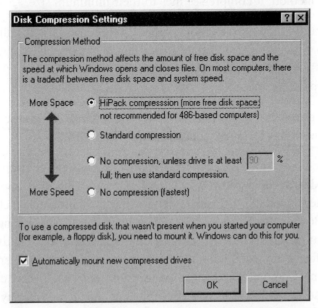

Fig. 4.9. The **Disk Compression Settings** dialog box

The DriveSpace 3 program includes several compression methods that determine the balance between compression and performance. In order to choose which method you would like to use, select the **Settings** command from the **Advanced** menu. The **Disk compression settings** dialog will appear (Fig. 4.9). The DriveSpace 3 program allows you to use one of three compression methods: standard, HiPack, or UltraPack. The HiPack method compresses the files to half of their normal size, and UltraPack to one third.

The Compression Agent Program

After compressing the drive using the DriveSpace 3 program, you can use the Compression Agent program to attain maximum results (Fig. 4.10). This program optimally compresses the files and allows you to use the powerful UltraPack method.

I should mention that the Compression Agent program processes all files stored on the logical disk and compressed with the DriveSpace program. Using the UltraPack method, it compresses files to their minimum size.

When using the Windows 95 operating system, this program is installed along with DriveSpace 3 from the Microsoft Plus! for Windows 95 software package. The Compression Agent program is included with Windows 95 OSR2 and Windows 98 operating systems.

To start the program, select the following commands from the **Start** menu: **Programs | Accessories | System Tools | Compression Agent**.

To set the compression parameters, click the **Settings** button (Fig. 4.10). The **Compression agent parameters** dialog box (Fig. 4.11) will appear. Although Windows 9x developers do not recommend using the UltraPack method on computers with 486 processors, the performance degradation after using this method is not significant. This means that the UltraPack algorithm is relatively fast. It is suitable even for legacy computers that can't be considered as powerful. After you complete setting Compression Agent's parameters, click **OK**, then click the **Start** button. After accomplishing its tasks, Compression Agent will display the results of the operation (Fig. 4.12).

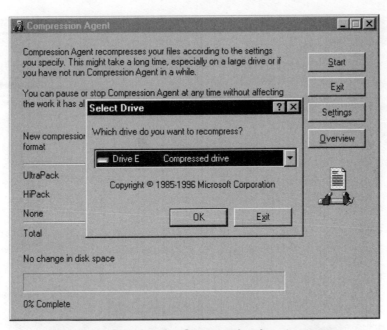

Fig. 4.10. Running the Compression Agent program

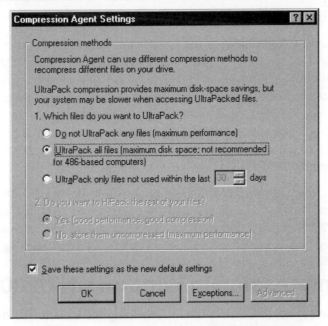

Fig. 4.11. Setting the compression parameters

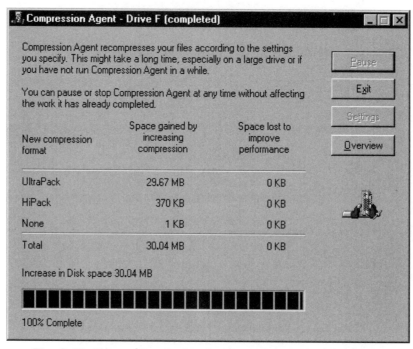

Fig. 4.12. The results of using the Compression Agent program

When discussing the capabilities of the DriveSpace program and other similar compression tools, it is necessary to point out that some users doubt the reliability of compressed information storage. In the past, these doubts were partially justified. However, storage technologies have significantly improved since that time. The newest reliability tools (implemented on both the software and hardware level), such as tools for error-proof encoding, S.M.A.R.T. technology, etc., have solved the reliability problem and made DriveSpace and other similar tools more attractive. Furthermore, the programs themselves now have built-in reliability tools.

However, even admitting all the advantages of the above described software tools, it is necessary to mention that the highest level of comfort and reliability are provided in Windows NT/2000 operating systems. If you have one of these OSs, the user can employ the NTFS-based built-in compression tools implemented in these operating systems.

File compression in Windows NT/2000

The NTFS file system (NT File System), providing the basis for modern, powerful operating systems, was developed a relatively long time ago. It was oriented towards the Windows NT operating system. However, it became widely accepted only after the release of the newer versions of Windows NT, such as Windows NT 4.0 and Windows 2000. Among other technologies implemented in NTFS, efficient data compression deserves special mention. It is widely used and commonly recognized by most advanced users.

NTFS provides the capabilities for compressing both whole volumes and individual files and folders, thus allowing you to significantly increase free disk space. Quite often, it allows you to increase hard disks of several GB by hundreds of MB. More advanced hard disks of larger capacity can be compressed to save several dozens of GB.

The user works with compressed data the same way as he or she would with normal (uncompressed) files or folders. Furthermore, as the practice has shown, data compression has no negative impact on system performance. This is achieved thanks to the simplicity of the compression/decompression methods and the algorithms implemented in NTFS. Besides this, the NTFS file system itself is conveniently integrated into modern high-performance operating systems.

When evaluating and discussing NTFS functionality, it is necessary to point out that for several years before its arrival, the DriveSpace program was the only popular and well-known compression tool. The third version of this program — DriveSpace 3 — was the most widely used.

The DriveSpace program is included with Microsoft operating systems, starting with Windows 95 OSR2. If you want to use this program when running Windows 95, you need to install the Microsoft Plus! for Windows 95 software, which includes the DriveSpace program. Notice, however, that despite its popularity, this program is neither included with Windows NT/2000, nor does Windows NT/2000 provide support for DriveSpace compression.

Certainly, it is necessary to mention that DriveSpace has several limitations. For example, this program allows you to compress only disks formatted for a FAT16 file system. Furthermore, it only allows you to compress the whole logical disk, and there is a disk space limitation: the compressed disk must not exceed 2 GB. Also, the disk space loss caused by the cluster size (32 KB) must not be neglected.

In contrast to FAT16, for which the DriveSpace program is intended, NTFS enables the user to compress individual files. The logical disk size limitation has also been practically removed (2 TB). The compression and decompression processes implemented in NTFS are also much easier, and run significantly faster.

When comparing the capabilities of the FAT and NTFS files systems, it is necessary to emphasize that the DriveSpace program stores compressed data within a single file. Because of this circumstance, the reliability of storing information compressed using DriveSpace is somewhat lower than that for data compressed using NTFS compression.

Thus, we can draw the conclusion that NTFS compression is preferable when it comes to such important characteristics as convenience, ease of use, working speed, and storage reliability.

Some NTFS-specific features of file and folder compression deserve special mention:

❑ Each file is compressed individually. Some files are compressed more efficiently than others

❑ Files or folders moved or copied to compressed folders (directories) will be compressed automatically

❑ Compressed files or folders moved or copied to uncompressed folders or volumes are automatically decompressed

❑ Files or folders created in compressed folders or on compressed volumes (disks) are automatically compressed

❑ Files or folders created in uncompressed folders or on uncompressed volumes are not compressed

Windows NT 4.0 Compression

First of all, it is recommended that you configure the system in such a way as to instruct Windows Explorer to display compressed files in alternate color (blue). This will provide you with the capability of visually distinguishing compressed files from uncompressed ones. To achieve this, proceed as follows:

1. Open the **My Computer** window by double-clicking the icon on the desktop.

2. Select the **Options** command from the **View** menu.

3. The **Options** window will open. Go to the **View** tab.

4. Set the **Display compressed files and folders with alternate color** checkbox.

5. Click **OK**.

Now, to compress a specific file (or group of files), do the following:

1. Open the folder containing the files that you need to compress, and select the file or group of files that you are going to compress.

2. Right-click any of the selected files with the mouse and select the **Properties** command from the context menu.

3. The **Properties** window will open.

4. Select the **Compressed** checkbox.

5. Click **OK**.

As a result of performing the above-described operations the selected files will be compressed. If you have configured the visual control option, the compressed files will be displayed in blue.

To compress individual folders or groups of folders, proceed in the same manner. The folders will be compressed after you set the **Compressed** attribute and click **OK**. As a result, the system will display a dialog box prompting you to compress all the folders nested within the selected folder(s). Select the appropriate option according to your requirements, and then click **OK**.

After you click **OK**, thus confirming the attribute selection, the system will display the **Compressing Files** window with the current information on file and folder compression. This window displays file and folder names, along with the number of compressed files and folders, the data size before and after compression, and the compression ratio. You can interrupt the compression process at any time.

You should proceed in the same way in order to compress an entire partition or logical drive, if needed. To do so, select the **Compression** option from the disk properties.

Windows 2000 Compression

As in the previous case, we recommend that you to configure the system to display compressed files using an alternate color (blue), since this option provides the rather convenient capability of visual control, enabling you to easily distinguish compressed files from uncompressed ones. To achieve this, do the following:

1. Open the **My Computer** window by double-clicking the icon on the desktop.

2. Select the **Folder Options** command from the **Tools** menu (Fig. 4.13).

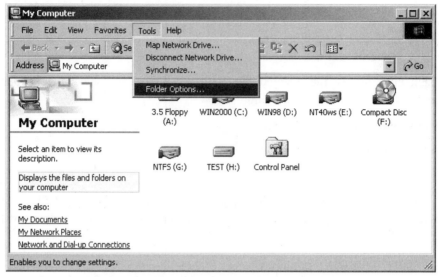

Fig. 4.13. The **Folder Options** command from the **Tools** menu

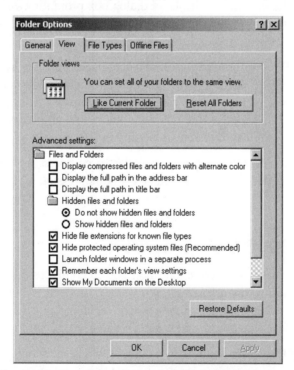

Fig. 4.14. The **View** tab in the **Folder Options** window

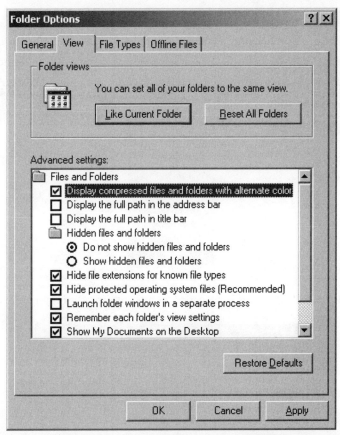

Fig. 4.15. To enable visual control over compressed and uncompressed files and folders, set the **Display compressed files and folders with alternate color** checkbox

3. The **Folder Options** window will open. Click the **View** tab (Fig. 4.14).

4. Set the **Display compressed files and folders with alternate color** checkbox (Fig. 4.15) and click **OK**.

Now, to compress an individual file or group of files, you need to proceed as follows:

1. Open the folder containing the required file(s) and select the ones that you want to compress. Right-click the selected files with the mouse and select the **Properties** command from the right-click menu (Fig. 4.16).

2. The **Properties** window will open (Fig. 4.17).

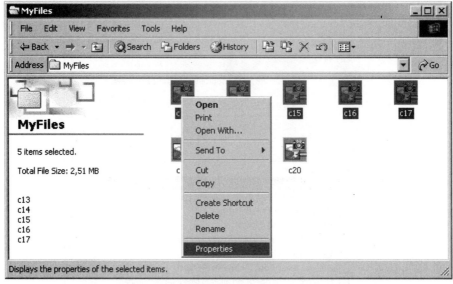

Fig. 4.16. Selecting the **Properties** command from the right-click menu

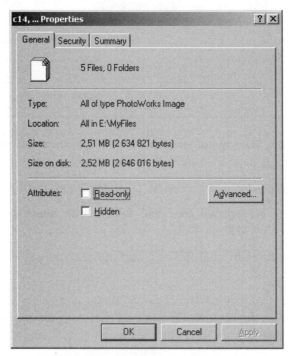

Fig. 4.17. The **Properties** window

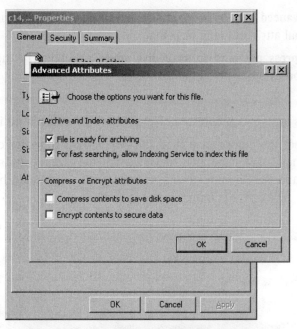

Fig. 4.18. The **Advanced Attributes** window

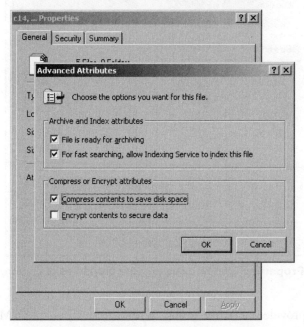

Fig. 4.19. Setting the compression attribute

3. Click the **Advanced** button to open the **Advanced Attributes** window that displays additional attributes (Fig. 4.18).

4. Set the **Compress contents to save disk space** checkbox in the **Compress or Encrypt attributes** option group (Fig. 4.19).

5. Click **OK**.

The selected files are now compressed. These files will be displayed in blue.

Now, if you select the compressed files and select the **Properties** command from the right-click menu, you'll be able to view both the size of the selected objects (the **Size** field) and the amount of disk space actually consumed by these objects (the **Size on disk** field) after compression (Fig. 4.20).

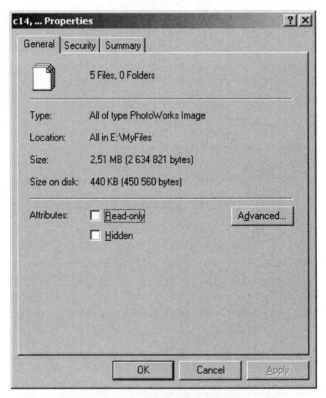

Fig. 4.20. The **Properties** window displaying the properties of compressed files and folders

In the example provided here, the group of files (total size — 2.81 MB) were compressed to 444 KB.

Do the same to compress individual folders and groups of folders. This capability will be available after you set the compression attribute and click **OK**. As a result of these actions, the system will display the **Confirm Attribute Changes** dialog box (Fig. 4.21) prompting you to select whether you want to compress only the selected folder, or the selected folder and all its contents, including both subfolders and files. Select the required option as necessary and confirm your selection by clicking **OK**.

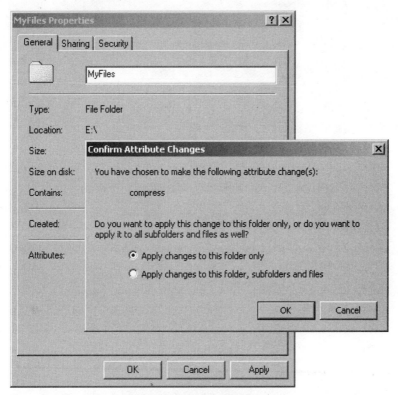

Fig. 4.21. The **Confirm Attribute Changes** window prompts you to apply the attribute change to the selected folder only or to the selected folder and all its contents (subfolders and files)

After you confirm your selection by clicking **OK**, the **Applying Attributes** dialog box appears (Fig. 4.22), displaying the progress indicator informing you of the compression's progress. This dialog displays both the file and folder names, along with the expected time required for accomplishing the operation. The compression process can be interrupted at any time.

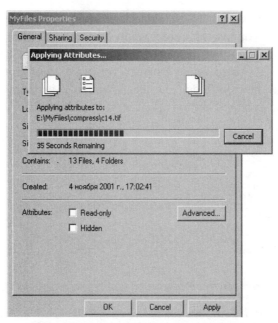

Fig. 4.22. The **Applying Attributes** window

Fig. 4.23. Compressing the whole partition or logical disk

You can also compress the whole partition or logical disk in a similar manner. Open the **Properties** window for the volume that you want to compress, and then set the **Compress drive to save disk space** checkbox (Fig. 4.23).

Decompressing Objects in Windows NT 4.0 and Windows 2000

The process of decompressing previously compressed file system objects (files, folders, logical disks) is quite similar to the compression procedure, with one exception — instead of setting the compression attribute, here you need to clear it.

The Command Line Method

Windows NT 4.0 and Windows 2000 operating systems provide the command-line tool for compressing file system objects. This operation is done by issuing the compact command from the command prompt. The syntax of this command is similar for both operating systems (the only difference is in the terms used: Windows NT 4.0 calls them *directories*, while Windows 2000 uses the word *folders*):

```
Displays or alters the compression of files on NTFS partitions.

COMPACT [/C | /U] [/S[:dir]] [/A] [/I] [/F] [/Q] [filename [...]]

    /C      Compresses the specified files.  Directories will be
            marked
            so that files added afterward will be compressed.
    /U      Uncompresses the specified files.  Directories will be
            marked
            so that files added afterward will not be compressed.
    /S      Performs the specified operation on files in the given
            directory and all subdirectories.  Default "dir" is the
            current directory.
    /A      Displays files with the hidden or system attributes.
            These
            files are omitted by default.
    /I      Continues performing the specified operation even
            after errors
            have occurred.  By default, COMPACT stops when an
            error is
            encountered.
    /F      Forces the compress operation on all specified files,
            even
            those which are already compressed.  Already-
            compressed files
            are skipped by default.
```

```
/Q        Reports only the most essential information.
Filename  Specifies a pattern, file, or directory.

Used without parameters, COMPACT displays the compression state of
the current directory and any files it contains. You may use
        multiple
filenames and wildcards.  You must put spaces between multiple
parameters.
```

Examples illustrating the usage of this command in Windows 2000 are provided below.

1. Starting the command in an uncompressed directory:

```
G:\TEXT\BOOK\PROG\C\Builder\Documentation\>compact

    Listing G:\TEXT\BOOK\PROG\C\Builder\Documentation\
    New files added to this directory will not be compressed.

    16874446 :  16874446 = 1.0 to 1   DG.PDF
    14156631 :  14156631 = 1.0 to 1   QS.PDF

    Of 2 files within 1 directories
    0 are compressed and 2 are not compressed.
    31 031 077 total bytes of data are stored in 31 031 077 bytes.
    The compression ratio is 1.0 to 1.
```

2. Compression — starting the command with the /c key:

```
G:\TEXT\BOOK\PROG\C\Builder\Documentation\>compact /c

    Setting the directory
    G:\TEXT\BOOK\PROG\C\Builder\Documentation\ to compress new
    files [OK]

    Compressing files in G:\TEXT\BOOK\PROG\C\Builder\Documentation\

    DG.PDF            16874446 :   8966144 = 1.9 to 1 [OK]
    QS.PDF            14156631 :   2811904 = 5.0 to 1 [OK]

    3 files within 2 directories were compressed.
    31 031 077 total bytes of data are stored in 11 778 048
    bytes.
    The compression ratio is 2.6 to 1.
```

3. Starting the compact tool in a directory containing compressed files:

```
G:\TEXT\BOOK\PROG\C\Builder\Documentation\>compact

    Listing  G:\TEXT\BOOK\PROG\C\Builder\Documentation\
    New files added to this directory will be compressed.

    16874446 :   8968192 = 1.9 to 1 C DG.PDF
```

```
14156631 :    2811904 = 5.0 to 1 C QS.PDF

Of 2 files within 1 directories
2 are compressed and 0 are not compressed.
31 031 077 total bytes of data are stored in 11 778 048 bytes.
The compression ratio is 2,6 to 1.
```

4. Decompression — starting the compact tool with the /u key:

```
G:\TEXT\BOOK\PROG\C\Builder\Documentation\>compact /u

    Setting the directory G:\TEXT\BOOK\PROG\C\Builder\Documentation\
    not to compress new files [OK]

    Uncompressing files in G:\TEXT\BOOK\PROG\C\Builder\Documentation\

    DG.PDF [OK]
    QS.PDF [OK]

    3 files within 2 directories were uncompressed.
```

Comparing DriveSpace 3 and NTFS Compression

To compare the compression efficiency of the DriveSpace 3 tool and NTFS compression, we performed the following experiment. Using DriveSpace 3, we created a compressed drive that was later populated with various data (including text files, image files, program source code files, etc.). To achieve maximum compression, the Compression Agent program was used. The parameters of the compressed drives obtained using the DriveSpace 3 program are presented below.

Information on the compressed drive E according to the DriveSpace data:

❑ Compressed drive E is physically located in the uncompressed drive H (in the H:\DRVSPACE.000 file)

❑ Used space: 1.56 GB

❑ Free space: 0 KB

❑ Compression ration: 2.4 to 1

Information on the drive H according to the DriveSpace data:

❑ Host drive for the drive E

❑ Used space: 533.23 MB

❑ Free space: 112 KB

The data provided below are displayed by the Windows GUI. The actual space consumed by all files and directories on the drive E is given. Notice that this information is slightly different: the drive E is full (1.55 GB), while the total space consumed by the files stored on this drive is only 1.00 GB. This difference is due to the internal organization of the data within the file stored at the host drive, the cluster size, etc.

Drive E properties:

❒ Local Disk (FAT)

❒ Used space: 1,671,364,608 (1.55 GB)

❒ Free space: 0 bytes

❒ Capacity: 1,671,364,608 (1.55 GB)

❒ Files: 20,035

❒ Folders: 1,792

❒ File and folder size: 1.00 GB (1,073,742,644 bytes)

Properties of the compressed file stored on the host drive that contains all information from the compressed drive E:

❒ File: Drvspace.000

❒ Size: 533 MB (559,091,200 bytes)

The following results have been obtained:

Useful information size, GB	1.00
Compressed data size, MB	533
Compression ratio	1.9 to 1

Thus, we managed to compress the information by 1.9 times.

After obtaining the data on DriveSpace 3 compression, it is necessary to repeat the whole process using NTFS compression. And so all information from the drive E was copied to the NTFS-formatted disk into a separate compressed directory. The properties of this directory are shown in Fig. 4.24.

The following results have been obtained:

Useful information size, GB	1.00
Compressed information size, MB	535
Compression ratio	1.9 to 1

Fig. 4.24. The compressed folder properties

Thus, we can draw the conclusion that, as a general rule, both methods provide nearly the same compression ratio. One could say that DriveSpace 3 provides somewhat better compression (usually several tenths of a percent). It should be especially emphasized that the data on the size of the NTFS-compressed information includes the loss due to cluster size, while the information compressed using DriveSpace 3 is stored in one large file (and thus the loss due to the cluster size is minimal). Fig. 4.25 shows the properties of an uncompressed folder containing the same information.

From this screenshot, it is evident that the losses due to cluster size (4 KB) are approximately 50 MB. If the drive were formatted with a cluster size of, say, 1 KB, this loss would be several times smaller. Thus, the NTFS compression algorithm is by itself much more efficient in comparison to such popular compression tools as DriveSpace.

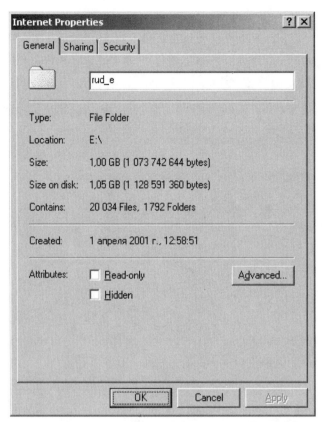

Fig. 4.25. The uncompressed folder properties

The example provided above and the rough analysis of the compression results demonstrate the advantage of NTFS built-in compression tools.

To conclude this chapter, we would like to emphasize that we have been using the above described compression tools for several years, on several hardware platforms, while running different operating systems, and on various hard drives from large variety of vendors.

It is also necessary that we mention that the compression tools discussed in this chapter provide highly efficient usage of the hard disk space. Additionally, the dynamic compression tools considered here provide for reliable storage of the compressed programs and data files, which is supported not only on the software level, but by special hardware components as well, allowing for reliable and fail-safe usage of the storage system. Such components are mandatory components of all modern hard drives.

Chapter 5

Caching Hard
and Compact Disks

You can increase the performance of the hard disk drives and CD-ROM drives by caching. When this mode is enabled, part of the available RAM is allocated for data buffering. Buffering is used during read/write operations when accessing the hard drive, and during read operations when accessing CD-ROM drive.

Caching allows you to optimize data transfer, and in the long run, boosts the overall performance of the computer. When caching is enabled, data exchange between the drive (HDD or CD-ROM), its controller, and all other hardware components of the system is not done in small fragments, but rather in blocks of significant length. This speeds up data exchange.

Modern devices have built-in controllers with built-in cache memory, but the size of this built-in cache memory is often insufficient for attaining the highest possible speed of data access and exchange. In such a case, it is possible to programmatically reserve some part of available RAM for additional data buffering. A memory buffer of significant size not only allows reading of the data necessary in the current reading cycle, but also of the data that might be needed in the next one(s). In accordance with the fairly complicated caching algorithms, the needed data is first sought in the cache memory (a specially allocated part of the RAM), and then on the disks in the chosen drive. This decreases the number of access operations to the HDD or CD-ROM drive. Accessing the RAM is much faster than accessing data stored on the hard disk or CD. This is due to the fact that electronic elements are much faster than mechanical ones. For mechanical movements the execution time of the command is measured in milliseconds (hard drives) and even tenths of milliseconds (CD-ROM drives). Searches in the RAM can be completed in tenths of nanoseconds, that is, hundreds of thousands times faster. Hence, saving data in the RAM section specifically reserved for caching will speed up data exchange and increase the general performance of the computer system. Caching can significantly increase the operating speed of the drives, which is especially true for CD-ROM drives.

Caching Implementation in MS-DOS and Windows 3.1x

When using the MS-DOS/Windows 3.1x combination, CD-ROM caching can be implemented using the *MSCDEX* driver. To enable the caching mode, use the /M:x key in the command line when loading the driver. In this case, x represents the number of buffers. For the given driver, a buffer is equal to 2 KB RAM. The speed of exchange and the performance of the computer will grow along with the reserved memory (the number of buffers). However, this growth is not arbitrary, since it is limited by the physical size of the available RAM. This may be either conventional memory, or the upper memory block (UMB). Usually, 10 buffers are used, so the command line used to load the MSCDEX driver may look like this:

```
c:\dos\mscdex /d:001 /m:10
```

Quite often, the *SmartDrive* driver is used for caching for both CD-ROM and hard and floppy disks. This driver, residing in conventional and/or partly in the UMB memory, provides the opportunity to use a relatively large amount of additional memory for caching — extended memory. Using SmartDrive allows you to significantly increase the size of the cache memory, and won't take up any conventional or UMB memory. Under these conditions caching can be enabled for any number of devices. Note that it's recommended to use SmartDrive only when no less than 8 MB RAM is available, which is quite a common characteristic for modern computers.

To activate the SmartDrive driver, you must run the smartdrv.exe file. For convenience of use, set the /v command line key. This will display information about the cached drives on the screen. For instance, after running the driver, the user may see the following:

```
Caching utility of Microsoft disks SmartDrive version 5.0
Copyright 1991,1994 Microsoft Corp.
Size of cache-memory: 2 097 152 bytes
Size of cache-memory under Windows: 2 097 152 bytes
Status of disk caching
disk cache reading cache writing bufferization
A:   yes    no     no
B:   yes    no     no
C:   yes    yes    no
F:   yes    no     no
To receive information, begin running Smartdrv /?
```

The example record provided above shows that the two floppy drives (A and B), the hard disk (C), and the CD-ROM drive (F) use the cache for reading. Only the hard disk (C) uses cache for writing. In the `bufferization` column, no drives are indicated, since it refers to so-called double bufferization which is rarely used. Using additional switches, you can perform a more detailed set-up of drive caching with SmartDrive.

Caching Implementation in Windows 95/98

In Windows 9x, the SmartDrive caching system was replaced by VCACHE caching system. Whereas SmartDrive is a 16-bit driver, VCACHE is a 32-bit driver that can dynamically change the size of the disk cache depending on the available disk space and application requirements.

When using Windows 95/98, drive caching can be set up using the following procedures.

To cache hard disks (Fig. 5.1):

1. Double-click the **My Computer** icon.

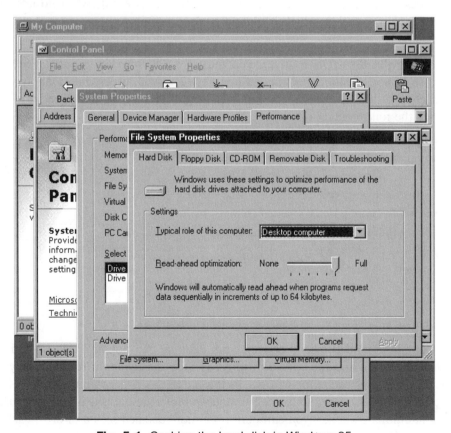

Fig. 5.1. Caching the hard disk in Windows 95

2. The **My Computer** window will appear. Double-click the **Control Panel** icon to open the **Control Panel** window. Then double-click the **System** icon.

3. In the **System Properties** dialog go to the **Performance** tab.

4. Click the **File System** button.

5. Go to the **Hard Disk** tab.

6. In the **Read-ahead optimization** field, move the slide to the rightmost position.

7. Confirm your settings by clicking **OK.**

To cache the CD-ROM drive (Fig. 5.2):

1. Double-click the **My Computer** icon.

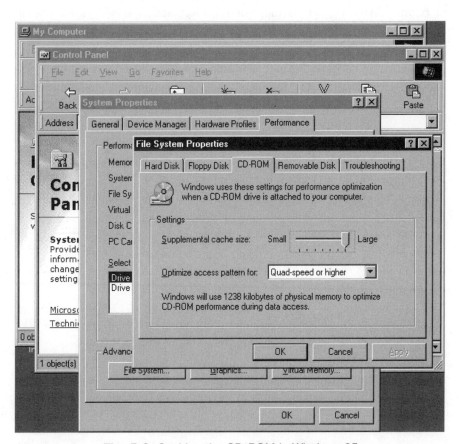

Fig. 5.2. Caching the CD-ROM in Windows 95

2. Open the **Control Panel** window; then start the **System** applet.

3. In the **System Properties** dialog, go to the **Performance** tab.

4. Click the **File System** button.

5. Go to the **CD-ROM** tab.

6. Select the necessary parameter in the **Optimize access pattern for** field, usually Quad speed or higher.

7. Set the necessary size of the cache memory in the **Supplemental cache size** field. Usually the slide is moved to the rightmost position.

8. Confirm your settings by clicking **OK**.

When booting Windows 9x in the MS-DOS emulation mode, drive caching is done using the same drivers as in MS-DOS or Windows 3.x.

Chapter 6

Optimizing
the Video Subsystem

The functional capabilities and performance of the video subsystem are determined by the parameters of the monitor, the video adapter, and the software used.

Adjusting the monitor using its built-in equipment will generally change the linear dimensions, the distortion compensation of the displayed image, and color, brightness, and contrast correction, etc. Usually, adjusting the monitor has no impact on the general performance of the video subsystem.

Modern video adapters, as a rule, don't have built-in set-up equipment. Normally, their elements never change during operation, except for, maybe, upgrading the video memory and, for certain models of video adapters, the use of a special daughterboard.

However, the video subsystem performance — the speed of processing video information and displaying it on the monitor — and often certain functional capabilities, depend on the settings specified in BIOS Setup — CMOS Setup. Furthermore, overall performance of the video subsystem depends on the functional capabilities of the installed application software and on the modes set by the operating system and its drivers.

You can access the CMOS Setup immediately after turning on your computer. The system provides you with this opportunity during the POST (Power-On Self Test) by prompting you to press a certain key or key combination to enter the Setup mode. It may be the <Delete> key, the <Insert> key, or a combination like <Ctrl>+<Alt>+<Esc>, and so on. Usually, this prompt will be displayed on the screen. For example:

```
PRESS <DEL> TO ENTER SETUP.
```

Certain versions of BIOS Setup have specific parameters that influence the speed of video output. For instance, if you have Award Modular BIOS (from Award Software), video subsystem performance can be increased by enabling settings such as **Video BIOS Shadow** and **Video BIOS Cacheable**.

The BIOS Setup routine provided by certain motherboards allows you to run AGP modes, for example, to enable or disable support of the AGP2x mode and choose the **Primary Video (PCI/AGP)** option. The choice of the given parameters depends on the type of video adapter used and on the modes that it supports. In order to support efficient functioning of the video adapter in the 3D modes, some BIOS Setup routines provide special parameters that control the video memory and/or the RAM. For example, the **AGP Aperture Size (MB)** parameter determines the size of the AGP-video adapter memory. As with the corresponding option in BIOS Setup, a section of the RAM is dynamically reserved for video adapter. It's usually in this section that the video adapter stores textures. Consequently, the frequency of accessing the hard disk is reduced. The speed of video output is increased as a result.

Setting up the monitor and video adapter drivers should be done according to the documentation supplied with these hardware devices. Often, driver installation and setup is done using special setup programs that come with the hardware.

The performance of the video subsystem is directly related to its operating modes, which are characterized by the color depth and resolution. In the standard VGA/SVGA, the following resolution values have become the most widely used for the most commonly used 14"—17" monitors: 640×480, 800×600, 1024×768, and 1280×1024. The color palette consists of the following values: 16 colors, 256 colors, High Color (16 bits), True Color (24 bits, 32 bits). For system and office programs, 256 colors are usually enough. For multimedia tasks you may want to use the High Color or True Color mode.

Setting the necessary parameters for video output may be done using Windows $9x$ built-in tools (Fig. 6.1).

Optimum Resolutions for 14- to 17-Inch Monitors

Monitor size, inches	Optimum resolution
14	640×480
15	800×600
17	1024×768

The capabilities of the video subsystem are determined by the video adapter and the size of its video memory, and of course by the quality of the monitor. User requirements are determined by the operating system and installed applications. Obviously, using a high resolution with a significant color depth will intensify the flow of digital data which the computer video subsystem must process within a limited period of time. Often, this demands a significant amount of the video adapters as well as of the other hardware components, such as the processor, available RAM, buses, hard disks, etc. Video modes with a low resolution and a small number of colors demand less hardware resources. In this case, the computer processes the video frames considerably faster. This is particularly important for the tasks related to multimedia information processing. For most modern video clips, playback is optimized for the following video mode: resolution − 640×480, and color palette − 256. It's also possible to use higher resolutions and higher-precision color modes. The actual capabilities of such modes are limited by the capabilities of the video adapter, the monitor, and by the amount of video memory, which is generally 0.5, 1, 2, 4, 8, 16 MB or more. Notice that for efficient usage of the video adapter in 3D mode, additional resources such as video memory and RAM are required. These resources are needed for storing textures.

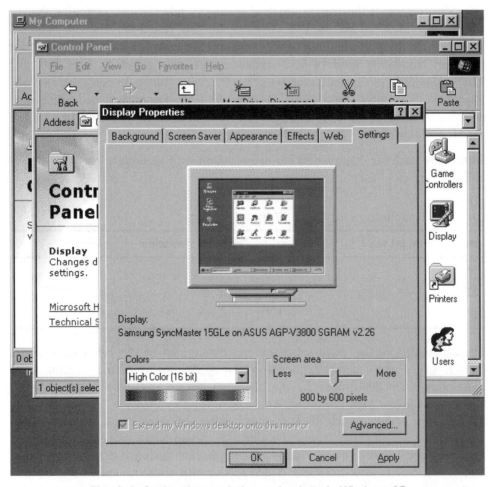

Fig. 6.1. Setting the resolution and palette in Windows 95

Resolutions, Palettes, and the Minimum Size of the Video Memory

Resolution	Palette	Video memory size
640x480	256 colors	0.5 MB
800x600	256 colors	0.5 MB
1024x768	256 colors	1 MB
1280x1024	256 colors	2 MB
1600x1200	256 colors	2 MB
640x480	High Color (16 bits)	1 MB
800x600	High Color (16 bits)	1 MB
1024x768	High Color (16 bits)	2 MB
1280x1024	High Color (16 bits)	4 MB
1600x1200	High Color (16 bits)	4 MB
640x480	True Color (24 bits)	1 MB
800x600	True Color (24 bits)	2 MB
1024x768	True Color (24 bits)	4 MB
1280x1024	True Color (24 bits)	4 MB
1600x1200	True Color (24 bits)	8 MB

Thus, both the speed of processing and output of video information often decrease, once that extraneous video output parameters have been set. Notice that extraneous parameters will not improve the output quality. If the video subsystem and other components of the computer don't actually support enhanced video modes, this will result in zooming-in the displayed image. Also, individual frames may slip out, and/or the image and sound may be distorted. Because of this, to guarantee maximum video performance it is not recommended to set higher-resolution and higher-precision color modes unless it is absolutely necessary. This is especially true for those cases when you need to provide high performance when using a relatively inexpensive video adapter. It's a well-known fact that the video cards of this class have inferior performance.

Windows $9x$ provides built-in tools intended for setting up the video adapter to work at maximum speed (Figs. 6.2, 6.3).

The power of modern advanced video adapters depends to a great extent on the efficiency of their respective drivers. Generally, improved versions of the video adapter drivers exploit acceleration features of the card to provide higher video processing and output speed. Sometimes, new drivers even enhance the adapter functionality. Some cases were reported in which upgraded drivers have accelerated video processing and output speed by 30—50%. This is often more than the actual performance increase generally achieved by replacing the video adapter with the next-generation one (using the new release of the video chipset).

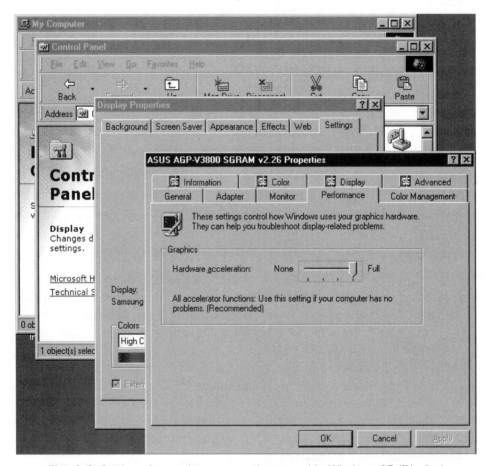

Fig. 6.2. Settings for maximum operating speed in Windows 95 (Display)

Video card manufacturers usually provide comprehensive support for their products through their distributors and dealers. They are the ones who sell the hardware and software, and take care of consulting and service. Most well known manufacturers provide support for their products for a long time after their release, and are constantly improving drivers and providing new APIs.

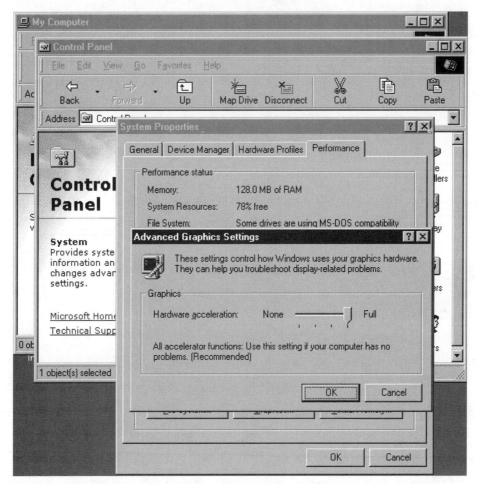

Fig. 6.3. Settings for maximum operating speed in Windows 95 (System)

Quite often, you can get the necessary advice or download new versions of drivers via the Internet. There you can also find many tips and recommendations concerning video card overclocking using software tools.

Chapter 7

Optimizing RAM

In the traditional PC architecture that uses the command system of Intel processors, the first megabyte of RAM has a special function. It's no wonder that the first 640 KB of RAM within that first megabyte (which is the only part of memory available for certain types of programs) is known as the *conventional* (or *basic*) *memory*. Part of this memory area is used by system programs; application programs take up the rest. Often, these programs are sensitive to the conventional memory concerns. For example, certain application programs require no less than 600 KB of conventional memory to run. If the amount of available conventional memory is insufficient, such programs will not run, and a message will appear informing you that there is not enough conventional memory. As a matter of fact, this will happen even in a system with a large amount of RAM that exceeds that program's requirements. In the case we are considering, however, this large amount of available RAM is practically useless, because the first 640 KB is the only area that the program can access. This is due to the fact that all memory above the first megabyte is of the *extended* type, which a normal DOS program can't use.

One of the most common methods of RAM optimization under Windows 9x is using the drivers specially developed for the particular Windows version. These drivers work in protected mode. To maximize conventional memory under Windows 9x, try to avoid if possible using drivers that require an MS-DOS compatibility mode (a real mode). This is because such drivers load in the first MB of memory, thus decreasing the available conventional memory, and resulting in performance degradation and a limited capability of running programs that need a large amount of conventional memory.

To detect real-mode drivers under Windows 95, do the following:

1. Click the **Start** button.

2. From the **Start** menu select **Settings | Control Panel**.

3. The **Control Panel** window will appear. Double-click the **System** icon.

4. In the **System Properties** window go to the **Performance** tab.

A list of real-mode drivers will be displayed. To get additional information on these drivers, click **Information (?)**.

The programs that run under Windows 9x in MS-DOS compatibility mode may require real-mode drivers. To use these drivers, you need to describe them in the appropriate manner in Autoexec.bat and Config.sys files. Real-mode drivers are loaded into conventional memory, and thus decrease the size of available conventional memory. To maximize conventional memory and increase the performance, it's recommended to try loading some of the real-mode drivers into the upper memory area (UMA), which is the upper 384 KB of the first megabyte of system memory, directly above conventional memory. To do this, you must add the following lines to the Config.sys configuration file:

```
DOS =HIGH, UMB
DEVICE=C:\WINDOWS\HIMEM.SYS
DEVICE=C:\WINDOWS\EMM386.EXE NOEMS HIGHSCAN
```

Then, in order to load the program in the high memory, you should use the DEVICEHIGH command in Config.sys and LH or LOADHIGH command in Autoexec.bat.

You can also optimize the location of the system programs within the first megabyte of memory and increase the size of conventional memory available for applications using the MemMaker utility specially designed for this purpose. This utility, included with MS-DOS version 6.0 and later versions, modifies the Config.sys and Autoexec.bat configuration files. After you execute MemMaker, device drivers and other resident programs that reside in the RAM will use the conventional memory in the most advantageous manner possible. If possible, MemMaker will try to load resident programs into the so-called UMB blocks. All of this maximizes free space within the conventional memory, thus making it available to user applications, such as, for example, games, educational programs, business applications, multimedia programs, etc.

Note that to run MemMaker, you need a computer that has at least an 80386 (or higher) processor and extended memory. Currently, most computers easily meet this requirement.

Before running MemMaker, do the following:

❑ Make sure that all the hardware installed in the system (especially the RAM) functions correctly.

❑ Exit all active programs, such as Windows, MS-DOS Shell, NC, etc.

❑ Load all the drivers and resident programs which you normally use (including device drivers and software applications).

While loading MemMaker, the user is given the opportunity to choose the mode: **Express Setup** (standard setup) or **Custom Setup**.

Later in this chapter we'll consider several aspects that should be taken into account when optimizing conventional memory in order to maximize the amount of available free space. Although the information provided here would be enough to complete this task, it's recommended that you also read the official Microsoft documentation that comes with MS-DOS in order to make your work with MemMaker easier.

Express Setup Mode

To use the MemMaker utility in Express Setup mode:

1. Start the MemMaker program. To do this, type MemMaker in the command line and press <Enter>. The first window will appear. To continue, select the **Continue** option and press <Enter>.

2. You will then be prompted to select the setup mode.

3. To use the standard mode, select the **Express Setup** option and press <Enter>. Then specify whether or not you need EMS memory.

4. If none of the programs requires space in the EMS memory, or if you're not sure, select **No** and press <Enter>. If you are going to use programs that require EMS memory, select **Yes** by pressing the <Space> bar, and then press <Enter>. You will then be asked if you want the computer to reboot in order to test the loading order of the device drivers and resident programs.

5. After that, MemMaker will optimize the memory configuration. Having finished the analysis, MemMaker will introduce all necessary changes into Config.sys and Autoexec.bat configuration files. Once again, it will prompt you to reboot the computer with the new configuration settings. To reboot, press <Enter>. After rebooting, MemMaker will prompt you to specify whether the system is functioning correctly.

6. If MemMaker did not display error messages during optimization, and the system functions properly after rebooting, select **Yes** and press <Enter>. If you have any doubts, press the <Space> bar to select **No**. Then follow the instructions that appear on the screen.

7. If you confirm that the system is working correctly, MemMaker will display a table summarizing the amount of free memory of each type both before and after optimization.

Custom Setup Mode

If MemMaker has encountered any errors caused by a specific device driver or by any program, reboot the computer and select the **Custom Setup** mode. Then, select the **Yes** option when prompted to answer the question **Specify which drivers and TSRs to include in optimization?**

The Custom Setup mode looks very similar to Express Setup. The difference is that after the question about EMS memory is displayed, an **Advanced Options** dialog appears. The options specified in this dialog determine the manner in which MemMaker will configure the memory during the optimization process.

If necessary, the user can change the options in the **Advanced Options** dialog. Use the up arrow <↑> and down arrow <↓> keys to select the option you need. To change the values, use the <Space> bar. For information on a particular option press the <F1> key.

Having set all the options, press <Enter> to continue. When necessary, MemMaker will prompt you to specify an option or answer a question. In such a case, you need simply answer correctly and/or follow the instructions. When optimization is completed, MemMaker will prompt you to restart the computer to test the loading order of the device drivers and resident programs.

After this, the process is similar to that in Express Setup.

MemMaker will modify the system configuration, and introduce changes into Config.sys, Autoexec.bat, and sometimes System.ini files. Before modifying the files, MemMaker will create backup copies, usually with the same names but with the .umb filename extension. In case of problems you will be able to use these backup copies to restore the original configuration. You can even undo the changes after you've exited MemMaker. To undo the changes, proceed as follows:

1. Exit all active programs.

2. From the command line, run the following command: `Memmaker /undo`. A message will appear prompting you to restore original configuration or to exit MemMaker.

3. To restore the original configuration files, press <Enter>. You'll see a message prompting you to restart the computer.

4. Press <Enter>.

Chapter 8

Updating the BIOS

The BIOS is responsible for the proper operation of the entire computer system. The overall stability and reliability of the computer system as well as its performance in various modes depends on BIOS's functionality, the quality of its code, and its efficiency. The motherboard manufacturers are constantly improving the BIOS code in co-operation with BIOS developers. As a result, new, improved BIOS versions are constantly being released, not only for newly created motherboards, but also for the older ones.

Improved BIOS versions are mainly intended for use with newly released components, taking into account particular features of their architecture. Updating the BIOS version often allows you to compensate for the drawbacks of legacy devices used in the computer system.

The architecture of modern motherboards uses electrically programmed flash memory chips for storing BIOS. These new generation ROM chips, so-called Flash ROMs, can be reprogrammed an infinite number of times by using a flash utility (software). In this case you will have to find the system/motherboard make, model and revision number, and then simply download the proper flash update and utility from the manufacturer's web- or FTP-site. Writing a new version of the BIOS code into the flash memory can be done on a computer that is using a motherboard with the BIOS that has to be updated.

Notice that certain computers based on legacy motherboards may not be supported by modern operating systems, such as Windows 98, Windows NT 4.0, and Windows 2000. In such a case it makes sense to update the BIOS version. This is an official recommendation of well-known motherboard manufacturers, such as Abit, ASUSTeK, and Chaintech, to those users that have legacy motherboards from one of the above-mentioned firms. Most other motherboard manufacturers also give similar advice. You should definitely consider updating your BIOS when you decide to purchase a newly released processor. For instance, it is recommended to update your BIOS if you are using Pentium III processors, because most motherboards are intended for use with a Pentium II processor. Consequently, these motherboards are usually good candidates for having their BIOS updated. In many cases, updating the BIOS is also a good idea for Pentium III processors with the Coppermine core.

For certain motherboards that have hidden potential, replacing the BIOS version allows you to discover their hidden capabilities and make them available for use. For a series of motherboards, for example, you will be able to widen the range of processor bus frequencies and supported processor core voltages. In many cases, it also allows you to use the newest processors with legacy motherboards. As an example, consider the well-known Asus P3B-F motherboard. Created before the release of the Pentium III (Coppermine) processor, the Asus P3B-F will be able to work with these processors after updating the BIOS.

Most motherboard manufacturers provide their distributors with BIOS update files. They also publish this information on their Web sites. Usually, the sites of these companies contain various BIOS versions. As a rule, you'll also find their BIOS updating utilities along with documentation describing the new capabilities available after updating the BIOS code.

BIOS Flashing Utilities

In order to update your BIOS you will need special flashing utilities. Notice that upgrading your BIOS through flashing is quite easy to do, but you'll have to consider the potential danger of this operation. Therefore, you have to proceed with this operation very carefully, strictly following the instructions provided by the motherboard manufacturer. As a general rule, you can download documents with instructions and analysis of possible errors from the same sites that contain BIOS updates and flashing utilities.

Updating BIOS means replacing all its data. When flashing your BIOS, there is always the possibility of error or power-down. If flashing has not been completed successfully, you will not be able to restart the computer. In such a case, you'll need to contact a specialist to repair the damage done to your system. Usually, to perform the repair procedures you'll need special equipment, or at least another working computer with the same type of the motherboard.

Keep in mind that the recommendations given below should only be taken as a general scenario of updating your BIOS. Before you actually start the procedure of flashing the BIOS, make sure that you have read and understood the available technical literature on the subject. Otherwise, contact a specialist, since in each particular case BIOS flashing has its own distinctive nuances that influence the final result.

Usually, you need to perform the following steps when updating your BIOS:

1. Determine exactly the model of your motherboard. For different motherboards you will need different BIOS-flashing utilities and different versions of BIOS

updates. Usually, data such as manufacturer, product name, and version are labeled on the motherboard itself.

2. Download the most recent BIOS version from Web or FTP site of manufacturer.

3. Unpack the downloaded file with the updated version of BIOS. Often the downloaded file will be a self-extracting archive with the .exe filename extension. To extract BIOS update, you'll simply need to run that executable file.

4. Disable the BIOS protection option in BIOS Setup. Certain motherboards have a **Flash BIOS Protection** option in the **SeePU & CHIPSET SETUP** menu in BIOS Setup. You must set this option to **Disabled** before you start updating BIOS.

5. Perform a "clean" boot, without loading any resident programs, such as memory managers and other similar programs. Some BIOS flashing utilities refuse to run in the presence of resident programs. Therefore, it is recommended to boot from the DOS-bootable diskette. Notice that besides DOS, this diskette should contain the flashing utility and the ROM image file(s). As an alternative, you may boot DOS or Windows 9x from the hard drive, but skip processing the autoexec.bat and config.sys files.

6. Run the flash utility.

7. Often the flashing utility is supplied with the motherboard. The image file for updating BIOS should reside in the same directory as the flashing utility. Make sure that you remember the exact name of the file that contains the new BIOS version.

Most often, flashing utilities are interactive programs that generally prompt the user to answer the following questions:

❏ the full name of the file containing updated BIOS version (including the filename extension);

❏ the full name of the file, to which the current version will be saved (for example, oldbios.bin);

❏ Confirmation of updating (y/n).

After flashing has finished, reboot the computer.

BIOS and Computer Performance

As you probably know, the functionality and overall performance of the computer are not determined by the CPU alone. They depend on all of the components of the system. A central, coordinating role is played by the motherboard, whose architecture includes the chipset and BIOS. And although the chipset, too, plays an important role in determining the motherboard parameters, it is a permanent feature that cannot be replaced. In contrast to the chipset, the BIOS code, which is recorded in the BIOS chip, can be replaced with a newer version by using special flashing utilities.

Improving and updating the BIOS code allows you both to correct any bugs discovered in the code itself or in the architecture of the motherboard and to make use of the new functionality provided by newer components and subsystems. It also comes with the ability to eliminate hardware conflicts and improve overall performance. Because of this, you should pay special attention to information on available BIOS updates as soon as you purchase your motherboard.

The functionality improvement and gain in performance that can be achieved by updating the BIOS can be demonstrated by the example of a computer with an ABIT BE6-II motherboard and a Pentium 550E processor. Note that the motherboard used is one of the best available, and has a wide range of functional capabilities. Nonetheless, as a result of changing the BIOS code, new parameters appeared in the BIOS Setup. The test results presented below illustrate performance gain.

Configuration of the System Used in Testing

❑ Motherboard: Abit BE6-II.

❑ Processor: Intel Pentium 550E (Coppermine core, 256 KB L2 cache memory operating at the full frequency of the processor's core, Slot 1, in-box version).

❑ Hard drive: IBM DPTA-372050 (20 GB, 2 MB cache memory, 7200 RPM, UltraDMA/66).

❑ RAM: 128 MB, PC100, M-Tech.

❑ Video adapter: Asus AGP-V3800 TV (TNT2 video chipset, 32 MB SGRAM video memory).

❑ CD-ROM: ASUS CD-S400/A (40x).

❑ OS: Windows 98 with installed drivers for UMDA/66 hard drive controller.

BIOS Version

Date of the original BIOS version:

❏ 30.12.1999 (beh_po)

Dates of the new BIOS version:

❏ 01.02.2000 (beh_qj)

❏ 08.05.2000 (beh_rv)

Modifying BIOS and Testing

The steps taken to update the BIOS code are illustrated by Figs. 8.1 and 8.2.

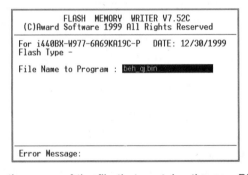

Fig. 8.1. Entering the name of the file that contains the new BIOS program code

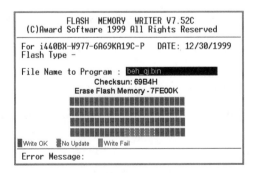

Fig. 8.2. BIOS flashing in progress

Program tests from the WinBench 99 v1.1 were used in testing, specifically the CPUmark99 and the FPU WinMark tests. Test results are illustrated in Figs. 8.3 and 8.4.

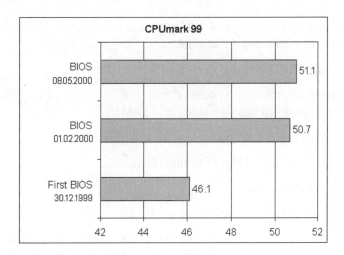

Fig. 8.3. Test results for computers with different BIOS versions

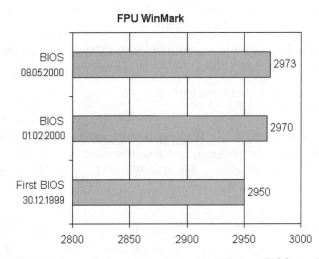

Fig. 8.4. Test results for computers with different BIOS versions

Test Results

Tests	Original BIOS code 30.12.1999	BIOS 01.02.2000	BIOS 08.05.2000
CPUmark 99	46.1	50.7	51.1
FPU WinMark	2,950	2,970	2,973

As a result of updating the original BIOS program code (beh_po) 30.12.1999 with a newer version, the following functional capabilities were added:

❑ BIOS (beh_qj) 01.02.2000:

- Elimination of problems associated with the operation of certain AGP video adapters at a system bus frequency of 133 MHz

- Support for Pentium III processors up to 800 MHz

- Improvement of the SDRAM compatibility

❑ BIOS (beh_rv) 08.05.2000:

- Improvement of the 133 MHz parameter for the system bus

- Elimination of malfunctions associated with certain hard drives when installing the CD-ROM drive at the first hard drive controller (IDE1); the capability to boot the operating system from a CD-ROM

- Elimination of the problem with incorrectly determined RAM size when running the Linux operating system

- Elimination of the problems with the video subsystem when using HighPoint with AHA-2940A and TNT AGP video adapters

- Elimination of the problems with Wake on Ring, Wake on Lan, and Wake on Alarm in Win98SE

- Improvement of the **CPU Warning Temperature** parameter (gives an alert when the processor temperature becomes close to critical) for fixing the problems that arise when using the Win98SE operating system when the processor is overheatead

According to the CPU test, the performance gain attained as a result of replacing the original BIOS version (30.12.1999) with the BIOS code from 01.02.2000 was almost 10%. The next modification had practically no influence on the performance whatsoever, which testifies to the fact that there is a limit to the growth in performance that can be attained from BIOS alone. Nonetheless, the rise in performance from replacing the original BIOS program code with an improved version is relatively large, practically the same as replacing the Pentium III 550E processor with a faster (and therefore more expensive) processor — the Pentium III 600E, for example. It's something to consider, anyway.

Chapter 9

Testing, Monitoring, and Diagnostics

Tuning and optimizing hardware and software is often related to the analysis and setting of a number of parameters. The problem of estimating the effectiveness of certain parameters and their values often arises. Also, it is necessary to evaluate the efficiency of the procedures selected when setting up the computer's hardware and software. Because the total number of parameters that should be taken into account is quite large, it's especially hard to analyze the influence that these parameters have as a whole, since they often depend one on another. Notice also that sometimes these parameters are mutually exclusive.

Incorrect decisions made in the process of installing, optimizing, and especially upgrading hardware and software not only prevent you from getting the full advantage from your computer's functionality, but are also often accompanied by additional and unnecessary financial losses. In such cases, objective criteria that simplify the decision-making process are of the utmost importance.

There are special software tools that estimate the effect of certain specific parameters and settings. Usually, various tests are exploited for this purpose, which allow you to analyze the efficiency and overall performance of the basic subsystems under different combinations of settings. The results obtained in the course of testing allow you to figure out the optimum values. Using this benchmarking software allows you to solve the problem of feedback, which brings a bit of objectivity into the process of setting the parameters and analyzing the results. This amount depends on the software used and the completeness of the testing.

Special programs that are oriented towards analyzing one of the subsystems of the computer are often used as tests. An example is estimating of the performance of the hard drive by the widely known HDDSpeed program, or of the processor with MIPS. There is similar software that can be used for testing RAM and cache memory. This software also allows you to change their working parameters — for example, time delays set in BIOS Setup — and to estimate the operating speed of the given subsystem and its effect on the overall performance. Benchmarking software often helps you to ascertain the abilities of the memory modules and optimize their work, thus using them as effectively as possible.

Often, fairly complex resource-consuming games are also used as tests that help to analyze the system stability. These are, for example, such popular games as Quake, Quake2, Quake 3, and Unreal that have become generally accepted as tests that can aid in estimating the overall performance of the computer as well as the performance of its specific subsystems. It has become almost a tradition to present the results of playing these games/tests in various display modes when estimating the performance of a processor or video adapter.

Despite the prevalence of these programs, the most popular methods of testing are those that allow you to perform a complex analysis of the computer subsystems. Some of the most famous programs used for testing components are SysInfo from the Norton Utilities package, CheckIt 3.0, and PC-CONFIG.

Presented in Figs. 9.1—9.4 are examples of testing a computer using the SysInfo, CheckIt 3.0, and PC-CONFIG programs.

Fig. 9.1. Display of data on the configuration and choice of tests in the SysInfo program

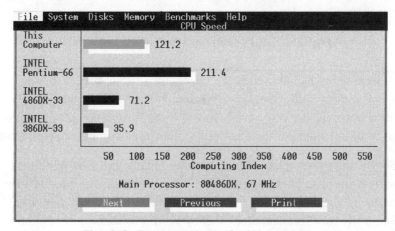

Fig. 9.2. Testing with the SysInfo program

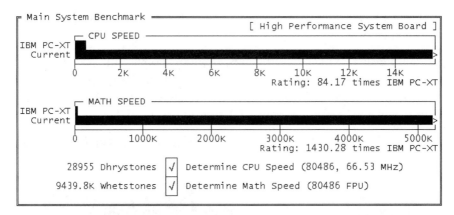

Fig. 9.3. Testing with the CheckIt 3.0 program

```
═══ Choose ═══          ═══════ Benchmark ═══════
 H - Hardware
 W -                    Speed compared with IBM-PC.: 8150%
 S - Software           Dhrystones, KWhetstones....: 24000, 6403
 B - Benchmark          VideoRAM throughput (text).: 5254 KByte/sec
 D - CD-Benchmark        Chars per second via BIOS..: 30590 Byte/sec
 P - Programs           Chars per second via DOS...:  8640 Byte/sec
 N - Devices            EMS speed..................: N/A
 I - Info               RAM disk speed.............: N/A
 V - Compare            DOS disk speed.............: E:  1070 KB/sec
 C - Chips-Info
 M - Mem-Timing
 Q - IRQs               Harddisk test:                HD1       HD2
 L - Drives             Rotations per minute.......: 2920      4500
 R - Restart            Linear read........in KB/S: 1537      1281
 E - Exit               Maximum throughput..in KB/S: 2131      1669
 X - Notes              Interleave seems to be.....:    1         1
                        Average accesstime.........: 11.5 ms   9.3 ms
                        Track to track.............:  3.2 ms   1.9 ms
 PC-CONFIG V7.27        Maximum accesstime.........: 20.6 ms  17.8 ms
```

Fig. 9.4. Testing with the PC-CONFIG program

For modern systems like Windows 9x, there are various benchmarking programs such as CheckIt, WinCheckIt, WinBench 98, WinBench 99, WinStone, 3D WinBench, etc. These programs help you to perform a complete analysis of the performance of individual devices as well as the overall computer performance.

Figs. 9.5—9.8 show examples of testing a computer with the WinBench 99 and WinCheckIt programs. These utilities are used for testing the products developed and released by the majority of hardware manufacturers, including Intel, AMD, VIA, ASUSTeK, etc. You can check this by visiting Web sites of respective manufacturers.

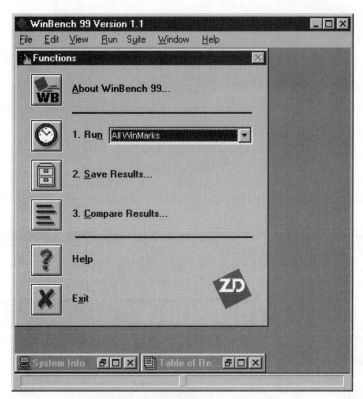

Fig. 9.5. The WinBench 99 program

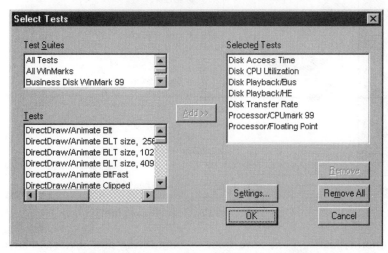

Fig. 9.6. Choice of tests in WinBench 99

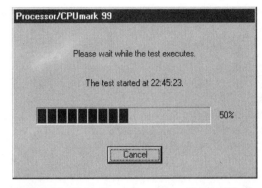

Fig. 9.7. An example of testing the processor with the WinBench 99 program

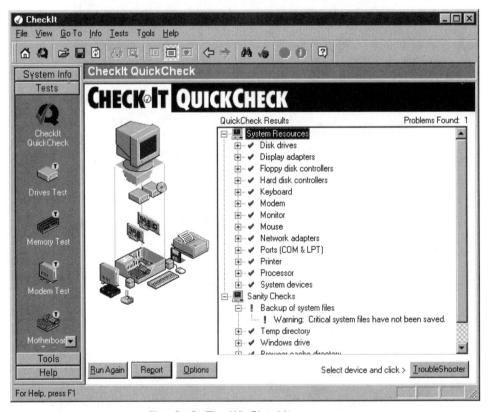

Fig. 9. 8. The WinCheckIt program

Modern motherboards often have built-in monitoring and management capabilities. An example of such a capability is Power Management, which is accessed through the **Power Management Setup** menu in BIOS Setup Award Software (Fig. 9.9). This menu allows you to set up the energy-saving mode option and provides visual control over electric and heat parameters for the processor and operation of the cooling fans and the power supply unit.

Power Management	: Disabled	**** System Monitoring & Alerting ****
PM Control by APM	: Yes	CPU Warning Temperature : 60 °C/140 °F
Video Off Method	: DPMS	Current System Temp. : 30 °C/77 °F
Video Off After	: Standby	Current CPU1 Temperature: 40 °C/77 °F
MODEM Use IRQ	: 3	Current CPU2 Temperature: 40 °C/77 °F
		Current CPUFAN Speed : 3600 RPM
Doze Mode	: Disabled	Current SYSFAN Speed : 3600 RPM
Standby Mode	: Disabled	+1.5V : 1.48V CPU(V): 2.49V
Suspend Mode	: Disabled	+3.3V : 3.32V +5V : 4.83V
HDD Power Down	: Disabled	+12V : 11.85V -12V : - 11.14V
Throttle Duty Cycle	: 62.5%	-5V : - 4.75V
VGA Active Monitor	: Disabled	
Soft-Off by PWR-BTTN	: Delay 4 Sec.	
Wake Up On LAN	: Disabled	
Power On By Modem	: Disabled	ESC : Quit ↑↓→← :Select Item
Power On By Alarm	: Disabled	F1 : Help PU/PD/+/- : Modify
		F5 : Old Values (Shift) F2 : Color
		F7 : Load Setup Defaults
IRQ 8 Break Suspend	: Disabled	

Fig. 9.9. Power Management tools in BIOS Setup

Windows 9*x* provides a built-in monitoring tool — System monitor — intended to help you analyze the computer performance.

Using this program allows you to determine the workload on the processor, RAM, hard drive(s), the size of swap files, etc. in real time without exiting any application or the system. As a result, it's not very difficult to find the hardware and software functions that are monopolizing the resources of the computer subsystems. Besides, having determined the requirements of the application programs in such areas as the RAM and virtual memory, it's easy to choose the best strategy for tuning and upgrading the computer. You now have the opportunity to increase the general performance of the computer while spending a minimal amount of money. For example, using the analysis of the results of testing and monitoring, you may now select the optimal size for a RAM modules to be installed in your computer. In addition, you can define the size and constant status of the swap file, which the virtual memory uses. Incidentally, in order to increase the operating speed of accessing this file, you should place it at the beginning of the hard drive (or at least in the first quarter), which is easily done after installing the system on a relatively large empty hard drive. This is generally accompanied by a significant gain in performance. From the size of the virtual memory, which is designated by the system for work with application and system programs, you may also estimate and choose the optimal size for the computer RAM.

To start this program, click the **Start** button and select the following commands from the **Start** menu: **Start | Programs | Accessories | System Tools | System monitor.**

The illustrations presented below (Figs. 9.10—9.12) demonstrate tuning and operation of the System Monitor program. In the first example, the first four peaks in the **Core: Using the processor** graph reflect the launching of the System monitor and MS Word 7 programs, loading of the file in MS Word 7, and launching MS Excel. In the last example, MS Word 97 was launched and the user was working with the files using that that program.

You can acquaint yourself with the System Monitor program by reading the technical documentation, the OS user guide, and Windows 9x on-line Help system.

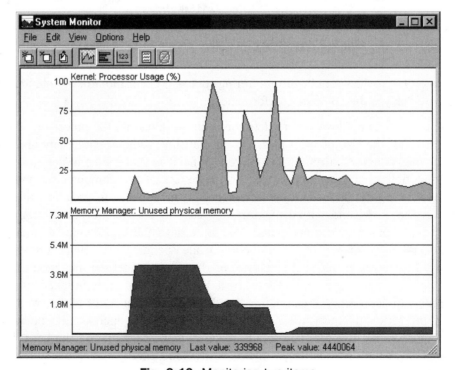

Fig. 9.10. Monitoring two items

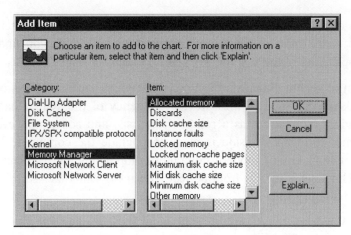

Fig. 9.11. Adding items in the System monitoring program

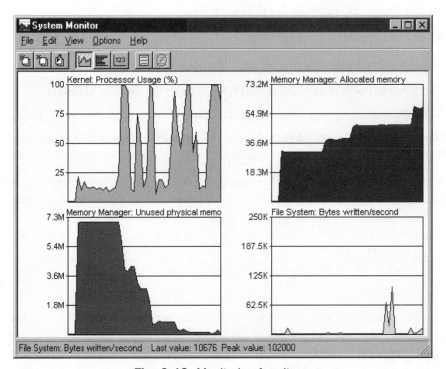

Fig. 9.12. Monitoring four items

Besides the system monitoring capabilities built into BIOS and Windows 9*x*, you can also use special programs developed and distributed by a number of manufacturers.

An example of one of these is the LANDesk Client Manager from Intel. This program is one of the most recognized monitoring programs. You can find out more about the capabilities of the LANDesk Client Manager on Intel's website.

The problem of system diagnostics is closely related to various aspects of monitoring as an instrument used to measure the efficiency of the system hardware and software. Indeed, sometimes as a result of analysis, and sometimes even without doing any monitoring, a decision is made to upgrade the computer. Taking into account the complexity of modern computer components and the fact that plug-and-play technology is still far from perfect, you must sometimes solve compatibility problem on your own.

Included in Windows 9x systems are built-in tools for compatibility analysis. These tools help you to figure out the configuration and analyze existing problems.

To launch them, you must do the following:

1. Right-click the **My computer** icon.

2. Select the **Properties** command from the right-click menu.

3. The **System Properties** window will open. Go to the **Device Manager** tab.

You will then see a list of all devices installed in the system. Conflicting devices will be marked with a special symbol. Fig. 9.13 shows an example of diagnosing the configuration that has a hardware conflict.

You should note that the conflict between devices does not always lead to the system crash. Often, you only notice it, when you need to access one of the conflicting devices. However, the presence of conflicts increases the time it takes to test the hardware while booting the system, and may decrease the operating speed of the computer. This is why, in order to reach maximum computer performance and take full advantage of its functional capabilities, you should resolve the hardware conflicts.

Most often, conflicts arise due to the fact that a number of devices try to use the same system resources, for instance, the addresses of input/output devices, the direct memory access channel (DMA), interrupt request lines (IRQ), etc. In order to fix such conflicts, you should attempt to change the value of the parameter that caused the conflict. It sometimes happens that the device is working incorrectly due to the hardware failure. It might be that the incorrect driver, or not all necessary drivers, are installed. In such a case, after appropriate diagnostics, you should add the necessary drivers. In many cases, you can find on the Internet FAQs and programs that can be of help.

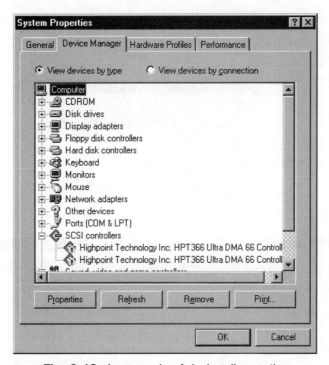

Fig. 9.13. An example of device diagnostics

For performance analysis, diagnostics, and troubleshooting, use the options provided in the **System Properties** window.

Sometimes it may be useful to get a report on system resources. The program can output the report both to the printer or to a PRN file.

The majority of hardware and software settings are stored in the system registry. Usually, most administrative and diagnostic tools change these settings in the registry. However, you can also edit these parameters directly in the system registry itself. This is done using the registry editor (REGEDIT.EXE) — special registry-editing tool that comes with Windows 9x.

To start registry editor proceed as follows:

1. Click the **Start** button.

2. Select **Run**.

3. In the **Run** window, type in the name of the program — REGEDIT — in the **Open** field.

4. Click **OK**.

Examples illustrating startup and operation of the REGEDIT program are shown in Figs. 9.14—9.15.

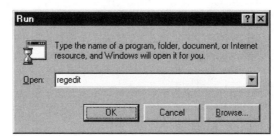

Fig. 9.14. Running the REGEDIT program

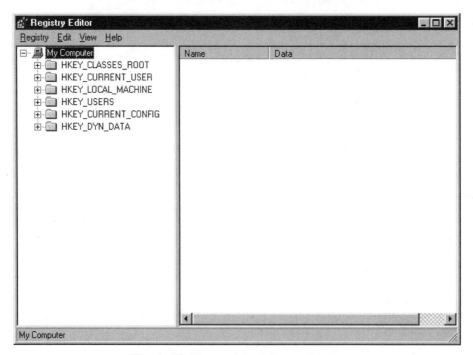

Fig. 9.15. The registry editor program

Notice that incorrect settings entered directly into the registry may easily render your system unbootable. The registry is vitally important system component, and it will require you significant skills and efforts to restore it. It's highly possible that to restore the damaged registry you'll have to reinstall the operating system. Furthermore, you may need to format the hard drive, which will guarantee a more radical and effective cleaning up of the storage device information space from the consequences of careless experimentation.

Because of the potential danger of correcting the hardware and software parameters by editing the system registry, this method can only be recommended to experienced users or professionals. This is also why it is recommended that you use safer methods of diagnosing and monitoring, such as those described earlier. Working with these methods generally is not dangerous to the functioning of the system and the hardware and software of the computer, and therefore can be recommended to those users who are trying to set and optimize the hardware and software of the computer themselves.

Hardware Implementation of Monitoring

Motherboard manufacturers often include special chips in the architecture of their products in order to provide support for diagnostic and management functions. As a general rule, these control various parameters, such as: temperature (of the processor, the motherboard, the air inside the case, etc.), voltage (to the processor, the motherboard's elements, etc.), and the rotation speed of the cooling fans (for the processor, the power supply unit, etc.).

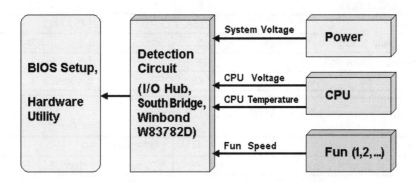

Fig. 9.16. A scheme for PC hardware monitoring

Hardware monitoring tools are gradually becoming not only highly desirable, but a mandatory component of contemporary high-end systems characterized by high performance and reliability. Such tools are increasingly often built into high-quality chipsets, such as the most commonly used North Bridge VT82C686A chip.

It is necessary to point out that some motherboard vendors, whose products are based on contemporary chipsets that include hardware monitoring tools, are not satisfied with their functional capabilities, and are therefore using special-purpose chips. Examples of such chips include LM78 and LM79 from National Semiconductor, and W83781D and W83782D from Winbond. The reason for this choice lies in the fact that specialized chips have higher parameters than the built-in chipset tools.

The main parameters of the W83781D and W83782D chips are listed below:

Parameter	W83781D	W83782D
Temperature control, input	3	3
Voltage control, input	5(+), 2(-)	9
Fan control, input	3	3
Body integrity control (open/closed), input	1	1
Typical values of the controlled voltages, V	VcoreA, VcoreB, 3.3, 5, 12, -12, -5	Vcore, 3.3, 5, 12, -12, -5, +5V Vsb, Vbat, 1 reserved
Voltage measurement precision, % (max.) +/-	1	1
Temperature measurement precision, % (max.) +/-	3	3
Built-in ADC, pulses	8	8
Interface	ISA, I^2C	ISA, I^2C
Power supply voltage, V	5	5
Consumed current, mA	1	5
Chip frame type	48p LQFP	48p LQFP

The main parameters of the LM78 and LM79 chips:

Parameters	LM78 and LM79
Temperature control, input	1 % sensor on chip
Voltage control, input	5(+), 2(-)
Fan control, input	3
Typical values of controlled voltages, V	2.5Va, 2.5Vb, 3.3, 5, 12, -5, -12
Voltage measurement precision, % (max.)	1

continues

Continued

Temperature measurement precision, % (max.)	3
FAN RPM measurement precision, % (max.)	10
Built-in ADC, pulses	8
Interface	ISA, I^2C
Power supply voltage, V	5
Consumed current, mA	1
Chip frame type	VGZ44A (PQFP)

Main methods of hardware monitoring in VT82C686A:

Temperature control, input	2 and 1 internal
Voltage control, input	4(+) and 1 internal
Fan control, input	2

For the measurement circuits to correctly function, they require appropriate sensors and meters, as well as co-ordination of their input resistance values depending on the input resistance values of the meters. This approach allows us to maximize the legitimate signal-to-noise ratio.

Instead of using the thermistor as a temperature sensor, it is possible to use the transistor in a diode-type circuit, as shown in Fig. 9.17a. The working principle of such a sensor is based on the dependence of the threshold-triggering voltage of the silicon p-n transition on the temperature. As a result, when the transistor temperature changes, the threshold voltage changes in practically linear dependence with a negative gradient of 2.3 mV/C (dV ~ 1/T).

Like the transistor scheme, other components can be used for controlling the processor temperature mode, such as a thermal diode built into the Pentium III chip. The thermal diode of the Pentium 4 processor is connected in a similar manner.

AMD processors (such as AMD Athlon (Thunderbird) and AMD Duron) and earlier products from Intel have no built-in on-chip temperature sensors. Because of this, temperature mode control for these processors must be done using external sensors, which are usually set either near Slot A and Slot 1 processors (Fig. 9.18) or within Socket A (Socket 462) or Socket 370 (Fig. 9.19) for PGA and FC-PGA processors. To guarantee the normal functioning of the thermal sensors and correct processor temperature values, motherboard vendors provide temperature contact between sensors and processor cases.

Hardware monitoring tools, whether implemented using special-purpose chips or built into the chipset's components and complemented with the appropriate sensors, usually only allow for measurement of the specified parameters.

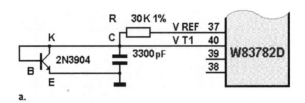

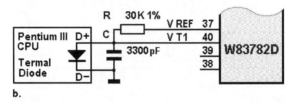

Fig. 9.17. Schemes for connecting semiconductor temperature sensors to the W83782D chip (a — 2N3904 transistor, b — built-in thermal diode of the Pentium III processor)

Fig. 9.18. External temperature sensor for Slot 1 processors

Fig. 9.19. External temperature sensor set within Socket A

Software

There are special programs that allow you to display this information on the monitor, perform a detailed analysis of the parameter values, and control these settings. Most often, the program that provides this kind of service is built into BIOS Setup.

As an example, consider the **PCHealth Status** menu, which appears in the BIOS Setup of Abit BE6-II motherboards (Fig. 9.20).

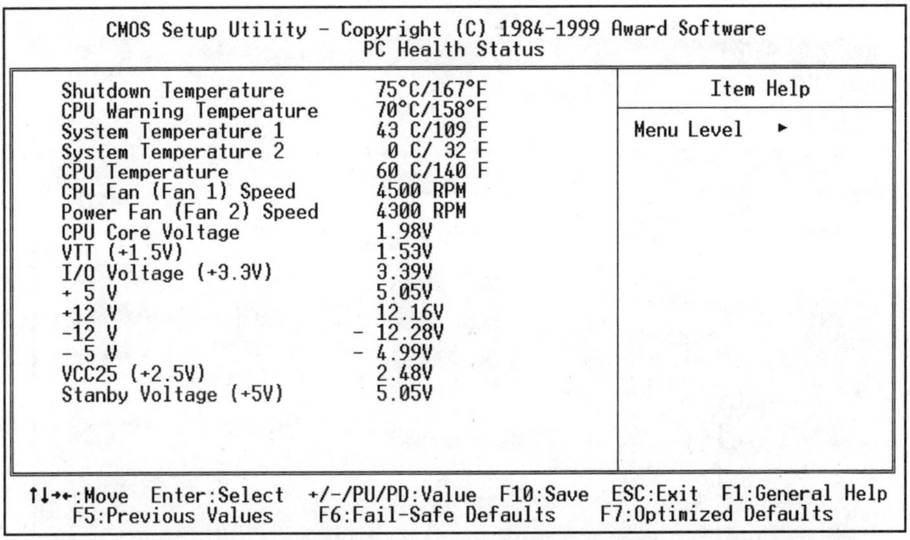

```
CMOS Setup Utility - Copyright (C) 1984-1999 Award Software
                      PC Health Status

  Shutdown Temperature          75°C/167°F          Item Help
  CPU Warning Temperature       70°C/158°F
  System Temperature 1          43 C/109 F       Menu Level  ▶
  System Temperature 2           0 C/ 32 F
  CPU Temperature               60 C/140 F
  CPU Fan (Fan 1) Speed         4500 RPM
  Power Fan (Fan 2) Speed       4300 RPM
  CPU Core Voltage              1.98V
  VTT (+1.5V)                   1.53V
  I/O Voltage (+3.3V)           3.39V
  + 5 V                         5.05V
  +12 V                        12.16V
  -12 V                       - 12.28V
  - 5 V                       - 4.99V
  VCC25 (+2.5V)                 2.48V
  Stanby Voltage (+5V)          5.05V

 ↑↓→←:Move  Enter:Select  +/-/PU/PD:Value  F10:Save  ESC:Exit  F1:General Help
     F5:Previous Values    F6:Fail-Safe Defaults    F7:Optimized Defaults
```

Fig. 9.20. Monitoring capabilities are often built-in to the BIOS Setup routine

There are other specialized programs, which allow you to control, analyze, and display the diagnostic parameters on the monitor using standard capabilities of widely spread operating systems, such as Windows. Usually, these programs are supplied by the motherboard manufacturers along with the motherboard. For example, let us consider the typical monitoring program Winbond Hardware Doctor included in the software package that comes with the Abit BE6-II. A screenshot illustrating operation of this program is shown in Fig. 9.21.

The Winbond Hardware Doctor program allows you to monitor the following parameters:

❑ **Voltage**:

- **Vcore** (processor core voltage)

- **Vtt** (additional processor voltage)

- **+3.3V** (chipset, oscillator, PCI bus)

- **+5V** (motherboard microcircuitry, PCI and ISA buses)

- **+12V** (ISA bus)

- **–5V** (ISA bus)

- **5Vsb** (suspended mode standby voltage)

- **VCC25**

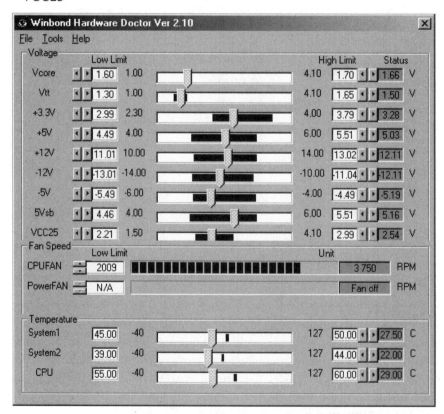

Fig. 9.21. The Winbond Hardware Doctor Ver 2.10 program

❑ **Fan Speed** (rotation speed):

- **CPUFAN**

- **PowerFAN** (power block fan)

❑ **Temperature**:

- **System1** (system temperature: motherboard or case)
- **System2** (system temperature: motherboard or case)
- **CPU**

Winbond Hardware Doctor allows you to specify the limits for the hardware operating modes. These limits determine the maximum (High Limit) and minimum (Low Limit) value allowed for each parameter (Fig. 9.22). For controlling the temperature, only the maximum value is important (Fig. 9.23), just as for the fan only the minimum value is key (Fig. 9.24). If the value of the controlled parameter exceeds the specified limits, a warning message will appear, accompanied by an audible alarm if necessary (Fig. 9.25).

You should keep in mind that the program described above has one drawback: it is bound to a specific model of the motherboard (or series of motherboards with identical diagnostic equipment). However, there exist universal system diagnostic programs. One of these is the Motherboard Monitor program (MBM). Version 4.12 of this program supports the following diagnostic chips: LM78, LM78-j, LM79, GL518SM, GL520SM, Winbond W83781D, Winbond W83782D, Winbond W83783S, and LM75.

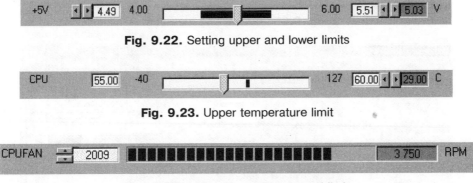

Fig. 9.22. Setting upper and lower limits

Fig. 9.23. Upper temperature limit

Fig. 9.24. Lower fan rotation speed limit

Examples that illustrate the usage of this program are presented in Figs. 9.26 and 9.27.

The following table lists examples of motherboards from some well-known manufacturers. These boards, according to data from the developers of MBM, support this program. Also included in the table are the chips integrated into the motherboard architecture. These chips ensure the monitoring of the basic parameters. The table also lists MBM versions, which started to provide support for monitoring parameters.

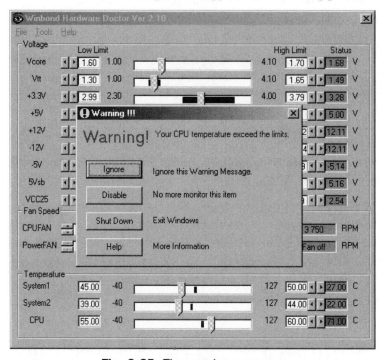

Fig. 9.25. The warning message

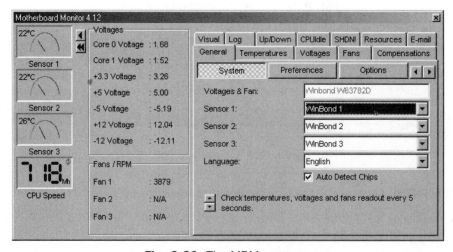

Fig. 9.26. The MBM program

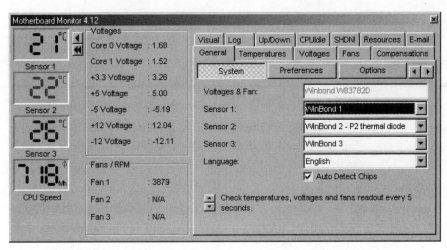

Fig. 9.27. A window in the MBM program with modified values

Motherboard Monitoring Capabilities

Motherboard	Voltage and speed of the fan rotation	System temperature	Processor temperature	MBM version
		Abit		
BH6	LM79	LM79	—	3.80
BM6	W83782D	Winbond 3	Winbond 2	3.80
BX6	LM79	LM79	—	3.80
BX6-2	W83782D	Winbond 1	Winbond 2 - P2 thermal diode (for the PII/III internal sensor) and Winbond 3 (for the external sensor)	3.80
LX6	—	—	—	3.80
TX6	—	—	—	3.80
ZM6	W83782D	Winbond 3	Winbond 2	3.80
BE6	W83783S core1 and -5 V not supported	Winbond 2	Winbond 1	4.09
BE6-2	W83782D	Winbond 1	Winbond 2 or Winbond 2 - P2 diode	4.16
BP6	W83782D	Winbond 3	Winbond 1, CPU 2 Winbond 2, CPU 1	4.09

continues

Continued

Motherboard	Voltage and speed of the fan rotation	System temperature	Processor temperature	MBM version
BF6	W83782D	Winbond 3	Winbond 2 - P2 thermal diode	4.13
VA6	VIA686A	VIA686-3	VIA686-2	4.13
KA6	VIA686A	VIA686-3	VIA686-2	4.17
A-Trend				
ATC 6220	W83781D	Winbond 1	Winbond 3	3.80
Acorp				
5TX52	—	—	LM75-5	3.80
5VIA77	—	—	—	4.09
Aopen				
AX6BC	GL518SM	—	GL518SM	4.03
AX6L	GL518SM	—	GL518SM	4.09
AX63	—	—	—	4.09
MX64	VIA686A	VIA686A-1	VIA686A-2	4.16
ASUSTeK				
P3V-4X	AS99127F	Asus 1	Asus 2 or Asus 3	4.17
P3C-2000	AS99127F	Asus 1	Asus 2 or Asus 3	4.13
P3C-E	AS99127F	Asus 1	Asus 2 or Asus 3	4.13
P3C-L	AS99127F	Asus 1	Asus 2 or Asus 3	4.13
P3C-S	AS99127F	Asus 1	Asus 2 or Asus 3	4.13
P3C-LS	AS99127F	Asus 1	Asus 2 or Asus 3	4.13
P3B-F	AS99127F	Asus 1	Asus 2 or Asus 3	4.10
P2B	W83781D	Winbond 1	Winbond 2 or 3 (if the sensors are enabled)	3.80
P2B-F	W83781D	Winbond 1	Winbond 2 or 3 (if the sensors are enabled)	3.80

continues

Continued

Motherboard	Voltage and speed of the fan rotation	System temperature	Processor temperature	MBM version
P2B-L	W83781D	Winbond 1	Winbond 2 or 3 (if the sensors are enabled)	3.80
P2B-S	W83781D	Winbond 1	Winbond 2 or 3 (if the sensors are enabled)	3.80
P2B-LS	W83781D	Winbond 1	Winbond 2 or 3 (if the sensors are enabled)	3.80
P2B-D	W83781D	Winbond 1	Winbond 2 or 3 (if the sensors are enabled)	3.80
P2B-DS	W83781D	Winbond 1	Winbond 2 or 3 (if the sensors are enabled)	3.80
P2L97	LM78	LM78	—	3.80
P2L97-S	LM78	LM78	—	3.80
P2L97-DS	LM78	LM78	—	3.80
P5A	W83781D	Winbond 1	Winbond 2	3.80
P5A-B	W83781D	Winbond 1	Winbond 2	3.80
P55T2P4S	—	—	—	3.80
TX-97	LM78	LM78	LM75-2	3.80
TX-97E	LM78	LM78	LM75-2	3.80
TX-97XE	LM78	LM78	LM75-2	3.80
TX-97X	LM78	LM78	LM75-2	3.80
TX-97XV	LM78	LM78	LM75-2	3.80
TX-97LE	LM78	LM78	LM75-2	3.80
KN-97X	LM78	LM78	—	3.80
K-7M	W83782D	Winbond 1	Winbond 2 (if the thermal sensor is connected to the TRCPU)	4.10
K-7V	W83782D	Winbond 1	Winbond 2	4.17
CUBX	AS99127F	Asus 1	Asus 2	4.17
BCM				
QS440BX	W83781D	Winbond 1	Winbond 2	4.03

continues

Continued

Motherboard	Voltage and speed of the fan rotation	System temperature	Processor temperature	MBM version
		Biostar		
M6TLA	—	—	—	3.80
M6TBA	W83781D	Winbond 1	Winbond 2 or 3	4.08
M7MKA	W83782D	Winbond 2	Winbond 1	4.16
		California Graphics		
Photon 100	W83781D	Winbond 1	Winbond 2	3.80
Photon 100 HC	W83781D	Winbond 1	Winbond 3	4.12
		Commate		
S7SXB	Sis 5595	—	Sis 5595-1	4.16
		ChainTech		
6BTM	W83781D	Winbond 1	Winbond 2	3.80
6LTM PII	LM78	LM78	—	3.80
CT-6ATA2	VIA686A	VIA686A-3	VIA686A-2	4.16
		Dell		
XPS R400	—	—	—	3.80
		DFI		
P5BV3+	—	—	—	3.80
DFI P2XBL/D rev. A1	W83781D	Winbond 1	LM75-2 & LM75-1	4.00
DFI K6XV3+/66	GL518SM	GL518SM	—	4.17
		DTK		
PRM-00761	LM78	LM78	—	3.80
		Elite		
6BX A+	W83781D	Winbond 1	Winbond 2	3.80
		Epox		
EP-51MVP3E-M AT	LM78	LM78	—	3.80

continues

Continued

Motherboard	Voltage and speed of the fan rotation	System temperature	Processor temperature	MBM version
EP-58MVP3C-M AT:				
the old version	LM78	LM78	—	3.80
the new version	W83781D	Winbond 1	Winbond 2	3.80
MVP3E-M	W83781D	Winbond 2	Winbond 3	3.80
MVP3G-M	W83781D	Winbond 3	Winbond 2	3.80
KP6 BS	LM78	LM78	ADM1021 - 7 Local	4.09
EP61 BXB-S	LM78	LM78	CPU0 = ADM1021-7	4.10
			CPU1 = ADM1021-8	
MVP4-A	VIA 686A	—	—	4.10
MVP3-G5	W83781D	Winbond 1	Winbond 2	4.16
EP-7KXA	VIA 686A	VIA 686A-3	VIA 686A-2	4.16
FIC				
VB 601	W83781D	Winbond 1	Winbond 2	3.80
VA 503A	VIA686A	VIA686A-2	VIA686A-1	4.11
SD 11	VIA686A	VIA686A-3 or VIA686A-2	VIA686A-2 or VIA686A-3	4.11
PA 2013	—	—	—	
PAG 2130	VIA686A	VIA686A-1 and/or VIA686A-2	VIA686A-3	4.16
Freetech				
P58F5	—	—	—	3.80
GigaByte				
GA-586 ATX	—	—	—	3.80
GA-5AX ATX	—	—	—	4.09
GA-686 LX	—	—	—	3.80

continues

Continued

Motherboard	Voltage and speed of the fan rotation	System temperature	Processor temperature	MBM version
GA-686 DLX	—	—	—	3.80
GA-686 BLX	—	—	—	3.80
GA-686 SLX	—	—	—	3.80
GA-686 LX2	—	—	—	3.80
GA-686 DL2	—	—	—	3.80
GA-686 LX3	—	—	—	3.80
GA-686 LX4	—	—	—	3.80
GA-686 BX	W83781D	Winbond 1 (or 3)	Winbond 2	3.80
GA-586 BA	W83781D	Winbond 1 (or 3)	Winbond 2	3.80
GA-6BXE	W83782D	Winbond 1	Winbond 2 (if the thermal sensor is connected) Winbond 3 - P2 thermal diode (for PII/III with a sensor inside)	3.80
GA-6BXS	W83781D	Winbond 1	Winbond 2	3.80
GA-BX2000	W83782D	Winbond 1	Winbond 2	4.05
7IX	W83782D	Winbond 1	Winbond 2	4.12
Intel				
Atlanta LX	—	—	—	3.80
Portland PD440FX	LM78	LM78	—	3.80
PR440FX	LM78	LM78	—	3.80
Tuscon TC430HX	—	—	—	3.80
VS440FX	—	—	—	3.80
SE440BX	ADM9240	ADM9240	—	4.06
SE440BX2	ADM9240	ADM9240	—	4.06

continues

Continued

Motherboard	Voltage and speed of the fan rotation	System temperature	Processor temperature	MBM version
Iwill				
BD100 Plus	W83781D	Winbond 2	Winbond 1	4.09
VD133	W83781D	Winbond 2	Winbond 1	4.16
Jbond				
PCI500K	—	—	—	3.80
JetWay				
J-P6LDX IDE PII	LM78	LM78	—	3.80
993N	—	—	—	4.16
Micron				
Millenia	—	—	—	3.80
Millenia XKU	—	—	—	4.01
Maxtium				
BXAD	W83781D	Winbond 1	Winbond 2	4.09
Microstar				
6-SBA	W83781D	Winbond 1	Winbond 2	3.80
MS-5158	LM78	LM78	—	3.80
MS-6119 (not for all of them)	W83781D	Winbond 1	Winbond 2	3.80
MS-6163	W83781D	Winbond 1	Winbond 2	4.08
OL-5158	LM78	LM78	—	3.80
MS-P6DBU	W83781D	Winbond 1	Winbond 2	4.16
MS-6309	VIA686A	VIA686A-3	VIA686A-2	4.16
MS-6199	W83782D	Winbond 1	Winbond 2	4.16
QDI				
Titanium 1B	—	—	—	3.80
BrilliantX IS	LM80	LM80	—	4.10

continues

Continued

Motherboard	Voltage and speed of the fan rotation	System temperature	Processor temperature	MBM version
BrilliantX I	LM80	LM80	LM80	4.10
PC Chips				
M575	—	—	—	3.80
M729	—	—	—	4.16
Shuttle				
Hot 591p	—	—	—	3.80
Hot 637	—	—	—	4.08
Soltek				
580VPX	—	—	—	4.04
Soyo				
6BA+	W83781D	Winbond 1	Winbond 2	3.80
6BA+ IV	W83782D	Winbond 1	Winbond 2 - P2 Diode	4.11
6BE+	W83781D	Winbond 1	Winbond 2	3.80
6Y6BB	W83781D	Winbond 1	Winbond 2	3.80
6BA	LM78	LM78	LM75-5	3.80
7IZB+	W83783S	—	Winbond 1 or Winbond 2	4.10
SY-6VBA	W83782D	Winbond 1	Winbond 2 - PII diode	4.12
SY-6VBA 133	W83782D	Winbond 1	Winbond 2 - PII diode	4.16
Supermicro				
P5MMS98	LM78-j	LM78	LM75-3	3.80
P5MMA98	LM78-j	LM78	LM75-3	3.80
P6SLS	LM78	LM78	with LM75-5 only	3.80
P6SLA	LM78	LM78	LM75-5	3.80
P6DLS	LM78	LM78	with LM75-5 only	3.80
P6DLA	LM78	LM78	with LM75-5 only	3.80
P6DLF	LM78	LM78	with LM75-5 only	3.80

continues

Continued

Motherboard	Voltage and speed of the fan rotation	System temperature	Processor temperature	MBM version
P6DLH	LM78	LM78	with LM75-5 only	3.80
P6DNF	LM78	LM78	with LM75-5 only	3.80
PMMS98	LM78	LM78	with LM75-5 only	3.80
P6DBS	W83781D	Winbond 1	Winbond 2 and Winbond 3	3.80
Elite P5SS-Me	—	—	—	4.09
P6SBA	W83781D	Winbond 1	Winbond 2	4.10
Tekram				
P6B40-A4X	LM78	LM78	LM78 - Tekram probe	4.08
TMC				
TI5VG+	W83781D	Winbond 1	Winbond 2	3.80
TI5VGF	W83781D	Winbond 1	Winbond 2	3.80
TYAN				
Dual Tiger 2 (S1692DL)	LM78	LM78	—	3.80
S1682D	LM78	LM78	—	3.80
S1836 DLU	LM79	LM79	LM75-5 and LM75-6	3.80
S1837 DLU	LM79	LM79	LM75-5 and LM75-6	3.80
Thunder 100 1836DLUAN-GX	LM79	LM79	LM75-5 and LM75-6	3.80
Tiger 100 S1832DL	LM78	LM78	LM75-5 and LM75-6	3.80
Trinity S1590S	—	—	—	3.80
Tsunami SLA	LM78	LM78	LM75-5	3.80
S1598	VIA686A	VIA686A-3	VIA686A-2	4.11
S1598c2	VIA686A	VIA686A-2	VIA686A-3	4.11
1832DL	LM79	LM79	LM75-5 and LM75-6	4.17

Chapter 10

Windows 9x/NT/2000 Local Area Networks

Organizing PCs into Local Area Networks (LANs) is an important factor in increasing their functional capabilities. This provides the computer with the ability to exchange information with other computers and efficiently use shared network resources. Efficient management of the shared network resources allows you to avoid unnecessary data redundancy and extra financial investments. The shared resources may include printers, modems, CD-ROM, DVD-ROM and floppy drives, hard disks and their partitions or logical drives, individual folders etc. Not only does it allow optimization of each individual computer, but also provides you with the ability to dedicate individual computers to specific tasks. The most important fact here is that LAN will allow you to efficiently use the PCs with relatively inferior performance, which otherwise would be of little use. Local Area Networks allow you to organize parallel processing of the data that an individual computer could not handle on its own, make several users work with the shared resources, distribute resource-consuming tasks between several computers, and so on.

Setting up the Network

Windows $9x$ operating systems provide built-in networking capabilities that allow you to organize a peer-to-peer network fairly easily. Such a network can be deployed in an office as well as at a home.

To interconnect two PCs into a Local Area Network (LAN), the following equipment is required:

❒ Network adapters (one for each of the networked PCs)

❒ Coaxial cable and a BNC connector, 2N-2 items, where N is the number of networked computers (Fig. 10.1)

❒ T-connector (N items, where N is the number of networked PCs) and two terminators with a resistance of 50 ohms (Fig. 10.2)

Let's consider for example the procedure of connecting two computers into a local area network.

To create this simple network, proceed as follows:

1. Open the computer's case and install the network card into a free slot. Then close the case.

2. Do the same for the second computer.

3. Connect the two network cards with a coaxial cable using a T-connector (Fig. 10.3).

4. Install a terminator (50 ohms) into the free jack of the T-connector.

Fig. 10.1. Coaxial cable and BNC connector

Fig. 10.2. T-connector and terminator (50 ohms)

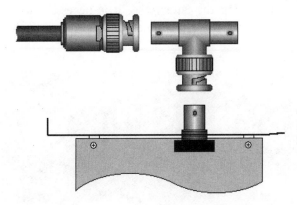

Fig. 10.3. Connecting the coaxial cable to the network adapter via a T-connector

Connection of the PC to the Local Area Network is shown in Fig. 10.4.

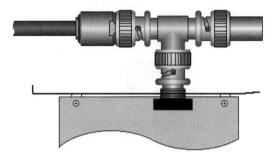

Fig. 10.4. Connecting the PC to the LAN

Don't connect the pieces of cable by soldering or twisting. Use a BNC barrel connector (Fig. 10.5).

Fig. 10.5. Connecting cable pieces using a BNC barrel connector

Within a LAN, computers might be interconnected both by coaxial cable and by the so-called twisted pair. In the latter case, it is necessary to use special cables and RJ-45 connectors. The network adapter must have an appropriate connector (Figs. 10.6 and 10.7).

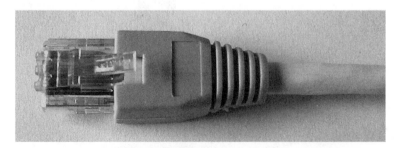

Fig. 10.6. RJ-45 connector with the twisted pair cable

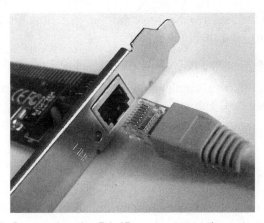

Fig. 10.7. Connecting the RJ-45 connector to the network adapter

To connect two or more computers to the network, you'll require additional equipment — hubs. Hubs are not needed when using coaxial cable.

Reboot both computers so that Windows 9x can analyze the hardware configuration changes and detect network adapters. If Windows 95 can't detect network adapters automatically, you can perform the installation manually (Fig. 10.8):

1. Open the **Control Panel** window and double-click the **Add New Hardware** icon.

2. The Add New Hardware wizard will open its first window. Click **Next** to continue.

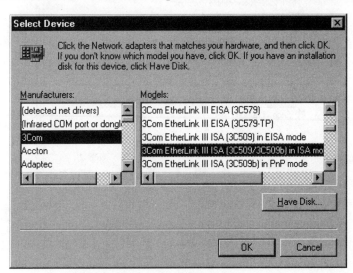

Fig. 10.8. Installing the network cards

3. In the next window, set the **No** radio button (the program will not search for hardware for you), and then click **Next**.

4. Select the **Network cards** option from the equipment list and click **Next**.

5. From the list in the next window, select an appropriate network card (the one that you have installed) and click **OK**.

6. Restart the computer.

Configuring the Network

In order to specify the network configuration for a computer running Windows 9x, do the following:

1. Open the **Control Panel** window and double-click the **Network** icon. The **Network** window will appear (Fig. 10.9).

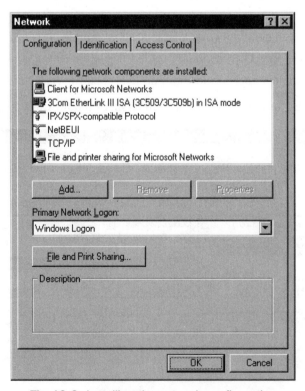

Fig 10.9. Installing the network configuration

2. This window will list network components that have already been installed in the system. Usually, this list includes the following components:

   - Microsoft network client

   - The network card driver

   - IPX/SPX-compatible protocol

   - NetBEUI

   - TCP/IP

   - File and printer sharing for Microsoft networks

3. Select the **Windows Logon** item from the **Primary Network Logon** drop-down list.

4. Click the **File and Print Sharing** button to open the File and Print Sharing dialog. Set the checkboxes **I want to be able to give others access to my files** and **I want to be able to allow others to print to my printer(s)**. Then click OK.

5. Go to the **Computer** tab (Windows 95) or to the **Identification** tab (Windows 98).

6. Enter any name for this computer (VR, for example) into the **Computer name** field.

7. Go to the **Workgroup** field and specify a name for the workgroup, to which the local computer will belong. Notice that in our example both computers must belong to the same workgroup, so this name must be the same for both computers.

8. The **Computer description** field is optional. You may fill it with any additional information on the local computer.

9. Click **OK** and restart the computer.

10. Thus, you have configured one of the two computers to participate in the network. To configure the second computer, follow the same procedure. (Note that the computer name must be unique, but both computers must belong to the same workgroup) After rebooting both computers, make sure that our small peer-to-peer network works correctly. To test the network, start Windows Explorer and open the Network Neighborhood folder. If the network is configured correctly, this folder will list the names of both computers. If this is not so, then something has gone wrong, and you need to detect and correct the error.

Organizing Access to Shared Resources

In order to provide a user of one networked computer with the ability to use the resources of another networked computer, it is necessary to organize access to the shared resources.

To do this, you need to install the *File and Print sharing for Microsoft networks* service on each computer that will contain shared resources, and then create the shared resources.

1. Double-click the **My Computer** icon to open the **My Computer** window.

2. Right-click the disk to which you need to provide access through the network.

3. Select the **Sharing** command from the right-click menu (Fig. 10.10).

4. Set the **Shared As** radio button.

5. Specify the network name for the shared resource. For convenience sake, the actual drive letter assigned to the logical drive is normally used (for example: C, D, etc.).

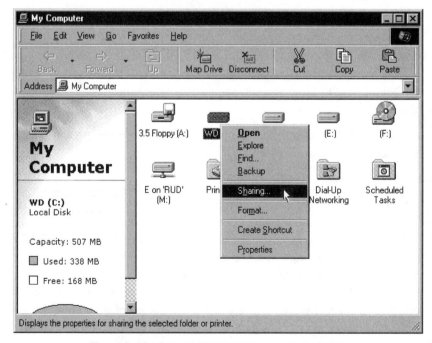

Fig. 10.10. Organizing access to a logical disk

6. Select one of the three types of access by setting one of the following options: **Read-Only**, **Full**, or **Depends on Password**.

7. Click **OK** (Fig. 10.11).

8. If there are other disks that you want to share, repeat the above-described procedure for each one, including the CD-ROM drive.

You can share not only logical disks, but individual folders (directories) as well.

1. Open **My Computer**.

2. Find the folder that you want to share and right-click it.

3. Select the **Sharing** command from the right-click menu (Fig. 10.12). The **Properties** window for that folder will appear opened to the **Sharing** tab. Set the **Shared As** radio button.

4. Enter the network name for the given folder. For convenience sake, the actual name of that folder is generally used.

5. Specify access type by selecting one of the following options: **Read-Only**, **Full**, or **Depends on Password** (Fig 10.13).

6. Click **OK**.

Repeat this procedure for all folders that you need to share.

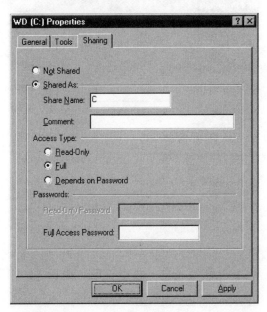

Fig 10.11. Setting up access to a logical disk

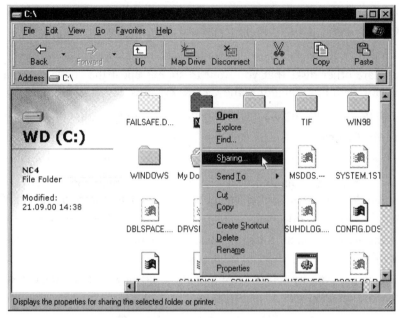

Fig. 10.12. Sharing a folder

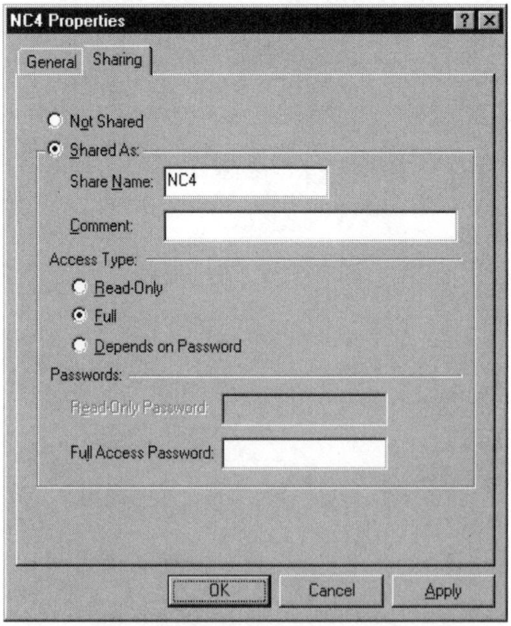

Fig. 10.13. Specifying access type to a folder

Mapping Network Drives

Now that the network has been installed and configured, and network shares have been created, you can start working in your new network environment. The **Network Neighborhood** folder provides the easiest way of browsing the network and accessing available shared resources. Double-click the **Network Neighborhood** icon to start browsing the network. After you select a computer, you'll be able to view all shared resources available there and access disks and folders to which access is granted. Working with shared disks and folders through the network is similar to the way you access the resources on your own computer.

Note that sometimes this method is inconvenient, because, for instance, you cannot use shared resources in DOS applications such as Norton Commander, DOS Navigator, and the like.

Mapping network drives and creating persistent network connections can solve many problems. After network drives are mapped, they can be used as if they were local resources on your computer.

To map network drive when working under Windows 95:

1. Open **My Computer**.

2. Click the **Map Network Drive** button on the toolbar. The **Map Network Drive** dialog will appear (Fig. 10.14).

3. Open the **Drive** drop-down list and select the drive letter for the shared resource to be mapped. This network share may be a network disk or shared folder. Subsequently, the mapped resource will be treated in the same manner as a logical disk on the local computer.

4. Go to the **Path** field and manually enter the fully qualified pathname of the network share to which you are going to connect. The path entered into this field must be in the Universal Naming Convention (UNC) format: `\\computer_name\share_name` (for example: `\\VR\C`, where `VR` is the name of the computer, and `C` is the name of the shared resource). If you have difficulties entering the UNC path to the shared resource manually, you can browse the drop-down list to select the one that you need.

5. You can also specify if you would like to create a persistent network connection by setting the **Reconnect at logon** checkbox. If you set this option, this connection will be restored any time you log on to Windows.

6. Click **OK**.

7. If everything has been done correctly, the icon for the mapped share will appear in the **My Computer** window.

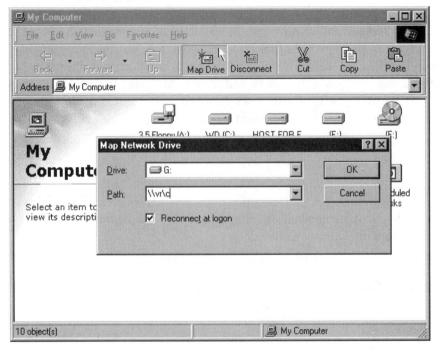

Fig. 10.14. Mapping the network drive

To map network shares under Windows 98:

1. Right-click the **My Computer** icon.

2. Select the **Map Network Drive** command from the right-click menu. The **Map Network Drive** dialog will appear.

3. Go to the **Drive** field and select the drive letter for the drive to be mapped. Notice that the network share to be mapped may represent a network disk or shared folder. Subsequently, the mapped resource will be treated in the same manner as a logical disk on the local computer.

4. Go to the **Path** field and enter the fully qualified path to the disk or shared folder that you are going to connect. The path you enter into this field should be in the UNC format: \\computer_name\share_name (for example, \\VR\C, where VR is the name of the computer, and C is the name of the shared

resource). If you have problems specifying the network path manually, you can browse the network to select the shared resource that you need to map.

5. You can also specify if you would like to create a persistent network connection by setting the **Reconnect at logon** checkbox. If you set this option, this connection will be restored any time you log on to Windows.

6. Click **OK**.

7. If everything has been done correctly, the icon for the mapped share will appear in the **My Computer** window.

Using Network Printers

If there is a computer within your network that has a printer connected to it, you may share that printer so that all network users can access it.

First, you must provide access to the printer for the network users. Sharing printers is done in the same manner as sharing other network resources such as disks or folders. Open the **Printers** window (**Start | Settings | Control Panel | Printers**) and right-click the printer that you want to share. Then select the **Properties** command from the right-click menu and go to the **Sharing tab**. Set the **Share As** radio button and enter the share name for the printer.

After this, you'll be able to access this network printer from other computers within your network. To achieve this, you'll need to specify this printer when installing the network printer on the other computers within your network. To install the network printer, follow these steps:

1. Click the **Start** button and select **Settings | Printers | Add Printer** from the **Start** menu.

2. The **Add Printer Wizard** window will appear. Click **Next >** to continue.

3. In the next window, set the **Network Printer** radio button, and then click **Next >**.

4. In the next window, press the **Browse** button to browse shared resources available in the network. Find computer that has the printer attached to it, browse the shared resources available there, and locate the printer you need to access. Select that printer and click **OK**.

5. Specify a name for the new printer and click **Next >**.

6. Click **Finish**.

After installing the network printer, it can be used just like a local printer, with the only difference being that it is physically connected to another computer.

This procedure is applicable for a LAN containing any number of computers. The network cards of the computers participating in the network interact with one another via network media (for example, thin Ethernet). In the example considered here, network adapters are connected to the network media (coaxial cable) through T-connectors. Terminators should be set in the unused T-connector jacks of the first and the last networked computers. Needless to say, the setup procedure for shared network printers must be done for all the computers that are providing and/or using shared resources.

Playing Games via the Network

Many programs provide multi-user mode, where a number of users can work simultaneously. Some popular games also provide multi-player mode. Having completed network setup, gamers can enjoy multi-player mode, if their favorite game supports it. For example, the most popular games supporting multi-player mode are DOOM, Quake, Duke 3D, WarCraft II, Red Alert, etc. If the game supports this mode, its menu contains a **Network Game** option, or something of the sort.

Creating Remote Networks

When you need to access the resources on another computer from a remote location (for example, the corporate network from home) and it is impossible to physically connect the computers by means of network adapters and coaxial or unshielded twisted pair (UTP) cables, remote access will help you accomplish this task. For this purpose, Windows 9x provides Dial-Up Networking functionality, which allows you to establish a physical connection between computers having modems to communicate over dial-up telephone lines.

To provide access to the remote network it is necessary to connect two computers using modems and a telephone line. One of these computers (the one that provides the access) is connected to the network. This computer is called the remote access server, while the other one is a client. Windows 98 is a convenient client platform for remote access, because its built-in Dial-Up Networking functionality provides connectivity to most popular remote access servers, and its Dial-Up Server component allows other users to access Windows 98 computers or home networks from remote locations. The most important consideration here is that both client and server have modems installed, and modems used with the server and with the client must be compatible with each other.

In order to establish a connection to a remote network, you must configure the remote access server. This procedure includes the following steps:

1. Planning and organizing access to the shared resources that will be accessible to remote users. This procedure was described earlier in this chapter when discussing the topic *"Organizing Access to Shared Resources"*.

2. Perform the Dial-Up Networking Server installation. The Dial-Up Networking Server component, which allows users to access the local computer from remote locations, is included with Microsoft Plus! software product.

3. Start Dial-Up Networking (**Start** | **Programs** | **Accessories** | **Dial-Up Networking**). Alternatively, you can open the **My Computer** window and double-click the **Dial-Up Networking** icon.

4. From the **Connections** menu, select the **Dial-Up Server** command (Fig. 10.15).

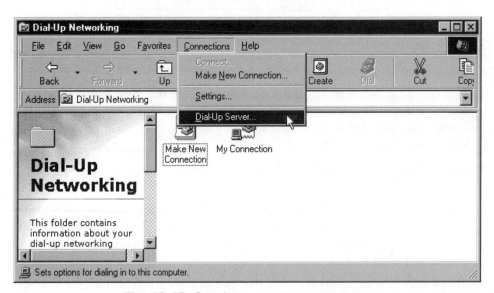

Fig. 10.15. Creating a remote access server

5. Set the **Allow caller access** radio button (Fig. 10.16) to enable remote access. This will enable Windows 98 to accept incoming calls and grant remote users access to shared resources on the local area network. Remote users will be able to access these resources as if they were establishing a connection to a local

network. To secure your local network you'll normally wish to specify a password for logging on to it.

Fig. 10.16. Window for setting up access to network resources for remote users

When all these tasks are completed, remote users may start dialing the server and accessing shared resources. To establish the connection, proceed as follows:

1. Start Dial-Up Networking, and then select the **Make New Connection** command from the **Connection** menu. You'll need to enter information on the new connection, such as the name, the server's phone number, and the password for logging on to the network.

2. When these tasks are completed, a new icon for this connection will appear in the **Dial-Up Networking** window.

3. To start the connection, open the **Dial-Up Networking** window and double-click the icon representing the connection you need. The **Connect To** dialog will appear, providing you with the opportunity to change certain connection properties before dialing.

4. To establish the connection, click the **Connect** button. The modem will then start dialing the phone number and attempt to log on to the remote network.

After the connection has been successfully established, you'll be able to take advantage of all the capabilities described earlier in this chapter.

The only drawback of remote access is the connection speed, which is limited by the modem baudrate characteristics and the telephonine throughput.

Windows NT/2000/XP Networks

Windows NT/2000, like Windows 9x, also has built-in networking capabilities. A Windows-based LAN can be comprised of computers running different operating systems, for example, Windows 98 and Windows 2000. However, a Windows NT/2000 network installation has its own specific features, the most important of which is the fact that only authorized users having user accounts can access system resources. If you are going to implement a LAN connecting Windows 9x and Windows NT/2000 computers, you'll need to create user accounts. For example, if there is a computer running Windows 9x in your LAN, you'll need to create at least one user account on that computer. On a Windows NT/2000 computer you'll need at least two user accounts. The first user account is intended for the user working in the local system, and the second one relates to the user who is going to access this computer through the network. Accounts are created for each networked computer, and you also can create an account for each user. Note that Windows NT/2000 has built-in user accounts. The first user account therefore already exists, and you thus only need to create accounts for other users. This task is fairly straightforward. For the sake of simplicity, we will consider this procedure based on the example of the simplest possible peer-to-peer network consisting of two computers.

Setting up of the Windows XP-based network is performed according to the similar scenario.

Creating a Windows 95/98 User Account

1. Open the **Control Panel** window and double-click the **Users** icon (Fig. 10.17).

2. The **Enable Multi-User Settings** window will appear. Click **Next** (Fig. 10.18).

3. The **Add User** window will appear. Enter the new username into the **User Name** field, then click **Next** (Fig. 10.19).

4. The **Enter New Password** window will appear. If necessary, specify the password for the new user, then click **Next** (Fig. 10.20).

5. Next, the **Personalized Items Settings** window will open. Here you can select personalized user settings for the new user. When finished, click **Next** (Fig. 10.21).

6. The **Enable Multi-User Settings** window is the final window that appears in the course of the procedure of creating new user accounts (Fig. 10.22). To conclude the process, click **Finish** and reboot the computer. After successful completion of the startup procedures, the system will prompt you to enter your username and password.

Fig. 10.17. Starting the Users applet in the **Control Panel** window (Windows 98)

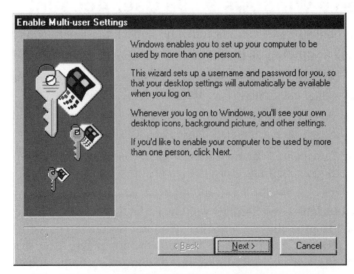

Fig. 10.18. The **Enable Multi-user Settings** window

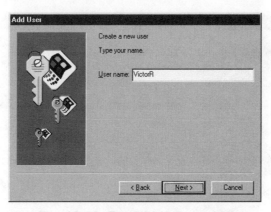

Fig. 10.19. The **Add User** window

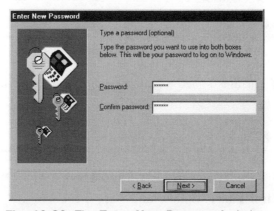

Fig. 10.20. The **Enter New Password** window

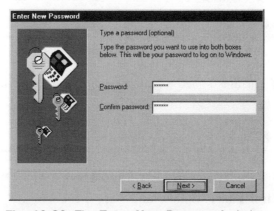

Fig. 10.21. The **Personalized Items Settings** window

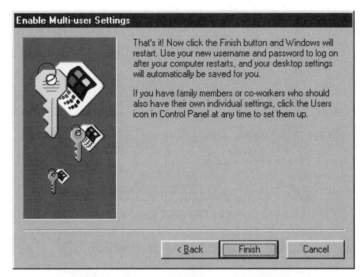

Fig. 10.22. The **Enable Multi-user Settings** window

The procedure of creating a new user account is illustrated by the screenshots shown in Figs. 10.17—10.22.

Creating a Windows NT/2000 User Account

To create a new user account in Windows 2000, proceed as follows:

1. Open the **Control Panel** window and start the **Users and Passwords** applet (Fig. 10.23).

2. You will then see the **Users** tab of the **Users and Passwords** window. This tab will display the list of users who have user accounts on the local computer. Click **Add** to create a new user account (Fig. 10.24).

3. The **Add New User** window will appear. Enter the new user name into the **User Name** field. Note that if this user will be accessing this system remotely, then there must be a user account with the same name on the client computer, from which that user will access the local system. You can also enter optional data, such as full name and description. Click **Next** when done (Fig. 10.25).

4. The system will prompt you to enter the password. Having done so, click **Next** (Fig. 10.26). Notice that the password is optional. If the password field is left blank, it will simplify things for the user, but it is not advisable from the security point of view.

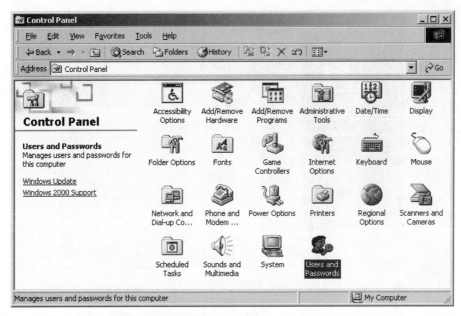

Fig. 10.23. Starting the **Users and Passwords** applet from the **Control Panel** window

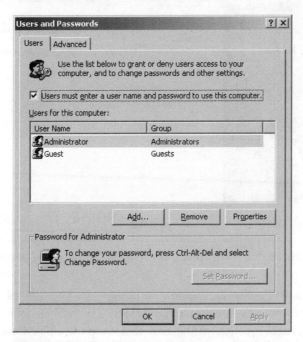

Fig. 10.24. The **Users and Passwords** window

Fig. 10.25. The **Add New User** window. Entering the user name

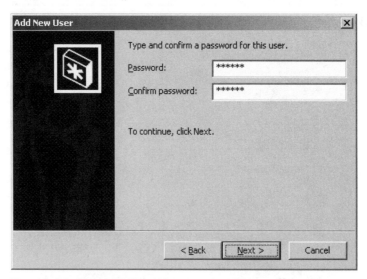

Fig. 10.26. The **Add New User** window. Entering the password

5. The **Users and Passwords** window will appear. The list of users contains the newly created user account (Fig. 10.27). The user account has thus been created. To cancel creation of the new user account, click **Cancel**. To confirm the results, click **OK**.

Fig. 10.27. The **Users and Passwords** window displays the list of users, including the newly created user

The process of creating new user accounts in Windows NT 4.0 has some differences from the procedure described above. To start the procedure of creating a new user account in Windows NT 4.0 start the **User manager** tool (Windows NT 4.0 Workstation) or **User Manager for Domains** tool (Windows NT 4.0 Server).

To initiate the procedure, select the following commands from the **Start** menu: **Start | Programs | Administrative tools (common) | User Manager**. As a result, the **User Manager** window will appear, containing the list of all existing user accounts. To create a new user account, select the **New User** command from the **User** menu. The **New User** window will appear. Enter the login name into the **Username** field. You can also specify and confirm the password for the new user, enter his or her full name and description, and specify other user-specific parameters. To complete the procedure of creating the new user account, click **OK**. As a result, new user account will be created, and the name of the new user will appear in the list of users.

Configuring a Windows NT/2000 Network

During Windows 2000 installation, the Setup program detects and configures the network adapter. It then prompts the user to select the network installation mode. The following two options are available: Default settings and Custom settings. If the user selects the automatic installation mode with default network settings, only one network protocol — TCP/IP — will be installed. Thus, if this protocol is not sufficient, you'll either need to select the custom network setup mode during Windows 2000 setup, or install additional network protocols later. This procedure can be done any time after Setup is completed. To install additional network protocols, proceed as follows:

1. Right-click the **My Network Places** icon at the desktop and select the **Properties** command from the right-click menu (Fig. 10.28).

2. The **Network and Dial-Up Connections** window will appear (Fig. 10.29).

3. Right-click the **Local Area Connection** icon and select the **Properties** command from the right-click menu (Fig. 10.30).

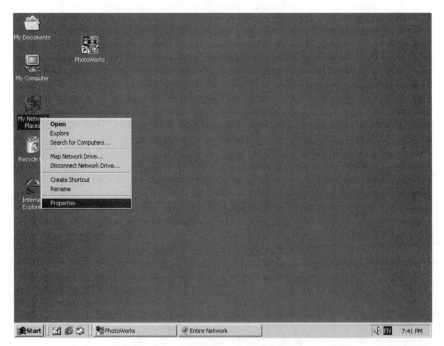

Fig. 10.28. Selecting the **Properties** command from **My Network Places** right-click menu

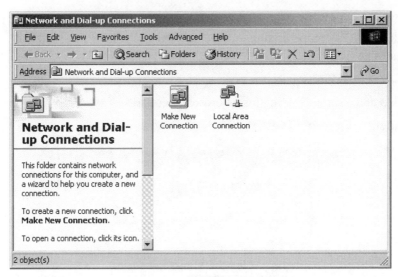

Fig. 10.29. The **Network and Dial-up Connections** window

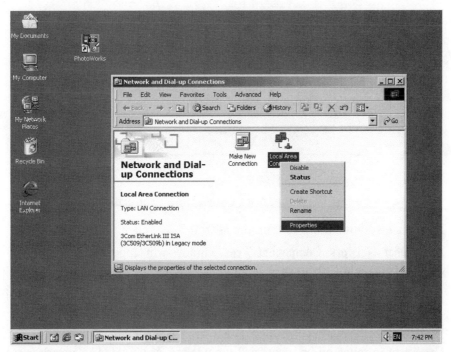

Fig. 10.30. Selecting the **Properties** command from the **Local Area Connection** right-click menu

4. The **Local Area Connections Properties** window will appear (Fig. 10.31). This window will list network components installed in the system. By default, this list includes the following:

- Client for Microsoft Networks
- File and Printer Sharing for Microsoft Networks
- Internet Protocol (TCP/IP)

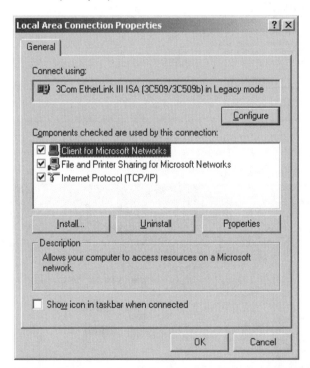

Fig. 10.31. The **Local Area Connection Properties** window

5. To include additional network protocols to this list, click the **Install** button.

6. The **Select Network Component Type** window will appear (Fig. 10.32). Here you'll need to select **Protocol** and click the **Add** button.

7. The **Select Network Protocol** window will appear. Select, for example, the **NetBEUI Protocol** option and click **OK** (Fig. 10.33).

8. The wizard will return you to the **Local Area Connections Properties** window. The list of installed components will include the newly added network protocol (Fig. 10.34).

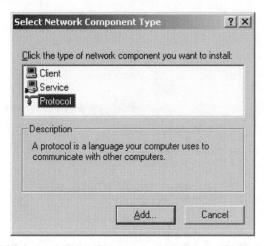

Fig. 10.32. Selecting the **Protocol** option in the **Select Network Component Type** window

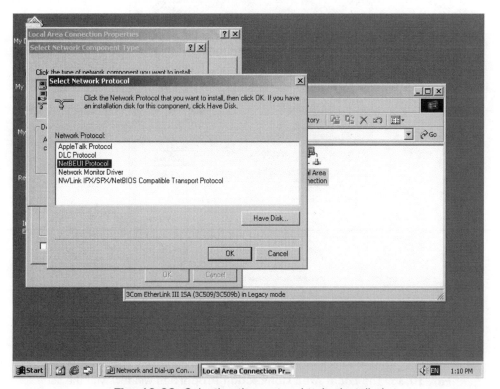

Fig. 10.33. Selecting the protocol to be installed

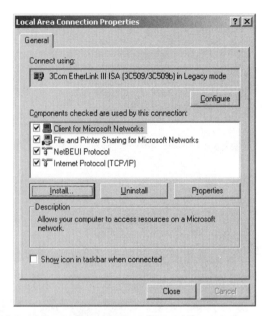

Fig. 10.34. The **Local Area Connection Properties** window contains the newly installed NetBEUI Protocol in the list of detected network components

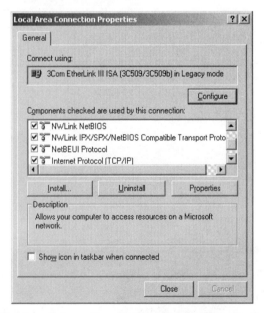

Fig. 10.35. The **Local Area Connection Properties** window with the list of all installed network components

9. Repeat items 5—8 to add the **NWLink IPX/SPX/NetBIOS Compatible Transport Protocol** to the protocol list.

10. As a result, the list of installed network components in the **Local Area Connections Properties** window will contain the following items (Fig. 10.35):

    - Client for Microsoft Networks

    - File and Printer Sharing for Microsoft Networks

    - NWLink NetBIOS

    - NWLinkIPX/SPX/NetBIOS Compatible Transport Protocol

    - NetBEUI Protocol

    - Internet Protocol (TCP/IP)

In a Windows NT 4.0 network, protocols are installed using a similar procedure in the **Protocols** tab of the **Network** window (**Start | Settings | Control Panel | Network**).

Thus, all necessary protocols are selected and the network has been installed and configured. As with the case of a peer-to-peer network based on Windows 95/98, you'll need to identify computers on the network by specifying computer names and the workgroup they belong to. Note that sometimes the names are set by default (the user can change these default values during the operating system setup or any time later).

To modify these parameters in Windows 2000, do the following:

1. Right-click the **My Computer** icon at the desktop and select the **Properties** command from the right-click menu.

2. The **System Properties** window will appear. Go to the **Network Identification** tab. This tab displays the current computer name (the **Full computer name** field) and workgroup name (the **Workgroup** field). The screenshot of this tab is shown in Fig. 10.36.

3. To rename the local computer, click the **Properties** button.

4. The **Identification Changes** window will appear (Fig. 10.37). Here you can rename the computer, and join another workgroup or domain.

5. Having made all the necessary changes, click **OK**.

6. You'll return to the **Network Identification** tab of the **System Properties** window. Notice the new names in the respective fields of this tab (Fig. 10.38).

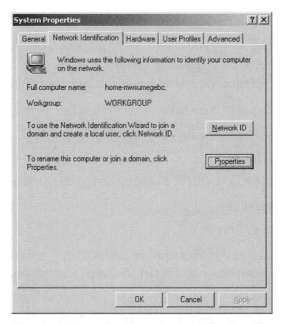

Fig. 10.36. The **Network Identification** tab of the **System Properties** window

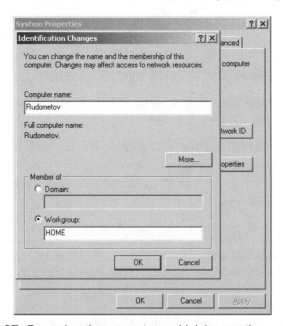

Fig. 10.37. Renaming the computer and joining another workgroup
in the **Identification Changes** window

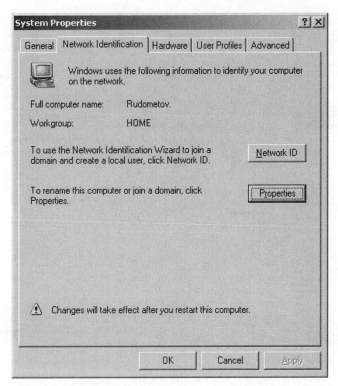

Fig. 10.38. The **Network Identification** tab of the **System Properties** window now contains new names

7. Now click **OK** and reboot the computer.

In Windows NT 4.0 you can change the computer name and group membership at the **Identification** tab of the **Network** window (**Start | Settings | Control Panel | Network**).

Organization of access to shared resources in Windows NT/2000 is very much similar to the procedure in Windows 95/98. To access network disks it is necessary to proceed as follows:

1. Right-click the **My Computer** icon (or **My Network Places** icon) and select the **Map Network Drive** command from the right-click menu (Fig. 10.39).

2. The **Map Network Drive** window will appear. Select the drivename letter and specify the network path to the shared resource (Fig. 10.40). If you need to re-connect this resource every time Windows starts, set the **Reconnect at logon** checkbox. When done, click **Finish**.

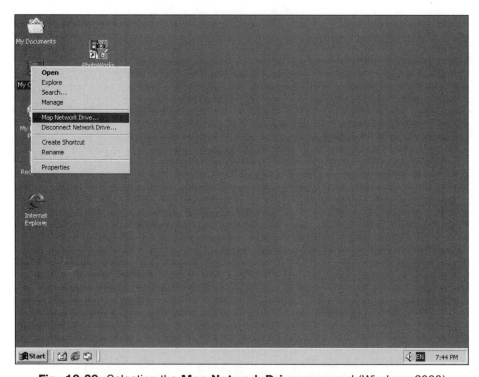

Fig. 10.39. Selecting the **Map Network Drive** command (Windows 2000)

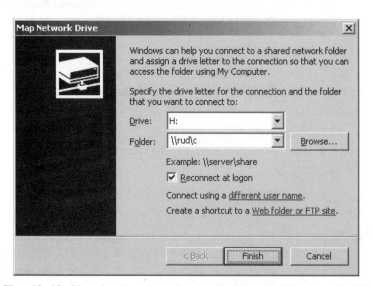

Fig. 10.40. Mapping the shared network resource (Windows 2000)

Chapter 11

Overclocking Modes

The general performance of the computer can be significantly increased by setting overclocked modes for some of its subsystems that will impose an increase in their operating speed. One of these subsystems is the processor, which plays the leading role in processing data and managing the other subsystems of the computer. By raising the processor operating frequency and/or the front-side bus frequency (which determines the processor operating frequency), you will be able to considerably improve the overall computer performance. The other subsystems, such as the video adapters and storage subsystem, often undergo a similar process. This method of increasing the operating speed is called "overclocking". This is the widely used and generally accepted term, used in computer-related literature and on the Internet. You should note that along with increasing the frequency you must often also increase the voltage to those components subject to overclocking.

In no case can the authors be held responsible for any damage resulting from an attempt to overclock any computer subsystem. Any overclocking is done at your own risk.

The main idea of setting overclocked modes for certain components and subsystems is to increase the computer's performance without serious financial investments into its upgrade.

In most cases, to switch the computer subsystems to overclocking mode, it is sufficient to change a few settings on the motherboard. Usually, this comes down to changing the position of a few jumpers or switches. Sometimes, however, you must replace or add a few elements. This is especially true for the elements intended to guarantee effective and reliable cooling of the system.

Not so long ago, overclocking meant no more than raising the clock frequency of the processor. For example, XT computers based on i8088 processors rated to run at 4.7 MHz, could be overclocked to run at the frequencies from 6 to 12 MHz. I80386 processors rated at 33 MHz could be overclocked to 40 MHz. This ability to be overclocked was often already included in the computer design by the manufacturers. Although they didn't usually advertise this, it was not unusual to find a Normal/Turbo button on the front panel of the system unit, which would switch the computer to run at a higher clock frequency.

Now, many users of computers based on Pentium, Pentium II, or Pentium III processors from Intel, or similar processors from other companies, have the opportunity to increase not only the internal clock frequency of the processor at which data is processed, but also the frequency of the processor system bus. The frequency of this bus determines the external frequency of the processor. Note that in technical literature, this bus is often referred to as the host bus, FSB (Front Side Bus), CPU Bus, or SB (System Bus). Raising the frequency of this bus can appreciably improve the computer performance, since this speeds up data exchange with the memory, the video adapter, the hard drive, etc.

Some Overclocking Problems

As was previously mentioned, the overclocking method has been in use for a relatively long time. Nonetheless, there are a several factors that limit the use of this mode that best exploits the components and subsystems of the computer.

First of all, you need to remember that overclocking increases the probability of failure of components running in forced mode. For instance, overclocked processors release larger amounts of heat. This disturbs the heat balance. As a result, the temperature of the processor case increases, and the semi-conductor chip located inside overheats. Sometimes, this overheating is so intense that the processor can fail. A similar problem may arise for the other overclocked elements, such as the video adapter chipset and its memory. Keep in mind that modern video adapters allow you to overclock these elements separately.

The problem of disturbing the heating rate of the overclocked elements can often be solved by more intense cooling. Incidentally, this applies not only to overclocked modes. Proper cooling, in general, serves as a precautionary measure, ensuring the stable and prolonged work of the computer components, even while working in the recommended modes. In overclocked modes, however, the problem of cooling is much more complicated. Often, even effective cooling is not sufficient to compensate for the negative effects of overclocking on the components. For this reason, the overclocked processor may possibly not last for the entire warranty period. Generally, this is not a matter of importance. As was mentioned before, the elements usually become obsolete much more quickly than they physically age. In the process of using the computer, many of its elements will be replaced by newer ones before they fail due to the irreversible processes in the semiconductors caused by overclocking. Furthermore, the reliability and life cycle of modern components are so impressive (hundreds of thousands of power-on hours before failure, more than 10 years of guaranteed trouble-free usage) that when overclocked within reasonable limits and with proper control over the heating mode, this reduction in the component's life cycle is insignificant. It's recommended that you replace your processor every 1 or 2 years, and this time period is showing a tendency to decrease. The same applies to video adapters and hard drives.

The next problem is perhaps more essential. When overclocked, the overall stability of the system is often disturbed. There is always the probability that after overclocking any component, your system will become unstable. Of course, it's not very wise to perform important tasks that demand a high level of reliability on computers whose components have been overclocked. Due to the possible instabilities, data may be damaged or even lost. This is exactly why you should test the computer thoroughly in every possible manner after the overclocking process is completed. It's recommended that you use such popular testing programs as WinStone, WinBench, and the like. In order to test the system, it makes sense to run applications that use the maximum amount of system resources. This may be a sufficiently complex application, or a game − Doom or Quake, for example. It's also advised that you initialize a number of tasks for simultaneous execution. If it appears that a certain component of the computer is not stable, you must figure out the reason for this, and change the functioning modes. In order to increase the functional stability of the overclocked components, you may need to carefully raise the voltage. Or, you might need to decrease the clock frequency, or even return everything back to its original state. There is no universal cure. Overclocking is a creative process. The result depends on the overclocker's experience and persistence, on the elements used and their interaction, and also on the drivers and programs used. Often, the result can even depends on the individual specimen.

Your most important task when overclocking, then, is to increase the performance while maintaining the stability of the entire computer system.

Clock Frequencies and Performance

Increasing the bus frequency and the internal and external clock frequency of the processor can raise the performance of a computer.

As mentioned earlier, the best and the simplest method of increasing the performance of the system is to raise the bus frequency. However, this can only be done if the specific motherboard model allows it. If it does not, you must be content with only increasing the clock frequency of the processor. The internal processor frequency is derived using the multiplier of the external frequency.

Note that the internal processor frequency is the rate at which the processor executes operations. External frequency is the rate of the host-bus (FSB, SB, CPU Bus), that is, the speed at which the chipset, the cache memory, and the RAM operate. Other components of the computer, device controllers for example, operate at the frequency of the buses that connect them to the system, for instance, through the PCI and AGP buses. For PCI buses, the operating rate, as a rule, is half of the host-bus frequency. For certain motherboards, it is either half or a third, depending on the frequency. Other input-to-output frequency ratios of the host bus are also possible. Modern video adapters in computers with Pentium II, Pentium III, and similar processors are generally connected to the other components of the computer by an AGP bus, the frequency of which also depends on the frequency of the host bus. This all means that any change in the frequency of the host-bus will lead to a change in the throughput of the PCI and AGP buses, and in the long run will change overall computer performance.

To track the interdependence of these frequencies, let us use an Intel Pentium-166 processor. The internal frequency of this processor, for which it is intended and at which it is recommended to perform internal data processing, is, as you can see from its name, 166 MHz. This frequency is determined by the host bus frequency and the multiplier. If the host bus frequency is 66 MHz, the multiplier will be 2.5 (2.5×66 MHz gives us 166 MHz). Thus, if the processor works at a clock frequency that is X times more than the host-bus frequency, the internal clock frequency of the processor is determined as follows:

```
Host-bus frequency x X = internal clock frequency.
```

where x is the multiplier.

In the above example, the frequency of the PCI bus is 33 MHz.

For Intel Pentium 150 processors, the internal clock frequency is 150 MHz, the external frequency is 60 MHz, the multiplier is 2.5, and the PCI frequency is 30 MHz.

Special jumpers on the motherboard usually determine the multiplier for Intel Pentium and similar processors from other companies. Less often, it is set in BIOS Setup.

Listed in the following tables are popular processors, their speeds, and the multiplier for the external frequency.

Intel Pentium Processors

Processor	Internal frequency/external frequency, MHz	Multiplier	External voltage/ core voltage, V
Pentium 60	60/60	1.0	3.5/3.5
Pentium 66	66/66	1.0	3.5/3.5
Pentium 75	75/50	1.5	3.5/3.5
Pentium 90	90/60	1.5	3.5/3.5

continues

Continued

Processor	Internal frequency/external frequency, MHz	Multiplier	External voltage/ core voltage, V
Pentium 100	100/66	1.5	3.5/3.5
Pentium 120	120/60	2.0	3.5/3.5
Pentium 133	133/66	2.0	3.5/3.5
Pentium 150	150/60	2.5	3.5/3.5
Pentium 166	166/66	2.5	3.5/3.5
Pentium 180	180/60	3.0	3.5/3.5
Pentium 200	200/66	3.0	3.5/3.5
Pentium MMX 166	166/66	2.5	3.3/2.8
Pentium MMX 200	200/66	3.0	3.3/2.8
Pentium MMX 233	233/66	3.5	3.3/2.8

Intel Pentium II Processors

Processor	Internal frequency/external frequency, MHz	Multiplier	Core voltage, V
Pentium II 233	233/66	3.5	2.8
Pentium II 266	266/66	4.0	2.8
Pentium II266	266/66	4.0	2.0
Pentium II 300	300/66	4.5	2.8
Pentium II 300	300/66	4.5	2.0
Pentium II 333	333/66	5.0	2.0
Pentium II 350	350/100	3.5	2.0
Pentium II 400	400/100	4.0	2.0
Pentium II 450	450/100	4.5	2.0

Intel Celeron Processors

Processor	Internal frequency/external frequency, MHz	Multiplier	Core voltage, V
Celeron 266	266/66	4.0	2.0
Celeron 300	300/66	4.5	2.0

continues

Continued

Processor	Internal frequency/external frequency, MHz	Multiplier	Core voltage, V
Celeron 300A	300/66	4.5	2.00
Celeron 333	333/66	5.0	2.00
Celeron 366	366/66	5.5	2.00
Celeron 400	400/66	6.0	2.00
Celeron 433	433/66	6.5	2.00
Celeron 466	466/66	7.0	2.00
Celeron 500	500/66	7.5	2.00
Celeron 533	533/66	8.0	2.00
Celeron 533A	533/66	8.0	1.50
Celeron 566	566/66	8.5	1.50
Celeron 600	600/66	9.0	1.50
Celeron 633	600/66	9.5	1.65
Celeron 667	600/66	10.0	1.65
Celeron 700	600/66	10.5	1.65

Intel Pentium III (SECC2) Processors

Processor	Internal frequency/external frequency, MHz	Multiplier	Core voltage, V
Pentium III 450	450/100	4.5	2.00
Pentium III 500	500/100	5.0	2.00
Pentium III 533B	533/133	4.0	2.00
Pentium III 533EB	533/133	4.0	1.65
Pentium III 550	550/100	5.5	2.00
Pentium III 550E	550/100	5.5	1.65
Pentium III 600	600/100	6.0	2.05
Pentium III 600B	600/133	4.5	2.05
Pentium III 600E	600/100	6.0	1.65
Pentium III 600EB	600/133	4.5	1.65

continues

Continued

Processor	Internal frequency/external frequency, MHz	Multiplier	Core voltage, V
Pentium III 650	650/100	6.5	1.65
Pentium III 667	667/133	5.0	1.65
Pentium III 700	700/100	7.0	1.65
Pentium III 733	733/133	5.5	1.65
Pentium III 750	750/100	7.5	1.65
Pentium III 800	800/100	8.0	1.65
Pentium III 800EB	800/133	6.0	1.65
Pentium III 850	850/100	8.5	1.65
Pentium III 866	866/133	6.5	1.65
Pentium III 933	933/133	7.0	1.70
Pentium III 1.08 GHz	1.08 GHz	7.5	1.70

Intel Pentium III (PGA370) Processors

Processor	Internal frequency/external frequency, MHz	Multiplier	Core voltage, V
500E	500/100	100	1.60
533EB	533/133	4.0	1.65
550E	550/100	5.5	1.60
600E	600/100	6.0	1.65
600EB	600/133	4.5	1.65
650	650/100	6.5	1.65
667	667/133	5.0	1.65
700	700/100	7.0	1.65
733	733/133	5.5	1.65
750	750/100	7.5	1.65
800	800/100	8.0	1.65
800EB	800/133	6.0	1.65
850	850/100	8.5	1.65

continues

Continued

Processor	Internal frequency/external frequency, MHz	Multiplier	Core voltage, V
866	866/133	6.5	1.65
933	933/133	7.0	1.65

AMD K5/K6 Processors

Processor	Internal frequency/external frequency, MHz	Multiplier	External voltage/core voltage, V
AMD-K5 PR75	75/50	1.5	—
AMD-K5 PR90	90/60	1.5	—
AMD-K5 PR100	100/66	1.5	—
AMD-K5 PR120	120/60	2.0	—
AMD-K5 PR133	133/66	2.0	—
K5 PR166	166/66	2.5	3.5/3.5
K6-166 (Model 6)	166/66	2.5	3.3/2.9
K6-200 (Model 6)	200/66	3.0	3.3/2.9
K6-200 (Model 7)	200/66	3.0	3.3/2.2
K6-233 (Model 6)	233/66	3.5	3.3/3.2
K6-233 (Model 7)	233/66	3.5	3.3/2.2
K6-266	266/66	4.0	3.3/2.2
K6-300	300/66	4.5	3.45/2.2
K6-3D-300	300/100	3.0	3.3/2.2
K6-3D-333	333/95	3.5	3.3/2.2
K6-2-266	266/66	4.0	3.3/2.2 (2.4)
K6-2-300	300/100	3.0	3.3/2.2 (2.4)
K6-2-333	333/95	3.5	3.3/2.2 (2.4)
K6-2-350	350/100	3.5	3.3/2.2 (2.4)
K6-2-366	366/66	5.5	3.3/2.2 (2.4)
K6-2-380	380/95	4.0	3.3/2.2 (2.4)
K6-2-400	400/66	6.0	3.3/2.2 (2.4)

continues

Continued

Processor	Internal frequency/external frequency, MHz	Multiplier	External voltage/core voltage, V
K6-2-400	400/100	4.0	3.3/2.2 (2.4)
K6-2-450	450/100	4.5	3.3/2.2 (2.4)
K6-2-475	475/95	5.0	3.3/2.2 (2.4)
K6-2-500	500/100	5.0	3.3/2.2 (2.4)
K6-2-533	533/97	5.5	3.3/2.2 (2.4)
K6-III-400	400/100	4.0	3.3/2.2 (2.4)
K6-III-450	450/100	4.5	3.3/2.2 (2.4)

AMD Athlon Processors (0.25 micron — Model 1)

Processor clock frequency, MHz	System bus frequency, MHz	Voltage, V
500	200	1.6
550	200	1.6
600	200	1.6
650	200	1.6
700	200	1.6

AMD Athlon Processors (0.18 micron — Model 2)

Processor clock frequency, MHz	System bus frequency, MHz	Voltage, V
550	200	1.6
600	200	1.6
650	200	1.6
700	200	1.6
750	200	1.6
800	200	1.7
850	200	1.7
900	200	1.8
950	200	1.8
1000	200	1.8

AMD Athlon Processors (0.18 micron — Model 4 [256 KB L2 on-chip])

Processor clock frequency, MHz	System bus frequency, MHz	Voltage, V
650	200	1.70
700	200	1.70
750	200	1.70
800	200	1.70
850	200	1.70
900	200	1.75
950	200	1.75
1000	200	1.75

AMD Duron Processors

Processor frequency, MHz	System bus frequency, MHz	Voltage, V
550	200	1.5
600	200	1.5
650	200	1.5
700	200	1.5

AMD Thunderbird Processors

Processor clock frequency, MHz	System bus frequency, MHz	Voltage, V
650	200	1.70
700	200	1.70
750	200	1.70
800	200	1.70
850	200	1.70
900	200	1.75
950	200	1.75
1000	200	1.75

Cyrix/IBM 6x86 Processors

Processor	Internal frequency/external frequency, MHz	Multiplier	External voltage/ core voltage, V
Cyrix 6x86 P120+	100/50	2.0	—
Cyrix 6x86 P133+	110/55	2.0	—
Cyrix 6x86 P150+	120/60	2.0	—
Cyrix 6x86 P166+	133/66	2.0	—
Cyrix 6x86 P200+	150/75	2.0	—
6x86L PR166+	133/66	2.0	3.3/2.8
6x86L PR200+	150/75	2.0	3.3/2.8
6x86MX PR166	150/60	2.5	3.3/2.9
6x86MX PR200	166/66	2.5	3.3/2.9
6x86MX PR166	133/66	2.0	3.3/2.9
6x86MX PR200	150/75	2.0	3.3/2.9
6x86MX PR233	188/75	2.5	3.3/2.9
6x86MX PR266	208/83	2.5	3.3/2.9
M II 300	233/66	3.5	3.3/2.9
M II 300	225/75	3.0	3.3/2.9
M II 333	250/83	3.0	3.3/2.9
6x86MX PR166	133/66	2.0	3.3/2.9
6x86MX PR200	150/75	2.0	3.3/2.9
6x86MX PR233	166/83	2.0	3.3/2.6
6x86MX PR233	166/83	2.0	3.3/2.9
6x86MX PR266	208/83	2.5	3.3/2.9
6x86MX PR300	233/66	3.5	3.3/2.9
6x86MX PR333	250/83	3.0	3.3/2.9
6x86MX PR333	250/100	2.5	3.3/2.9

IDT Processors

Processor	Internal frequency/ external frequency, MHz	Multiplier	External voltage/ core voltage, V
C6-DS180GAEM	180/60	3	3.52/3.52
C6-DS200GAEM	200/66	3	3.52/3.52
C6-DS225GAEM	225/75	3	3.52/3.52
WinChip2-3DE200GA	200/66	3	3.52/3.52
WinChip2-3DE225GA	225/75	3	3.52/3.52
WinChip2-3DE240GA	240/60	4	3.52/3.52

The tables list only the standard parameters, which are set by default. By modifying these parameters you may be able to realize a substantial gain in performance.

You should remember, however, that to attain maximum performance you must first raise the host bus frequency, or at least, after having set the parameters of the chosen mode, try not to lower its frequency.

For example, having changed the arrangement of the jumpers from assigning an internal clock frequency of 166 MHz (2.5×66 MHz) to one of 180 MHz (3×60 MHz), you risk lowering the real performance of the system. It would seem that since the processor clock frequency has gone up from 166 to 180 MHz, you would obviously gain in performance. And truly, the performance of the processor seems to improve. But don't forget about another very important parameter — the external frequency, or the host-bus frequency. This frequency plays one of the most important roles in transferring data between the processor and the memory (cache, RAM), and also defines the operating speed of the rest of the subsystems, that is, it has a significant influence on the overal performance of the entire computer system. As for the growth in the processor performance, in this case it is reflected mostly in operations that don't demand intensive data exchange with the memory and with other computer subsystems.

When changing from a clock frequency of 133 MHz (2×66 MHz) to a clock frequency of 150 MHz (3×50 MHz) you also are risking loss of speed, and thus decreasing the actual performance of the system.

Thanks to the increase in the processor clock frequency it actually will work more intensively. However, taking into account the decreased bus frequency, the speed of data transfer will fall. And, therefore, when performing tasks that require intense data transfer between the processor and the cache memory or the RAM, the performance of the computer will suffer as well.

Keep in mind that, nominally, Pentium, Pentium Pro, and AMD K5 processors use bus frequencies of 50, 60, and 66 MHz. The choice of bus frequency depends on the processor and the chipset. The official bus frequencies for 6×86 processors are 50, 55, 60, 66, or 75 MHz. However, there are motherboards that allow you to attain bus frequency values higher than the generally accepted ones, so called "undocumented bus frequencies". These are frequencies of 75 and 83 MHz. It should be noted that there are some motherboards with a documented bus frequency of 75 MHz, that is, the manufacturer of the motherboard guarantees its capability to operate at that frequency. These are boards from, for instance, ASUSTeK.

Using the non-standard bus frequency of 75 MHz for Intel processors and chipsets, you can attempt to raise the performance of the computer by overclocking the Pentium processor even without increasing the internal clock frequency. For example, let us take the Pentium-150, which can be overclocked from 150 (2.5×60 MHz) to 150 MHz (2×75 MHz). Based on the facts provided above, the overall computer performance will increase, but without increasing the internal clock frequency of the processor and without practically any change in its heating rate. You should note, however, that the load of the RAM and the cache memory is increased, and they will have to work at a higher clock frequency, which is essentially overclocking of the memory (and certain other subsystems).

In order to change the clock frequency of the host bus, you must consult the documentation supplied with the motherboard. There you will find all the information you need for this. More specifically, you'll need to know which jumpers are responsible for this clock frequency, which combination you must choose to set the required bus frequency, and if possible, the multiplier.

Using increased bus frequencies, like 75 and 83 MHz, can lead to certain consequences that you should be aware of before attempting overclocking.

When using frequencies of 75 or 83 MHz, the PCI bus will generally work at frequencies of 37.5 or 41.6 MHz, respectively. The effect of these frequencies may be seen in the work of the video adapter, for example, which is set to the PCI bus, and in the work of the disk controller, which is connected through the same PCI bus. At higher frequencies (in overclocked modes), certain devices maintain their serviceability. However, when functioning at these higher frequencies, they may become overheated. In such a case, you must implement proper cooling of such components. Certain other devices may become unstable. If this is the case, you should either stop using a higher frequency, or replace the devices with ones that are better adapted to working at such high frequencies.

The speed of the EIDE controller depends not only on the PIO or DMA modes, but also quite heavily on the PCI bus frequency. This is exactly why it's advantageous to use a higher frequency. However, there are cases where a hard drive will work reliably and quickly at a frequency of 75 MHz, but at 83 MHz its performance abruptly declines to, for example, PIO 2. The same can be said of the CD-ROM drive. Obviously, such a mode is undesirable, since the general performance of the system decreases.

You may also expect to run into problems with the memory. At the frequency of 83 MHz, it's only possible to use SDRAM-type memory, or a special High-End EDO DRAM. But there are exceptions when certain memory chips, against their type and nature, maintain the same level of efficiency at increased frequencies. Nevertheless, it's better to use those types of memory that are intended for work at high frequencies.

Switching Modes through BIOS Setup

Preparing the subsystems of the computer is accomplished by arranging the corresponding jumpers and switches on the motherboard and expansion cards. In addition to this, you must adjust a series of parameters found in BIOS Setup. There do exist certain motherboards, however, that allow you to carry out this adjustment by simply changing these parameters in BIOS Setup. These are motherboards that use Soft-Menu technology. In the case of one of these motherboards, you don't need to open the case of the computer and look for the appropriate jumpers and switches. Setting the appropriate modes is done through parameters that control the FSB, PCI, and AGP bus frequencies, the voltage supplied to the processor, the value of the multiplier (if possible), certain features of the memory functioning, etc. Setting the values of these parameters is done in the appropriate menus in BIOS Setup, those like Advanced Chipset Setup, BIOS Features Setup, and Chipset Features Setup. You should, however, note, that before choosing the necessary modes and beginning the set up you ought to become acquainted with the documentation that accompanies both the computer motherboard and extension cards.

Changing the Multiplier

As was previously mentioned, the internal clock frequency of the processor is determined by the bus frequency and the multiplier. The multiplier value is assigned by the processor itself, but is often chosen and set on the motherboard.

❑ Intel Pentium processors support the following multipliers: ×1.5, ×2, ×2.5, ×3

❑ Intel Pentium Pro − ×2.5, ×3, ×3.5, ×4

❑ 6x86 series processors − ×2, ×3; for M2 − ×2, ×2.5, ×3, ×3.5

As for the K5 series processors, the situation is a bit different. Changing the internal clock frequency of a K5 processor is often difficult. In all cases, the PR75, PR90, PR100, and PR133 models only support a multiplier of ×1.5; the more perfected K5 processors PR150 and PR166 support a multiplier of ×2. The problem is that multipliers of K5 processors cannot be adjusted, nor can those of K6 processors. A similar situation is found with Intel Pentium II, Pentium III, and Celeron processors. There are certain series of these lines of processors for which this is still possible. But this generally refers to the first releases of Pentium II and Celeron.

The multiplying factor, just as the host bus frequency, is set on the motherboard with the help of jumpers. To change the factor, you need to change the arrangement of the jumpers. Before you do this you must read all information concerning this rearrangement in the documentation supplied with the motherboard. Look for the heading *CPU to BUS Frequency Ratio Selection*, or something similar to it. There are usually only two jumpers on the motherboard that determine this feature.

Increasing the Voltage and Cooling

When overclocking, you should keep in mind that in order to guarantee the functional stability of the processor at high frequencies − the values of which can be more than 1.5 times than the clock frequency set by the manufacturer − you must also increase the CPU voltage. The necessity of this is clear, and stems from the theory of the digital device operation at high frequencies. According to this theory, in order to guarantee steep front impulses for high frequency signals and a high performance for the semiconductor elements, a relatively high level of current and voltage is necessary. You should note that raising voltage should be done very carefully, since there is a possibility of the irreversible failure of the given element. Besides, at a high voltage more electrical power is used. As a result, the heat flux rises, and without an additional heatsink, the processor under these conditions will get extremely hot. Therefore, it's advised to intensify the cooling system of the processor by, for instance, installing a more powerful fan. There are instances where Intel Pentium processors will work reliably with a voltage of 4.6 V, which is significantly higher than the standard level recommended for and set for processors of this type.

When overclocking components, always remember to effectively and reliably cool them. This may sometimes require that you install a more powerful cooling fan or cooler for the processor. It may also require additional cooling of certain other devices. Indeed, as was previously stated, raising the frequency of the processor bus influences the functioning of most of the computer subsystems. When beginning the procedure of overclocking, you must be prepared for these problems.

When it comes to cooling, it's best not to risk it; otherwise, there is the possibility that a component may fail due to extremely high temperatures. Besides this, you should once again recall that intensive heating an element shortens its trouble-free operating life.

Chapter 12

Requirements for Overclocked Elements

The Processor

Generally, overclocking suits processors from Intel — for example, Pentium, Pentium MMX, Pentium II, Pentium III, and Celeron processors — although other companies' processors also often take to the procedure as well. There are no processors that can be characterized as "overclockable" or "non-overclockable". Everything depends on the specific configuration of the computer, the processor type, series, and even the particular instance.

Based on the experience of overclocking processors of the same type but intended for different clock frequencies, the following trend becomes obvious. The best overclocking results can be achieved with the first processors released after significant changes in technology, core architecture, etc. This is reasonably explained by the fact that the first releases of the new generation of processors evidently have a large technological reserve. Of course, the first batches of processors contain a lower percentage of consistently stable chips released. This, though, is the problem of the manufacturer. Those processors that have been tested and released, however, allow you to significantly increase the clock frequency. Subsequent releases of processors are more difficult to overclock. This situation has occurred in Pentium, Pentium MMX, Pentium II, and Celeron processors. For example, Pentium processors with the clock frequencies of 75—100 MHz and Pentium MMX 166 overclocked very well. Certain Pentium 75 processors allowed you to increase the clock frequency to 112 MHz, while Pentium MMX could be overclocked to 208 MHz. Within the Pentium II processor family, the following processors were overclocking leaders: Celeron 266 and Celeron 300 (the first of the Celeron processors), Celeron 300A and Celeron 333 (the first of the family of processors with the new Mendocino core and with a built-in L2 cache memory that works at the frequency of the processor). When overclocking these processors, it was possible to increase the clock frequency by more than 50% with, of course, a corresponding rise in performance. The subsequent, more powerful processors, with clock frequencies already increased by the manufacturer, show weaker results in an overclocked mode. However, there is a basis to claim that the forthcoming first members of the Celeron processor family, intended for a host bus frequency of 100 MHz and created by new technology and with new cores, will live up to the expectations of overclocking enthusiasts.

It's worth mentioning that Pentium II and Pentium III processors are significantly different from their predecessors. This difference lies not only in the more complex internal architecture, but also in the construction of the processor, which now uses a SEC cartridge connected through Slot 1. An important feature of processors of this type is the fact that, besides the processor chip, this cartridge contains a controlling chip and a level two cache memory (L2) intended for work at half of the frequency of the processor core. Unfortunately, in many cases the chip used in the processor is not noted for its high-speed abilities. This greatly reduces the possibilities of overclocking. Sometimes, however, a series of processors can be found that do have high-speed chip. These processors are the preferred ones for overclocking. Incidentally, Celeron processors with clock frequencies of 266—300 MHz do not have the L2 cache memory with its relatively slow chip, and this is exactly the reason that these processors with Slot 1 can reach such a high level when overclocked. The next generation of Celeron processors, Celeron 300A, Celeron 333, etc. were released with a high speed L2 cache memory inside the processor chip, able to work at the frequency of the processor core. The code name of this core is Mendocino. Processors of this type possess a high performance level and make a good showing as a processor that takes well to overclocking. Both processors in SEC cartridges with Slot 1 and processors in PPGA cases with Socket 370 have been released.

The existence of a huge quantity of falsely labeled (re-marked) processor instances complicates choosing the best processor. You must try to avoid re-marked processors. A "re-marked" or "sawed-off" processor is one whose original label has been filed off and replaced with a new one. Remarking is illegal, and done in clandestine laboratories in some countries. A falsely labeled processor allows it to pass for a more powerful one than it actually is, and therefore will be sold at a higher price. This is what happened to, for example, the AMD 486DX2-66, series 25253, which was "transformed" into a 486DX4-100. Because of this, in 1995 AMD had to stop the release of the DX2/DX4 series with a changeable multiplier. Later on, fake labels were being made for Intel processors too: Pentium, Pentium MMX, Pentium II, and Celeron.

Telling a real processor from a remarked one is not as easy as it may seem at first glance. You should take into consideration the fact that false marking is relatively competently done, with the use of modern technical instruments and technology, including lasers. This is why there is no unambiguous way to tell if a processor has been remarked. There are a few indirect ways by which you can judge the probability of a processor having been falsely marked. For example:

❑ The processor becomes unstable at the clock frequency immediately following the rated one. However, keep in mind that this may happen with genuine processors as well.

❑ The processor only works while cold. When the temperature of the case reaches the region of 70—80°C*, you begin to get errors; but again, this may also be the case with real processors, that is, ones that haven't been re-marked.

❑ The symbols of the label are not engraved, but are drawn on or raised, or the depth of the engraving is very shallow. This does not apply to Texas Instruments processors, which are not engraved at all.

❑ The symbols of the label, after a careful, strongly magnified examination, look as if they were smeared, or carelessly done, etc.

❑ The frequency mark on the lower side of the case (if there is one) does not coincide with the frequency written on the upper side.

❑ Identification data given by such programs as SysInfo, CPUID, and similar programs do not match the data for the type or series of processor that you are supposedly using.

In order to minimize the possibility of buying a re-marked processor, you are advised to buy one from an authorized dealer or distributor.

You should note that certain firms that deal in the assembly and sale of computers overclock their processors with the aim of increasing their profit. Of course, they don't inform the customer of this fact. Thus, they are simply cheating you, which, by the way, is prosecutable by law. Usually, these are smaller firms that usually don't stay in business for very long.

Incidentally, the BIOS of modern motherboards is generally able to define the clock frequency of Pentium II processors. To do this, you need simply go into BIOS Setup to the appropriate parameters. Checking this may serve as a test of the computer for its overclocking possibilities, and will also help to defend you from unprincipled salesmen. However, this test will not always help in identifying re-marked processors, as their architecture and construction has undergone certain changes.

You should pay attention to the fact that re-marked processors seem as if they were intended for work in an overclocked mode. Indeed, the mode set to match the false marking on the case of the processor will correspond to one of the overclocked modes. From here you can see that it will be difficult to further overclock the processor. Although, if you increase the CPU voltage, you may be able to make even a re-marked one work a little faster and perform a little better.

---

* °F = 9/5°C + 32 or °F = 9/5 (°C + 40) – 40.

The Motherboard

A successful attempt at overclocking depends to a great extent on the quality of the motherboard. Overclocking has become so popular that many companies tout the overclocking abilities of their processors in their ad campaigns. However, as stressed repeatedly, low quality motherboards may lead to frequent hang-ups, failures, or the system may just refuse to work altogether at the higher frequencies. For this reason it is recommended that you use only high quality motherboards when planning to overclock the computer. Examples of such brands are Abit, ASUSTeK, Chaintech, Shuttle, Giga-Byte, and the like. You should note as well that motherboards from Intel, whose products are always high quality (and high priced!) are generally not the best choice for your goals. This is due to the hard-line position of Intel, who implacably and on principle fights against the overclocking of their processors and whose motherboards usually are not compatible with third-party processors.

Be aware of the fact that not every motherboard will support higher host bus frequencies like 75 and 83 MHz. These values were most important for overclocking processors with bus frequencies of 50−66 MHz. For Pentium, Pentium MMX and similar processors from other manufacturers, these boards are among those released in the very beginning of the heyday of these processors, and are relatively rare. For the motherboards intended for the more powerful Celeron, Pentium II, and Pentium III processors and advanced chipsets, these frequencies are more a mandatory attribute than an exception. Moreover, the range and amount of bus frequencies supported by modern motherboards has grown substantially. For motherboards that are intended for Pentium II, Pentium III, and other similar processors, the standard host bus frequency has become 100 MHz. There are already many motherboards that will support bus frequencies higher than the standard 66 and 100 MHz. Some have the ability, for example, to set and support host bus frequencies of 103, 105, 112, 124, 133, and 150 MHz. Of course, these motherboards can also support the standard 75 and 83 MHz. A strong tendency towards further widening of the range and number of frequencies can be observed as well. Some boards have begun supporting 90 and 95 MHz. This allows you to more precisely choose the optimum mode that will give the highest performance possible while maintaining the stability of all of the computer's subsystems.

Many motherboards are advertised as being specially designed for overclocked modes, for example: Abit BH6, Abit BX6, Abit BM6, Abit BE6, and Abit BE6-II, all from Abit; ASUS P2B-B, ASUS P2B-F, and ASUS P3B-F from ASUSTeK; and CT-6BTM, CT-6BTM2, CT-6ATA2 and CT-6ATA4 from Chaintech. There have also been some good reviews of HOT-679 and HOT-681 from Shuttle, and many users are fans of boards from companies like Micro Star and Giga-Byte.

The products from the manufacturers listed above are known for their high quality. They are convenient in their set up, maintain stability, operate reliably, are well documented, and come with a guarantee and support. On the official sites of their respective manufacturers, you can always find a number of updated BIOS versions, a detailed description of its abilities, updated hardware drivers, and utilities for updating the BIOS code.

Having given the products of these popular companies their due, it's necessary to note that the recognized and undisputed leader is Abit, who puts out high quality motherboards that include various tools for setup and management of overclocking modes. Their motherboard Abit BE6-II, developed on the basis of the widely known and popular i440BX chipset, has become the standard by which other companies products are evaluated. When it comes to performance, stability, and popularity among users, the closest competitor of the Abit BE6-II is the ASUS P3B-F motherboard from ASUSTeK. It also was designed based on the i440BX chipset. Among motherboards using the VIA Apollo Pro133A chipset, one of the most popular is the CT-6ATA4 from Chaintech.

Despite their relatively high prices, the motherboards from the aforementioned companies are popular, and deservedly so. You should be warned against buying motherboards from minor companies, whose products are usually inexpensive and of poor quality.

In later sections, more information on motherboards that support higher bus frequencies will be presented. This data was gathered on the Internet and FidoNet from users of these boards. You'll also find information on the particular jumpers that are responsible for frequency level.

Besides a wide range of host bus frequencies, a motherboard must also support a changeable multiplier and provide the ability to adjust the CPU voltage (voltage tweaking). If you want or have to use an overclocked mode for a relatively new model processor that supports MMX technology, or just need to lower the voltage of a Pentium MMX, Pentium II, Pentium III, Celeron, M2, K5/K6, or a similar processor, you need a motherboard that provides *split voltage*.

The optimal motherboards for overclocking must, within a wide range of possible voltages for the processor, be able to adjust the voltage in small steps of 0.1 V or even 0.05 V.

RAM

In a computer that has been set to one of the overclocked modes, the RAM plays a huge role. At a raised host bus frequency, this important element has the ability to either augment the general performance of the system, or significantly slow it down and weaken the effect of overclocking.

Often, increasing the host bus frequency has a negative effect on the RAM modules installed in the computer. In such a case you may encounter errors, your computer may freeze or refuse to work, etc. To make the RAM, and thus your computer, once again function properly, you need to introduce additional wait-loops into the work cycle of the RAM modules, which affect time delays when working with the modules of the memory. This procedure is usually executed in BIOS Setup, in the **Advanced Chipset Setup** menu. Note, though, that this will affect the general performance, sometimes lowering it to an unacceptable level. This is why the values of the wait loops should be minimal when working with the RAM modules.

In order to ensure the stability of the system and maintain a high level of overall performance at increased host bus frequencies, it's advised that you use RAM modules of a type that best supports increased frequencies. The memory type most suitable and strongly recommended for Pentium-type and higher processors, beginning with the i82430VX chipset, is SDRAM. Usually, memory chips of this type are released and used in the form of special modules in DIMM form factor. In certain situations, you may be able to use High-End EDO DRAM modules. Similar modules have been adapted for work at high frequencies. But, at a bus frequency of 83 MHz or higher, you should in any case use an SDRAM or a more perfected and higher performance memory type, such as, for instance, DDR SDRAM.

Frequency Properties of Selected Types of Memory Modules

Bus frequency, MHz	FPM DRAM, nsec	EDO DRAM, nsec	SDRAM, nsec
033	70	—	—
050	70	70	—
060	70	70	12
066	60	60	12

continues

Continued

Bus frequency, MHz	FPM DRAM, nsec	EDO DRAM, nsec	SDRAM, nsec
075	—	50	12
083	—	50	10
100	—	—	7 or 10 PC100
133	—	—	PC133

To guarantee the stability and reliability of the computer at high bus frequencies, it's recommended that you use RAM modules that meet PC100 or even PC133 specifications.

Chapter 13

Overclocking the Processor

Overclocking 286, 386, and 486 Processors

Computers based on 286 processors are now obsolete. Of course, you can enhance their performance using optimal settings; you can also overclock the processor. But no matter what you do, their data processing frequency will be tens of times as slow as even computers with a 486 processor. However, you might want to use these computers as experimental ground, and increase their performance as a type of training. Besides, these computers can continue to be used as simple word processors.

Computers based on i80286 processors can hardly be upgraded. This is basically because you would need to replace almost every component. This means the monitor, the ISA video adapter — generally CGA or EGA standard, the motherboard, the processor, the hard drive — whose capacity is, by today's standards, inadequate and doesn't usually exceed 80 MB, and the slow RAM with an outdated form factor. The rest of the computer is no better. You'll even have a hard time finding a use for the keyboard that has an 8088/80286 switch.

You can increase the performance of a computer with a 286 processor significantly by increasing the clock frequency. However, using the TURBO mode, which automatically increases the computer operating speed by raising the clock frequency, is pretty much the same as overclocking.

Generally, raising the clock frequency of these processors doesn't present a huge problem. This is because for the majority of the systems two quartz resonators are used: one is related to the timer, the other establishes the clock frequency of the processor. Replacing the second one allows you to increase the operating speed. For example, in a system where the processor clock frequency equals 12 MHz, the quartz resonator is usually set to a frequency of 25 or 30 MHz. Replacing it with a quartz resonator of 33 or 66 MHz allows you to increase the operating seed by up to 16 MHz. Further increase of the processor clock frequency is done in a similar manner.

Overclocking computers with 386 processors, as was the case with the 286 models, more often than not, is not a task with a worthy goal. Instead, it's preferable to upgrade such computers, by replacing the motherboard with, for instance, one with a 486 or even a Pentium processor. Considering the current prices, this doesn't really cost much. There may be certain situations, however, that for whatever reason, such an upgrade is not advisable (even if it is possible). Excluding a computer for which a user has developed a personal affection, examples of these may be, for example, computers with a Slim or UltraSlim case. There are also computers with an exotic type of construct, such as booksize. There are more than a few of these types of computers, and finding a suitable motherboard for them is not an easy task. In such cases, your best bet is to look for some other way of increasing the computer performance. In certain cases, this might just be overclocking.

The particular features of the 386 processor and its motherboard did not well anticipate the next generation of processors. However, these processors were released with the intention of their being able to work at different clock frequencies, for example, at 25, 33, and 40 MHz. In order to keep costs down, motherboards often permitted using processors of various clock frequencies. This is the reason that there have been cases where a motherboard that allows a relatively high clock frequency has adapted to a processor with a lower frequency. In a case like this you can try to raise the performance by running in a mode with a higher clock frequency. This is usually done by adjusting the jumpers and switches that determine the clock frequency of the processor. More rarely, this can be done using BIOS Setup settings. Sometimes, you can raise the clock frequency by replacing the elements of the timing circuit, for example by replacing the quartz resonator or changing the divider.

Usually, motherboards intended for i80386 processors provide no voltage tweaking options.

Information on the capabilities of the motherboard and its modes can be found in the technical literature that comes along with the computer. Often, the necessary explanations of the purpose of the jumpers are shown directly on the board. You can also try to find necessary information on the Internet.

In case it comes down to it, the temperature conditions of the processor may be improved by installing a heatsink with special thermal grease.

The architecture of the motherboards intended for 486 processors is both more complete and more diverse. The clock frequencies of the buses — the processors' internal frequencies — are 25, 44, 40, and 50 MHz. They use processors from Intel, AMD, Cyrix, TI, and IBM. These processors may be of the SX or DX type, and may be able to have their external frequency increased by 2—4 times. Changing the multiplier is usually not provided for in the standard capabilities of the motherboard. The factor is generally a parameter of the internal architecture of the processor.

For motherboards with 486 processors whose case construction is not suited to replacing the processor, the same problems and the same recommendations as given for the 386 processor apply.

The architecture of the majority of motherboards intended for use with 486 processors uses special sockets, which allow you to easily replace the processor on the motherboard. This design raises the level of unification of the motherboard and allows you to reduce its nomenclature for every manufacturer. As a result, many motherboards were created for a wide range of processors with different operating frequencies. It is critical that BIOS recognize them (actually, this is the most important aspect). Information on this is contained in the motherboard manual. There should also be a list there of the possible clock frequencies and voltages for the processor, and instructions on setting these values.

Overclocking motherboards intended for use with a wide spectrum of 486 processors comes down to the procedure of setting them to a higher frequency than was originally intended. For example, for 486SX/25 and 486SX2/50 processors, an external frequency of 33 or 40 MHz is set; for 486SX/33, 486DX/33, 486SX2/66, and 486DX2/66 processors — 40 or even 50 MHz; for 486DX4/75 — 33 MHz, and for 486DX4/100 — 40 MHz. Really good results can be achieved with an AMD processor, the 486DX4/133, which can be overclocked to a bus frequency of 40 MHz. In this mode the 486DX4/133 works at a clock frequency of 160 MHz. As such, for certain tasks the processor performance is equal to that of an Intel Pentium-100 processor.

Overclocked modes demand proper cooling of the processor. You must remember that for 486 processors it is necessary to set them to the voltage for which they were intended. This is why the voltage setting of 486 processors does not depend on the mode and allows you the choice of one of two values, 5 or 3 V.

Overclocking Intel Pentium and Pentium MMX Processors

Intel Pentium processors produce good results when overclocked. However, the level of overclocking often depends not only on the series, but also on the individual processor.

Intel Pentium MMX processors also take to overclocking very well, in some cases better than the traditional Pentium. This, though, usually depends on the individual processor. One feature of the Pentium MMX processor is that it requires a voltage of about 2.8 V. However, many of the motherboards that support Pentium MMX processors can support voltages higher than the standard 2.8 V, a voltage of 2.9 or 2.93, for instance. This ability may help you find the best level to which to overclock this type of processor. Take, for example, the Intel

Pentium MMX 200, which works just as well at 208/83 (clock frequency — 208 MHz; host bus frequency — 83 MHz) as it does at 227/75. For the Pentium MMX 200, a mode of 250/83 is also possible, but in order to maintain stability you must raise the voltage to 2.9 V. Note, of course, that raising the voltage to levels higher than the recommended ones produces an unfavorable effect on the reliability and power-on hours of the components. However, this processor, as a rule, will successfully withstand a voltage increase of up to 2.9 V.

Hence, in order to successfully overclock your processor, you should keep in mind certain important facts and perform some of the procedures that have been mentioned:

❏ If possible, try to increase the host bus frequency, which determines the external (input/output) frequency of the processor.

❏ When choosing the multiplier, don't lower the bus frequency; this may reduce the overall gain in performance.

❏ To improve the stability of the processor's behavior in an overclocked mode, you may try to increase its voltage by increments of 0.1 or 0.2 V, as long as you provide adequate cooling.

❏ Try to avoid buying re-marked processors.

❏ When making the decision to overclock a processor, bear in mind that overclocking significantly increases the probability of failure due to overheating or voltage that is too high.

Achieving stability for a Pentium 166 overclocked to 208 MHz (2.5×83 MHz) is relatively difficult. To achieve this target clock frequency you need high quality components, such as SDRAM memory, etc.

The Pentium 150 processor is intended to run at 2.5×66 MHz. This processor will, however, be stable at 166 MHz (2.5×66 MHz). Still, the best mode for this processor is 150 MHz (2×75 MHz).

The following Pentium and Pentium MMX processors are the best ones for overclocking purposes:

❏ Pentium 150 — this processor is popular among overclockers, especially since it has practically the same core as the Pentium 166, but is less expensive.

❏ Pentium 166 and the Pentium 166 MMX — these processors run well at 187.5 MHz (2.5×75 MHz), and in most cases are stable at 200 MHz (3×66 MHz) as well.

❏ Pentium 133 — can be successfully overclocked to 150 MHz (2×75 MHz) or 166 MHz (2×83 MHz).

❏ Most Pentium 75 processors run well at 90 MHz (1.5×60 MHz), and some can even be overclocked to 100 MHz (1.5×66 MHz).

❏ Pentium 200 (and Pentium 200 MMX as well), run wonderfully at 208 MHz (2.5×83 MHz), 225 MHz (3×75 MHz), and 250 MHz (3×83 MHz), when the voltage is also raised.

When overclocking the Pentium 133 processor, it's wise to avoid, if you can, processors marked SY022 and SU073.

Listed in the following tables are the basic Pentium processors and the possible combinations of parameters that allow the processor to run in overclocked mode. The tables include both the processor's clock frequency and the Front Side Bus frequency.

```
Clock frequency = Multiplier × host bus frequency
```

Intel Pentium Processors and Combinations of Their Parameters in Overclocking Mode

Pentium	Option I	Option II	Option III	Option IV
75	112.5 MHz = 1.5 × 75 MHz	100 MHz = 1.5 × 66 MHz	90 MHz = 1.5 × 60 MHz	83 MHz = 1.5 × 55 MHz
90	125 MHz = 1.5 × 83 MHz	112.5 MHz = 1.5 × 75 MHz	100 MHz = 1.5 × 66 MHz	
100	125 MHz = 1.5 × 83 MHz	112.5 MHz = 1.5 × 75 MHz		
120	125 MHz = 1.5 × 83 MHz	133 MHz = 2 × 66 MHz	112.5 MHz = 1.5 × 75 MHz	
133	166 MHz = 2 × 83 MHz	150 MHz = 2 × 75 MHz	166 MHz = 2.5 × 66 MHz	
150	166 MHz = 2 × 83 MHz	187.5 MHz = 2.5 x 75 MHz	200 MHz = 3 × 66 MHz	150 MHz = 2 × 75 MHz
166	208 MHz = 2.5 × 83 MHz	166 MHz = 2 × 83 MHz	187.5 MHz = 2.5 × 75 MHz	200 MHz = 3 × 66 MHz
200	250 MHz = 3 × 83 MHz	225 MHz = 3 × 75 MHz	208 MHz = 2.5 × 83 MHz	

To produce a more accurate analysis of the temperature conditions of the computer and to estimate the capabilities of the cooling facilities, it's very useful to have data on the electric power (Watts) of the processor at hand. The two tables provided below include data on the Pentium and Pentium MMX processors' power consumption.

Power Consumption of Pentium Processors

Pentium	Usual power consumption, W	Maximum power consumption, W
75 MHz	3.00	8.00
90 MHz	3.50	9.00
100 MHz	3.90	10.10
120 MHz	5.06	12.81
133 MHz	4.30	11.20
150 MHz	4.90	11.60
166 MHz	5.40	14.50
200 MHz	6.50	15.50

Power Consumption of Pentium MMX Processors

Pentium	Usual power consumption, W	Maximum power consumption, W
166 MHz	6.1	13.1
200 MHz	7.3	15.7
233 MHz	7.9	17.0

Overclocking Intel Pentium Pro Processors

It is commonly supposed that Intel Pentium Pro processors are not suitable for overclocking. However, processors of this type run in overclocked modes just as well as other processors of the Pentium and Pentium MMX classes.

Everything that was said about the Pentium and Pentium MMX processors applies as well to the Intel Pentium Pro. The main goal of the overclocker when dealing with this processor is raising the host bus frequency.

Intel Pentium Pro processors are intended for use at a bus frequency of 50 or 60 MHz. Overclocking this type of processor requires that you set a higher host bus frequency — 66 MHz for example. The noticeable performance gain that you will achieve is due to both the higher clock frequency of the processor as well as the faster speed of data transfer by the host bus.

**Intel Pentium Pro Processors and Combinations
of Their Parameters in Overclocking Mode**

Pentium Pro	Option I	Option II
150	166 MHz = 2.5 × 66 MHz	
180	233 MHz = 3.5 × 66 MHz	200 MHz = 3 × 66 MHz
200	266 MHz = 4 × 66 MHz	233 MHz = 3.5 × 66 MHz

The most significant performance growth is achieved for Pentium Pro 180 MHz overclocked to 233 MHz, and for Pentium Pro 200 MHz overclocked to 266 MHz. However, this is not always possible by simply raising the bus frequency. As in the case of the Intel Pentium and Pentium MMX processors, you'll need to increase the voltage supplied to the processor to guarantee stability.

Taking into account relatively high prices of these processors, you must be very careful when increasing the voltage in the course of the overclocking procedure — although several cases were reported where processors of this type worked reliably at a voltage of 4.6 V for a long time period.

You must remember that an overclocked processor needs proper cooling.

Despite all the difficulties, Intel Pentium Pro processors are worth experimenting with to find the most effective overclocked mode as long as you take all the necessary precautions and always keep in mind how much the processor costs.

To analyze the temperature conditions of the computer more precisely and to estimate which cooling facilities are necessary, it is useful to have data on the power consumption. The table provided below contains data concerning the power consumption of Pentium Pro processors.

Data on the Power Consumption of Pentium Pro Processors

Pentium Pro	Usual power consumption, W	Maximum power consumption, W
150 MHz, 256 KB L2	23,0	29.2
166 MHz, 512 KB L2	27.5	35.0
180 MHz, 256 KB L2	24.8	31.7
200 MHz, 256 KB L2	27.3	35.0
200 MHz, 512 KB L2	32.6	37.9

Overclocking Intel Pentium II and Pentium III Processors

Basic Principles of Overclocking Pentium II and Pentium III Processors

Unfortunately, Intel Pentium II and Intel Pentium III processors cannot be overclocked by means of adjusting the multiplier, which establishes the ratio between the clock frequency and FSB frequency. Intel has developed a number of methods intended to prevent overclocking of their processors as much as possible. As a result, in all newer processors the multiplier is locked. By locking the multiplier, Intel protects its processors from re-marking. Besides, Intel also protects its market by preventing inexpensive processors overclocked from competing with faster and more expensive genuine Intel processors.

Beginning with the Pentium MMX-166, Intel processors generally do not allow you to change the clock frequency by adjusting the multiplier, although there may be a chance that you have an Intel CPU manufactured before the company started to lock the multiplier. This, however, is a very rare exception from the general rule.

Thus, Intel Pentium II and Intel Pentium III processors can actually be overclocked only by increasing the bus frequency. So, for instance, a Pentium II 266 (4×66 MHz) can be overclocked to 300 MHz (4×75 MHz) or even to 333 MHz (4×83 MHz). A Pentium III-500 processor (5×100 MHz) can be overclocked to 560 MHz (5×112 MHz). Generally, this can be successfully done without increasing the processor voltage.

Examples of Overclocked Pentium II Processors

Processor	Overclocking mode	
Intel Pentium II 300	processor: 333 MHz	processor: 375 MHz
	host bus: 75 MHz	host bus: 83 MHz
	multiplier: 4.5	multiplier: 4.5
Intel Pentium II 266	processor: 300 MHz	processor: 333 MHz
	host bus: 75 MHz	host bus: 83 MHz
	multiplier: 4	multiplier: 4
Intel Pentium II 233	processor: 266 MHz	processor: 300 MHz
	host bus: 75 MHz	host bus: 83 MHz
	multiplier: 3.5	multiplier: 3.5

Examples of Overclocked Pentium III Processors

Processor	Overclocking mode	
Intel Pentium III 500	processor: 515 MHz	processor: 560 MHz
	host bus: 103 MHz	host bus: 112 MHz
	multiplier: 5	multiplier: 5
Intel Pentium II 450	processor: 464 MHz	processor: 504 MHz
	host bus: 103 MHz	host bus: 112 MHz
	multiplier: 4.5	multiplier: 4.5

Note that as processor manufacturing technology becomes more advanced, manufacturers lower the levels of voltage supplied to the processor in order to reduce power consumption and therefore decrease heat release. It's not uncommon that processors of the same type, characterized by the same clock frequency and bus frequency but manufactured at different times and therefore having different serial numbers, also differ by the voltage they consume. The BIOS of most modern motherboards usually detects the power supply voltage required by the processor correctly and without much trouble. However, in order to maintain stability at faster frequencies, you'll need to supply your CPU with more power. Of course, the required voltage levels will be different for different processors. Also, the methods of tweaking the voltage will differ. This is exactly why different sets of parameters may prove optimal for different motherboards and processors. For example, the voltage used may differ from the recommended values. For some other motherboards, overclocking is simply impossible. Such motherboards automatically determine all modes for the processor, and provide no way of changing them. But in any case, before you begin experimenting, you should provide efficient extra cooling for both the processor and the other components.

Re-marked Intel Pentium II Processors — an Obstacle to Overclocking

Changing the mark on a processor, i. e. re-marking, is an illegal practice. Re-marking began almost as soon as the first processors appeared on the market. This practice became common and widespread with 486 and Pentium processors. Essentially, the re-marking procedure itself is simple enough. Using a special machine or even a saw, the re-marker removed a thin layer from the case enclosing the microchip. After polishing the surface, the re-marker placed a fake mark onto it, usually with an overrated clock frequency. Often, other information, such as data on the manufacturer, was forged as well. Distinguishing a re-marked processor from the genuine product is not an easy task. Processors of the same generation are often very similar in technology, and, most often, even the same semiconductor wafers were used to produce them. Re-marked processors usually work just as well as real ones. Because of this, many companies (Intel, for example) developed a number of defense strategies for their processors. This defense also relates to protecting processors from overclocking.

In the relatively new and modern Pentium II processor, additional defense measures are implemented. For example, the multiplier is now locked using a special circuitry that prevents setting the multiplier value to anything other than the value set by the manufacturer. Unfortunately, professional re-markers usually have little trouble removing this multiplier lock. They simply open up the cartridge and remove the bothersome defense circuitry.

There does exist certain software that is able to tell a real Intel Pentium II 300 processor from a fake. This is done by analyzing the cache memory in the processor's cartridge. This is possible because an Intel Pentium II 266 uses a level 2 cache memory without ECC (error correction code), while Intel Pentium II 300 processors are supplied with a cache memory that includes ECC. However, according to some sources, Intel did release some Pentium II processors rated to both 233 and 266 MHz, and both using ECC. These processors were mostly meant for use in servers. It turns out, then, that the test for ECC isn't completely reliable, and doesn't always produce correct results.

The fastest and more advanced high-performance Intel Pentium processors rated to run at 350, 400, and 450 MHz also have a built-in circuitry intended to protect them from overclocking. Basically, this consists of the multiplier lock. There are also additional protective circuits related to the use of certain L2 cache memory chips. This cache memory works well at the manufacturer-specified frequency, but produces persistent errors when the operating frequency is significantly increased. This method, however, is under development, and because of this has not been introduced on a wide scale. As it is, however, it may be a big disappointment to professionals and to overclocking enthusiasts.

You should note that you are least likely to find a re-marked processor among the in-box products. These processors are much harder to re-mark than, for example, OEM versions.

There are other methods of protection, which as of yet are being planned by Intel and other processor manufacturers. For example, the manufacturers are planning to introduce various identification circuits into the processor architecture, similar to the ones used in the Intel Pentium III. There has also been a proposal to fix all of the frequency parameters. Fortunately for overclocking enthusiasts, this is still only a future possibility for the manufacturing firms.

Increasing the Bus Frequency

With the appearance of Intel i440BX chipset, a good number motherboards appeared on the market that were built on its basis. These motherboards were the first to support a standard host bus frequency of 100 MHz. Support for a bus frequency of 100 MHz provides the ability to significantly increase the processor clock frequency, and therefore the overall performance of the system. Some manufacturers widened the range of supported bus frequencies by adding even higher values, such as 133 MHz or even 150 MHz. This is undoubtedly a significant technological advance towards increasing computer performance by means of overclocking.

Many motherboards were released that strictly followed Intel specifications (Intel's own boards for example). Unfortunately, these boards allow setting of the bus frequency to 100 MHz for Intel Pentium II processors only, with the clock frequency no less than 350 MHz. This relates to the fact that Intel Pentium II and Intel Celeron processors assign their own bus frequency. That is, depending on the processor you use, the host bus will function at 66 or 100 MHz.

However, like any other protective measure of this type, automatic setting of the bus frequency can be easily removed.

On the processor chip, there is a special pin responsible for automatically setting the value of the bus frequency. Its number is well known — pin B21.

All you need to do is to disconnect pin B21, which will allow you to work at a bus frequency of 100 MHz with a processor that normally would only support a bus frequency of 66 MHz. Thus, you will be able to overclock the processor and the other subsystems by means of increasing the bus frequency. Disconnecting this particular pin is a relatively simple task, which, however, still demands care and accuracy. There are several methods of accomplishing this task.

First, you could simply cut the pin off, but this certainly can't be considered the best method.

Second, you could put some adhesive tape around the pin. This also isn't the best way to accomplish your goal. Plus, the glue from the adhesive tape will gradually oxidize the pin and may slide into the motherboard plug.

Third, you could try to cover pin B21 with an insulating varnish. This may be, for example, a special colored or colorless varnish, nail polish, or even parquet lacquer. This is probably the most effective method. However, if the temperature gets too high, the lacquer's structure may change. This may result in the isolating properties of the lacquer being lost, or, just as bad, the polymer film may turn into glue. Epoxy lacquer works very well, and you might want to use epoxy resin instead of lacquer altogether.

Having attained a higher bus frequency, you must keep in mind that components like the processor, the video card, etc. need proper and effective cooling. As a rule, you will need to use additional cooling equipment.

If the processor begins to work unstably, and you can't find a way of resolving the problem, you will have to restore contact to pin B21.

For a more in-depth analysis of the temperature conditions within the computer, and estimates on which cooling facilities you might need, the tables below contain data on the power dissipated by Pentium II and Pentium III processors.

Pentium II

Clock frequency, MHz	Maximum power dissipated by the chip, W	Maximum power dissipated by the case, W
233	34.8	33.6
266	38.2	37.0
300	43.0	41.4
333	23.7	21.8
350	21.5	20.8
400	24.3	23.6
450	27.1	26.4

Pentium III (SECC)

Clock frequency, MHz	Maximum power dissipated by the chip, W
450	25.3
500	28.2

Pentium III (SECC2)

Clock frequency, MHz	L2 cache memory, KB	Maximum power dissipated by the chip, W
450	512	25.3
500	512	28.0
533B	512	29.7
533EB	256	14.0
550	512	30.8
550E	256	14.5
600	512	34.5
600B	512	34.5
600E	256	15.8
600EB	256	15.8
650	256	17.0
667	256	17.5

continues

Continued

Clock frequency, MHz	L2 cache memory, KB	Maximum power dissipated by the chip, W
700	256	18.3
733	256	19.1
750	256	19.5
800	256	20.8
800EB	256	20.8
850	256	22.5
866	256	22.9
933	256	25.5
1.0B GHz	256	33.0

Pentium III (PGA370)

Clock frequency, MHz	L2 cache Memory, KB	Maximum power dissipated by the chip, W
500E	256	13.2
533EB	256	14.0
550E	256	14.5
600E	256	15.8
600EB	256	15.8
650	256	17.0
667	256	17.5
700	256	18.3
733	256	19.1
750	256	19.5
800	256	20.8
800EB	256	20.8
850	256	22.5
866	256	22.9
933	256	24.5

Overclocking Celeron Processors
Some Characteristics of Celeron Processors

As newer Intel products appear on the processor market, the choice of processor becomes more and more complicated. In order to make the best choice, you need to analyze a good number of parameters. Usually, these parameters include performance, compatibility, price, etc. It also makes sense to assess the overclocking potential.

In the table below, certain characteristics of various processors are listed: performance index according to the iCOMP 2.0 test, average price (as of September 1998), and, of course, the price/performance ratio.

Comparative Parameters of Certain Intel Processors

Processor	iCOMP 2.0	Price (09/98), $	Price/performance*
iPentium MMX 233	203	145	0.714
Celeron-266	213	105	0.493
Celeron-300	226	125	0.553
iPentium II 233 (512 KB L2)	267	175	0.655
iPentium II 266 (512 KB L2)	303	200	0.660
iPentium II 300 (512 KB L2)	332	245	0.738
iPentium II 333 (512 KB L2)	366	350	0.956
iPentium II 350 (512 KB L2)	386	450	1.166
iPentium II 400 (512 KB L2)	440	645	1.465

* The rounded-off result of dividing the price by its iCOMP 2.0 performance rating.

As you can see from the table and the graph (Fig. 13.1), the least expensive processor with the best price/performance ratio is the Celeron 266. The second position is held by the Celeron 300. This tendency has not changed. Both of these processors are relatively new products from Intel. Both of these processors lack an L2 cache memory, and this is exactly why they are so much cheaper than Pentium II processors, which are intended for the same clock frequencies as the Celeron. Thanks to the absence of the L2 cache memory, they not only have the best price/performance characteristics, but are also good candidates for overclocking.

Indeed, the only thing that somewhat prevents Intel Pentium II processors from being overclocked is the relatively low frequency of the L2 cache memory microcircuit which is located on the processor chip.

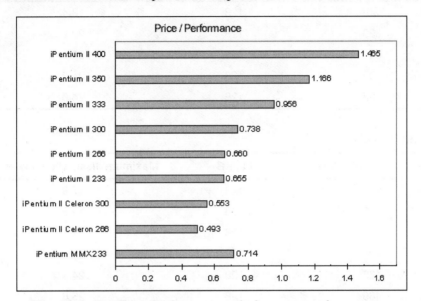

Fig. 13.1. The Price/Performance ratio for a range of processors

There are two Celeron processors without an L2 cache memory — the Celeron 266 and the Celeron 300. The clock frequency is derived in the following manner: 4×66 MHz = 266 MHz and 4.5×66 MHz = 300 MHz. The multipliers in the processors are locked at values of 4 and 4.5, respectively. Therefore, the only way to overclock these processors is by increasing the bus frequency. As test results have shown, there is a real possibility for a Celeron 266 processor to be overclocked to 400 MHz with a host bus frequency of 100 MHz, and even to achieve a clock frequency of 448 MHz with a host bus frequency of 112 MHz. By setting the same bus frequencies for a Celeron 300, it is possible to overclock them to 450 or even 504 MHz.

Celeron (S.E.P.P.)

Clock frequency, MHz	L2, KB	Maximum dissipation power, W
266	0	16.6
300	0	18.4

continues

Continued

Clock frequency, MHz	L2, KB	Maximum dissipation power, W
300A	128	18.4
333	128	20.2
366	128	22.2
400	128	24.2
433	128	24.6

Celeron (PPGA)

Clock frequency, MHz	L2, KB	Maximum dissipation power, W
300A	128	17.8
333	128	19.7
366	128	21.7
400	128	23.7
433	128	24.1
466	128	25.6
500	128	27.0
533	128	28.3

Choosing the Best Celeron Processor

As with other processors, the overclocking results depend to a large extent on the individual processor, and may be different even among processors of the same version and series.

There are several types of Celeron processors on the market, and each one has its own advantages and drawbacks, especially in regard to overclocking. There are specific features according to which the processors can be divided into three groups:

1. Processors without a cooling fan, but with a heatsink. These are usually found among the first Celeron processors released.

2. So-called OEM processors, which come with just a chip, that is, without a heatsink or cooling fan.

3. Intel processors with both a heatsink and cooling fan from Intel.

More precisely, there are six such groups, three for processors rated to run at clock frequencies of 266 and three for those rated to run at 300 MHz.

There is a large variety of opinions as to which processor is the best for overclocking. Some sources claim that the first type of processor provides more stability in overclocked modes, while others say that retail (in-box) processors are the best. Unfortunately, there is no unified opinion on this subject, although many users cling to in-box processors, mainly because there is less chance of getting a remarked processor.

There is another group of characteristics of Celeron processors to which you should pay close attention when choosing a processor. These are the so-called specifications and code versions of processors.

On the computer market you can find at least two different microcodes for Celeron 266 and Celeron 300 processors: dA0 and dA1. It's generally accepted that dA1 is the best choice. You can easily determine this parameter using the CPUID program, which designates dA0 as 0650 and dA1 as 0651. Of course, the best way is to check this parameter when buying the processor.

When selecting the processor, you should also pay attention to the specification (S-Spec), which is usually indicated on the back side of the processor along with the other parameters.

Additional Characteristics Important for Choosing a Processor

In Box S-Spec	SL2YN	SL2QG	SL2Z7	SL2Y2
OEM S-Spec	SL2SY	SL2TR	SL2YP	SL2X8
Frequency, MHz	266	266	300	300
Code number	dA0	dA1	dA0	dA1
Data from CPUID	0650	0651	0650	0651

When buying a processor, figuring out its specifications is fairly simple. You just need to read the box and/or chip of the processor carefully.

On the processor chip, you can find the S-Spec in the marking, in which are shown the serial number, then the specification, then the clock frequency, and then the country of origin.

On the box, the specification is shown at the bottom, under the bar code at the end of the prod. code line.

Overclocking statistics confirm that optimal processors are those with the SL2QG specification, that is, Celeron 266s (in-box versions). It's been confirmed that they can run at 448 MHz. For Celeron 300 processors the SL2Y2 is the best.

Note that some Internet resources provide information about Celeron processors that overclock poorly. These include, for example, Celeron 300-A processors with Slot 1 and the SL2WM specification.

Parameters of Overclocked Celeron 266/300 Processors

As experience has shown, you can receive a huge boost in performance by over-clocking Celeron 266 and Celeron 300 processors. Theoretically there exist a large number of possible overclocking modes that can be set by changing the bus frequency. Some of these modes are listed in the table below.

Parameters of Overclocked Celeron 266/300 Processors

Celeron 266	Celeron 300
$266 = 4 \times 66$	$300 = 4.5 \times 66$
$272 = 4 \times 68$	$306 = 4.5 \times 68$
$300 = 4 \times 75$	$338 = 4.5 \times 75$
$333 = 4 \times 83$	$374 = 4.5 \times 83$
$400 = 4 \times 100$	$450 = 4.5 \times 100$
$413 = 4 \times 103$	$464 = 4.5 \times 103$
$448 = 4 \times 112$	$504 = 4.5 \times 112$

You should realize that there are certain motherboards that support a host bus frequency of more than 112 MHz. The practice has shown, however, that overclocking processors and other components to such a frequency is usually impossible without increasing the voltage. As for a bus frequency of 112 MHz, it is only attainable for a very few of the Celeron 266 and Celeron 300 processors.

Normally, if you have chosen the components of your computer right, Celeron 266 and Celeron-300 processors will do well in a mode where the host bus frequency is set to 83 MHz, which will result in a clock frequency of 333 and 374 MHz, respectively.

The overclocking limit for Celeron 266 is 400 MHz, and for Celeron 300 — 450 MHz. These values mean that the host bus frequency is 100 MHz. Note that a few lucky users may be able to overclock their Celeron processors to run at a bus frequency of 112 MHz.

Once again, we need to emphasize the fact that all overclocking modes require appropriate cooling, the intensity of which should grow along with the host bus frequency.

Parameters of Overclocked Celeron 300A/333 Processors

On August 24, 1998, Intel announced the first new processors in the Celeron family. These processors received the names Intel Celeron 300A and Celeron 333.

These new processors were developed using the same 0.25-micron technology, but differ from their predecessors in that they contain a new core, known as the Mendocino.

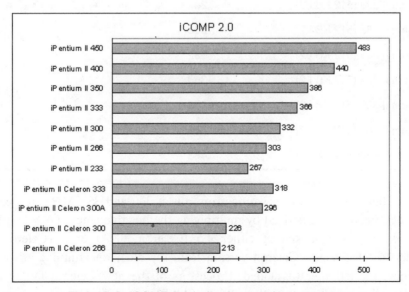

Fig. 13.2. iCOMP 2.0 index for certain processors

These processors of the new Celeron family contain 128 KB of second-level cache memory, which is located on the chip itself.

Recall that Pentium II processors have a cache memory of 512 KB, which is located on the processor chip inside the SEC cartridge that uses Slot 1. Here, the cache memory works at the half of the clock frequency. Celeron 266/300 processors did not have a cache memory at all.

In the newer Celeron 300A and 333 processors, the cache memory works at a frequency equal to that of the processor core. This has greatly increased the performance of the processor (Fig. 13.2).

iCOMP 2.0 Performance Index for Processors

Processor	ICOMP 2.0
Celeron 266	213
Celeron 300	226
Celeron 300A (128 KB L2)	296
Celeron 333 (128 KB L2)	318
iPentium II 233 (512 KB L2)	267
iPentium II 266 (512 KB L2)	303
iPentium II 300 (512 KB L2)	332
iPentium II 333 (512 KB L2)	366
iPentium II 350 (512 KB L2)	386
iPentium II 400 (512 KB L2)	440
iPentium II 450 (512 KB L2)	483

Celeron 300A and Celeron 333 processors run at 300 and 333 MHz, respectively. This clock frequency is derived by multiplying the bus frequency (66 MHz) by the multiplier, which is locked at either 4.5 (Celeron 300A) or 5 (Celeron 333). In order to tell the new Celeron version from the older one running at the same frequency, the letter A was added. Processors of the new Celeron family should work on all motherboards with i440LX, i440EX, i440BX chipsets etc. as long as they are supported by BIOS. For those motherboards released earlier, a new version of BIOS can be obtained on the Internet sites of their respective manufacturers.

The processors from the new Celeron family have a smaller cache memory size than the Intel Pentium II. But when it comes to performance, they are comparable to the Pentium II and sometimes, due to the smaller and faster cache memory, may even outperform the Pentium II. For example, reading information from the memory in blocks from 16 to 128 KB (the size of the new Celerons' L2 cache) can be done by the Celeron 333 approximately twice as fast as by Pentium II 333. But, when using large blocks, from 128 to 512 KB (the size of the Pentium II L2 cache), the Pentium II 333 works faster. Thus, depending on the applications, the Celeron processors with the Mendocino core and the on-chip cache memory can at times outperform, and at times lag behind the Pentium II with the same clock frequency (Fig. 13.3).

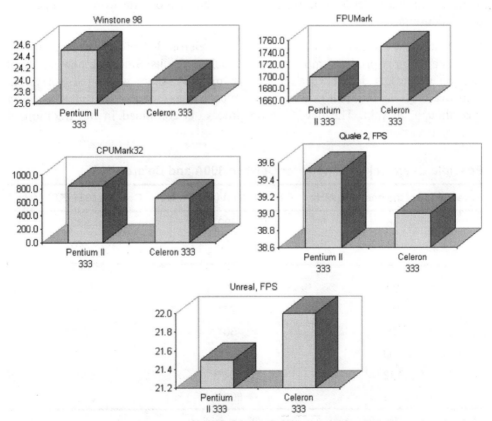

Fig. 13.3. Comparison of processors' performance

Comparison of the Performances of Celeron 333 and Pentium II 333

	Intel Pentium II 333	Intel Celeron 333	Difference
Winstone 98	24.5	24	−2%
CPUMark32	8350	655	−22%
FPUMark	1700	1750	+3%
Quake2, FPS	39.5	39	−1%
Unreal, FPS	21.5	22	+2%

From the test results, we can see that these processors have very close performance parameters. Regardless of the fact that CPUMark32 showed that the Celeron 333 lagged behind by 22%, the test results shown in games such as Quake 2 and Unreal demonstrate that Celeron processors with a cache memory are worthy competitors of the Pentium II.

It is widely known that the Celeron 266 and Celeron 300 processors without the L2 cache memory produce impressive overclocking results. Since the new family of Celeron processors does have an L2 cache memory, there was some worry that their overclocking capabilities would be similar to those of Pentium II. The worry was, though, in vain. The new Celeron processors continued in the tradition of their predecessors.

Possible Overclocking Modes for Celeron 300A and Celeron 333

Frequency of the host bus, MHz	Celeron 300A (x4.5), MHz	Celeron 333 (x5.0), MHz
66	300	333
68	306	340
75	337	375
83	375	416
95	427*	475*
100	450*	500**
103	463*	515**
112	504**	560**
133	600**	666**

* In most cases the processor will require additional cooling.
** In most cases, even with additional cooling, the system will not be stable.

Overclocking Pentium III Processors (Coppermine)

Based on the experience of overclocking processors of the same type but intended to run at different clock frequencies, one can formulate the following rule that underlies overclocking success. This rule relates to the fact that after a change in technology, architecture of the core or cache memory, any modification introduced to the internal functional algorithms, etc., the first releases of the processor are the ones most suitable for overclocking. Usually, this is explained by the large technological reserve, which is the most apparent in the first members of a line of new processors. This is true for all processor families, including Pentium, Celeron processors with the Deshutes core, Celeron processors with the Mendocino core, and for Pentium II processors. Practically all processors can be overclocked to some extent, but it is especially the first processors of a new line that produce the best overclocking results. Indeed, it's enough to look at the example of the Pentium processors of 75—100 MHz, and the Celeron 266, Celeron 300A, and Pentium II processors with frequencies of 266—300 MHz. The Pentium III processor with a Coppermine core is no exception to this rule.

Pentium III processors with a Coppermine core were developed based on the experience accumulated early on from repeated use of Pentium II, Pentium III, and Celeron (Mendocino) processors. The first representatives of the new line were introduced at the end of 1999. Pentium III processors with a Coppermine core were developed with the new 0.18-micron semiconductor technology. As with earlier Pentium III processors with the Katmai core, the new processors that replaced them support MMX and SSE. Unlike their predecessors, they have a built-in 256 KB L2 cache memory intended for operation at the core frequency, which makes them to some extent relatives of Celeron processors with the Mendocino core. However, the larger size of the L2 cache memory, the internal bus which has been expanded from 64 to 256 bits, the more advanced functional algorithm (256-bit Advanced Transfer Cache), and its improved architecture, allow it to perform better not only in comparison to overclocked Celeron (Mendocino) processors, but also when compared to Pentium III (Katmai) processors with a 512 KB cache memory used at the same frequencies. You should note that in the line of Pentium III processors with the Coppermine core, there are certain models intended for operation at bus frequencies of 100 and 133 MHz. The ones intended for 133 MHz are designated as such by the letter "B" when it is necessary to differentiate them from those that work at a bus frequency of 100 MHz. The models intended ed to run at the same clock frequencies as Pentium III processors with the Katmai core are designated by the letter "E" used in the name.

As a packaging for the processors, SECC2 (Slot 1) and FC-PGA (Socket 370) were chosen with the idea to subsequently reduce the number issued of the first type and gradually increase production of the second. Processors with this type of architecture, using the FC-PGA construct, had become predominant by the end of 2000.

Keep in mind that all Pentium III (Coppermine) processors have a locked multiplier, which establishes the ratio between the processor clock frequency and the bus frequency. Therefore, these processors can only be overclocked by increasing the bus frequency.

Many of the first released processors in the Pentium III (Coppermine) line are intended for use at a bus frequency of 100 MHz, and without trouble allow you to raise the FSB frequency to 133 MHz and even higher. However, such high FSB frequency values impose certain requirements on the components that are working in overclocked mode.

In order to ensure successful overclocking of the processor and the stable functioning of the computer at a bus frequency of 133 MHz, all of the basic components must satisfy at least the following requirements:

☐ The RAM modules must meet PC133 specifications or have the ability to work at a frequency of 133 MHz. Otherwise, the chipset on which the motherboard is based must provide the ability to decrease the memory bus frequency in relation to the FSB frequency (Intel 810/810E, VIA Apollo Pro133/Pro133A, etc.).

☐ The video adapter must tolerate an AGP bus frequency of 89 MHz, when the divisor of the AGP bus frequency is 2/3 (i440BX, i440ZX, VIA Apollo Pro/Pro+).

☐ The motherboard must either have a frequency divisor of for the PCI bus, or all the PCI-devices and the hard drive must work reliably at 44 MHz.

Pentium III processors with the Coppermine core have repeated the success of their predecessors by retaining their overclocking abilities on a large scale, due to the significant reserve of technology that exists in this line of processors. This reserve gives you the ability to increase the clock frequency and the bus frequency by a relatively large amount, which in turn leads to an adequate gain in the performance of the processor, and thus to a gain in overall computer performance.

For a more precise analysis of the temperature conditions of the computer and estimates of the necessary type of cooling, the table below gives some data on the power dissipated by Pentium III Coppermine processors.

Pentium III (SECC2)

Clock frequency, MHz	L2 cache memory, KB	Maximum power dissipated by the chip, W
533EB	256	14.0
550E	256	14.5
600E	256	15.8
600EB	256	15.8
650	256	17.0
667	256	17.5
700	256	18.3
733	256	19.1
750	256	19.5
800	256	20.8
800EB	256	20.8
850	256	22.5
866	256	22.9
933	256	25.5
1.0B GHz	256	33.0

Pentium III (PGA370)

Clock frequency, MHz	L2 cache memory, KB	Maximum power dissipated by the chip, W
500E	256	13.2
533EB	256	14.0
550E	256	14.5
600E	256	15.8
600EB	256	15.8

continues

Continued

Clock frequency, MHz	L2 cache memory, KB	Maximum power dissipated by the chip, W
650	256	17.0
667	256	17.5
700	256	18.3
733	256	19.1
750	256	19.5
800	256	20.8
800EB	256	20.8
850	256	22.5
866	256	22.9
933	256	24.5

In the table below, you will find a comparison of the power dissipated by Pentium III Coppermine (256 KB L2) and Pentium III Katmai (512 KB L2) processors.

Pentium III (SECC2)

Clock frequency, MHz	L2 cache memory, KB	Maximum power dissipated by the chip, W
450	512	25.3
500	512	28.0
533B	512	29.7
533EB	256	14.0
550	512	30.8
550E	256	14.5
600	512	34.5
600B	512	34.5
600E	256	15.8
600EB	256	15.8

Overclocking Celeron (Coppermine) Processors

Soon after developing and releasing the first representatives of the Pentium III line of processors with the Coppermine core, Intel announced the release of a similar processor line oriented towards Low End computers — the Celeron with a Coppermine core. These processors appeared as the result of Intel policy of dividing the computer market into sectors by the performance and cost of the computer in order to optimize their price/performance index.

Celeron processors that have the Coppermine core, unlike their more powerful relatives, have a smaller L2 cache memory of 128 KB (256-digit Advanced Transfer Cache) and are intended for a bus frequency of 66 MHz. In all other respects, the architecture of these processors is almost the same as that of the Pentium III (Coppermine), including support of not only MMX, but also SSE, which before was a characteristic of only Pentium III (Katmai) processors oriented towards High End computers.

Celeron (Coppermine) processors are released in the FC-PGA (Socket 370) construct.

The core voltage in the first representatives of this line, which includes the Celeron 533A (Coppermine), is 1.5 V, which is somewhat less than for Pentium III (Coppermine) processors, whose core voltages are 1.6 and 1.65. This generally allows you to safely raise the voltage of the Celeron (Coppermine) processors to a level of 1.6—1.65 V, provided, of course, that you implement adequate cooling. This has a positive effect on the stability of the processor under extreme overclocking conditions. Later, for the higher performance Celeron models, the core voltage was raised to the standard level, characteristic for processors with a Coppermine core. This increase of the core voltage widens the possibilities of overclocking for these processors. For example, the Celeron 667 (Coppermine) can be overclocked to 1,000 MHz. In general, Celeron (Coppermine) processors are stable in overclocked modes even at the standard core voltage, which generally allows you to raise the bus frequency by 30% without much trouble. For certain models, you can raise the standard values for the clock frequency and bus frequency by more than 50%.

For a more precise analysis of the computer temperature conditions and more accurate assessments of the necessary type of cooling, the table below gives some data on the power dissipated by the first members of the line of Celeron processors with the Coppermine core.

Celeron (FC-PGA)

Clock frequency, MHz	L2 cache memory, KB	Dissipation power, W
533A	128	11.2
566	128	11.9
600	128	12.6
633	128	16.5
667	128	17.5
700	128	18.3

Overclocking Pentium 4 (Willamette) Processors

The Pentium 4 processor, earlier known as the Willamette processor, is a product based on principally new architecture. It was developed on the basis of Intel Net-Burst micro-architecture, and contains 42 million transistors. The well-known and reliable 0.18 µm technology, tested on the previous generation of processors, was used in its creation. The core's code name is Willamette.

The usage of hyper-pipelining technology in Pentium 4 architecture enabled Intel to significantly increase the processor frequency. This line of processors starts with models intended to run at frequencies of 1.3, 1.4, and 1.5 GHz.

To provide continuous functioning of a pipeline of such a large length (more than 20 steps) running at high frequency, significant changes to the core's internal architecture were introduced. For example, the new Advanced Dynamic Execution Engine technology improves branch prediction, while Arithmetic Logic Units (ALUs) run at frequency double the one used bythe processor's core.

High performance is also provided by the efficient L1 cache memory (L1 = 8 KB) and L2 cache memory (L2 = 256 KB), integrated on-chip. As with the Pentium III processors with the Coppermine core, the L2 cache memory provides a 256-bit data throughput channel (Advanced Transfer Cache). It runs at the processor's core frequency, thus providing a high performance.

In order to optimize the internal core components, the command set was further enhanced. The extended command set, which represents the further enhancement of the MMX and SSE technologies, has the name of SSE2 (Streaming SIMD Extensions 2), and includes 144 new instructions.

As a result of above-listed innovations, Pentium 4 is positioned as a powerful processor oriented towards performing tasks such as Internet and/or multimedia applications with minimal branching. As a matter of fact, the number of such applications is constantly increasing.

It should be mentioned that the high processor frequency required the developers not only to change the internal structure of the processor, but also to introduce the appropriate changes into the computer architecture. The new physical signaling scheme of quad pumping enables the 100 MHz-clocked system bus to transfer data with a frequency of 400 MHz, and process the address part with a frequency of 200 MHz (2X). This next standard raises the bus speed to 133 MHz, which enables you to transfer data at a frequency of 533 MHz and delivers a data rate of 4.3 GB/sec.

Pentium 4 processors with the Willamette core are supplied in two variations of the FCPGA (Flip Chip Pin Grid Array), using Socket 423 and Socket 478. The core voltage (Vcore) of Socket 423 processors is 1.7 and 1.75 V, and for Socket 478 processors, it is 1.75 V.

Especially for Pentium 4 processors, Intel has developed the following chipsets: i850 (MCH+ICH2+FWH), supporting two Rambus memory channels, i845 — SDRAM (PC133), i845 B-step (i845D) — DDR SDRAM. Third-party vendors, such as VIA and Sis, have also released their chipsets: P4X266 — DDR SDRAM and SiS645 — DDR333 SDRAM.

The above-listed components have became the bases of the respective motherboards. They provide capabilities of implementing the high potential of the new core architecture as well as new, promising technologies. At the same time, the architectures of most motherboards also include the appropriate overclocking facilities, which, combined with the hardware monitoring tools, are gradually becoming a mandatory component of contemporary motherboards. Despite the fact that, as with previous releases, such motherboards traditionally use fixed multipliers, these motherboards provide a significant overclocking potential for Pentium 4 processors, thanks to the possibilities of increasing the FSB frequency. For example, the 1.7 GHz models (Socket 478) can be overclocked to increase the performance by up to 20%, while some 1.4 GHz models (Socket 478) can be increased by as much as 25—30%. According to overclocking theory and practice, an even higher potential is expected for models based on more advanced technological processes, such as the first representatives of the Pentium 4 processors with the Northwood core (Socket 478), based on the 0.13 μm technology, and any further developments based on 90 nm (100 nm = 0.1 μm), 65 nm, 45 nm technological processes, and so on.

Processor Thermal Design Power Processor 4 (Socket 423)

Processor, GHz/ Vcore, V	Thermal design power (W)	Minimum Tcase (°C)	Maximum Tcase (°C)
1.30 / 1.7	48.9	5	69
1.40 / 1.7	51.8	5	70
1.50 / 1.7	54.7	5	72
1.30 / 1.75	51.6	5	70
1.40 / 1.75	54.7	5	72
1.50 / 1.75	57.8	5	73
1.60 / 1.75	61.0	5	75
1.70 / 1.75	64.0	5	76
1.80 / 1.75	66.7	5	78
1.90 / 1.75	69.2	5	73
2.0 / 1.75	71.8	5	74

Processor Thermal Design Power Processor 4 (Socket 478)

Processor, GHz	Thermal design power (W)	Minimum Tcase (°C)	Maximum Tcase (°C)
1.50	57.9	5	73
1.60	60.8	5	75
1.70	63.5	5	76
1.80	66.1	5	77
1.90	72.8	5	75
2.0	75.3	5	76

Increasing the Voltage of the Processor

Pentium II and Celeron

Unfortunately, with the changeover to the new architecture of the Pentium II with Slot 1, users practically lost the ability to manually set the voltage to the processor. And as is generally known, increasing this voltage is sometimes absolutely necessary in order to ensure the stable functioning of the processor in an overclocked mode. When overclocking a Pentium, it was often necessary to increase the voltage by 5–10%, and you were then able to get a very good result. Processors with Slot 1 automatically assign the necessary voltage to the processor with the help of a binary code set by five power leads. They are named VID 0, VID 1, VID 2, VID 3, and VID 4, VID being an abbreviation of Voltage Identification.

Voltage Identifications for Pentium II

Voltage, V	VID 0	VID 1	VID 2	VID 3	VID 4
1.80	1	0	1	0	0
1.85	0	0	1	0	0
1.90	1	1	0	0	0
1.95	0	1	0	0	0
2.00	1	0	0	0	0
2.05	0	0	0	0	0
2.10	0	1	1	1	1
2.20	1	0	1	1	1
2.30	0	0	1	1	1
2.40	1	1	0	1	1
2.50	0	1	0	1	1
2.60	1	0	0	1	1
2.70	0	0	0	1	1
2.80	1	1	1	0	1
2.90	0	1	1	0	1
3.00	1	0	1	0	1

continues

Continued

Voltage, V	VID 0	VID 1	VID 2	VID 3	VID 4
3.10	0	0	1	0	1
3.20	1	1	0	0	1
3.30	0	1	0	0	1
3.40	1	0	0	0	1
3.50	0	0	0	0	1

The motherboard will automatically assign the necessary level of voltage to the processor by analyzing the code of the power leads VID 0, VID 1, VID 2, VID 3, and VID 4.

Certain motherboards, designed with overclocking in mind, provide the user with the ability to change the processor voltage. If you are going to overclock, it's best to use such motherboards.

In those cases where you must increase the voltage to the motherboard, but the motherboard doesn't provide such an opportunity, the only way to increase the voltage is by changing the code for the VID 0, VID 1, VID 2, VID 3, and VID 4 pins. This can be done by cutting off the appropriate contact using tape, lacquer, etc. As a result of this, a value of 1 is set for the pin.

For processors with a voltage of 2.8 V, changing the voltage in this manner is impossible. These processors are the Intel Pentium II: 333, 350, 400, and 450 MHz, and the Intel Celeron: 266, 300, 300A, and 333.

Arrangement of VIDs 0–4 on the Processor Chip

Power lead	VID 0	VID 1	VID 2	VID 3	VID 4
Pin	B120	A120	A119	B119	A121

Pins A1—A121 are located on the same side as the cooler or heatsink, and pins B1—B121 can be found on the opposite side. They are relatively easy to find; you need only count the number of the pins from those whose numbers are written on the processor chip.

The table below lists the pins which you may isolate (marked with an asterisk [*]) in order to achieve the desired voltage.

Assigning the Processor Voltage

Voltage, V	B119	B120	A119	A120	A121
2.0					
2.2	*		*		*
2.4	*			*	*
2.6	*				*
2.8			*	*	*
3.0			*		*
3.2				*	*
3.4					*

You can cover the necessary pins with lacquer (nail polish, etc.) or adhesive tape. You can also cut the pin off completely. There are many ways to get around this problem. However, you should always be very careful. If you isolate the wrong pin, you may accidentally increase the voltage to such a level that the processor core will be destroyed as soon as you power on your computer.

When increasing the voltage to the processor, don't forget that the power consumed by the processor increases accordingly. Therefore, you will need to make sure that appropriate cooling is provided.

Pentium III

When overclocking, it is often necessary to increase the voltage of the processor to ensure the processor stability. Unfortunately, most motherboards on the market are not capable of this.

As in the case of the Pentium II, the Pentium III processor automatically assigns the necessary voltage for the processor by using a binary code set by five power leads, again named VID 0, VID 1, VID 2, VID 3, and VID 4, VID being an acronym of Voltage IDentification.

Voltage Identifications for Pentium III

Voltage, V	VID 0	VID 1	VID 2	VID 3	VID 4
1.30	1	1	1	1	0
1.35	0	1	1	1	0

continues

Continued

Voltage, V	VID 0	VID 1	VID 2	VID 3	VID 4
1.40	1	0	1	1	0
1.45	0	0	1	1	0
1.50	1	1	0	1	0
1.55	0	1	0	1	0
1.60	1	0	0	1	0
1.65	0	0	0	1	0
1.70	1	1	1	0	0
1.75	0	1	1	0	0
1.80	1	0	1	0	0
1.85	0	0	1	0	0
1.90	1	1	0	0	0
1.95	0	1	0	0	0
2.00	1	0	0	0	0
2.05	0	0	0	0	0
2.10	0	1	1	1	1
2.20	1	0	1	1	1
2.30	0	0	1	1	1
2.40	1	1	0	1	1
2.50	0	1	0	1	1
2.60	1	0	0	1	1
2.70	0	0	0	1	1
2.80	1	1	1	0	1
2.90	0	1	1	0	1
3.00	1	0	1	0	1
3.10	0	0	1	0	1
3.20	1	1	0	0	1
3.30	0	1	0	0	1
3.40	1	0	0	0	1
3.50	0	0	0	0	1

The motherboard will automatically assign the necessary level of voltage to the processor by analyzing the code of the power leads VID 0, VID 1, VID 2, VID 3, and VID 4.

Certain motherboards that were designed with overclocking in mind give you the ability to change the processor voltage. If you are going to overclock, such motherboards are the best choice.

In those cases when you must increase the voltage to the motherboard, but the motherboard doesn't provide you with such an opportunity, the only way to accomplish this task is by changing the code for the VID 0, VID 1, VID 2, VID 3, and VID 4 pins. This can be done by isolating the appropriate contact using tape, lacquer, etc. As a result of this, a value of 1 is set for the pin.

Arrangement of VIDs 0–4 on the Processor Chip

Power lead	VID 0	VID 1	VID 2	VID 3	VID 4
Pin	B120	A120	A119	B119	A121

Pins A1–A121 can be found on the same side as the cooler or heatsink, and pins B1–B121 are located on the opposite side. They are relatively easy to find; you need only count the number of the pins from those whose numbers are written on the processor's chip.

You can cover the necessary pins with lacquer (nail polish, etc.) or adhesive tape. You can also cut the pin off completely. There are many ways to get around this problem. However, you should always be very careful. If you isolate the wrong pin, you might accidentally increase the voltage to such a level that the processor core will be destroyed when you turn on your computer.

When increasing the voltage to the processor, don't forget that the power consumed by the processor increases accordingly. Therefore, make sure to provide effective cooling.

Overclocking Cyrix/IBM 6x86 Processors

Because of the fact that Cyrix/IBM 6x86 processors heat up very quickly, they are practically unsuitable for overclocking. You should keep in mind that by overclocking these processors you might very easily cause them to fail due to over-heating. There are many examples of Cyrix/IBM 6x86 processors that have failed completely and permanently as a result of an unsuccessful overclocking attempt.

The distinctive property of Cyrix/IBM processors is that they demand an extremely high level of power even in standard modes. This puts a heavy load on the special circuitry located on the motherboard and responsible for supplying power to the processor. Certain motherboards cannot ensure the necessary reserve of power for processors of this type, even when running in the modes recommended by manu-facturers. Overclocked modes increase power demand greatly. As a result, the power supply circuitry may fail, thus rendering the motherboard permanently unusable.

Thus, overclocking of the 6x86 processor is limited by a number of factors. The most important limitations are the intense heating of the chip and the significant power demand.

Several architectural features of the Cyrix processor also influence overclocking strategy. First, it's necessary to emphasize the fact that this particular processor supports only two multipliers, ×2 and ×3. Note that the ×3 multiplier is not rec-ommended for use at all, since it greatly increases the probability of damaging the processor. To avoid this damage, you may need to set the 3×50 MHz configura-tion, which is generally inefficient because of decreased throughput of the host bus. Thus, you are reduced to selecting the multiplier of ×2, which as a matter of fact means that you have no real choice.

Still, if you decide to attempt overclocking of the 6x86 processor, it makes sense to do it gradually, while ensuring constant control over the temperature conditions.

The overclocking sequence for 6x86 processors is as follows:

❏ from 120+ (100 MHz) to 133+ (110 MHz)

❏ from 133+ (110 MHz) to 150+ (120 MHz)

❏ from 150+ (120 MHz) to 166+ (133 MHz)

Note that the transition from P166+ (133 MHz) to P200+ (150 MHz) is a rela-tively large step, which heavily increases the processor workload. At the same time, you are taking a huge risk of damaging the processor for the sake of a relatively small performance increase.

Intensive cooling of 6x86 processors is mandatory if you plan to use such processors in overclocked modes. You'll most definitely need to install a huge and powerful cooling fan to reduce the risk of damaging the processor due to overheating.

Thus, overclocking the 6x86 processors is not recommended, due to the risk of badly damaging the processor caused by intense heating. Because of the high power consumption of these processors in overclocked modes, you may even burn certain essential elements on the motherboard. Still, regardless of all the difficulties, there are many cases where users reported successful overclocking of these processors.

For a more precise analysis of the computer temperature conditions and estimates of the necessary cooling facilities, the table below provides some data on the power consumption of Cyrix 6x86MX processor.

Cyrix

Processor	Frequency, MHz	Power consumption, W
6x86-P120+	100	19.4
6x86-P133+	110	20.9
6x86-P150+	120	22.0
6x86-P166+	133	23.8
6x86-P200+	150	25.2
6x86-P90+	80	16.9
6x86L-P120+	100	14.2
6x86L-P133+	110	15.1
6x86L-P150+	120	16.0
6x86L-P166+	133	16.6
6x86L-P200+	150	18.2

Cyrix 6x86MX (PR)

6x86MX	Normal, V	Maximum, V
150 MHz (PR166)	11.4	18.9
166 MHz (PR200)	12.1	20.2
188 MHz (PR233)	13.1	21.8
200 MHz (PR233)	13.7	22.9
225 MHz (PR266)	15.7	26.1
233 MHz (PR266)	16.2	27.0

Overclocking AMD-K5 and AMD-K6 Processors

K5 processors from AMD appeared a comparatively short time ago, but immediately proved their relatively high level of performance. The most recent AMD-K5 models successfully compete with Pentium processors. At the same time, the price of AMD-K5 processors is significantly lower.

As for overclocking these processors, you should remember that AMD produced a large variety of 486 processors that could be successfully overclocked. These were the Am486DX/40, overclockable to 50 MHz, the Am486DX4/100, which could be overclocked to 120 MHz, and the very well known and popular Am486DX4/133 (Am5x86-133). This last processor worked excellently at 166 MHz, and to this day is a worthy competitor of systems based on the Pentium 100. Don't forget that the Pentium 100 requires a compatible motherboard, while overclocking the Am5x86 allows you to attain a relatively high level of performance without replacing the motherboard, which means no extra effort or financial investments.

Unfortunately, the recent models of the K5 processors with P-ratings of PR75, PR90, and PR100 do not overclock as well as processors of the previous generation. The problem is the same as with the Cyrix 6x86 processors — excessive heating while overclocked. In overclocked modes, these processors will overheat and may fail or even burn out. In order to protect the processor from overheating in overclocked modes you must provide sufficient cooling.

The newer models, such as PR120 and PR133, are better suited to overclocking. They aren't subject to such excessive overheating. However, even for these processors you must provide adequate cooling.

Overclocking AMD-K6 processors can be done using the same methods that were used for Pentium II processors. The table presented below shows some examples of overclocking parameters.

Examples of Overclocked AMD-K6 Processors

Processor	Overclocking mode		
AMD-K6–233	processor: 290 MHz host bus: 83 MHz multiplier: 3.5	processor: 263 MHz host bus: 75 MHz multiplier: 3.5	processor: 250 MHz host bus: 83 MHz multiplier: 3

continues

Continued

Processor	Overclocking mode		
AMD-K6–200	processor: 250 MHz host bus: 83 MHz multiplier: 3	processor: 225 MHz host bus: 75 MHz multiplier: 3	processor: 233 MHz host bus: 66 MHz multiplier: 3.5
AMD-K6–166	processor: 225 MHz host bus: 75 MHz multiplier: 3	processor: 208 MHz host bus: 83 MHz multiplier: 2.5	processor: 200 MHz host bus: 66 MHz multiplier: 3

For a more precise analysis of the computer temperature conditions and evaluation of the necessary cooling facilities, the tables below provide data on the power consumption of the AMD-K5 and AMD-K6 processors.

AMD-K5

K5	Power consumption, W
PR75	11.9
PR90	14.3
PR100	15.8
PR120	12.6
PR133	14.0
PR166	16.4

AMD-K6 (Model 6)

K6	Normal power consumption, W	Maximum power consumption, W
166 MHz (2.9 V)	10.3	17.2
200 MHz (2.9 V)	12.0	20.0
233 MHz (3.2 V)	17.0	28.3

AMD-K6 (Model 7)

K6	Normal power consumption, W	Maximum power consumption, W
200 MHz (2.2 V)	10.60	12.45
233 MHz (2.2 V)	11.25	13.50

continues

Continued

K6	Normal power consumption, W	Maximum power consumption, W
266 MHz (2.2 V)	12.85	14.55
300 MHz (2.2 V)	13.45	15.40

AMD-K6-2 (2.4 V)

Clock frequency, MHz	Maximum power consumption, W	Normal power consumption, W
266	14.7	8.85
300	17.2	10.35
333	19.0	11.40
350	19.95	11.98
366	20.80	12.48
380	21.60	12.95
400	22.70	13.65
450	28.40	17.50
475	29.60	17.75

AMD-K6-2 (2.2 V)

Clock frequency, MHz	Maximum power consumption, W	Normal power consumption, W
400	16.90	10.15
450	18.80	11.30
475	19.80	11.90
500	20.75	12.45
533	20.75	12.45

AMD-K6-III

Clock frequency, MHz	Core voltage, V	Maximum, W	Normal, W
400	2.2	18.1	10.85
450	2.2	20.2	12.15

continues

Continued

Clock frequency, MHz	Core voltage, V	Maximum, W	Normal, W
400	2.4	26.8	16.10
450	2.4	29.5	17.70

Overclocking AMD Athlon (K7) Processors

AMD Athlon processors were developed based on previous experience accumulated in the course of using previously released AMD-K6-2 and AMD-K6-III processors. The first representatives of the new line were released in 1999. AMD Athlon processors are manufactured using 0.25 micron and 0.18 micron technology. The processor core contains more than 20 million transistors. Like its predecessors developed by AMD, this processor supports MMX and 3DNow! technologies.

Not only are AMD Athlon processors just as good as popular and widely used Pentium III processors, but by certain parameters even prove their superiority.

AMD Athlon processors are not electrically or logically Intel-compatible, but the two families of processors are compatible at the software level. AMD Athlon processors use Slot A, which is mechanically compatible with Slot 1. They require special motherboards with chipsets that support them.

The advanced technology used as the basis of AMD Athlon processors guarantees a high performance index. In some cases, they also support higher values of performance parameters not only in comparison with the Pentium II and Pentium III (Katmai), but also when compared to the newer Pentium II processors built on the basis of the Coppermine architecture. The tables presented below show the results (according to data from **www.anandtech.com**) of testing the AMD Athlon (EPoX EP-7KXA motherboard with VIA Apollo KX133) and the Intel Pentium III (Coppermine, 133 MHz FSB, and Tyan Trinity 400 Rev.D motherboard with VIA Apollo Pro133A).

Content Creation Winstone 2000

Processor clock frequency, MHz	AMD Athlon	Pentium III
1,000	33.7	31.6
800	30.6	29.2
600	27.0	25.6

SYSMark 2000

Processor clock frequency, MHz	AMD Athlon	Pentium III
1,000	171	186
800	153	155
600	127	132

AMD Athlon processors have a significant technological reserve. According to the data provided by some reliable sources, KryoTech, known for extreme cooling methods, can overclock the AMD Athlon 600 to 800 MHz. The architecture of the AMD Athlon processor has the following distinguishing features: a 128 KB L1 cache memory; a 512 KB L2 cache memory which, similar to Intel Pentium II and Pentium II (Katmai) processors, is located on the processor PCB (printed circuit board); an improved FPU block; a core voltage of 1.6—1.8 V; and a new type of processor bus, the EV6, which differs from processor buses used by Intel, etc.

Increasing the Bus Frequency

AMD Athlon processors are intended for use with the Alpha EV6 bus, developed by DEC for Alpha processors and licensed by AMD for their products that resemble the Athlon.

The Alpha EV6 bus, used as a processor bus (FSB), ensures a double-data rate when transferring data. This increases the bus throughput, thus increasing overall system performance. At a clock frequency of 100 MHz, the Alpha EV6 FSB, usually called, simply, the EV6, guarantees data transfer at 200 MHz. In contrast to the EV6, GTL+ and AGTL+ buses used by Intel Celeron, Pentium II, and Pentium III have the same bus frequency and data transfer rate.

However, despite all of its advantages, the high operating frequency of the EV6 system bus creates certain problems for overclockers. Its growth potential is usually limited to an additional 10—15 %.

When considering overclocking capabilities, you should pay attention to the fact that AMD Athlon processors, just as Intel Pentium II and Pentium III processors (Katmai, Coppermine), have a fixed multiplier, which connects the bus frequency and internal clock frequency of the processor. As a result, overclocking is usually done by increasing the external frequency — the operating speed of the FSB, the EV6 in this case. Note that because this bus has limited overclocking capabilities, the method itself also is very limited.

Fig. 13.4. External view of the Athlon processor

However, in addition to this traditional method, AMD Athlon processors can be overclocked using alternate methods. These methods are based on using some of the specific features of the construction of this type of processor.

Overclocking AMD Athlon processors may be accomplished by either resoldering the resistors that define the basic characteristics of the processor, or by using their internal technological sockets.

Modifying the Layout of the Resistors

Note that the voltage, multiplier, and FSB frequency of the Athlon processor are determined by special resistors located on the processor PCB. Therefore, you can change these technical parameters by changing the combinations of special resistors soldered to the processor PCB. However, if you do plan to use this technique, remember that by opening the processor case you automatically lose any warranties, to speak nothing of the processor marketability. If such a processor fails or burns out, even if the failure is not caused by overclocking, you won't be able to exchange it for a new, working one. Also, keep in mind that only qualified persons should perform overclocking, especially in cases when it's necessary to open the case and resolder the resistors on the processor PCB. In the case under consideration, you need to have experience in opening the case and in soldering SMD resistors. Besides, you'll need appropriate, professional-quality equipment.

The layout of the resistors that determine the parameters of the AMD Athlon processor is presented in Figs. 13.5 and 13.6.

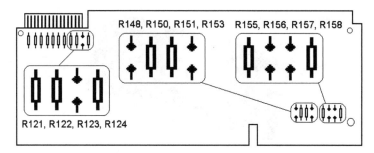

Fig. 13.5. Layout of the resistors on the rear side of the AMD Athlon processor PCB

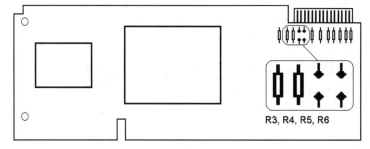

Fig 13.6. Layout of the resistors on the front side of the AMD Athlon processor PCB

The resistors are either present in their appropriate positions, or their respective slots may be empty. In the latter case, you will see two pins to which you can solder the resistor if necessary. Resistors R3, R4, R5, R6, R121, R122, R123, R124 determine the frequency; R148, R150, R151, R153 specify the voltage; and R155, R156, R157, R158 are responsible for setting the multiplier. On both sides of the processor board there are 16 resistors (or mounting slots to which they can be soldered) that determine the basic parameters of the processor.

The overclocking procedure can be divided into four steps. Each step corresponds to the modification of the combination of resistors in the groups listed above.

1. Setting the multiplier (R155, R156, R157, R158). A detailed drawing of the part of the processor PCB that contains the resistors determining the multiplier is presented in Fig. 13.7. The group of resistors responsible for voltage selection is located directly to the left.

Fig. 13.7. Resistors for changing the multiplier

All the resistors in question are so-called SMD resistors with a resistance of 1,000 ohms. The next table shows the correct arrangement of these four resistors for the corresponding modes (clock frequencies) of the processor ("yes" means that the slot is bridged by the resistor, while "—" means that the slot is open).

Setting the Multiplier

Clock frequency, MHz	R155	R156	R157	R158
500	yes	—	yes	yes
550	yes	—	yes	—
600	yes	—	—	yes
650	yes	—	—	—
700	—	yes	yes	yes
750	—	yes	yes	—
800	—	yes	—	yes
850	—	yes	—	—
900	—	—	yes	yes
950	—	—	yes	—
1,000	—	—	—	yes
1,050	—	—	—	—

2. Setting the clock frequency (R121, R122, R123, R124).

Fig. 13.8. Resistors for changing the clock frequency

The diagram shown in Fig. 13.8 illustrates the positioning of the corresponding resistors on the processor PCB.

All of the resistors are SMD resistors ('102') with the resistance of 1,000 ohms. The following table shows the correct arrangement of these four resistors for the corresponding mode (clock frequency) of the processor ("yes" means that the slot is bridged by the resistor, while "—" means that the slot is open).

Setting the Frequency

Clock frequency, MHz	R121	R122	R123	R124
500	—	yes	—	yes
550	—	yes	—	—
600	yes	yes	—	yes
650	yes	yes	—	—
700	—	—	yes	yes
750	—	—	yes	—
800	yes	—	yes	yes
850	yes	—	yes	—
900	—	yes	yes	yes
950	—	yes	yes	—
1,000	yes	yes	yes	yes
1,050	yes	yes	yes	—

3. Setting the clock frequency (R3, R4, R5, R6).

A detailed drawing of the location of the corresponding resistors on the processor PCB is shown in Fig. 13.9.

Again, all resistors used to bridge the slots are SMD resistors with a resistance of 1,000 ohms. Notice that the first resistor in this group is R3 (rather than the one, labeled R2). The following table shows the correct arrangement of these four resistors for the corresponding mode (clock frequency) of the processor. (As usual, "yes" means that the slot is bridged, and "—" means that the slot is open.)

Fig. 13.9. The resistors for changing the clock frequency

Setting the Frequency

Frequency, MHz	R3	R4	R5	R6
500	—	yes	—	yes
550	yes	yes	—	yes
600	—	yes	—	—
650	yes	yes	—	—
700	—	—	yes	yes
750	yes	—	yes	yes
800	—	—	yes	—

continues

Continued

Frequency, MHz	R3	R4	R5	R6
850	yes	—	yes	—
900	—	—	—	yes
950	yes	—	—	yes
1,000	—	—	—	—
1,050	yes	—	—	—

Thus, having made the right adjustments for the multiplier and corresponding clock frequencies, you should now check all the settings. After that, you can reassemble the processor and try to boot the computer with the newly over-clocked Athlon processor. The situations where you also need to increase the voltage are rare. But even if you must, it is not recommended that you raise it more than by 0.05 V.

4. Setting the voltage (R148, R150, R151, R153). According to the data officially provided by AMD (AMD Athlon Processor Data Sheet), the minimum, normal, and maximum values of the core voltage needed for stable operation under normal conditions are presented in the table below. Model 1 processors have a 0.25-micron core, Model 2 processors have a 0.18-micron core, and Model 4 processors have a 0.18-micron core with on-chip L2 cache.

Processor Core Voltage Values under Normal Conditions

Core	Frequency, MHz	Minimum voltage, V	Normal voltage, V	Maximum voltage, V
Model 1	500—700	1.50	1.60	1.70
Model 2	550—750	1.50	1.60	1.70
	800—850	1.60	1.70	1.80
	900—1,000	1.70	1.80	1.90
Model 4	650—850	1.60	1.70	1.80
	900—1,000	1.65	1.75	1.85

Fig. 13.10 shows a detailed diagram of the location of the voltage selection group of resistors.

Fig. 13.10. Voltage selection resistors on the AMD Athlon PCB

All resistors belonging to this group are of the SMD type ('101') with a resistance of 100 ohms. The following table shows the correct arrangement of these four resistors for the corresponding mode (internal frequency) of the processor ("yes" means that the slot is bridged, "—" means that the slot is open).

Setting the Voltage

Voltage, V	R148 (VID0)	R150 (VID1)	R151 (VID2)	R153 (VID3)
1.30	—	—	—	—
1.35	yes	—	—	—
1.40	—	yes	—	—
1.45	yes	yes	—	—
1.50	—	—	yes	—
1.55	yes	—	yes	—
1.60	—	yes	yes	—
1.65	yes	yes	yes	—
1.70	—	—	—	yes
1.75	yes	—	—	yes
1.80	—	yes	—	yes
1.85	yes	yes	—	yes

continues

Continued

Voltage, V	R148 (VID0)	R150 (VID1)	R151 (VID2)	R153 (VID3)
1.90	—	—	yes	yes
1.95	yes	—	yes	yes
2.00	—	yes	yes	yes
2.05	yes	yes	yes	yes

Once again, it should be noted that any overclocking requires you to consider improving the cooling system, and this is especially true if you have increased the voltage.

Using the Athlon Technological Connector

Repositioning the resistors on the processor PCB demands considerable qualifications and skill from the user and is often a relatively dangerous operation. The result may be very disappointing for the owner of the processor.

If you are not very careful, you may irreversibly damage your processor to the point of complete loss of serviceability. Fortunately, there is a different method of modifying the multiplier, which makes the overclocking procedure significantly easier. The architecture of the AMD Athlon processor incorporates an extra connector (Fig. 13.11), which can be used in a way similar to the resistors on the processor PCB to set overclocked processor modes.

To overclock an AMD Athlon using this method, you need to connect a small overclocking card to this connector via a special plug. This overclocking device consists of a small PCB, where all the DIP switches and resistors necessary for setting the desired operating modes are mounted. There are several methods of connecting the card to the processor connector. For example, it is possible to directly solder all the wires to it, which certainly isn't the best solution. The reason is that this method is messy and potentially dangerous. If you are not careful, some of these wires may disconnect or break, thus causing a sharp voltage increase that would certainly burn out the processor almost immediately. The most professional method of approaching this problem is to use a special plug that will ensure reliable contacts (Figs. 13.12 and 13.13).

After making a decision on the method of connecting the overclocking device to the technological processor connector, you may start implementing the circuit shown in Fig. 13.14.

Athlon processor connector

Fig. 13.11. Connector used for overclocking

Fig. 13.12. Professional plug for connecting an overclocking card to the Athlon technological connector (the general view)

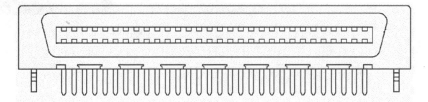

Fig. 13.13. Professional plug for Athlon connector (the bottom view)

All resistors used to implement this circuit are SMD resistors with a resistance of 56 ohms. When on, they consume a power of around 440 mW. This is a relatively large amount, which thus demands that you use appropriate resistors. Otherwise, you'll have to accept the fact that these elements (and, accordingly, your AMD Athlon processor) won't last for long. The above mentioned resistors serve to "disable" the selection set by the 1,000-ohm SMD resistors on the processor PCB. According to the opinion of some researchers, resistors of higher resistance (for example, 220 ohms) can be used successfully as external elements. In this case, the dissipation power is 113 mW, which is significantly smaller than when using resistors of 56 ohms.

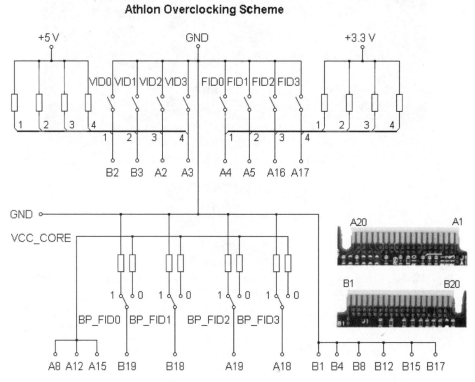

Fig. 13.14. Circuitry of the card for overclocking Athlon processors

Notice that the circuit suggested here is relatively simple, since it comprises only resistors and on/off switches. It requires +5 V, +3.3 V, and also "ground" (GND) voltages. You can use a CPU-external voltage supply and a small voltage-regulator to produce +3.3 V. Users that don't feel comfortable or skilled enough to implement such a circuit on their own can try to find a similar device in specialized computer stores. An example of just such a device is shown in Fig. 13.15.

The necessary arrangement of the switches is presented in the following tables ("enable" means just that: enable, "—" means disable, "0" means set the switch to the 0 position, and "1" means set the switch to the 1 position).

Fig. 13.15. Device for overclocking Athlon processors

Setting the Multiplier

Frequency, MHz	FID3	FID2	FID1	FID0
500	enable	—	enable	enable
550	enable	—	enable	—
600	enable	—	—	enable
650	enable	—	—	—
700	—	enable	enable	enable
750	—	enable	enable	—
800	—	enable	—	enable
850	—	enable	—	—
900	—	—	enable	enable
950	—	—	enable	—
1,000	—	—	—	enable
1,050	—	—	—	—

Setting the Frequency

Frequency, MHz	BP_FID0	BP_FID1	BP_FID2	BP_FID3
500	1	1	0	1
550	0	1	0	1
600	1	0	0	1
650	0	0	0	1
700	1	1	1	0
750	0	1	1	0
800	1	0	1	0
850	0	0	1	0
900	1	1	0	0
950	0	1	0	0
1,000	1	0	0	0
1,050	0	0	0	0

AMD recommendations for the processor voltage are given in the following table. Model 1 are processors with a core made with 0.25 micron technology, Model 2 are processors made with 0.18 micron technology, and Model 4 are processors made with 0.18 micron technology and with on-chip L2 cache (256 KB).

AMD Recommendations

Core	Clock frequency, MHz	Minimum voltage, V	Standard voltage, V	Maximum voltage, V
Model 1	500—700	1.50	1.60	1.70
Model 2	550—750	1.50	1.60	1.70
	800—850	1.60	1.70	1.80
	900—1,000	1.70	1.80	1.90
Model 4	650—850	1.60	1.70	1.80
	900—1,000	1.65	1.75	1.85

Setting the Voltage

Voltage, V	R148 (VID0)	R150 (VID1)	R151 (VID2)	R153 (VID3)
1.30	—	—	—	—
1.35	enable	—	—	—
1.40	—	enable	—	—
1.45	enable	enable	—	—
1.50	—	—	enable	—
1.55	enable	—	enable	—
1.60	—	enable	enable	—
1.65	enable	enable	enable	—
1.70	—	—	—	enable
1.75	enable	—	—	enable
1.80	—	enable	—	enable
1.85	enable	enable	—	enable
1.90	—	—	enable	enable
1.95	enable	—	enable	enable
2.00	—	enable	enable	enable
2.05	enable	enable	enable	enable

For a more precise analysis of the temperature conditions of the computer and an evaluation of the necessary cooling facilities, the table below provides data on the power consumption of the Athlon (K7) processors with cores made with 0.18 and 0.25 technology.

AMD Athlon (0.25 micron — Model 1)

Processor clock frequency, MHz	Normal power consumption, W	Maximum power consumption, W
500	38	42
550	41	46
600	45	50
650	48	54
700	45	50

AMD Athlon (0.18 micron — Model 2)

Processor clock frequency, MHz	Normal power consumption, W	Maximum power consumption, W
550	28	31
600	30	34
650	32	36
700	34	39
750	35	40
800	43	48
850	45	50
900	53	60
950	55	62
1,000	60	65

Athlon (0.18 micron — Model 4, 256 KB L2 on the crystal)

Processor clock frequency, MHz	Normal power consumption, W	Maximum power consumption, W
650	32.4	36.1
700	34.4	38.3
750	36.3	40.4
800	38.3	42.6
850	40.2	44.8
900	44.6	49.7
950	46.7	52.0
1,000	48.7	54.3

Overclocking AMD Duron and Athlon Thunderbird

AMD Duron and Thunderbird processors are sold in PGA packaging. The motherboard for these processors must have a special socket, a PGA socket, called Socket A (462 contacts). The Duron processor has a 128 KB L1 cache memory and a 64 KB L2 cache memory (Fig. 13.16). The Thunderbird processor (Fig. 13.17) is also often called simply Athlon, meaning Athlon for Socket A. The Thunderbird processor differs from the Duron processor only by the L2 cache size (256 KB).

Fig. 13.16. AMD Duron processor

Fig. 13.17. AMD Althlon (Thunderbird) processor

The above-mentioned processors are intended for work with the Alpha EV6 bus, developed by DEC for Alpha processors and licensed by AMD for use with its products.

The Alpha EV6 bus is used as the processor's front-side bus (FSB), and provides data transfer on both fronts of clock pulses (double-data-rate). This increases the throughput, thus increasing the overall system performance. At a clock frequency of 100 MHz, the Alpha EV6 bus (also known simply as EV6) provides for a data transfer rate of 200 MHz, in contrast to the GTL+ and AGTL+ buses used in Intel Celeron, and Pentium II/III processors, for which the data transfer frequency and clock frequency are the same.

Because of the specific features of the AMD processor architecture, AMD Athlon and Duron processors require the use of specalized motherboards, with the chipsets supporting these processors. Such motherboards support stable functioning of these processors, provided that sufficiently poweful supply sources are used, ones generally no less than 235 W.

AMD Athlon and Duron processors have a significant technological reserve, which enables you to increase the performance thanks to the use of the overclocked modes, such as increasing the processor bus frequency.

AMD Duron and Thunderbird processors released in the Socket A construct have locked frequency multipliers. Due to their Socket A construct, which bars you from changing the resistors as was possible in the case of AMD Athlon, it is only possible to change the multiplier using special hardware facilities and software tools, which are currently only supported by a limited number of motherboards.

You should note that the processor core voltage can only be increased by no more than 5—10% above the standard level. AMD recommended voltage levels for Athlon processors are shown in the following table. This information often changes with time, and therefore the tables provided below also give the dates the information and recommendations were posted in the AMD documentation.

Permissible Voltage Levels for AMD Athlon and Duron Processors (06/2000)

Processor	Clock frequency, MHz	Minimum voltage, V	Standard voltage, V	Maximum voltage, V
Thunderbird	650—850	1.60	1.70	1.80
	900—1,000	1.65	1.75	1.85
Duron	550—700	1.40	1.50	1.60

Permissible Voltage Levels for AMD Duron Model 7 Processors (10/2001)

Minimum voltage AC/DC, V	Nominal voltage, V	Maximum voltage AC/DC, V
1.65/1.70	1.75	1.80/1.90

Permissible Voltage Levels for AMD Athlon and Duron Model 3 Processors (11/2001 and 06/2001)

Processor	Clock frequency, MHz	Minimum voltage, V	Standard voltage, V	Maximum voltage, V
Thunderbird	650—1,400	1.65	1.75	1.85
Duron	600—950	1.50	1.60	1.70

For a more precise analysis of the temperature conditions of the computer and more accurate assessments of the necessary cooling facilities, the following table provides information on the power consumption of AMD Duron and AMD Thunderbird processors.

Power Consumption of AMD Thunderbird Processors (06/2000)

Processor clock frequency, MHz	Normal power, W	Maximum power, W
650	32.4	36.1
700	34.4	38.3
750	36.3	40.4
800	38.3	42.6
850	40.2	44.8
900	44.6	49.7
950	46.7	52.0
1,000	48.7	54.3

Power Consumption of AMD Thunderbird Processors (11/2001)

Processor clock frequency, MHz	Normal power, W	Maximum power, W
900	45.8	51.0

continues

Continued

Processor clock frequency, MHz	Normal power, W	Maximum power, W
950	47.6	53.1
1,000	49.5	55.1
1,100	54.1	60.3
1,133	55.7	62.1
1,200	58.9	65.7
1,266	60.1	66.9
1,300	61.3	68.3
1,333	62.6	69.8
1,400	64.7	72.1

Power Consumption of AMD Duron Processors (06/2000)

Processor clock frequency, MHz	Normal power, W	Maximum power, W
550	18.9	21.1
600	20.4	22.7
650	21.8	24.3
700	22.9	25.5

Power Consumption of AMD Duron Processors (06/2001)

Processor clock frequency, MHz	Normal power, W	Maximum power, W
600	24.5	27.4
650	26.4	29.4
700	28.2	31.4
750	30.0	33.4
800	31.8	35.4
850	33.6	37.4
900	35.4	39.5
950	37.2	41.5

Power Consumption of AMD Duron Model 7 Processors (11/2001)

Processor clock frequency, MHz	Normal power, W	Maximum power, W
900	38.3	42.7
950	39.8	44.4
1,000	41.3	46.1
1,100	45.1	50.3

AMD Athlon and Duron processors have a significant technological reserve, which enables you to increase the performance thanks to the use of overclocking modes, such as increasing the processor bus frequency.

Overclocking by Increasing the FSB Frequency

When considering the capabilities of using overclocking modes, it is necessary to take into account the fact that processors such as AMD Athlon and Duron, just like Intel Pentium II, and Pentium III (Katmai, Coppermine) have a fixed frequency multiplier relating the internal and external frequencies.

Because the Socket A construct doesn't allow you to modify the layout of the resistors, which was possible with AMD Athlon for Slot A, you can only change the frequency multiplier using special software and hardware tools supported by a limited number of motherboards.

Specific features and secrets of using these tools to correct the Socket A AMD Athlon and Duron Socket frequency multipliers will be analyzed in the next section. Here, let's concentrate on the traditional method, based on increasing the bus clock frequencies.

As a result of implementing this method, AMD Duron and Athlon processors are overclocked by increasing the external frequency — the frequency of the EV6 front-side bus (FSB EV6).

The selection and setting of the required FSB value, depending on the motherboard, is performed either using DIP switches, or using the appropriate menu items in BIOS Setup.

Despite all its advantages, a high clock frequency of the EV6 bus, at which data transfer is performed, limits the ability to overclock processors by increasing the processor bus frequency.

When using widely recognized motherboards based on popular chipsets such as VIA Apollo KT133, one usually manages to increase the FSB frequency by no more than by 10—15% (moderate overclocking), or by 12—17% when using extreme overclocking modes. The upper limit of the possible FSB EV6 increase and, consequently, the resulting peformance gain, depends on the motherboard (topology, quality, special features of the components used).

The performance gain obtained for AMD Duron and AMD Athlon processors resulting from overclocking via FSB EV6 is illustrated by the tables and graphs provided below.

Overclocking the AMD Duron Processor

CPU Clock Speed = FSB frequency × multiplier	CPUmark 99	FPU WinMark
600 = 100 × 6	51.4	3,260
690 = 115 × 6	59.4	3,760

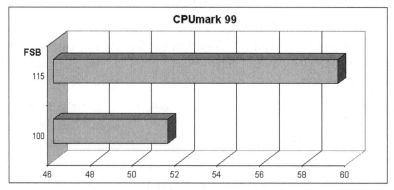

Fig. 13.18. AMD Duron overclocking results

Overclocking of AMD Athlon (Thunderbird) Processors

CPU Clock Speed = FSB frequency × multiplier	CPUmark 99	FPU WinMark
700 = 100 × 7	64.7	3,810
784 = 112 × 7	72.5	4,270

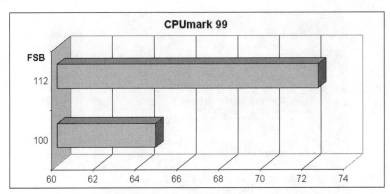

Fig. 13.19. AMD Athlon (Thunderbird) overclocking results

Detailed overclocking results for AMD Duron and AMD Athlon processors will be presented in the appropriate section in *Chapter 19*.

However, despite the quite moderate values of the performance gain obtained by increasing the FSB EV6 bus speed in systems based on the VIA Apollo KT133 chipset, this method has become widely used and even more popular since the release of the more advanced VIA Apollo KT133A chipset. Supplemented with the ability to change the frequency multiplier values of the AMD Duron and AMD Athlon processors, this method allows you to obtain even more impressive results, which can be adequately evaluated and assesed only after looking at the method of overclocking by changing the multipliers.

Overclocking by Changing Multipliers

As a matter of fact, AMD Athlon (Thunderbird) and AMD Duron have a fixed frequency multiplier. Despite this fact, some motherboards (such as Soltek SL-75KV+ and Abit KT7) still provide the ability to change this multiplier.

The capability of changing the frequency multiplier is related to the fact that its value can be changed using the FID0–FID3 contacts. This, however, concerns only the first releases of the processors. Beginning at a certain moment, AMD removed this capability by cutting the signal lines that allowed you to change the multiplier frequency. However, and fortunately for overclocking fans, AMD performs this operation with L1 jumpers, positioned externally on the processor case's surface (Fig. 13.20).

Fig. 13.20. Position of L1 jumpers

Locked capabilities of changing the frequency multiplier can be restored by simply connecting the broken contacts. This can be easily done using a sharpened soft pencil with a high percentage of graphite, which, is actually a good conductor. Take the pencil and rub the graphite over the gaps between L1 jumper contacts, trying to provide a better contact. When doing so, it is important to avoid contacts between neighouring jumpers. The results of this procedure are shown in Figs. 13.21 (cut bridges) and 13.22 (restored contacts), which show fragments of the AMD Duron processor surface.

Fig. 13.21. Interrupted contacts of the L1 bridges

Fig. 13.22. Restored contacts of the L1 bridges

The most important advantage of this method is that you can quickly restore the processor's marketability with a cloth and some rubbing alcohol.

An even better result can be obtained using a special silver pencil, generally used for correcting printed circuits, and a piece of solder in the form of a thin wire (used in a similar manner). Furthermore, the broken contacts of the L1 bridges can be restored by quickly soldering them using low-temperature soldering materials, or with special glues that contain fine solder powder. However, these methods have one common drawback — they are irreversible, and don't allow you torestore the processor's marketability.

After restoring the broken L1 contacts on the AMD Duron and Athlon processors, you'll be able to change the frequency multiplier using the built-in tools of the motherboards that provide this capability.

If the L1 contacts are not interrupted (Fig. 13.23), this procedure is not required.

Fig. 13.23. L1 bridges that don't need to be restored

The performance gain of the AMD Duron and AMD Athlon processors obtained by changing the frequency multiplier is illustrated by the tables and graphs provided below.

Overclocking AMD Duron

CPU Clock Speed = FSB frequency × multiplier	CPUmark 99	FPU WinMark
600 = 100 × 6	51.4	3,260
900 = 100 × 9	68.3	4,900

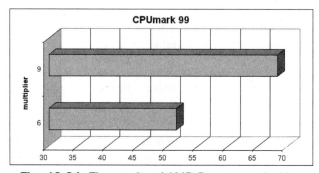

Fig. 13.24. The results of AMD Duron overclocking

Overclocking the AMD Athlon (Thunderbird)

CPU Clock Speed = FSB frequency × multiplier	CPUmark 99	FPU WinMark
700 = 100 × 7	64.7	3,810
800 = 100 × 8	71.8	4,350

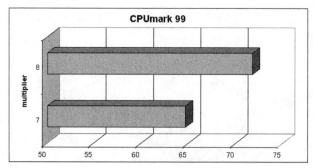

Fig. 13.25. The results of overclocking AMD Athlon (Thunderbird)

More detailed results of AMD Duron and AMD Athlon overclocking will be provided in *Chapter 19*.

Combining Both Methods

In order to achieve a significant performance gain, it is advisable to combine both methods: increase the FSB EV6 bus frequency and change the frequency multiplier of the processor. By setting different combinations of bus frequencies and multiplier values, and evaluating the result, you can then select the optimal combination that will provide you with the maximum performance gain.

Provided below are the results of overclocking for AMD Duron using a combination of the two above-described overclocking methods.

Overclocking the AMD Duron

CPU Clock Speed = FSB frequency × multiplier	CPUmark 99
600 = 100 × 6	51.4
690 = 115 × 6	59.4
900 = 100 × 9	68.3
896 = 112 × 8	71.2

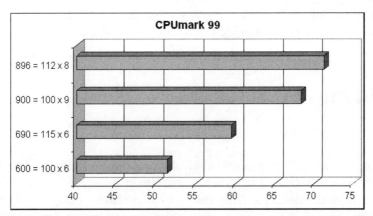

Fig. 13.26. The overclocking results of the AMD Duron processor using a combination of overclocking methods

It is necessary to mention that in the example provided here, maximum performance is obtained with an FSB frequency of 112 MHz and a multiplier value equal to 8 (112 MHz × 8 = 896 MHz). This is despite the fact that the maximum processor frequency corresponds to an FSB frequency of 100 MHz and a multiplier of 9 (100 MHz × 9 = 900 MHz). According to the results of the CPUmark 99, it comes to approximately 5%.

Higher performance generally comes with combinations with higher FSB frequencies, which, by the way, is used to clock other PC buses. By increasing the FSB frequency, the user increases the throughput of this and other buses, and at the same time increases the performance of the processor and other subsystems, including the video adapter, hard disks, PCI devices, etc. The performance gain, however, is limited not only by the architecture and technological capabilities of these devices, but also by the motherboard design and architectrure of the chipsets used. Furthermore, when you approach the value limits, the system might develop the first indications of instability.

Cases when the potential capabilities of the processor can't be fully used are quite frequent when overclocking by just increasing the FSB frequency, due to the above mentioned limitations. This is why it makes sense to use an approach where both methods are combined: increasing of the FSB EV6 frequency and changing the frequency multiplier.

Thus, the combination of both overclocking methods allows you to increase the overall performance of the system, while maintaining the required stability.

To conclude this section, it is necessary to remind you that changing the frequency multiplier is possible only when using a motherboard that supports this function. Individual examples of overclocking will be covered in detail in *Chapter 19.*

Identifying Processors

Intel

In order to identify Intel processors, you can use the Intel Processor Frequency ID Utility for Windows (Fig. 13.27). This program can be downloaded from Intel website for free. Besides identifying the type of processor using standard CPUID functionality (Fig. 13.28), it also gives you the opportunity to detect the FSB frequency and the internal clock frequency of the processor (Fig. 13.29).

Fig. 13.27. Frequency ID Utility

Such a specialized program that identifies the parameters of a processor is indispensable when battling the multitude of fake, re-marked processors. Intel itself says that the Intel Processor Frequency Utility was developed in order to tell whether or not an Intel processor is working at a clock frequency higher than normal. However, this program is also useful for users who wish to overclock, or who have already overclocked, elements of their computers. Note that the aforementioned program gives the correct data on the frequencies, even if they are higher than normal (recommended) for the given processor. If, though, the frequency is higher than the recommended one, the program gives a warning about all of the unpleasant consequences of overclocking (Figs. 13.30 and 13.31).

Unfortunately, the CPUID program does not support processors from other manufacturers. Those functions that identify clock frequency also have some limitations on the processor type. Listed below are the types of processors CPUID supports.

Processors supported by Frequency ID Utility:

❑ Intel Pentium III

❑ Intel Pentium III Xeon

❑ Intel Celeron with clock frequencies from 533A MHz

❑ Mobile Intel Pentium III

❑ Mobile Intel Celeron with clock frequencies from 450 MHz

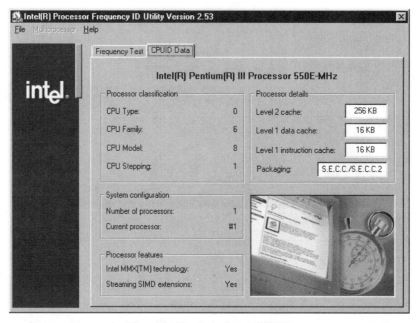

Fig. 13.28. Data from CPUID

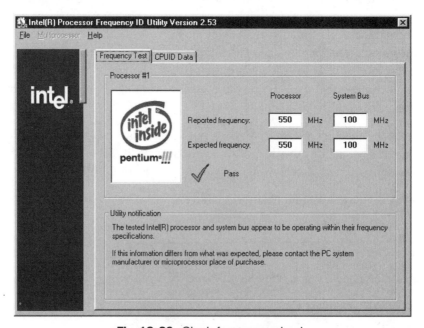

Fig.13.29. Clock frequency check

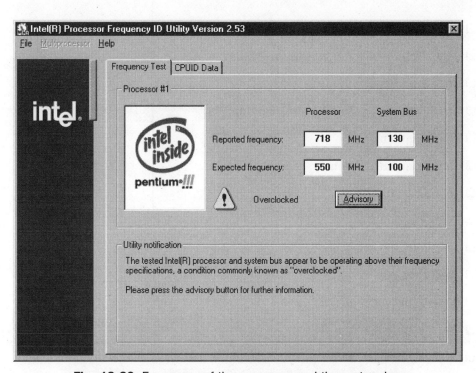

Fig. 13.30. Frequency of the processor and the system bus

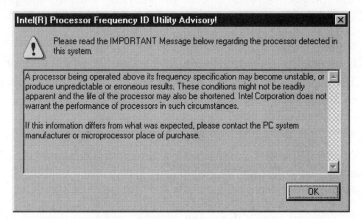

Fig. 13.31. Warning message

Processors supported by CPUID:

❑ Intel Pentium

❑ Intel Pentium MMX

❑ Intel Pentium OverDrive

❑ Intel Pentium OverDrive with MMX technology

❑ Intel Pentium Pro

❑ Intel Pentium II OverDrive for Pentium Pro

❑ Intel Pentium II

❑ Intel Pentium II Xeon

❑ Intel Celeron

❑ Intel Pentium III

❑ Intel Pentium III Xeon

❑ Intel Pentium

❑ Mobile Intel Pentium II

❑ Mobile Intel Pentium III

❑ Mobile Intel Celeron

Note that this program is also capable of analyzing each of the processors in a multiprocessor system running operating systems such as Windows 2000 or Windows NT.

The CPUID program will provide you with a good deal of information about the processor. This information can be very useful when, for example, looking for the most overclockable processors, since processors that may be alike in many ways ("almost identical") may have important differences when it comes to their ability to overclock. To find out which processor is the best from the overclocking point of view, you should acquaint yourself with the appropriate parameters in more detail. Besides using the Frequency utility, there are other methods of obtaining PUID information.

For example, consider the DOS version of Intel cpuid.exe program (Fig. 13.32), which gives you information on these parameters when running MS-DOS.

To view the information on the processor, you need only check the corresponding register of the processor. Beginning with the i486 series, processors have a built-in identifier made up of five blocks (Fig. 13.33).

```
C:\Dist\Dist1\cpu soft\cpiid>cpuid.exe
(C) Copyright 1994, 1997, 1998 Intel Corp. All rights reserved.
This Intel Microprocessor Identification Utility is designed to identify
the type of Intel microprocessor your PC contains.  It is intended for use
on systems containing Intel processors which are running in real mode.  If
your system is not running in real mode, either contact your system OEM or
consult the README.TXT file on how to execute this utility from a bootable
floppy disk.

This system has a Genuine Intel Pentium(R) II processor
Processor Family: 6
Model:            8
Stepping:         1


C:\cid>
```

Fig. 13.32. Results of the CPUID program

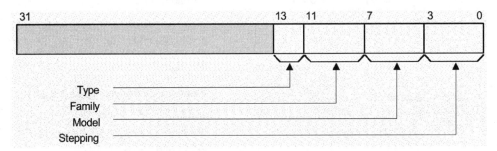

Fig. 13.33. How information about the processor is stored

Usually, these programs will give you the following information about the processor:

❑ *Name of the Intel processor*

This is the name of the specific processor given to it by Intel, for example, Intel Pentium III. Sometimes the program will not give you the full name of the processor, but you can easily figure it out by using of the following table. (Data is given in binary code.)

Processor Identification Parameters

Type	Family	Model	Name
00	0100	0000 and 0001	i486 DX
00	0100	0010	i486 SX
00	0100	0011	i486 DX2

continues

Continued

Type	Family	Model	Name
00	0100	0011	i486 DX2 Overdrive
00	0100	0100	i486 SL
00	0100	0101	i486 SX2
00	0100	0111	Write-Back Enhanced i486 DX2
00	0100	1000	i486 DX4
00 and 01	0100	1000	i486 DX4 Overdrive
00	0101	0001	iPentium 60 and 66 MHz
00	0101	0010	iPentium 75, 90, 100, 120, 133, 150, 166, 200 MHz
01	0101	0001	iPentium Overdrive 60 and 66 MHz
01	0101	0010	iPentium Overdrive 75, 90, 100, 120, 133 MHz
01	0101	0011	iPentium Overdrive for systems on a i486 base
00	0101	0100	iPentium MMX
01	0101	0100	iPentium MMX Overdrive 75, 90, 100, 120, 133 MHz
00	0110	0001	iPentium Pro
00	0110	0011	iPentium II, model 3
00	0110	0101	iPentium II and iCeleron, model 5; iPentium II Xeon
00	0110	0110	iCeleron, model 6
00	0110	0111	iPentium III and iPentium III Xeon
01	0110	0011	iPentium II Overdrive

Notice that i386 processors also have an identifier, but it is stored in a different format (Fig. 13.34).

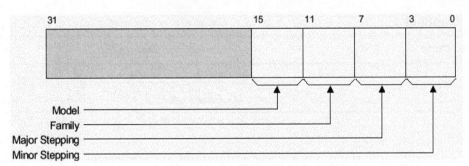

Fig. 13.34. Storage format of the processor information for the i386

The basic parameters for identifying i386 processors are shown in the table below.

Identification Parameters for i386 Processors

Type	Family	Major Stepping	Processor
0000	0011	0000	i386 DX
0010	0011	0000	i386 SX
0010	0011	0000	i386 CX
0010	0011	0000	i386 EX
0100	0011	0000 and 0001	i386 SL

❑ *Processor type*

According to Intel, the type of the processor shows who should install the given Intel processor, the buyer (the end-user), or a professional PC system integrator, service company, or manufacturer. Intel holds that a type 1 processor means that the approved microprocessor is intended for installation by the end-user (for example, when upgrading the PC by installing the Intel Overdrive processor). Type 0 means that a professional PC system integrator, service company, or manufacturer should install the processor.

Decoding the "Type" Parameter

Code	Processor description
00	OEM
01	Overdrive

continues

Continued

Code	Processor description
10	Dual
00	Reserved

❑ *Processor family*

The family of the processor is the same as its generation. For example, family 6 (sixth generation) includes the following processors: Intel Pentium Pro, Intel Celeron, Pentium II/III, and Pentium II/III Xeon. Family 5 consists of Pentium and Pentium MMX processors.

❑ *Processor model*

The processor model indicates the technology used in creating the processor and the design generation (for example, Model 4). The model number is used along with the family number to determine exactly which processor of a specific family the computer contains.

Besides this, there is additional information saved inside the processor.

❑ *Information on the cache memory*

Information on the processor cache memory usually includes the size of the L2 cache memory (if indeed the processor has one and it is enabled), as well as level 1 data and instruction cache sizes. In certain older mobile systems this function is disabled, and you will be told that the information is not available (N/A).

❑ *The processor packaging type* (SECC, PPGA, etc.)

❑ Additional characteristics of the processor (presence of an internal coprocessor, whether or not MMX is supported, etc.)

AMD

Fig. 13.35 depicts an external view of the AMD Athlon processor, which shows the set of identification symbols on the case. AMD processors also have a CPUID identification number (Fig. 13.36).

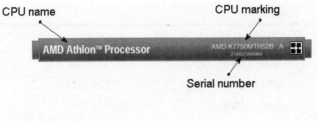

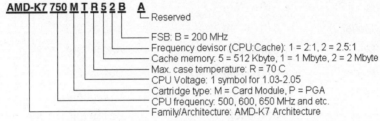

Fig. 13.35. Athlon marking

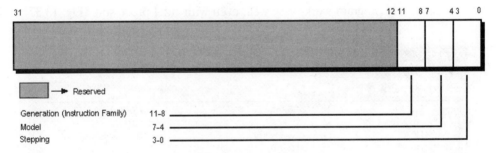

Fig. 13.36. CPUID for the Athlon

In the following table, the values for bits of the register are shown for certain models of AMD processors.

Identification Parameters for AMD Processors

Processor	Family Instruction	Model
Am486 and Am586	0100b (4h)	yyyy
AMD- K5 (Model 0)	0101b (5h)	0000b (0h)
AMD- K5 (Model 1)	0101b (5h)	0001b (1h)
AMD- K5 (Model 2)	0101b (5h)	0010b (2h)

continues

Continued

Processor	Family Instruction	Model
AMD- K5 (Model 3)	0101b (5h)	0011b (3h)
AMD- K6 (Model 6)	0101b (5h)	0110b (6h)
AMD- K6 (Model 7)	0101b (5h)	0111b (7h)
AMD- K6-2 (Model 8)	0101b (5h)	1000b (8h)
AMD- K6- III (Model 9)	0101b (5h)	1001b (9h)
AMD Athlon (Model 1)	0110b (6h)	0001b (1h)
AMD Athlon (Model 2)	0110b (6h)	0010b (2h)
AMD Athlon (Model 4)	0110b (6h)	0100b (4h)
AMD Duron	0110b (6h)	0011b (3h)

To obtain this information, you can use, for example, the program amdcpuid from AMD. This handy program works very well, even with Intel processors (Fig. 13.37).

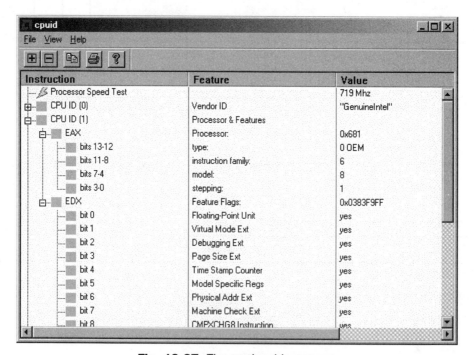

Fig. 13.37. The amdcpuid program

Additional Information

Besides the information obtained from CPUID, every processor has certain other characteristics, such as S-Spec, Core Stepping, the serial number, the country of origin, and many more. Below are tables that give these characteristics for Celeron, Pentium II, Pentium III, Pentium, Pentium MMX, and Pentium Pro processors.

In Figs. 13.38 and 13.39 an external view of the Celeron SEPP and Celeron PPGA processors is pictured.

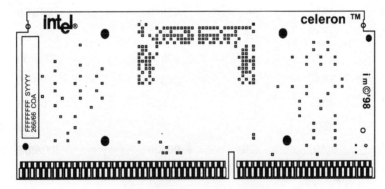

Fig. 13.38. Celeron SEPP

In Fig. 13.38: SYYYY is the S-Spec, 266/66 is the frequency of the processor/frequency of the bus (MHz), COA is the country of assembly.

In Fig. 13.39: AAAAAAA is the code, ZZZ is the frequency of the processor (MHz), LLL is the size of the L2 cache memory (KB), SYYYY is the S-Spec.

Fig. 13.39. Celeron PPGA

Identification Information for Celeron (SEPP) Processors

S-Spec	Core stepping	L2 cache, KB	Data from CPUID	Frequency of the processor/frequency of the bus, MHz
SL2SY	dA0	—	0650h	266/66
SL2YN	dA0	—	0650h	266/66
SL2YP	dA0	—	0650h	300/66
SL2Z7	dA0	—	0650h	300/66
SL2TR	dA1	—	0651h	266/66
SL2QG	dA1	—	0651h	266/66
SL2X8	dA1	—	0651h	300/66
SL2Y2	dA1	—	0651h	300/66
SL2Y3	dB0	—	0652h	266/66
SL2Y4	dB0	—	0652h	300/66
SL2WM	mA0	128	0660h	300A/66
SL32A	mA0	128	0660h	300A/66
SL2WN	mA0	128	0660h	333/66
SL32B	mA0	128	0660h	333/66
SL376	mA0	128	0660h	366/66
SL37Q	mA0	128	0660h	366/66
SL39Z	mA0	128	0660h	400/66
SL37V	mA0	128	0660h	400/66
SL3BC	mA0	128	0660h	433/66

Identification Information for Celeron (PPGA) Processors

S-Spec	Core stepping	L2 cache, KB	Data from CPUID	Frequency of the processor/frequency of the bus, MHz
SL35Q	mB0	128	0665h	300A/66
SL36A	mB0	128	0665h	300A/66

continues

Continued

S-Spec	Core stepping	L2 cache, KB	Data from CPUID	Frequency of the processor/frequency of the bus, MHz
SL35R	mB0	128	0665h	333/66
SL36B	mB0	128	0665h	333/66
SL36C	mB0	128	0665h	366/66
SL35S	mB0	128	0665h	366/66
SL3A2	mB0	128	0665h	400/66
SL37X	mB0	128	0665h	400/66
SL3BA	mB0	128	0665h	433/66
SL3BS	mB0	128	0665h	433/66
SL3EH	mB0	128	0665h	466/66
SL3FL	mB0	128	0665h	466/66
SL3FY	mB0	128	0665h	500/66
SL3LQ	mB0	128	0665h	500/66
SL3FZ	mB0	128	0665h	533/66
SL3PZ	mB0	128	0665h	533/66

Identification Information for Celeron (FC-PGA) Processors

S-Spec	Core stepping	L2 cache, KB	Data from CPUID	Frequency of the processor/frequency of the bus, MHz
SL3KZ	mB0	128	0683h	500A/66
SL46R	mB0	128	0683h	500A/66
SL46S	mB0	128	0683h	533A/66
SL3W6	mB0	128	06 83h	533A/66
SL46T	mB0	128	0683h	566/66
SL3W7	mB0	128	0683h	566/66

continues

Continued

S-Spec	Core stepping	L2 cache, KB	Data from CPUID	Frequency of the processor/frequency of the bus, MHz
SL46U	mB0	128	0683h	600/66
SL3W8	mB0	128	0683h	600/66
SL3VS	mB0	128	0683h	633/66
SL3W9	mB0	128	0683h	633/66
SL48E	mB0	128	0683h	667/66
SL4AB	mB0	128	0683h	667/66
SL48F	B0	128	0683h	700/66
SL4EG	B0	128	0683h	700/66

Figs. 13.40 and 13.41 illustrate the three-line marking and the regular marking for the Pentium II processor.

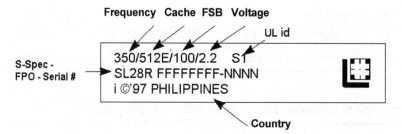

Fig. 13.40. Three-line marking of the Pentium II

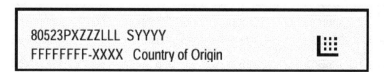

Fig. 13.41. Regular marking of the Pentium II

In Fig. 13.41: ZZZ is the frequency of the processor (MHz), LLL is the size of the L2 cache memory (KB), SYYYY is the S-Spec, and XXXX is the serial code.

Identification Information for Pentium II (SEPP) Processors

S-Spec	Core stepping	Data from CPUID	Frequency of the processor/frequency of the bus, MHz	TagRAM/ stepping	ECC/ non-ECC	Core voltage, V
SL264	C0	0633h	233/66	T6/B0	non-ECC	2.8
SL265	C0	0633h	266/66	T6/B0	non-ECC	2.8
SL268	C0	0633h	233/66	T6/B0	ECC	2.8
SL269	C0	0633h	266/66	T6/B0	ECC	2.8
SL28K	C0	0633h	233/66	T6/B0	non-ECC	2.8
SL28L	C0	0633h	266/66	T6/B0	non-ECC	2.8
SL28R	C0	0633h	300/66	T6/B0	ECC	2.8
SL2MZ	C0	0633h	300/66	T6/B0	ECC	2.8
SL2HA	C1	0634h	300/66	T6/B0	ECC	2.8
SL2HC	C1	0634h	266/66	T6/B0	non-ECC	2.8
SL2HD	C1	0634h	233/66	T6/B0	non-ECC	2.8
SL2HE	C1	0634h	266/66	T6/B0	ECC	2.8
SL2HF	C1	0634h	233/66	T6/B0	ECC	2.8
SL2QA	C1	0634h	233/66	T6/B0	non-ECC	2.8
SL2QB	C1	0634h	266/66	T6/B0	non-ECC	2.8
SL2QC	C1	0634h	300/66	T6/B0	ECC	2.8
SL2KA	dA0	0650h	333/66	T6P/A3	ECC	2.0
SL2QF	dA0	0650h	333/66	T6P/A3	ECC	2.0
SL2K9	dA0	0650h	266/66	T6P/A3	ECC	2.0
SL35V	dA1	0651h	300/66	T6P-e/A0	ECC	2.0
SL2QH	dA1	0651h	333/66	T6P-e/A0	ECC	2.0
SL2S5	dA1	0651h	333/66	T6P-e/A0	ECC	2.0
SL2ZP	dA1	0651h	333/66	T6P-e/A0	ECC	2.0
SL2ZQ	dA1	0651h	350/100	T6P-e/A0	ECC	2.0
SL2S6	dA1	0651h	350/100	T6P-e/A0	ECC	2.0

continues

Continued

S-Spec	Core stepping	Data from CPUID	Frequency of the processor/frequency of the bus, MHz	TagRAM/ stepping	ECC/ non-ECC	Core voltage, V
SL2S7	dA1	0651h	400/100	T6P-e/A0	ECC	2.0
SL2SF	dA1	0651h	350/100	T6P-e/A0	ECC	2.0
SL2SH	dA1	0651h	400/100	T6P-e/A0	ECC	2.0
SL2VY	dA1	0651h	300/66	T6P-e/A0	ECC	2.0
SL33D	dB0	0652h	266/66	T6P-e/A0	ECC	2.0
SL2YK	dB0	0652h	300/66	T6P-e/A0	ECC	2.0
SL2WZ	dB0	0652h	350/100	T6P-e/A0	ECC	2.0
SL2YM	dB0	0652h	400/100	T6P-e/A0	ECC	2.0
SL37G	dB0	0652h	400/100	T6P-e/A0	ECC	2.0
SL2WB	dB0	0652h	450/100	T6P-e/A0	ECC	2.0
SL37H	dB0	0652h	450/100	T6P-e/A0	ECC	2.0
SL2KE	TdB0	1632h	333/66	C6C/A3	ECC	2.0
SL2W7	dB0	0652h	266/66	T6P-e/A0	ECC	2.0
SL2W8	dB0	0652h	300/66	T6P-e/A0	ECC	2.0
SL2TV	dB0	0652h	333/66	T6P-e/A0	ECC	2.0
SL2U3	dB0	0652h	350/100	T6P-e/A0	ECC	2.0
SL2U4	dB0	0652h	350/100	T6P-e/A0	ECC	2.0
SL2U5	dB0	0652h	400/100	T6P-e/A0	ECC	2.0
SL2U6	dB0	0652h	400/100	T6P-e/A0	ECC	2.0
SL2U7	dB0	0652h	450/100	T6P-e/A0	ECC	2.0
SL356	dB0	0652h	350/100	T6P-e/A0	ECC	2.0
SL357	dB0	0652h	400/100	T6P-e/A0	ECC	2.0
SL358	dB0	0652h	450/100	T6P-e/A0	ECC	2.0
SL37F	dB0	0652h	350/100	T6P-e/A0	ECC	2.0
SL3FN	dB0	0652h	350/100	T6P-e/0	ECC	2.0

continues

Continued

S-Spec	Core stepping	Data from CPUID	Frequency of the processor/frequency of the bus, MHz	TagRAM/ stepping	ECC/ non-ECC	Core voltage, V
SL3EE	dB0	0652h	400/100	T6P-e/0	ECC	2.8
SL3F9	dB0	0652h	400/100	T6P-e/A0	ECC	2.0
SL38M	dB1	0653h	350/100	T6P-e/A0	ECC	2.0
SL38N	dB1	0653h	400/100	T6P-e/A0	ECC	2.0
SL36U	dB1	0653h	350/100	T6P-e/A0	ECC	2.0
SL38Z	dB1	0653h	400/100	T6P-e/A0	ECC	2.0
SL3D5	dB1	0653h	400/100	T6P-e/A0	ECC	2.0
SL3J2	dB1	0653h	350/100	T6P-e/A0	ECC	2.0

Presented in Fig. 13.42 is the three-line marking of Pentium III processors.

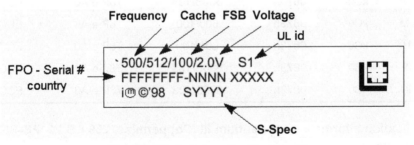

Fig. 13.42. Label on the Pentium III

Identification Information for Pentium III (SECC2, 512 KB L2) Processors

S-Spec	Core stepping	Data from CPUID	Frequency of the processor/ frequency of the bus, MHz	TagRAM/ stepping	ECC/non-ECC
SL364	kB0	0672h	450/100	T6P-e/A0	ECC
SL365	kB0	0672h	500/100	T6P-e/A0	ECC
SL3CC	kB0	0672h	450/100	T6P-e/A0	ECC

continues

Continued

S-Spec	Core stepping	Data from CPUID	Frequency of the processor/ frequency of the bus, MHz	TagRAM/ stepping	ECC/non-ECC
SL3CD	kB0	0672h	500/100	T6P-e/A0	ECC
SL38E	kB0	0672h	450/100	T6P-e/A0	ECC
SL38F	kB0	0672h	500/100	T6P-e/A0	ECC
SL35D	kC0	0673h	450/100	T6P-e/A0	ECC
SL37C	kC0	0673h	450/100	T6P-e/A0	ECC
SL35E	kC0	0673h	500/100	T6P-e/A0	ECC
SL37D	kC0	0673h	500/100	T6P-e/A0	ECC
SL3F7	kC0	0673h	550/100	T6P-e/A0	ECC
SL3FJ	kC0	0673h	550/100	T6P-e/A0	ECC
SL3BN	kC0	0673h	533B/133	T6P-e/A0	ECC
SL3E9	kC0	0673h	533B/133	T6P-e/A0	ECC
SL3JM	kC0	0673h	600/100	T6P-e/A0	ECC
SL3JT	kC0	0673h	600/100	T6P-e/A0	ECC
SL3JP	kC0	0673h	600B/133	T6p-e/A0	ECC
SL3JU	kC0	0673h	600B/133	T6P-e/A0	ECC

Identification Information for Pentium III (Coppermine, 256 KB L2, FC-PGA) Processors

S-Spec	Core stepping	Data from CPUID	Frequency of the processor/ frequency of the bus, MHz	ECC/non-ECC
SL3Q9	cA2	0681h	500E/100	ECC
SL3R2	cA2	0681h	500E/100	ECC
SL3VF	cA2	0681h	533EB/133	ECC
SL3VA	cA2	0681h	533EB/133	ECC
SL3QA	cA2	0681h	550E/100	ECC
SL3R3	cA2	0681h	550E/100	ECC

continues

Continued

S-Spec	Core stepping	Data from CPUID	Frequency of the processor/ frequency of the bus, MHz	ECC/non-ECC
SL3VH	cA2	0681h	600E/100	ECC
SL3NL	cA2	0681h	600E/100	ECC
SLVG	cA2	0681h	600EB/133	ECC
SL3VB	cA2	0681h	600EB/133	ECC
SL3VJ	cA2	0681h	650/100	ECC
SL3NM	cA2	0681h	650/100	ECC
SL3VK	cA2	0681h	667/133	ECC
SL3T2	cA2	0681h	667/133	ECC
SL3VL	cA2	0681h	700/100	ECC
SL3T3	cA2	0681h	700/100	ECC
SL3VM	cA2	0681h	733/133	ECC
SL3T4	cA2	0681h	733/133	ECC
SL3VN	cA2	0681h	750/100	ECC
SL3VC	cA2	0681h	750/100	ECC
SL3WB	cA2	0681h	800EB/133	ECC
SL3VE	cA2	0681h	800EB/133	ECC
SL3X4	cA2	0681h	800/100	ECC
SL3VD	cA2	0681h	800/100	ECC
SL444/SL446	cB0	0683h	500E/100	ECC
SL45R	cB0	0683h	500E/100	ECC
SL3XS	cB0	0683h	533EB/133	ECC
SL45S	cB0	0683h	533EB/133	ECC
SL44G	cB0	0683h	550E/100	ECC
SL45T	cB0	0683h	550E/100	ECC
SL3XT	cB0	0683h	600EB/133	ECC
SL45V	cB0	0683h	600EB/133	ECC
SL3XU	cB0	0683h	600E/100	ECC

continues

Continued

S-Spec	Core stepping	Data from CPUID	Frequency of the processor/ frequency of the bus, MHz	ECC/non-ECC
SL45U	cB0	0683h	600E/100	ECC
SL3XV	cB0	0683h	650/100	ECC
SL45W	cB0	0683h	650/100	ECC
SL3XW	cB0	0683h	667/133	ECC
SL45X	cB0	0683h	667/133	ECC
SL3XX	cB0	0683h	700/100	ECC
SL45Y	cB0	0683h	700/100	ECC
SL45Z	cB0	0683h	733/133	ECC
SL3XY	cB0	0683h	733/133	ECC
SL3XZ	cB0	0683h	750/100	ECC
SL462	cB0	0683h	750/100	ECC
SL3Y2	cB0	0683h	800EB/133	ECC
SL464	cB0	0683h	800EB/133	ECC
SL3Y3	cB0	0683h	800/100	ECC
SL463	cB0	0683h	800/100	ECC
SL43H	cB0	0683h	850/100	ECC
SL49G	cB0	0683h	850/100	ECC
SL43J	cB0	0683h	866/133	ECC
SL49H	cB0	0683h	866/133	ECC
SL44J	cB0	0683h	933/133	ECC

Fig. 13.43. Examples of Pentium III processors (FC-PGA and SECC2) marking

Identification Information for Pentium III (Coppermine, 256 KB L2, SECC2) Processors

S-Spec	Core stepping	Data from CPUID	Frequency of the processor/ frequency of the bus, MHz	ECC/non-ECC
SL3H7	cA2	0681h	600EB/133	ECC
SL3NB	cA2	0681h	600EB/133	ECC
SL3KV	cA2	0681h	650/100	ECC
SL3NR	cA2	0681h	650/100	ECC
SL3KW	cA2	0681h	667/133	ECC
SL3ND	cA2	0681h	667/133	ECC
SL3S9	cA2	0681h	700/100	ECC
SL3SY	cA2	0681h	700/100	ECC
SL3SB	cA2	0681h	733/133	ECC
SL3SZ	cA2	0681h	733/133	ECC
SL3H6	cA2	0681h	600E/100	ECC
SL3N6	cA2	0681h	533EB/133	ECC
SL3SX	cA2	0681h	533EB/133	ECC
SL3V5	cA2	0681h	550E/100	ECC
SL3N7	cA2	0681h	550E/100	ECC
SL3NA	cA2	0681h	600E/100	ECC
SL3WC	cA2	0681h	750/100	ECC
SL3V6	cA2	0681h	750/100	ECC
SL3Z6	cA2	0681h	800/100	ECC
SL3V7	cA2	0681h	800/100	ECC
SL3WA	cA2	0681h	800EB/133	ECC
SL3V8	cA2	0681h	800EB/133	ECC
SL3XG	cB0	0683h	533EB/133	ECC
SL44W	cB0	0683h	533EB/133	ECC
SL3XH	cB0	0683h	550E/100	ECC
SL44X	cB0	0683h	550E/100	ECC

continues

Continued

S-Spec	Core stepping	Data from CPUID	Frequency of the processor/frequency of the bus, MHz	ECC/non-ECC
SL43E	cB0	0683h	600E/100	ECC
SL44Y	cB0	0683h	600E/100	ECC
SL3XJ	cB0	0683h	600EB/133	ECC
SL44Z	cB0	0683h	600EB/133	ECC
SL3XK	cB0	0683h	650/100	ECC
SL452	cB0	0683h	650/100	ECC
SL3XL	cB0	0683h	667/133	ECC
SL453	cB0	0683h	667/133	ECC
SL3XM	cB0	0683h	700/100	ECC
SL454	cB0	0683h	700/100	ECC
SL3XN	cB0	0683h	733/133	ECC
SL455	cB0	0683h	733/133	ECC
SL3XP	cB0	0683h	750/100	ECC
SL456	cB0	0683h	750/100	ECC
SL3XQ	cB0	0683h	800EB/133	ECC
SL458	cB0	0683h	800EB/133	ECC
SL3XR	cB0	0683h	800/100	ECC
SL457	cB0	0683h	800/100	ECC
SL43F	cB0	0683h	850/100	ECC
SL47M	cB0	0683h	850/100	ECC
SL43G	cB0	0683h	866/133	ECC
SL47N	cB0	0683h	866/133	ECC
SL4FP	cB0	0683h	1.0B GHz/133	ECC
SL48S	cB0	0683h	1.0B GHz /133	ECC

In the next table, those processors that support MMX technology are indicated with the added symbol "x" (under manufacturing stepping), while mobile processors are indicated with an "m".

Identification Information for Pentium/Pentium MMX Processors

Type	Family	Model	Stepping	Manufacturing stepping	Frequency of the processor/ frequency of the bus, MHz	S-Spec
0	5	2	1	B1	75/50	Q0540
2	5	2	1	B1	75/50	Q0541
0	5	2	1	B1	90/60	Q0542
0	5	2	1	B1	90/60	Q0613
2	5	2	1	B1	90/60	Q0543
0	5	2	1	B1	100/66	Q0563
0	5	2	1	B1	100/66	Q0587
0	5	2	1	B1	100/66	Q0614
0	5	2	1	B1	75/50	Q0601
0	5	2	1	B1	90/60	SX879
0	5	2	1	B1	90/60	SX885
0	5	2	1	B1	90/60	SX909
2	5	2	1	B1	90/60	SX874
0	5	2	1	B1	100/66	SX886
0	5	2	1	B1	100/66	SX910
0	5	2	2	B3	90/60	Q0628
0 or 2	5	2	2	B3	90/60	Q0611
0 or 2	5	2	2	B3	90/60	Q0612
0	5	2	2	B3	100/66	Q0677
0	5	2	2	B3	75/50	Q0606
0	5	2	2	B3	75/50	SX951
0	5	2	2	B3	90/60	SX923
0	5	2	2	B3	90/60	SX922
0	5	2	2	B3	90/60	SX921
2	5	2	2	B3	90/60	SX942
2	5	2	2	B3	90/60	SX943

continues

Continued

Type	Family	Model	Stepping	Manufacturing stepping	Frequency of the processor/ frequency of the bus, MHz	S-Spec
2	5	2	2	B3	90/60	SX944
0	5	2	2	B3	90/60	SZ951
0	5	2	2	B3	100/66	SX960
0 or 2	5	2	4	B5	75/50	Q0704
0 or 2	5	2	4	B5	75/50	Q0666
0 or 2	5	2	4	B5	90/60	Q0653
0 or 2	5	2	4	B5	90/60	Q0654
0 or 2	5	2	4	B5	90/60	Q0655
0 or 2	5	2	4	B5	100/66	Q0656
0 or 2	5	2	4	B5	100/66	Q0657
0 or 2	5	2	4	B5	100/66	Q0658
0	5	2	4	B5	120/60	Q0707
0	5	2	4	B5	120/60	Q0708
0	5	2	4	B5	75/50	SX975
0 or 2	5	2	4	B5	75/50	SX961
0 or 2	5	2	4	B5	75/50	SZ977
0 or 2	5	2	4	B5	90/60	SX957
0 or 2	5	2	4	B5	90/60	SX958
0 or 2	5	2	4	B5	90/60	SX959
0 or 2	5	2	4	B5	90/60	SZ978
0 or 2	5	2	4	B5	100/66	SX962
0	5	2	5	C2	75/50	Q0725
0 or 2	5	2	5	C2	75/50	Q0700
0 or 2	5	2	5	C2	75/50	Q0749
0 or 2	5	2	5	C2	90/60	Q0699
0 or 2	5	2	5	C2	100/50 or 66	Q0698

continues

Continued

Type	Family	Model	Stepping	Manufacturing stepping	Frequency of the processor/ frequency of the bus, MHz	S-Spec
0 or 2	5	2	5	C2	100/50 or 66	Q0697
0	5	2	5	C2	120/60	Q0711
0	5	2	5	C2	120/60	Q0732
0	5	2	5	C2	133/66	Q0733
0	5	2	5	C2	133/66	Q0751
0	5	2	5	C2	133/66	Q0775
0	5	2	5	C2	75/50	SK079
0 or 2	5	2	5	C2	75/50	SX969
0 or 2	5	2	5	C2	75/50	SX998
0 or 2	5	2	5	C2	75/50	SZ994
0 or 2	5	2	5	C2	75/50	SU070
0 or 2	5	2	5	C2	90/60	SX968
0 or 2	5	2	5	C2	90/60	SZ995
0 or 2	5	2	5	C2	90/60	SU031
0 or 2	5	2	5	C2	100/50 or 66	SX970
0 or 2	5	2	5	C2	100/50 or 66	SX963
0 or 2	5	2	5	C2	100/50 or 66	SZ996
0 or 2	5	2	5	C2	100/50 or 66	SU032
0	5	2	5	C2	120/60	SK086
0	5	2	5	C2	120/60	SX994
0	5	2	5	C2	120/60	SU033
0	5	2	5	C2	133/66	SK098
0	5	2	5	mA1	75/50	Q0686
0	5	2	5	mA1	75/50	Q0689
0	5	2	5	mA1	90/60	Q0694
0	5	2	5	mA1	90/60	Q0695

continues

Continued

Type	Family	Model	Stepping	Manufacturing stepping	Frequency of the processor/ frequency of the bus, MHz	S-Spec
0	5	2	5	mA1	75/50	SK089
0	5	2	5	mA1	75/50	SK091
0	5	2	5	mA1	90/60	SK090
0	5	2	5	mA1	90/60	SK092
0 or 2	5	2	B	cB1	120/60	Q0776
0 or 2	5	2	B	cB1	133/66	Q0772
0 or 2	5	2	B	cB1	133/66	Q0773
0 or 2	5	2	B	cB1	133/66	Q0774
0 or 2	5	2	B	cB1	120/60	SK110
0 or 2	5	2	B	cB1	133/66	SK106
0 or 2	5	2	B	cB1	133/66	S106J
0 or 2	5	2	B	cB1	133/66	SK107
0 or 2	5	2	B	cB1	133/66	SU038
0	5	2	B	mcB1	100/66	Q0884
0	5	2	B	mcB1	120/60	Q0779
0	5	2	B	mcB1	120/60	Q0808
0	5	2	B	mcB1	100/66	SY029
0	5	2	B	mcB1	120/60	SK113
0	5	2	B	mcB1	120/60	SK118
0	5	2	B	mcB1	120/60	SX999
0 or 2	5	2	C	cC0	133/66	Q0843
0 or 2	5	2	C	cC0	133/66	Q0844
0 or 2	5	2	C	cC0	150/60	Q0835
0 or 2	5	2	C	cC0	150/60	Q0878
0 or 2	5	2	C	cC0	150/60	SU122
0 or 2	5	2	C	cC0	166/66	Q0836

continues

Continued

Type	Family	Model	Stepping	Manufacturing stepping	Frequency of the processor/ frequency of the bus, MHz	S-Spec
0 or 2	5	2	C	cC0	166/66	SY055
0 or 2	5	2	C	cC0	166/66	Q0841
0 or 2	5	2	C	cC0	166/66	Q0886
0 or 2	5	2	C	cC0	166/66	Q0890
0	5	2	C	cC0	166/66	Q0949
0 or 2	5	2	C	cC0	200/66	Q0951F
0	5	2	C	cC0	200/66	Q0951
0	5	2	C	cC0	200/66	SL25H
0 or 2	5	2	C	cC0	120/60	SL22M
0 or 2	5	2	C	cC0	120/60	SL25J
0 or 2	5	2	C	cC0	120/60	SY062
0 or 2	5	2	C	cC0	133/66	SL22Q
0 or 2	5	2	C	cC0	133/66	SL25L
0 or 2	5	2	C	cC0	133/66	SY022
0 or 2	5	2	C	cC0	133/66	SY023
0 or 2	5	2	C	cC0	133/66	SU073
0 or 2	5	2	C	cC0	150/60	SY015
0 or 2	5	2	C	cC0	150/60	SU071
0 or 2	5	2	C	cC0	166/66	SL24R
0 or 2	5	2	C	cC0	166/66	SY016
0 or 2	5	2	C	cC0	166/66	SY017
0 or 2	5	2	C	cC0	166/66	SU072
0	5	2	C	cC0	166/66	SY037
0 or 2	5	2	C	cC0	200/66	SY044
0	5	2	C	cC0	200/66	SY045
0	5	2	C	cC0	200/66	SU114

continues

Continued

Type	Family	Model	Stepping	Manufacturing stepping	Frequency of the processor/ frequency of the bus, MHz	S-Spec
0	5	2	C	cC0	200/66	SL24Q
0	5	7	0	mA4	75/50	Q0848
0	5	7	0	mA4	75/50	Q0851
0	5	7	0	mA4	90/60	Q0849
0	5	7	0	mA4	90/60	Q0852
0	5	7	0	mA4	100/66	Q0850
0	5	7	0	mA4	100/66	Q0853
0	5	7	0	mA4	75/50	SK119
0	5	7	0	mA4	75/50	SK122
0	5	7	0	mA4	90/60	SK120
0	5	7	0	mA4	90/60	SK123
0	5	7	0	mA4	100/66	SK121
0	5	7	0	mA4	100/66	SK124
0	5	2	C	mcC0	100/66	Q0887
0	5	2	C	mcC0	120/60	Q0879
0	5	2	C	mcC0	120/60	Q0880
0	5	2	C	mcC0	133/66	Q0881
0	5	2	C	mcC0	133/66	Q0882
0	5	2	C	mcC0	150/60	Q024
0	5	2	C	mcC0	150/60	Q0906
0	5	2	C	mcC0	150/60	Q040
0	5	2	C	mcC0	75/50	SY056
0	5	2	C	mcC0	100/66	SY020
0	5	2	C	mcC0	100/66	SY046
0	5	2	C	mcC0	120/60	SY021
0	5	2	C	mcC0	120/60	SY027

continues

Continued

Type	Family	Model	Stepping	Manufacturing stepping	Frequency of the processor/ frequency of the bus, MHz	S-Spec
0	5	2	C	mcC0	120/60	SY030
0	5	2	C	mcC0	133/66	SY019
0	5	2	C	mcC0	133/66	SY028
0	5	2	C	mcC0	150/60	SY061
0	5	2	C	mcC0	150/60	SY043
0	5	2	C	mcC0	150/60	SY058
0	5	2	6	E0	75/50	Q0846
0 or 2	5	2	6	E0	75/50	Q0837
0 or 2	5	2	6	E0	90/60	Q0783
0 or 2	5	2	6	E0	100/50 or 66	Q0784
0 or 2	5	2	6	E0	120/60	Q0785
0	5	2	6	E0	75/50	SY009
0 or 2	5	2	6	E0	75/50	SY005
0 or 2	5	2	6	E0	75/50	SU097
0 or 2	5	2	6	E0	75/50	SU098
0 or 2	5	2	6	E0	90/60	SY006
0 or 2	5	2	6	E0	100/50 or 66	SY007
0 or 2	5	2	6	E0	100/50 or 66	SU110
0 or 2	5	2	6	E0	100/50 or 66	SU099
0 or 2	5	2	6	E0	120/60	SY033
0 or 2	5	2	6	E0	120/60	SU100
0 or 2	5	2	6	E0	90/60	SL2WW
0 or 2	5	4	4	xA3	150/60	Q020
0 or 2	5	4	4	xA3	166/66	Q019
0 or 2	5	4	4	xA3	200/66	Q018
0 or 2	5	4	4	xA3	166/66	SL23T

continues

Continued

Type	Family	Model	Stepping	Manufacturing stepping	Frequency of the processor/ frequency of the bus, MHz	S-Spec
0 or 2	5	4	4	xA3	166/66	SL23R
0 or 2	5	4	4	xA3	166/66	SL25M
0 or 2	5	4	4	xA3	166/66	SY059
0 or 2	5	4	4	xA3	166/66	SL2HU
0 or 2	5	4	4	xA3	166/66	SL239
0 or 2	5	4	4	xA3	166/66	SL26V
0 or 2	5	4	4	xA3	166/66	SL26H
0 or 2	5	4	4	xA3	200/66	SL26J
0 or 2	5	4	4	xA3	200/66	SY060
0 or 2	5	4	4	xA3	200/66	SL26Q
0 or 2	5	4	4	xA3	200/66	SL274
0 or 2	5	4	4	xA3	200/66	SL23S
0 or 2	5	4	4	xA3	200/66	SL25N
0	5	4	4	mxA3	150/60	Q016
0	5	4	4	mxA3	150/60	Q061
0	5	4	4	mxA3	166/66	Q017
0	5	4	4	mxA3	166/66	Q062
0	5	4	4	mxA3	150/60	SL22G
0	5	4	4	mxA3	150/60	SL246
0	5	4	4	mxA3	166/66	SL22F
0	5	4	4	mxA3	166/66	SL23Z
0 or 2	5	4	3	xB1	166/66	Q125
0 or 2	5	4	3	xB1	166/66	Q126
0 or 2	5	4	3	xB1	200/66	Q124
0 or 2	5	4	3	xB1	200/66	Q430
0 or 2	5	4	3	xB1	166/66	SL27H

continues

Continued

Type	Family	Model	Stepping	Manufacturing stepping	Frequency of the processor/ frequency of the bus, MHz	S-Spec
0 or 2	5	4	3	xB1	166/66	SL27K
0 or 2	5	4	3	xB1	166/66	SL2HX
0 or 2	5	4	3	xB1	166/66	SL23X
0 or 2	5	4	3	xB1	166/66	SL2FP
0 or 2	5	4	3	xB1	166/66	SL23V
0 or 2	5	4	3	xB1	200/66	SL27J
0 or 2	5	4	3	xB1	200/66	SL2FQ
0 or 2	5	4	3	xB1	200/66	SL23W
0 or 2	5	4	3	xB1	200/66	SL2RY
0 or 2	5	4	3	xB1	200/66	SL2S9
0 or 2	5	4	3	xB1	233/66	SL27S
0 or 2	5	4	3	xB1	233/66	SL2BM
0 or 2	5	4	3	xB1	233/66	SL293
0	5	4	3	mxB1	120/60	Q230
0	5	4	3	mxB1	133/66	Q130
0	5	4	3	mxB1	133/66	Q129
0	5	4	3	mxB1	150/60	Q116
0	5	4	3	mxB1	150/60	Q128
0	5	4	3	mxB1	166/66	Q115
0	5	4	3	mxB1	166/66	Q127
0	5	4	3	mxB1	200/66	Q586
0	5	4	3	mxB1	133/66	SL27D
0	5	4	3	mxB1	133/66	SL27C
0	5	4	3	mxB1	150/60	SL26U
0	5	4	3	mxB1	150/60	SL27B
0	5	4	3	mxB1	166/66	SL26T
0	5	4	3	mxB1	166/66	SL27A

continues

Continued

Type	Family	Model	Stepping	Manufacturing stepping	Frequency of the processor/ frequency of the bus, MHz	S-Spec
0	5	4	3	mxB1	200/66	SL2WK
0	5	8	1	myA0	166/66	Q255
0	5	8	1	myA0	166/66	Q252
0	5	8	1	myA0	166/66	SL2N6
0	5	8	1	myA0	200/66	Q146
0	5	8	1	myA0	233/66	Q147
0	5	8	1	myA0	200/66	SL28P
0	5	8	1	myA0	233/66	SL28Q
0	5	8	1	myA0	266/66	Q250
0	5	8	1	myA0	266/66	Q251
0	5	8	1	myA0	266/66	SL2N5
0	5	8	1	myA0	266/66	Q695
0	5	8	1	myA0	266/66	SL2ZH
0	5	8	2	myB2	266/66	Q766
0	5	8	2	myB2	266/66	Q767
0	5	8	2	myB2	266/66	SL23M
0	5	8	2	myB2	266/66	SL23P
0	5	8	2	myB2	300/60	Q768
0	5	8	2	myB2	300/66	SL34N

Identification Information for Pentium Overdrive Processors

Code	Type	Family	Model	Stepping	Manufac- turing stepping	Frequency of the processor/ frequency of the bus, MHz	S-Spec
PODP5V63	1	5	3	1	B1	63/25	SZ953
PODP5V63	1	5	3	1	B2	63/25	SZ990

continues

Continued

Code	Type	Family	Model	Stepping	Manufac-turing stepping	Frequency of the processor/ frequency of the bus, MHz	S-Spec
PODP5V63	1	5	3	1	C0	63/25	SU013
PODP5V83	1	5	3	2	C0	83/33	SU014
PODP5V133	0	5	1	A	tA0	120/60, 133/66	SU082
PODP3V125	0	5	2	C	aC0	125/50	SU081
PODP3V150	0	5	2	C	aC0	150/60	SU083
PODP3V166	0	5	2	C	aC0	166/66	SU084
PODPMT60X150	1	5	4	4	oxA3	125/50, 150/60	SL24V
PODPMT66X166	1	5	4	4	oxA3	166/66	SL24W
PODPMT60X180	1	5	4	3	oxB1	180/60	SL2FE
PODPMT66X200	1	5	4	3	oxB1	200/66	SL2FF

Chapter 14

Overclocking Video Adapters and Hard Drives

The reliability and performance of hard drives and video adapters depends significantly on the modes in which they are used.

The working modes of hard disks and video adapters depend on the frequency of the buses to which these devices are connected, along with their controllers. For hard disks, the frequency modes are determined by the PCI bus. For a video adapter this might be either the AGP bus or PCI bus, depending on the device type. Notice that for motherboards manufactured several years ago and oriented towards 486 or 386 processors, these might be other buses, such as the VLB, MCA, ISA, or EISA.

The frequencies of buses such as PCI, AGP, and, quite often, their legacy predecessors, depend on the frequency of the processor's front side bus (GTL+/AGTL+, Alpha EV6). Usually, the frequencies of the PCI and AGP buses are set by dividing the FSB frequency. An example provided below lists the most commonly used FSB, AGP, and PCI frequencies often implemented in motherboards.

Here are the most common frequencies implemented in motherboards with the i440BX chipset:

FSB, MHz	AGP, MHz	PCI/IDE, MHz
66	66	33
75	75	38
83	83*	42*
100	66	33
103	69	34
112	75	37
124	83*	41*
133	89*	44*

* Instability is probable.

The architecture of most motherboards provides tools allowing you to correct the AGP and PCI frequencies not only by changing the FSB frequency, but also by changing the appropriate bus frequency multipliers. This can be achieved either by setting special parameters in BIOS Setup or with special switches or jumpers on the motherboard. Changing the bus frequency enables you to select the optimal mode for the devices managed by the corresponding buses.

The standard software and hardware tools generally don't provide special capabilities for overclocking hard drives. However, hard drive performance depends on the frequency of the PCI bus to which they are connected via the respective controllers. The existence of such dependence is illustrated by the results produced by testing a PC in the overclocking mode with the WinCheckIt program (v2.03) at various values of the FSB frequency. The FSB frequency determines the PCI frequency, and via this frequency it influences the hard drive's performance. The table provided below shows the results of performance evaluation for the hard drive when using the WinCheckIt (v2.03) program at various values of the PCI bus frequency.

Hard disk performance for different PCI frequency values obtained by WinCheckIt program:

PCI frequency, MHz	33	38	42
Hard disk performance	6,686	7,395	8,141

Hard disk performance for different PCI frequency values according to the data obtained by WinMark 99 test:

PCI frequency, MHz	33	38	42
Business Disk WinMark 99	1,700	1,770	1,850
High-End Disk WinMark 99	6,250	6,490	6,690

Notice that not all hard drives can satisfactorily tolerate overclocking via increase of the bus frequency. For some drives you will see a performance gain, while for other drives you may even notice a performance degradation. The results of such overclocking depend both on the device type and on the specific device instance. Most modern hard drives with a capacity larger than 10 GB will work well at overclocking frequencies (for example, 42 MHz or even higher), provided that you are using high-quality motherboards. If you are using smaller hard disks (less than 1 GB), such modes are normally impossible, because the technologies and components of such devices are not as advanced as the ones used in newer hard disks. However, despite the fact that most high-capacity hard disks are able to function at high PCI frequencies, it is not recommended that you set the bus frequency higher than 40 MHz. Such modes increase the probability of failure when performing data reads and writes (and, consequently, the risk of data loss). Besides this, they make the temperature mode worse for both the electronic and mechanical components of the hard disk. Note that most high-performance disks with a large amount of built-in cache memory (up to 2 MB) and a high rotation speed (7200 RPM, for example) often require additional cooling, even in nominal modes. This is especially true when using several such devices within a small system unit along with other high-performance components characterized by excessive heat emission. If this is the case, it is advisable to use adequate cooling facilities not only for the processor or video adapter, but also for the hard drive(s). Unfortunately, this can't always be implemented. Thus, the limitations caused by temperature modes and insufficient speed parameters of the electronic and mechanical components of hard drives are the most important factors preventing hard disks from being overclocked.

Modern high-performance video adapters based on advanced components tolerate more significant changes in their respective buses (AGP) as compared to hard disks. However, they also are not always stable at the high frequencies obtained as a result of processor overclocking. The table provided above illustrates this fact rather well. As with hard disks, the influence of increased AGP frequencies on the video output performance can be traced when analyzing practical overclocking examples.

Somewhat increasing the AGP frequency provides performance gain when processing video output. Furthermore, increasing the frequency of this bus also increases the bandwidth, which, in turn, increases the data transfer rate. As a result, the video subsystem performance increases proportionally to the increase of its bus speed. On the other hand, certain specific architecture improvements and frequency characteristics of the electronic components that provide the basis for a modern video adapter tolerate a significant increase of the AGP frequency. For example, some devices using modern high-performance components and the most advanced technologies are capable of working at frequencies up to 100 MHz, which is approximately 50% larger than the nominal value of 66 MHz, standard for the AGP bus.

However, the capabilities of this overclocking method are also limited. As a rule, the limits of the growth in AGP frequency are applicable only to individual high-quality instances of video adapters. Normally, these values are somewhat lower. Furthermore, heightening the possible video adapter frequency and performance is limited by individual components whose functional capabilities don't allow them to work at higher frequencies. If this is so, the potential capabilities of other elements that can tolerate overclocking will not be implemented.

A significant and, more importantly, well-balanced increase of the video adapter's speed can be achieved using specialized software utilities. Usually, such tools allow you to perform selective overclocking of the chipset and video memory, which together provide the basis for the video adapter. Overclocking capabilities intended for increasing the video subsystem performance can be supplemented by increasing the video adapter bus (AGP bus).

The PowerStrip utility developed by EnTech Taiwan (**http://entechtaiwan.com**) can be considered an example of universal software intended for video subsystem overclocking.

This utility provides tools for changing the working modes of the video adapter and monitor. The range in which you can change the monitor's vertical sweep (refresh frequency) encompasses up to 200 Hz, and is limited only by the capabilities of the video adapter and the monitor itself. Besides controlling this frequency, PowerStrip allows you to change the frequencies of the video chipsets and video memory, and enables you to test video adapters.

PowerStrip supports video chipsets from the following vendors 3Dfx, 3Dlabs, ATi, Cirrus Logic, Intel, nVidia, Matrox, S3, SiS, Trident, Tseng Labs, etc. The list of supported chipsets includes, for example ATi Rage II Pro, CL GD543x/544x/546x, i740, Matrox G100, Permedia, PowerVR, Riva128/128ZX, S3 Vision86x, S3 Vision968, S3 Trio32/64, S3 TrioV+, S3 TrioV2/DX, S3 TrioV2/GX, S3 Trio3D, S3 ViRGE, S3 ViRGE/VX, S3 ViRGE/DX, S3 ViRGE/GX, S3 ViRGE/GX2, SiS 6326, Trident ProVidia 9685, ET6000, ET6100 and many more.

This program works under Windows 9x and Windows NT, and allows you to control the functioning of practically all models of monitors, including ones provided by such well-known vendors as Hitachi, MAG, Mitsubishi, NEC, Nokia, Panasonic, Philips, Sony, ViewSonic, etc.

There are other universal programs that support a large variety of video adapters and monitors. However, most vendors provide special software tools and utilities along with their products. Besides testing and optimal tuning, this software provides tools for optimizing the video chipset and video memory. Quite often, such tools can be downloaded from the Internet or obtained from firms specializing in selling and supporting video adapters.

Besides commercial software intended to control the operating modes of your video subsystem, which is generally developed by video adapter manufacturers, there are lots of shareware and freeware utilities developed by overclocking enthusiasts. There are tons of such software on the Internet. Some Web addresses, where you can find such programs and support information, are provided in *Chapter 20*.

To conclude this chapter, let us consider an example of overclocking the Matrox Millennium G200 video adapter. Overclocking in this example was accomplished using the standard motherboard hardware.

❑ Test: 3D WinBench 98 (800×600×32)

❑ Motherboard: Asus P2B-S

❑ RAM: 128 MB CAS2 SDRAM

❑ Video adapter: Matrox Millennium G200, AGP, 250 MHz RAMDAC, 8 MB SGRAM, 128 MB Graphics Aperture Size

❑ Processor: Intel Celeron 300A

❑ Overclocking parameters: increasing the bus frequency to 75/83/103 MHz

❑ OS: Windows 98

The overclocking of the components was performed by increasing the FSB starting from the standard value (66 MHz) and going up to 103 MHz. The resulting performance gain of the video subsystem is illustrated by Figs. 14.1—14.3.

Test Results

	300/66	340/75	375/83	466/103
3D WinBench 98/3D Processing	23	25.8	28.7	35.5
3D WinBench 98/3D Scene/User Defined (Frames/Sec)	12.5	14.1	15.6	18.8
3D WinBench 98/3D WinMark	1,000	1,110	1,220	1,420

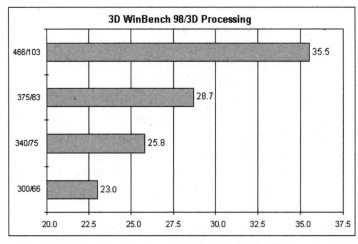

Fig. 14.1. Test results from 3d WinBench 98/3D Processing

Fig. 14.2. Test results from 3D WinBench 98/3D Scene

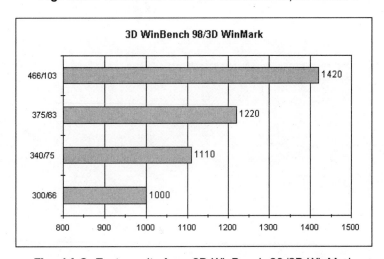

Fig. 14.3. Test results from 3D WinBench 98/3D WinMark

Chapter 15

Overclocking: Step-by-Step

1. Turn off the computer, remove the case from the system unit, and open the manual supplied with your motherboard.

2. Make sure that you follow all safety rules, which need to be observed when performing any tasks with the case open. There is a danger of static electricity. Therefore, it is wise to touch the case before you begin. Better yet, keep one hand on the case at all times while working. Try not to allow any foreign items, especially metallic ones, to touch the adapters. If anything does get inside, remove it immediately. Be sure of everything you are doing, but be careful and accurate.

3. Carefully read all of the basic characteristics of the processor from what is labeled on it. It makes sense to record this data.

4. Consult your motherboard manual to find out which jumpers control the multiplier, the bus frequency and the core voltage supplied to the processor.

5. Check to see if the jumpers are set according to the motherboard manual. Figure out the exact values of the multiplier, the host bus speed and the core voltage. Record this information as well.

6. Now consider how you are going to intensify the cooling of your processor. This is extremely important.

7. Consider how you are going to overclock the processor, what settings you are going to change, and by how much, etc.

8. Follow the instructions provided in the documentation to change the bus speed and/or the multiplier.

9. Check to see if all the jumpers are set correctly according to the instructions provided in the manual.

10. Turn the computer on.

11. If POST completes successfully and you see the boot-up screen with the BIOS information, skip steps 12 and 13, and go on to step 14.

12. If the computer doesn't boot, your CPU doesn't seem to be able to be overclocked to the speed that you are trying to set. Turn it off and try to increase the voltage supplied to the processor (if possible). Before tweaking the voltage, consult your motherboard manual.

13. Turn the computer on. If BIOS doesn't boot, you should abandon attempts to overclock your CPU to the frequency you are trying to set. Try more conservative settings for the multiplier and host bus frequency.

14. Go to BIOS Setup and, if necessary, change the appropriate settings.

15. Reboot the computer and allow the operating system to complete the boot process. If your operating system starts successfully, start testing your system's reliability at the increased frequency. It is recommended that you use various tests, such as WinStone, WinBench, BAPCo Suite, and any other tests available to you. The more tests you run the better.

16. If the system doesn't crash and everything runs normally, you have successfully overclocked your system.

17. If your system crashes, return to 12—16 steps.

18. General recommendations: Don't raise the voltage supplied to the processor except for the cases when it is absolutely necessary, since this increases CPU temperature. Cooling is the most important thing, one that you should never forget about, especially when overclocking.

To conclude this chapter, it should be mentioned that Windows 9x may become unstable after overclocking, while DOS and Windows 3.x may remain reliable. This is due to the more stringent hardware requirements imposed by Windows 9x. Thus, Windows 9x can itself be considered as a kind of test. If the computer doesn't pass this test, this means the system is unstable.

Chapter 16

Testing Overclocked Systems

The ASUSTeK P/I-P55T2P4 Rev. 3.0 motherboard with the 82430HX chipset supports increased host bus frequencies of 75 and 83 MHz. In order to estimate the maximum performance you can expect from a computer at higher frequencies, appropriate tests have been performed under Windows 95. Performance was measured using the standard tests: WinStone 96 and WinBench 96 (Fig. 16.1).

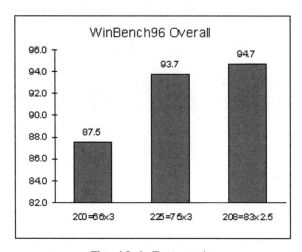

Fig. 16.1. Test results

Configuration of the Computer Tested

Motherboard	Asus P/I-P55T2P4 rev 3.0
BIOS	AWARD 4.51PG, #401A0–107
L2 cache (KB), type	512, PB (256 KB on-board + 256 KB CELP)
RAM (KB), type, nsec	32, EDO, 60 nsec
Processor	Intel Pentium-200
Video	Matrox MGA Millennium, with 2 MB RAM (1024×768×256×SF×75 Hz)
Hard drive	Quantun Fireball TM 1280AT
Sound card	Vibra 16S
CD-ROM drive, sec	Acer 685A, 8 sec
MB System BIOS Setup	Setup default + PM = disabled

Test Results

Bus frequency, MHz	66	75	83
Frequency multiplier	3.0	3.0	2.5
Internal frequency of the processor, MHz	200	225	208
WB96 Overall	87—88	93—94.4	94.4—95
WB96 CPU Mark16	357—363	401—408	402—417
WB96 CPU Mark32	358—364	406—408	407—418
WB96 Disk Winmark, thousand b/sec	1,160—1,180	1,180—1,230	1,220—1,250
WB96 Graphics Winmark, million pixels/sec	46.4—46.9	50.3—51.4	50.3—51.5

The following table lists test results for twenty systems overclocked using the technique of increasing the host bus frequency. Tested configurations include various motherboards, processors, and RAMs. The table lists all of the testing data, including information on the rate of data exchange between the CPU and the RAM, L1, and L2 cache memories (columns 2, 3, and 4, respectively). The table also includes information on the type and size of the L1 and L2 cache memories, and the RAM, along with the data on chipsets, processors, etc.

Test Results for Overclocked Systems

Mother-board	RAM MB/sec	Cache L1 Mb/sec	Cache L2 Mb/sec	Chipset	Cache L2 type	Processor	Host bus frequency	RAM
Asus P/I-P55TVP4	57.3	621.6	75.5	Intel Triton VX 430VX	Synchronous Burst Cache 512 KB	IP P54C without MMX 150 MHz	75 MHz	32 MB EDO 60 nsec
Asus P/I-P55T2P4	56.8	892.3	84.2	Intel Triton II 430HX	Pipelined Burst Cache 512 KB	IP P54C without MMX 208 MHz	83 MHz	32 MB EDO 50 nsec
Asus P/I-P55PTV4	56.6	435.6	116	Intel Triton VX 430VX	Pipelined Burst Cache 512 KB	Cyrix/IBM 6x86 – M1 150 MHz	75 MHz	32 MB SDRAM
FIC PT-2010	56.4	428.1	108.2	Intel Triton VX 430VX	Pipelined Burst Cache 512 KB	Cyrix/IBM 6x86 – M1 150 MHz	75 MHz	32 MB SDRAM

continues

Continued

Mother-board	RAM MB/sec	Cache L1 Mb/sec	Cache L2 Mb/sec	Chipset	Cache L2 type	Processor	Host bus frequency	RAM
Shuttle/ Spacewalker HOT 557	55.8	949.1	75.6	Intel Triton VX 430VX	Pipelined Burst Cache 512 KB	IP P54C without MMX 222 MHz	75 MHz	32 MB SDRAM 50 nsec
Asus P/I-P55T2P4	55.3	699.3	86.1	Intel Triton II 430HX	Pipelined Burst Cache 512 KB	IP P54C without MMX 166 MHz	83 MHz	16 MB EDO 60 nsec
Asus P/I-P55T2P4	55.3	699.3	86.1	Intel Triton II 430HX	Pipelined Burst Cache 512 KB	IP P54C without MMX 166 MHz	83 MHz	16 MB EDO 60 nsec
Asus P/I-P55T2P4	54.3	700.3	83.7	Intel Triton II 430HX	Pipelined Burst Cache 512 KB	IP P54C without MMX 166 MHz	83 MHz	64 MB EDO 60 nsec
Asus P/I-P55T2P4	54.2	703.3	84.2	Intel Triton II 430HX	Pipelined Burst Cache 512 KB	IP P54C without MMX 166 MHz	83 MHz	32 MB EDO 60 nsec
Asus P/I-P55T2P4	54.2	698.2	83.8	Intel Triton II 430HX	Pipelined Burst Cache 256 KB	IP P54C without MMX 166 MHz	83 MHz	32 MB EDO 60 nsec
fki SL586 VT II	53.1	426.7	76.4	VIA 580 VP Apollo VP1	Pipelined Burst Cache 512 KB	Cyrix/IBM 6x86 – M1 150 MHz	75 MHz	16 MB EDO 60 nsec
Supermicro P6DOF 2xP6	52.9	1016.3	315.5	Intel Orion 450GX	CPU Internal Cache 256 KB	IP Pro 256 KB L2 200 MHz	66 MHz	128 MB FPM 60 nsec
Asus P/I-P55T2P4	52.7	812.9	78.2	Intel Triton II 430HX	Pipelined Burst Cache 512 KB	IP P54C without MMX 187.5 MHz	75 MHz	64 MB EDO 55 nsec
Asus P/I-P55T2P4	52.2	893.3	84.1	Intel Triton II 430HX	Pipelined Burst Cache 512 KB	IP P54C without MMX 208 MHz	83 MHz	64 MB EDO 60 nsec
Asus P/I-P55T2P4	52.1	701	84.1	Intel Triton II 430HX	Pipelined Burst Cache 512 KB	IP P54C without MMX 166 MHz	83 MHz	16 MB EDO RAM 60 nsec

continues

Continued

Mother-board	RAM MB/sec	Cache L1 Mb/sec	Cache L2 Mb/sec	Chipset	Cache L2 type	Processor	Host bus frequency	RAM
QDI P5i430VX-250DM	52.1	792.8	75.5	Intel Triton VX 430VX	Pipelined Burst Cache 256 KB	IP P54C without MMX 187.5 MHz	75 MHz	32 MB SDRAM
Pine PT-7502	52	952.2	75.6	Intel Triton VX 430VX	Pipelined Burst Cache 256 KB	IP P54C without MMX 225 MHz	75 MHz	16 MB SDRAM
Asus P/I-P55T2P4	51.2	705.5	84.1	Intel Triton II 430HX	Pipelined Burst Cache 512 KB	IP P54C without MMX 166 MHz	83 MHz	32 FPM 60 nsec
Asus P/I-P55T2P4	50.7	623.6	75.2	Intel Triton II 430HX	Pipelined Burst Cache 256 KB	IP P54C without MMX 150 MHz	75 MHz	16 EDO 60 nsec
Asus P/I-P55T2P4	50.6	789.1	75.3	Intel Triton II 430HX	Pipelined Burst Cache 256 KB	IP P54C without MMX 187.5 MHz	75 MHz	64 EDO 60 nsec

Chapter 17

Motherboards and Chipsets for Overclocking Modes

Motherboards Supporting Increased Bus Frequency

When considering overclocking problems, keep in mind that one of the main overclocking aims is to improve the performance of legacy computers without significant financial investment. In many cases, the hardware configuration of such computers includes components whose parameters can't exactly be called modern or promising. However, such legacy systems still exist, and, what's more, adequately serve their users' purposes.

The following table contains a list of motherboards for Pentium processors. These motherboards support non-standard host bus frequency values of 75 and 83 MHz. This data may help you in choosing the optimum mode for overclocking the computer components.

The first column lists motherboard manufacturers; the second column specifies the name of the board. The remaining three columns contain the version number (X.X+ means X.X and higher) and recommended jumper positions for the corresponding bus frequency. Settings for the jumpers that specify bus frequency are listed in ascending order according to their respective numbers: 0 means open, 1 means short, combinations like 1—2 or 2—3 mean numbers of pins to be connected by jumper. Before you start overclocking, make sure that you have carefully studied the motherboard manual. The values shown in the table presented here should only be considered as an example illustrating overclocking methods. Note that the data provided in the table may not correspond exactly to your motherboard, as manufacturers of specific motherboards may introduce some changes into its design without notification. It is therefore strongly recommended that you check this data before overclocking and make sure that this information is consistent with the instructions provided in the motherboard manual. This is the only way to avoid regrettable mistakes. Some of this material, along with updated information, can be found on the Internet at the addresses **www.sysopt.com/mb83mhz.html** and **www.sysopt.com/mb100mhz.html**.

Motherboards Supporting High Bus Frequencies

Manufacturer	Motherboard	Version	75 MHz	83 MHz
Abit	IT5H	1.5+	SoftMenu	SoftMenu
AOpen	AX5		SoftMenu	SoftMenu

continues

Continued

Manufacturer	Motherboard	Version	75 MHz	83 MHz
	SM5		SoftMenu	
	AP5T		1–2	2–3
			2–3	1–2
			2–3	2–3
	AX5T		1–2	
			2–3	
			2–3	
Acorp	586VT-II		3–4	
	J-656VXC	3	0	
			0	
			1	
	SL586V-Plus	1.1	0	1
			1	0
			0	0
ASUSTeK	P/I-P55T2P4	3.0+	1–2	1–2
			2–3	1–2
			1–2	2–3
	P/I-P55TVP4	2.3+	1–2	2–3
			2–3	1–2
			1–2	1–2
	TX97		2–3	
	TX97-X		2–3	
			1–2	
	TX97-E	1.04	2–3	2–3
			2–3	1–2
			1–2	1–2
	TX97-XE		1–2	2–3
			2–3	1–2
			1–2	1–2
	VX97		1–2	2–3
			2–3	1–2
			1–2	1–2
DATA EXPERT	EXPERTBOARD 8661	1.0+	0	
			0	
			1	
FIC	VT-501		1–2	1–2
			2–3	1–2
			1–2	2–3

continues

Continued

Manufacturer	Motherboard	Version	75 MHz	83 MHz
	PA-2006		1–2 2–3 1–2	
	PT-2010	2.1		1–2 2–3 2–3
Iwill	P55V2	0.5A	0 0 1 1–2 2–3	
Jet Board	J656-VXC		0 0 1	
Lucky Star	5I-VX-C1 "Geminy"	1.1+	2–3 1–2 2–3	1–2 2–3 2–3
	5I-VX-1B 5I-VX-2B "APus"	H	2–3 1–2 2–3	1–2 2–3 2–3
	LSP54CE	D		0 1 1
	LSP55CE	D		0 1 1
Shuttle	HOT-555		0 1 0	1 0 0
	HOT-557	1.5		0 0 1
Super Micro	AP5P2			1 0 0
	P5MMS			1–2 1–2 2–3
Tomato	5DTX	1.1	1–3 4–6 1–2	2–4 3–5 1–2
Tyan	TYAN TURBO		JP45	1

Motherboards Supporting the Host Bus Frequency of 83 MHz

Motherboard	Chipset	Switches and jumpers for setting a frequency of 83 MHz
All Abit Motherboards	Intel HX, VX, TX	CPU SoftMenu
A-Trend 5130	ALi	—
AIR P5TX-A	Intel 430TX	—
AIR P5TX-I	Intel 430TX	SW2=ON, SW3=ON, SW4=ON
Amptron 8500 TXPro	TXPro	JP5: 1-2, JP6: 1-2
Amptron PM-8500	TXPro	JP5: 2-3, JP6: 1-2, JP7: 1-2
AOpen AP5T-2	Intel 430TX	—
AOpen AX5T-3	Intel 430TX	—
ASUS HX97	Intel 430HX	FS0=1-2, FS1=1-2, FS2=2-3
ASUS SP97-V	SiS 5598	FS0=2-3, FS1=1-2, FS2=1-2
ASUS P/I P55S2P4	Intel 430HX	—
ASUS P/I-P55T2P4	Intel 430HX	JP8 1-2, JP9 1-2, JP10 2-3
ASUS PI55TP4	Intel 430HX	—
ASUS VX97	Intel 430VX	FS0:2-3, FS1:1-2, FS2:1-2
ASUS TP4XE	Intel 430FX	—
ASUS P2L97	Intel 440LX	FS0=2&3, FS1=1&2, FS2=2&3
CHINESE SL586V-PLUS	Intel 430VX	J7:2-3, J8:1-2, J9:1-2
Elite Micro Systems 5VX-A	Intel 430VX	—
Elite P5TX-Bpro	Intel 430TX	—
EliteGroup P5VX-BE	Intel 430VX	—
FIC PA-2002	VIA 570 VP Apollo Master	—
FIC PA-2006	VIA 580VP	—
FIC PT-2010	VIA580VP	CLK1=1-2, CLK2=2-3, CLK3=2-3
FIC VA-502	VIA580VPX	—
FordLian 5IHXA	Intel 430HX	—
Free Technology Falcon P5F76	Intel 430VX	JP6 1-2, JP7 1-2, and JP8 2-3

continues

Continued

Motherboard	Chipset	Switches and jumpers for setting a frequency of 83 MHz
Gigabyte GA-586SG (w/AGP!)	SiS 5591	—
HSB-Labs Huron	—	CPU SoftMenu
Houston Technology M-549	Intel 430VX	JP7: A=1-2, B=1-2, C=2-3
Hsin Tech	ALI Aladdin IV (TxPRO)	JP5=2-3, JP6=2-3
Iwill P55XPlus	ALI Aladdin IV	JP5:T83
Jet-Way J-656VXDP	Intel 430VX	FS0: closed, FS1: open, FS2: open
Kamei KM-T5-T1	Intel 430TX	JP20: closed, JP3: open, JP2: open
Lucky Star TX1	Intel 430TX	JP1: 2-3, JP2: 2-3, JP3: 1-2
Megatrends FX83-A	Intel 440FX	J36=on, J37=on
M-Tech. Mustang R-534	SiS 5571	JP10: open, JP11: closed, JP12: closed
Micronics Twister AT	Intel 430TX	JP6: 1-2, JP7: 1-2, JP8: 2-3
Mtech R541	Intel 430TX	Change in BIOS Setup
Octek Rhino 12	VIA Apollo VP-1 580	JCK1: 1-2, JCK2: 1-2, JCK3: 2-3, or JCK1: open, JCK2: 1-2, JCK3: 1-2
Protac MB 8600	Intel TX-Pro	JP5=2-3, JP6=1-2, JP7=1-2
QDI Titanium 1b	Intel 430TX	—
QDI Titanium-1 (P5I430TX-250)	Intel 430TX	Download Speedeasy BIOS v2.2 for 83 MHz
QDI Explorer IV	Intel 430VX	JC1=closed, JC2=open, JC3=open
Shuttle HOT-555a	Intel 430VX	JP37: 1-2=open, 3-4=open, 5-6=closed
Shuttle HOT-557	Intel 430VX	JP36: 1-2 open, 3-4 open, 5-6 closed
Shuttle HOT-565	Intel 430TX	JP36: 1-2 off, 3-4 off, 5-6 on
Shuttle HOT-569	Intel 430TX	SW1 & SW3 = ON, SW2 = OFF
Shuttle HOT-603	AMD-640	—

continues

Continued

Motherboard	Chipset	Switches and jumpers for setting the frequency of 83 MHz
Spring ST586	Intel 430VX	—
SuperMicro AP5P2	Intel 430HX	JP29 open, JP31 off, JP28 closed
SuperMicro P5MMA98	Intel 430TX	JP5:1-2, JP6:1-2, JP7:2-3
SuperMicro P5MMS98	Intel 430TX	JP5:1-2, JP6:1-2, JP7:2-3
Tekram P5T30-B4		JFS0: 3-2, JFS1: 1-2, JFS2: 3-2
Tyan Titan Turbo AT-2 (S1571S)	Intel 430TX	JP9:1-2, JP10:OFF
UpgradeTech Computer UT-586TX	Intel 430TX	—

ASUS TX97 Motherboards

Model	Oscillator	75 MHz			83 MHz		
		FS0	FS1	FS2	FS0	FS1	FS2
TX97	ICS9147-09	2&3	2&3	1&2	2&3	1&2	1&2
TX97-X	ICS9147-09	2&3	2&3	1&2	2&3	1&2	1&2
TX97-E	ICW W48C67-03	2&3	2&3	1&2	2&3	1&2	1&2
TX97-XV	ICS9147-03	2&3	2&3	1&2	X	X	X
TX97-XE	ICS9169-27	1&2	2&3	1&2	2&3	1&2	1&2

Motherboards Supporting Host Bus Frequencies of 100 and 133 MHz

Model	Chipset	133 MHz	Setting of the jumpers
Abit BX6	Intel 440BX	*	CPU SoftMenu
Abit LX6	Intel 440LX		CPU SoftMenu
Abit AV5	—		—
AOpen AX6B	Intel 440BX	*	—
Asus P2B	Intel 440BX	*	—
AOpen AX59PRO	VIA Apollo MVP3		—
AOpen AX6B	Intel 440BX	*	—
Chaintech 5AGM2	VIA Apollo MVP3		—

continues

Continued

Model	Chipset	133 MHz	Setting of the jumpers
Chaintech 6BTM	Intel 440BX	*	—
Epox EP-58MVPC-M	VIA Apollo MVP3		JP3: 25-26, closed
Epox EP-51MVP3E-M	VIA Apollo MVP3		—
DFI P2BXL	Intel 440BX	*	BIOS Setup
DFI P5BV3+	VIA Apollo MVP3		—
Elitegroup P6BX	Intel 440BX		—
FIC PA-2013	VIA Apollo MVP3		—
FIC VB-601	VIA Apollo MVP3		—
FIC VA-503+	VIA Apollo MVP3		—
Gigabyte GA-686BX(DS)	Intel BX		JP6 1-2-3, open
Gigabyte GA-5AX	Aladdin ALi V		—
Iwill BS100	Intel BX	*	—
Lucky Star 5MVP3	VIA Apollo MVP3		—
Microstar MS-6119	Intel BX	*	BIOS Setup
QDI P6144BX (Brilliant I)	Intel BX	*	BIOS Setup
Shuttle HOT-591P	VIA Apollo MVP3		—
Soyo 5EH5/M	VIA Apollo MVP3		to 112 MHz (DIP)
SuperMicro P6SBA	Intel BX		Auto 66/100 MHz
SuperMicro P6DGE	Intel GX		—
SuperMicro P6DGS	Intel GX		—
SuperMicro P6DGU	Intel GX		—
SuperMicro P6DBE	Intel BX		—
SuperMicro P6DBS	Intel BX		—
SuperMicro P6DBU	Intel BX		—
Tekram P6B40-A4X	Intel BX	*	Auto 100, 103, 112, 133 MHz
Tyan Thunder 100 Pro	Intel BX		Auto 66/100 MHz
Tyan Trinity S1570s	—		—
Tyan Trinity S1590s	Apollo MVP3		—
Zida 6ABX	Intel BX		Auto 66/100 MHz

The next table lists certain parameters of popular motherboards that provide for high performance of the CPU, and therefore, improve overall system performance.

Characteristics of Certain Motherboards, in brief

Motherboard	Chipset	DIMM, slots/max., MB	FSB frequency, MHz	PCI/ISA/AGP slots	Form factor
BX6	i440BX	4/512	66, 83, 100, 103, 112, 133	4/3/1	ATX
BX6 Rev.2.0	i440BX	4/1024	66, 68, 75, 83, 100, 103, 112, 117, 124, 129, 133, 138, 143, 148, 153	5/2/1	ATX
BH6	i440BX	3/384	66, 75, 83, 100, 112, 124, 133	5/2/1	ATX
ASUS P2B	i440BX	3/768	66, 75, 83, 100, 103, 112, 133	4/3/1	ATX
ASUS P2B Rev.1.10			66, 75, 83, 100, 103, 105, 110, 112, 115, 120, 124, 133, 140, 150		
ASUS P2B-B	i440BX	3/768	66, 75, 83, 100, 103, 105, 110, 112, 115, 120, 124, 133, 140, 150	3/2/1	Baby AT
CT-6BTM	i440BX	4/512	66, 83, 100, 103, 112, 133	4/3/1	ATX

There are a few words to be said concerning the choice of a modern motherboard that is intended for use in overclocking modes.

Contemporary motherboards have a wide range of supported bus frequency values. However, if you were to compare motherboards according to this aspect only, you would notice that different boards vary not only by their supported bus frequency values, but also by their distribution within the frequency range. Usually, the supported values are not distributed evenly, but rather are grouped around a few areas within the entire range. This is due to the fact that the architecture of these newer motherboards uses different frequency synthesizer chips. This may affect the choice of the motherboard best suited for processor overclocking. Usually, brand name boards like Abit and ASUSTeK are very good for overclocking. These could be, for instance, the Abit BX6 Rev. 2.0 or the ASUS P2B Rev. 1.10. Both of these boards are noted for their support of a relatively large number of processor bus frequencies. However, most of the optimum overclocking frequencies provided by Abit BX6 Rev.2.0 are concentrated in the 112—133 MHz range, while the best overclocking frequencies provided by ASUS P2B Rev.1.10 are grouped within the 100—124 MHz range. This grouping of supported frequencies influences the fields of optimum application for each motherboard. For example, when overclocking Celeron processors intended for the bus frequency of 66 MHz, the best results can be achieved when using ASUS P2B Rev. 1.10 motherboards, since they provide you with the ability to gradually increase the bus frequency within the range of 100—124 MHz. If you are going to overclock a Pentium II, consider the fact that all Pentium II processors intended for a bus frequency of 100 MHz usually run reliably at a frequency of 112 MHz. Because of this, motherboards like Abit BX6 Rev. 2.0 are of particular interest for this case. These motherboards allow you to set the maximum bus frequency (higher than the usual 112—115 MHz), because it allows you to gradually increase the bus frequency in the range of 100—124 MHz.

As was mentioned earlier, CPU stability at high processor bus frequencies can be achieved by increasing the voltage supplied to the processor. If there are no built-in tools for voltage tweaking, you can accomplish this task using insulating varnish or adhesive tape according to the directions given in Chapter 13. This is possible with practically all modern motherboards.

Note that currently, support for processor bus frequencies above 150 MHz is not necessarily a crucial advantage that plays a decisive role when choosing a motherboard, despite that for the moment there are certain motherboards on the market that are advertised as supporting bus frequencies up to 200 MHz. This is due to the fact that for the moment it is still difficult to find hardware components for such motherboards — memory modules, for example — that would tolerate such high frequencies. Besides, the Celeron and Pentium II processors intended for standard bus frequencies of 66 and 100 MHz, respectively, don't allow such a drastic increase in their external frequencies. Not even all representatives of the Pentium III family support such a high values for the processor bus frequency. For example, not all specimens of Pentium III with the Coppermine core, intended for use at an FSB frequency of 100 MHz and allowing relatively high values of the bus frequency will be stable and reliable at FSB frequencies approaching 150 MHz. The only exception is the Pentium III that is rated to run at an FSB frequency of 133 MHz. For such processors, the bus frequency of 150 MHz is of specific interest, but again, as usual, only for the first representatives of this line.

However, when estimating the possibility of using one of these increased bus frequencies supported by your motherboard, you should also consider the fact that the AGP and PCI bus frequencies are determined by the FSB frequency. Bus frequency values set for these buses depend on the motherboard architecture and on the functional capabilities of their chipsets. If extremely high frequencies are set for these buses, it may lead to the malfunctioning or failure of the components connected to them, for example, DIMM SDRAM modules, video adapters (AGP or PCI), hard drives, etc.

Now let us discuss some specific features of the motherboards that support high processor bus frequencies.

Many motherboard manufacturers advertise new technologies used in the architecture of their product. This advertising is often a bit misleading, because technologies proclaimed as "new" may have been in use for a while before manufacturers felt that they were sure of its reliability. Consider, for example, the SoftMenu technology, which allows you to set and manage overclocking modes via BIOS Setup. This technology is widely advertised by Abit, but has been in use in QDI motherboards for a relatively long time. You should also understand that all of these innovations are based on the specifications and the architecture of modern processors. For instance, choosing the motherboard name **Chaintech 6BTM** from the **Overclocker BIOS** menu allows you to control external processor frequencies using SoftMenu. However, there is still a switch on the motherboard itself that assigns the Sel 66/100# amplitude levels and that in a normal mode sets the external frequency. At the same time, the actual frequency the processor uses is chosen in BIOS Setup. After setting the JP7 Sel66/100# level to **Low**, that is, to 66 MHz, the processor that is used to running on 100 MHz "frees" the multiplier. As a result, you gain the opportunity to set any external frequency and any multiplier you want in BIOS Setup. In many cases, this will allow you to get around the problem of locked multipliers. This technique is described at **www.ixbt.com** and has been tested on the Chaintech 6BTM motherboard. You might also try it with other motherboards that allow users to set the external frequency both in BIOS Setup and by switches.

Popular Motherboards

When estimating the capabilities of modern motherboards, it makes sense to carefully examine the parameters of the most popular, highly efficient motherboards from well-known manufacturers, which are often used in systems whose elements are being used in overclocking mode.

Abit BE6-II — ATX (305×200 mm), i440BX AGPset chipset. Socket: Slot 1. Processors: Pentium III, Pentium II, and Celeron 233−800 MHz. FSB frequencies: 66, 75, 83−200 MHz with increments of 1 MHz. Processor voltage: 1.3−2.3 V, with increments of 0.05 V. RAM: 3 DIMM (168 pins; 8, 16, 32, 64, 128, 256 MB), up to 768 MB SDRAM, ECC. AGP 1X/2X. 2 UltraDMA/33 IDE ports and 2 UltraDMA/66/33 (HPT366) IDE ports. I/O: 2 serial ports, 1 (ECP/EPP) parallel port, 2 USB, PS/2, IrDA TX/RX header, floppy. ACPI, hardware monitoring, Wake on LAN header, Wake on Ring header, etc. Activation from the keyboard, mouse, network, and modem. BIOS: Award BIOS v.6, Plug and Play, Write-Protect Anti-Virus, SoftMenu III (or DIP switches for setting CPU parameters). Slots: 5 PCI, 1 ISA, 1 AGP.

The general view of the Abit BE6-II is shown in Fig. 17.1.

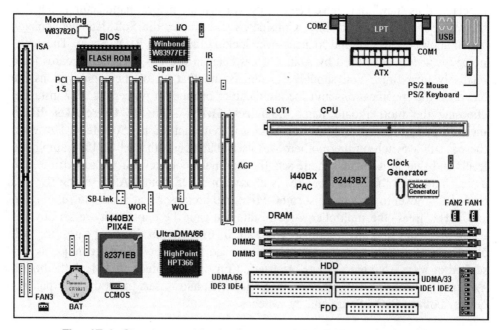

Fig. 17.1. Structure and basic elements of Abit BE6-II motherboards

Abit BE6 — ATX (305×210 mm), i440BX AGPset chipset. Socket: Slot 1. Processors: Pentium III, Pentium II and Celeron 233−700 MHz. FSB frequencies: 66, 75, 83, 100 MHz, etc. RAM: 3 DIMM (168 pins; 8, 16, 32, 64, 128, 256 MB), up to 768 MB SDRAM, ECC. AGP 1X/2X. 2 UltraDMA/33 IDE ports and 2 UltraDMA/66/33 IDE ports. I/O: 2 serial ports, 1 parallel port (ECP/EPP), 2 USB,

PS/2, IrDA TX/RX header, floppy. ACPI, hardware monitoring, Wake on LAN header, Wake on Ring header, etc. BIOS: Award BIOS, APM, DMI, Plug and Play, Write-Protect Anti-Virus, SoftMenu II. Slots: 5 PCI, 2 ISA, 1 AGP.

Abit BF6 — ATX (305×200 mm), i440BX AGPset chipset. Socket: Slot 1. Processors: Pentium III, Pentium II and Celeron 233—800 MHz. FSB frequencies: 66, 75, 100 MHz, etc. RAM: 3 DIMM (168 pins; 8, 16, 32, 64, 128, 256 MB), up to 768 MB SDRAM, ECC. AGP 1X/2X. 2 UltraDMA/33 IDE ports. I/O: 2 serial ports, 1 parallel port (ECP/EPP), 2 USB, PS/2, IrDA TX/RX header, floppy. ACPI, hardware monitoring, Wake on LAN header, Wake on Ring header, etc. Activation from the keyboard, mouse, network, and modem. BIOS: Award BIOS v.6, Plug and Play, Write-Protect Anti-Virus, SoftMenu III (or DIP switches for setting CPU parameters). Slots: 6 PCI, 1 ISA, 1 AGP.

Abit BM6 — ATX, i440BX AGPset chipset. Socket: Socket 370. Processors: Pentium III, Pentium II, and Celeron. FSB frequencies: 66, 75, 83, 100, 103, 105, 110, 112, 115, 120, 124, 133 MHz. RAM: 3 DIMM, up to 768 MB SDRAM. AGP 1X/2X. 2 UltraDMA/33 IDE. I/O: 2 serial ports, 1 parallel port (ECP/EPP), 2 USB, PS/2, IrDA TX/RX header, floppy. BIOS: Award BIOS, APM, DMI, Plug and Play, Anti-boot Virus, SoftMenu II. Slots: 5 PCI, 2 ISA, 1 AGP.

Abit KT7 — ATX (305x230 mm), chipset: VIA Apollo KT133 (VT8363+VT82C686A). Socket: Socket A (Socket 462). Processors: AMD Athlon and AMD Duron. FSB frequency: 100 MHz DDR (Alpha EV6). Overclocking: processor core voltage is 1.1—1.85 V with the increment of 0.25 V; processor bus brequencies are 100, 101, 103, 105, 107, 110, 112, 115, 117, 120, 122, 124, 127, 133, 136, 140, 145, 150, 155 MHz. RAM: 3 DIMM (168 pins, 3.3 V), up to 1.5 GB PC100/PC133 SDRAM. Memory bus frequency: 100/133 MHz. AGP 1X/2X/4X. BIOS. 2 IDE ports (up to 4 Ultra DMA/66/33 devices), 2 PS/2 slots for keyboard and mouse, 1 floppy port, 1 parallel port (EPP/ECP), 2 serial ports, 2 USB ports (+2 additional), etc. BIOS: Award Plug and Play. Slots: 1 AGP, 6 PCI, 1 ISA.

There is also an extended variation of the Abit KT7 motherboard — Abit KT7-RAID. The main distinguishing feature of this motherboard is that it uses the HPT-370 chip in the motherboard architecture. Besides implementing UltraDMA/100, this also allows to provide RAID functionality. RAID provides the ability to increase the disk subsystem's performance and improve the reliability of data storage on hard drives. Thanks to the presence of the HPT-370 chip, this motherboard configuration allows you to increase the number of IDE devices up to 8.

The Abit KT7 motherboard belongs to the motherboard class that allows you to unlock fixed frequency multipliers. Currently, this class is relatively small in number. However, you can only unlock frequency multipliers if the L1 bridges on the surface of the AMD Athlon and AMD Duron processors were not cut by the vendor in the course of production and testing. If this is not the case, you can restore the bridges. If you can't overclock by changing the processor frequency multiplier, you're limited to either the nominal modes or to overclocking via increasing the FSB frequency.

It must be noted that despite the fact that the VT82C686A chip is used as a South Bridge, and that this chip contains built-in AC'97 tools, the Abit KT7 motherboard architecture doesn't support audio functions. This, of course, limits the functionality of the product. It is also possible that this circumstance might even scare some potential purchasers. However, taking into account the relatively low quality of such audio capabilities, their lack can't be considered a significant drawback of this motherboard. Furthermore, it must be pointed out that the Abit KT7 motherboard is not intended for low-end systems.

On the other hand, this motherboard has several advantages. One of these advantageous features is the presence of cooling facilities for the North Bridge chip of the chipset. Besides the traditional on-chip heatsink, there is also a fan. According to the idea of the motherboard designers, the supplementary fan installed on the North Bridge VT8363 chip in addition to the powerful processor cooler should improve the system's stability and reliability (Fig. 17.2). Stability is one of the distinguishing characteristic of Abit products.

Fig. 17.2. Heatsink and fan installed on the North Bridge chip

After the release of the VIA Apollo KT133A chipset, Abit developed a newer variation of the motherboard, named Abit KT7A. This motherboard, in contrast to its prototype, is distinguished by an extended range of supported FSB frequencies, allowing to the system to run reliably and remain stable. Combined with the capability of changing the processor frequency multiplier, this feature provides for optimal overclocking and a boosted performance.

ASUS P2B-B — Baby AT (220×228 mm), 100 MHz i440BX AGPset chipset with PIIX4E South Bridge. Socket: Slot 1. Processors: Pentium II 233–450 MHz, Celeron. Bus frequency: 66/100 MHz; AGP: 66/133 MHz; overclocking: 66, 75, 83, 100, 103, 105, 110, 112, 115, 120, 124, 133, 140, 150 MHz. RAM: 3 DIMM (168 pins), up to 768 MB PC100 SDRAM, ECC. 2 UltraDMA/33 IDE that support a high-capacity HDD (more than 8.4 GB), ATAPI IDE CD-ROM and LS–120. I/O: 2 serial ports, 1 parallel port (ECP/EPP). Ports: USB, IrDA, 2 PS/2, floppy (up to 2.88 MB), AT-keyboards. Voltage: AT/ATX — 12 V, 5 V, 3 V — 20-pin ATX, 12-pin AT, supports enabling and disabling programs using the keyboard (with ATX). BIOS: 2 MB Flash EPROM Award AGP BIOS, ACPI, Plug and Play, Anti-boot Virus. Slots: 3 PCI, 2 ISA, 1 AGP.

ASUS P3B-F — ATX (192×304 mm), i440BX AGPset chipset with PIIX4E South Bridge. Socket: Slot 1. Processors: Pentium III, Pentium II, Celeron, 233–450 MHz and higher. FSB frequencies: 66/100 MHz; AGP 1X/2X 66/133 MHz; overclocking: 66, 75, 83, 100, 103, 105, 110, 112, 115, 120, 124, 133, 140, 150 MHz. RAM: 4 DIMM 13 (168 pins; 8, 16, 32, 64, 128, 256 MB), from 8 to 1024 MB PC100 SDRAM, ECC. AGP 1X/2X. 2 UltraDMA/33 IDE. Supports ATAPI IDE CD-ROM and LS-120. I/O: 2 serial ports, 1 parallel port (ECP/EPP), 2 USB ports, IrDA, 2 PS/2, floppy (up to 2.88 MB). Hardware monitoring. Activation from the keyboard. BIOS: 2 MB Flash Award BIOS v.6.0, ACPI, Plug and Play, Anti-boot Virus. Slots (3 options): 6 PCI, 0 ISA, 1 AGP; 6 PCI, 1 ISA, 1 AGP; 5 PCI, 0 ISA, 1 AGP.

The ASUS P3B-F motherboard is one of the most popular high-performance boards. Its structure, outward appearance, and elements are shown in Figs. 17.3 and 17.4.

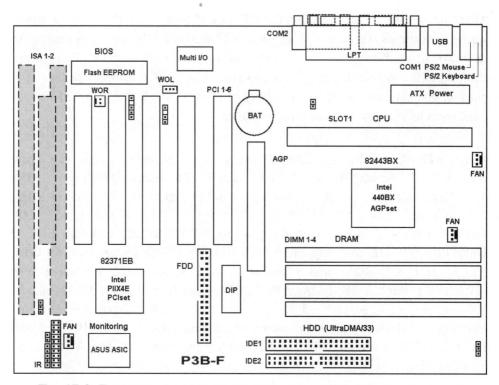

Fig. 17.3. The structure and basic elements of the ASUS P3B-F motherboard

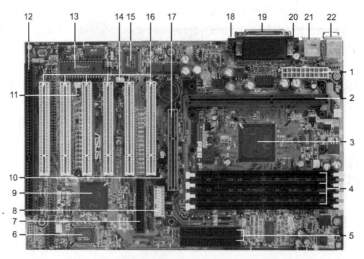

Fig. 17.4. The ASUS P3B-F motherboard

Components of the ASUS P3B-F Motherboard

1. ATX Power connector	12. 1 or 2 ISA slots
2. Slot 1 Processor socket	13. Programmable Flash EEPROM
3. 82443BX chip (North Bridge)	14. Wake-On-LAN socket
4. 4 DIMM	15. Multi I/O
5. 2 ports for connecting four IDE	16. 5 or 6 PCI slots
6. ASUS ASIC System monitoring chip	17. AGP port
7. Floppy disk drive connection	18. Serial port
8. DIP switches	19. Parallel port
9. 82371EB microcircuitry (South Bridge — PIIX4E)	20. Serial port
	21. 2 USB ports
10. LED	22. Slots for a PS/2 mouse and PS/2 keyboard
11. Wake-On-Ring socket	

ASUS CUSL2 — ATX (208×305 mm), i815E chipset (82815, 82801BA, 82802). Socket: Socket 370. Processors: FCPGA Pentium III (450−933 MHz and higher), Celeron (333−566 MHz and higher). FSB frequencies: 66/100/133 MHz; AGP 1X/2X/4X; overclocking: from 66 to 216 MHz (using the ICS 94201CF programmable frequency synthesizer), the bus frequency parameters are shown in the table below. Using the built-in tools, you can increase the processor core voltage by 0.3 V in increments of 0.05 V, and you can also set three voltage values to be used for input/output — 3.3 V (standard), 3.4 V (set for the ASUS CUSL2), and 3.6 V. RAM: 3 DIMM, up to 512 MB PC100/PC133 SDRAM. 2 UltraDMA/33/66/100 IDE. I/O: 2 serial ports, 1 parallel port (ECP/EPP), 2 built-in and 3 additional USB ports, 2 PS/2, floppy. Built-in graphics (i752), AC'97 audio, hardware monitoring. Activation from the modem, the mouse, the keyboard, the network, and the timer. BIOS: 4 MB Flash Award BIOS, ACPI, DMI, Green, Plug and Play, Trend Chip Away Virus, and Symbios SCSI BIOS. Slots: 6 PCI, 0 ISA, 1 AGP Pro, 2 CNR.

Bus Frequency Parameters for the ASUS CUSL2

Set FSB/SDRAM frequency ratio	FSB frequency, MHz		SDRAM/FSB frequency ratio	AGP/FSB frequency ratio	PCI/FSB frequency ratio
	min	max			
66/100	66	97	3/2	1	1/2
100/100	100	132	1	2/3	1/3
133/133	133	166	1	1/2	1/4
133/100	133	216	3/4	1/2	1/4

ASUS K7V — ATX (245×305 mm), VIA Apollo KX133 chipset (VT8371+ VT82C686A). Socket: Slot A. Processors: AMD Athlon 550–1000 MHz. FSB (EV6) clock frequency: 100 MHz; overclocking: 90, 92, 95, 97, 100, 101, 103, 105, 107, 110, 112, 115, 117, 120, 122, 124, 127, 130, 133, 136, 140, 145, 150, 155 MHz. You can change the voltage to the processor from 1.3 V to 2.05 V in increments of 0.05 V, and you can also raise the voltage to the AGP, the memory, and the chipset to 3.56 V. RAM: 3 DIMM (168 pins), up to 1.5 GB PC100/PC133 SDRAM and VC100/VC133 VCM. AGP Pro that can use AGP 1X/2X/4X modes. 2 UltraDMA/66 IDE ports. I/O: 2 serial ports, 1 parallel port, 2 built-in USB ports and 2 additional USB ports, 2 PS/2, floppy. AC'97 audio (Cirrus Logic CrystalClear SoundFusion CS4299 3D audio compression/decompression). Hardware monitoring (ASIC ASUS AS99127F microcircuitry). BIOS: Award AGP BIOS that supports Enhanced ACPI, DMI, Green, PnP Features plus Trend Chip Away Virus and Symbios SCSI BIOS. Slots: 5 PCI, 0 ISA, 1 AGP Pro, 1 AMR.

CT-6BTM — ATX, i440BX AGPset chipset. Socket: Slot 1. Processors: Pentium II (up to 600 MHz). Bus frequency: 66/100 MHz; overclocking: 68, 75, 83, 103, 112 MHz. RAM — up to 512 MB — 4 DIMM (168 pins) EDO (only 66 MHz) and SDRAM, ECC support. 2 IDE ports that support PIO mode 4, multiword DMA mode 2, and UltraDMA/33. I/O: 2 serial ports, 1 parallel port (SPP/ECP/EPP), 2 USB ports, floppy. Award System BIOS that supports Plug and Play, APM, DMI, ChipAwayVirus. Slots: 4 PCI, 3 ISA, 1 AGP. Supports SeePU technology.

CT-6ATA2 — ATX, VIA Apollo Pro133 chipset (VT82C693A+VT82C686A). Socket: Slot 1. Processors: Pentium II and Pentium III (up to 733 MHz) and Celeron (up to 466 MHz). FSB frequency— 66/100/133 MHz, overclocking — 68, 75, 83 MHz and from 100 to 152 MHz in increments of 1 MHz (RTM520-39C clock frequency synthesizer). RAM — up to 768 MB SDRAM — 3 DIMM (168 pins, 3.3 V), ECC support (1 bit). AGP 1X/2X. 2 IDE ports that support PIO mode 4, multiword DMA mode 2, and UltraDMA/33/66. I/O — 2 serial ports, 1 parallel port (SPP/ECP/EPP), 4 USB ports (2 USB on the board sockets), floppy, Audio Line-in/out. AC'97 v2.1 CODEC for software support of sound functions and the modem. Supports: Wake-On-LAN, Modem Ring, RTC Alarm, ACPI, Hardware Monitoring, etc. Award System BIOS that supports Plug and Play (v1.0a), APM (v1.2), DMI (v2.0), with the ability to boot from hard and floppy disks, LS120, ZIP ATAPI, CD-ROM. Slots: 4 PCI, 2 ISA, 1 AGP.

The structure and the basic elements of the CT-6ATA2 motherboard are presented in Fig. 17.5.

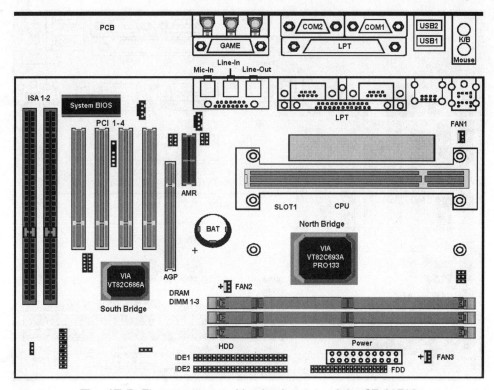

Fig. 17.5. The structure and basic elements of the CT-6ATA2

CT-6ATA4 — ATX, VIA Apollo Pro133A chipset (VT82C694X+VT82C686A). Socket: Slot 1. Processors: Pentium II and Pentium III (up to 750 MHz) and Celeron (up to 466 MHz). FSB frequency: 66/100/133 MHz; overclocking: 68, 75, 83 MHz and from 100 to 152 MHz in increments of 1 MHz. RAM — up to 768 MB SDRAM — 3 DIMM (168 pins, 3.3 V), ECC support (1 bit). AGP 1X/2X/4X. 2 IDE ports that support PIO mode 4, multiword DMA mode 2, and UltraDMA/33/66. I/O: 2 serial ports, 1 parallel port (SPP/ECP/EPP), 2 USB ports, floppy, Audio Line-in/out. AC'97 v2.1 CODEC for software support of sound functions and the modem. Supports: Wake-On-LAN, modem ring, RTC Alarm, ACPI, hardware monitoring, etc. Award System BIOS that supports Plug and Play (v1.0a), APM (v1.2), DMI (v2.0), with the ability to boot from hard and floppy disks, LS120, ZIP ATAPI, CD-ROM. Slots: 5 PCI, 1 ISA, 1 AGP, 1 AMR.

The structure and the basic elements of the CT-6ATA4 motherboard are presented in Fig. 17.6.

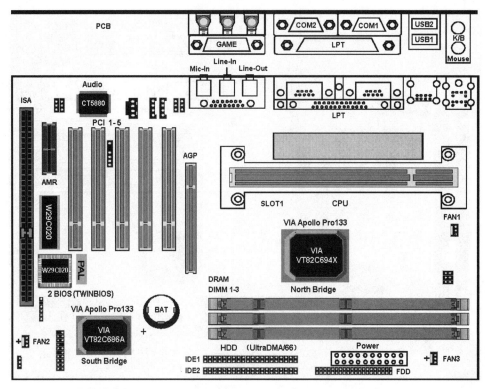

Fig. 17.6. The structure and basic elements of the CT-6ATA4

The performance and the functional capabilities of the computer depend to a large extent on the specialized system logic microcircuitry — the chipsets that are the basis of the motherboard.

Chipsets such as Intel's specialized sets (i440BX AGPset, i440ZX AGPset, i815) or similar products from VIA (VIA Apollo Pro Plus, VIA Apollo Pro133, VIA Apollo Pro133A, VIA Apollo KX133, VIA Apollo K133, for example) are the ones most commonly found in high performance motherboards used in overclocked systems.

Soltek SL-75KV+ — ATX (305x220 mm), chipset: VIA Apollo KT133 (VT8363+VT82C686A). Socket: Socket A (Socket 462). Processors: AMD Athlon and AMD Duron. FSB frequency: 100 MHz DDR (Alpha EV6). Overclocking: FSB frequency is set either using DIP switches — 100, 103, 105, 110, 112, 115, 120, 124, 133.3, 140, 150 MHz, or via BIOS Setup — 100, 103, 105, 112, 115, 120, 124 MHz. Processor core voltage: 1.5–1.85 V with the increment of 0.25 V. RAM: 3 DIMM (168 pins, 3.3 V), up to 768 MB PC100/PC133 SDRAM. Memory bus frequency: 100/133 MHz. AGP 1X/2X/4X. BIOS. 2 IDE ports (up to 4 Ultra DMA/66/33 devices), 2 PS/2 connectors for keyboard and mouse, 1 floppy port, 1 parallel port (EPP/ECP), 2 serial ports, 2 USB ports (+2 add.), etc. BIOS: Award Plug and Play. Slots: 1 AGP (Pro), 5 PCI, 1 ISA.

This motherboard belongs to the relatively tiny class of motherboards that provide built-in tools for unlocking the fixed processor frequency multipliers. Considering the capabilities of overclocking the processor via changing the multiplier, it is necessary to mention that this capability is only provided for processors with uninterrupted L1 bridges. If this is not the case, you can try to restore the cut bridges using the bridge restoring technology.

Among Soltek products, it is necessary to mention the SL-75KAV and SL-75KAV-X motherboards. These products implement the newest technologies that provide hardware diagnostics, along with automatic or semi-automatic selection of the processor overclocking mode.

Popular Chipsets

Intel Chipsets

i440BX AGPset. The i440 BX AGPset is optimal for working in systems based on sixth generation processors (Pentium II and Pentium III) with DIB (Dual Independent Bus) architecture using BSB (Back Side Bus) interface that ensures the efficiency of the L2 cache memory.

The 440BX AGPset supports an FSB frequency of 100 MHz for Pentium II and Pentium III processors. Configurations using two processors are also possible.

The i440BX AGPset has a built-in tool for controlling the FSB frequency that supports: all Celerons, Pentium II, and Pentium III processors with Slot 1 and Socket 370; SMP (Symmetric MultiProcessor) protocol for systems with one or two processors; bufferization, dynamic command execution, and a pipeline method of data transmission, I/O APIC; FSB frequencies of 60, 66, and 100 MHz (64 bit Host Bus GTL+); etc.

The built-in memory controller supports: a 64/72-bit memory bus (64+8 ECC); EDO DRAM or SDRAM memory (60, 66, 100 MHz) with a maximum capacity from 8 MB to 1 GB; a 3.3 V DIMM (Single/Double density), for EDO DRAM no more than 60 nsec, for SDRAM 66 or 100 MHz (PC100); at the frequency of 66 MHz, both EDO DRAM and SDRAM, and at the frequency of 100 MHz, only SDRAM, memory microcircuitry of 16- and 64-bit DRAM, and up to 4 double-sided DIMMs (8 rows); parity control and ECC (only for SDRAM); unbuffered and registered SDRAM (x-1-1-1 at 66 MHz, x-1-1-1 at 100 MHz; a DIMM plug-and-play using the Serial Presence Detect (SPD) mechanism, which uses the SMB interface, etc. The chipset will not support using both an EDO DRAM and an SDRAM at the same time.

The frequency of the memory bus is always equal to the processor FSB frequency.

The built-in interface controllers and other means of control support: AGP Rev 1.0 (4/12/96) with 1X/2X modes (66/133 MHz, 3.3 V); AGP side-band; PCI Rev. 2.1, 3.3 and 5 V, 33 MHz, 32 bit; up to 5 PCI components (in addition to the I/O bridge — PIIX4/PIIX4E); Bus Mastering; UltraDMA/33; 2 IDE ports (4 IDE devices); 2 USB ports (2×127 USB devices); System Management Bus (SMB); Power Management; ACPI power management (PC'98 ACPI power-management specification) for mobile and desktop systems; Wired for Management (WfM); and other functions and devices. Within systems created on the basis of the i440BX chipset, it is also possible to use UltraDMA/66 hard drives. However, such drives will function only in UltraDMA/33 mode.

The AGP and PCI bus frequencies are related to the frequency of the processor bus. In the i440 BX chipset, one of two ratios is used to obtain the frequency of the AGP bus from the frequency of the FSB — 1:1 and 2:3. For the PCI bus, you have three options when setting the ratio — 1:2, 1:3, and 1:4. Not all motherboards will support the last option, but it is exactly this ratio that is of the most interest for users experimenting with overcloking modes.

The i440BX AGPset consists of two chips: the 82443BX and the 82371/EB. The 82443BX chip is the Host Bridge/Controller PCI AGP (PAC). The 82371/EB is the PCI-TO ISA/IDE Xcelerator (PIIX4/PIIX4).

The structure of a computer with the i440BX AGPset is presented in Fig. 17.7.

Motherboard manufacturers generally use the following workaround for the problem of the lack of support of the UltraDMA/66 protocol, which is favored by all modern storage devices of this class. They include an additional UltraDMA/66 controller that is implemented using special microcircuitry, such as, for example, HighPoint HPT 366. This solution is used in certain motherboards from Abit and other manufacturers. The scheme shown in Fig. 17.8 illustrates the usage of the UltraDMA/66 controller (HighPoint HPT 377) in the architecture of computers based on the i440BX AGPset chipset.

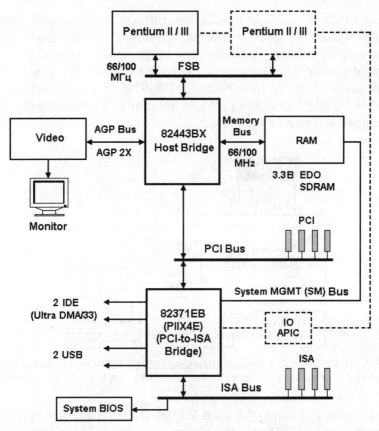

Fig. 17.7. Structure of a computer with the i440BX AGPset chipset

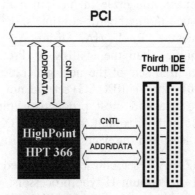

Fig. 17.8. UltraDMA/66 controller (HighPoint HPT 366) in the architecture
of a computer with the i440BX AGP set chipset

In addition to the means of supporting the UltraDMA/66 protocol, motherboard manufacturers often use specialized chips that ensure hardware monitoring, which is a mandatory attribute of the architecture of all modern systems. This capability is implemented using special chips such as Winbond W83782D. The diagram illustrating the usage of Super I/O (Winbond W83977EF) and hardware monitoring (Winbond W83782D) controllers in the architecture of computers with the i440BX AGPset chipset is shown in Fig. 17.9.

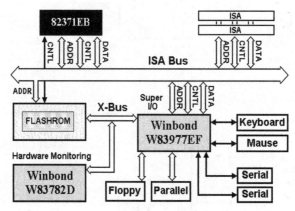

Fig. 17.9. The Super I/O controller (Winbond W83977EF) and hardware monitoring (W83782D) in the architecture of computers with the i440BX AGPset chipset

The above-mentioned chips, Winbond W83782D and HighPoint 366, are not an integral part of the i440BX AGPset chipset. However, they are used along with certain other elements for improving the functional capabilities of this chipset. They also prolong its reasonable life cycle in modern high performance motherboards. The production of such motherboards continues, despite the appearance of new chipsets from companies like Intel, VIA, Ali and SiS, architecture of which has more functional capabilities than the i440BX AGPset. However, even after Intel released the first specialized sets of the next generation, which included the i810, the i820, and the i820E, the i440BX AGPset did not lose its importance. It remains one of the most stable and most productive chipsets with an optimal price/performance ratio. Motherboards built for the i440BX AGPset also ensure a relatively high performance level and the necessary level of functionality.

i440ZX AGPset. The i440ZX AGPset chipset is intended for high-performance computers with Pentium II or Pentium II type processors. The chipset is built on the basis of the same core architecture as the i440BX AGPset, but is simpler and less expensive than its prototype. This specialized set appeared as a result of Intel's policy of dividing up the computer market according to performance and price with the aim of optimizing the price/performance index of their products. The performance and functional abilities of the i440ZX are slightly less than those of the i440BX, due, of course, to its simpler architecture.

This chipset is oriented towards Celeron, Pentium II, and Pentium III processors with Slot 1 or Socket 370, and an FSB frequency of 66 or 100 MHz.

The built-in memory controller supports: SDRAM memory — from 8 to 256 MB; 2 DIMM modules; 64 bit interface; PC66/100 SDRAM; 16-, 64-bit microcircuitry; you may use an EDO DRAM (60 nsec), etc. Supports plug-and-play mode for DIMM modules through the Serial Presence Detect (SPD) mechanism, using the SMBus interface.

Built-in to the AGP and the PGI are means of supporting: PCI Rev.2.1 3.3 V and 5 V, 33 MHz; 4 PCI; AGP Rev.1.0 with 1X/2X modes, 66/133 MHz 3.3 V; 2 USB ports, 2 IDE ports with UltraDMA/33, ACPI, and other functions and components.

However, in contrast to the i440BX AGPset, besides the lowering of the maximum amount of memory allowed, this chipset will not support two-processor architecture, parity control, or ECC.

The i440ZX AGPset consists of two chips: the 82443ZX Host Bridge (492 BGA) and the 82371EB (PIIX4E).

i815. The i815, i815E and i815EP chipsets are built on the basis of Accelerated Hub Architecture, and are intended for high-performance computers based on Pentium II/Pentium III-type processors with Slot 1 and Socket 370 and an FSB frequency of 66/100/133 MHz.

The built-in memory controller supports: SDRAM memory — up to 512 MB, up to 3 DIMM modules, 64 bit interface, PC100/133 SDRAM, etc.

This chipset also has built-in support of: AGP 1X/2X/4X, integrated graphics on an i752 basis (i815, i815E), up to 6 PCIs, 2 (i815) or 4 (i815E, i815EP) USB ports, 2 IDE ports with either UltraDMA/33/66 (i815) or UltraDMA/33/66/100 (i815E, i815EP), LAN (i815E, i815EP) controller, AC'97 audio with 2 (i815) or 6 (i815E, i815EP) channels, ACPI and other functions and components.

The i815 chipset consists of three chips: the 82815 Graphics and Memory Controller Hub (GMCH), the 82801AA I/O Controller Hub (ICH), and the 82802 Firmware Hub (FWH).

The i815E chipset consists of 3 chips: the 82815 Graphics and Memory Controller Hub (GMCH), the 82801BA I/O Controller Hub (ICH2), and the 82802 Firmware Hub (FWH).

The i815EP chipset consists of 3 chips: the 82815EP Memory Controller Hub (MCH), the 82801BA I/O Controller Hub (ICH2), and the 82802 Firmware Hub (FWH).

There are also variations of the i815 chipset that support Pentium III and Celeron processors based on the Tualatin core. These chipsets are marked as B-step.

i850. The i850 chipset is built based on Accelerated Hub Architecture, and is intended for high-performance computers using Pentium 4 processors with either Socket 423 or Socket 478 and an FSB frequency of 100 MHz (400 MHz Data Bus and 200 MHz Address Bus).

The built-in memory controller supports: 2 RDRAM memory channels — up to 2 GB, up to 4 RIMM modules, PC800 RIMM, etc.

This chipset also has built-in support of: AGP 1X/2X/4X, up to 6 PCIs, 4 USB ports, 2 IDE ports with UltraDMA/33/66/100, LAN controller, AC'97 audio with 6 channels, ACPI, and other functions and components.

The i850 chipset consists of 3 chips: the 82850 Memory Controller Hub (MCH), the 82801BA I/O Controller Hub (ICH2), and the 82802 Firmware Hub (FWH).

i845. The i845 and i845D chipsets are built on the basis of Accelerated Hub Architecture, and are intended for high-performance computers using Pentium 4 processors with Socket 478 (there are also Socket 423 motherboards) and an FSB frequency of 100 MHz (400 MHz Data Bus and 200 MHz Address Bus).

The built-in memory controller of the i845 supports: SDRAM memory — up to 3 MB, up to 3 DIMM modules, 64-bit interface, PC133 SDRAM, etc.

The built-in memory controller of the i845D supports DDR SDRAM memory.

This chipsets also have built-in support of: AGP 1X/2X/4X, up to 6 PCIs, 4 USB ports, 2 IDE ports with UltraDMA/33/66/100, LAN controller, AC'97 audio with 6 channels, ACPI, and other functions and components.

The i845 chipset consists of 3 chips: the 82845 Memory Controller Hub (MCH), the 82801BA I/O Controller Hub (ICH2), and the 82802 Firmware Hub (FWH).

VIA Chipsets

VIA Apollo Pro Plus. This chipset was developed by VIA Technologies. This is an improved version of the VIA Apollo Pro chipset with an expanded set of power management functions. It is oriented towards high-performance mobile and desktop systems based on processors with Slot 1 (Intel Pentium II) and Socket 370 (Intel Celeron). This chipset is intended to operate at a processor bus frequency of 66 and 100 MHz and at an internal frequency of 450 MHz and higher. It supports: a 64-bit memory bus, parity control and ECC, FP DRAM, EDO DRAM, and SDRAM memories — up to 1 GB, 8 memory banks in case of using more than one type of memory, pipelined — up to 533 MB/sec. Besides, it supports: EIDE, UltraDMA/33, USB v.1.0, AGP 1.0 with 1/2, PCI 2.1 (up to 5 PCIs), ISA, Side-Band Addressing (SBA) mode, ACPI, etc.

The chipset consists of two chips included in the standard BGA packages: VT82C693 — North Bridge, VT82C596A — South Bridge (Mobile South).

Besides the set consisting of the VT82C693 and the VT82C596A, there is a version of the VIA Apollo Pro Plus that instead of the VT82C596A uses the VT82C686A chip — South Bridge (Super South), with built-in support of UltraDMA/66, AC'97 (which allows you to utilize inexpensive built-in sound and modem software), etc.

With the aim of perfecting the architecture of the VIA Apollo Pro and the VIA Apollo Pro Plus, the developers created a better-performance product, engineered using the newest accomplishments in computer technology. One of the most interesting and likely most important characteristics of the new specialized set is its ability to use raised frequencies for the processor bus and the memory bus. This chipset was the first set to support a frequency of 133 MHz, which was reflected by the product name itself. The new chipset was given the name VIA Apollo Pro133.

VIA Apollo Pro133. The VIA Apollo Pro133 chipset was developed by VIA Technologies. This chipset is oriented towards high-performance systems such as those with Pentium Pro, Celeron, Pentium II, and Pentium III processors with Socket 8, Slot 1, or Socket 370. The VIA Apollo Pro 133 is intended for work at processor bus frequencies of 66, 100, and 133 MHz. It supports an asynchronous 64-bit memory bus, parity control and ECC, FP DRAM, EDO DRAM, SDRAM, and VCM (Virtual Channel Memory) SDRAM memories — up to 1.5 GB in 8 memory banks, UltraDMA/33 and UltraDMA/66, 4 USBs, AGP 1.0 with 1/2, PCI 2.1

(up to 5 PCIs), ACPI, etc. The architecture of this chipset is able to support a new frequency divider for the AGP bus: 1/2, which allows setting the standard 66 MHz frequency for AGP bus, even when using a processor bus frequency of 133 MHz.

The VIA Apollo pro133 chipset, like most traditional chipsets, consists of two chips within standard BGA packaging: the VT82C693A — North Bridge, and the VT82C686A — South Bridge — Mobile Bridge.

There is also a more perfected version of this chipset released under the name of VIA Apollo Pro133A.

In addition to the functionality supported by VIA Apollo Pro 133, this version also includes additional capabilities, among which is AGP 4X.

Among the important characteristics of the VIA Apollo Pro 133A, you should note that it supports: 66/100/133 MHz FSB GTL+ standard; synchronous and pseudo-synchronous bus modes, which allow you to set the frequency higher for memory modules (+33 MHz); SDRAM, VCM SDRAM, ESDRAM, and EDO DRAM memories, with the ability to use different types at the same time in order to use them most efficiently, up to a maximum capacity of 2 GB, and 8 memory banks, etc. Note that the PC133 specifications recommend a limit of three DIMM modules or six banks at 133 MHz as the maximum capacity of a 1.5 GB RAM.

Synchronous and pseudo-synchronous bus modes allow you to set the frequency of the memory modules higher (+33 MHz) or lower (–33 MHz) than the FSB frequency.

The chipset also supports: AGP 2.0 specifications with AGP 1X/2X/4X modes, PC 2.1 specifications, UltraDMA/33/66 modes for EIDE and USB ports, Keyboard/PS2-Mouse interfaces, and RTC/CMOS included in the VT82C694X chip.

The VIA Apollo Pro133A chipset includes two chips: the VT82C694X — North Bridge, and the VT82C596B — Mobile Bridge — South Bridge.

The structure of computers with the VIA Apollo Pro133A chipset is presented in Fig. 17.10.

Within the VIA Apollo Pro133A chipset, a VT82C686A might be used as a South Bridge. The set, consisting of the VT82C694X and the VT82C686A chips, allows you to create a high-performance multimedia system. In such a case, the VT82C694X North Bridge is responsible for interaction with the processor, memory, and graphics, while the VT82C694X South Bridge deals with all peripheral devices. The VT82C694X South Bridge includes support for UltraDMA/66, AC'97 (which allows you to utilize inexpensive built-in sound and modem software, but at the cost of a loss in overall performance of approximately 10% due to the additional burden on the CPU), 2 USBs, etc. This chip is used relatively often in VIA chipsets, including the VIA Pro Plus133 A, a chipset that has become one of the most popular chipsets released by VIA Technology.

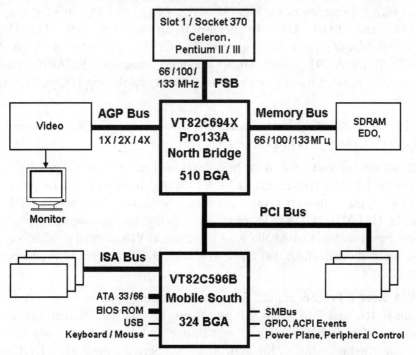

Fig. 17.10. The structure of a computer with the VIA Apollo Pro 133A chipset

VIA Apollo KX133. This chipset has also been developed by VIA Technology. It is oriented towards systems that use AMD Athlon processors with Slot A, and that work with an EV6 bus as the FSB, which guarantees data transfer on both fronts of the clock pulse. The chipset supports an asynchronous 64-bit memory bus with a frequency of 66/100/133 MHz; PC133 and PC100 SDRAM, VCM SDRAM, and EDO DRAM memory types in various combinations up to 2 GB; UltraDMA/33 and UltraDMA/66; PCI 2.2; up to 5 PCI components; 4 USB ports; AGP 1X/2X/4X; AC'97 audio; MC'97 modem; integrated IO/APIC; hardware monitoring; advanced mobile power management; clock stop, PC98/99 compatibility, etc.

The VIA Apollo KX133 chipset consists of two chips: the VT8371 — North Bridge, and the VT82C686A — South Bridge.

VIA Apollo KT133. This chipset was developed by VIA Technology. It is oriented towards systems that use AMD Duron and the AMD Athlon processors with Socket A (Socket 462). They are intended for work with an EV6 bus as the FSB. The standard clock frequency of the FSB EV6 is 100 MHz, which guarantees data transfer at a frequency of 200 MHz. It supports an asynchronous 64-bit memory bus with a frequency of 66/100/133 MHz; PC133 and PC100 SDRAM, VCM SDRAM, and EDO DRAM memories up to 1.5 GB; UltraDMA/33 and UltraDMA/66; PCI 2.2; up to 5 PCI components; 4 USB ports; AGP 1X/2X/4X AC'97 audio; MC'97 modem; integrated IO/APIC; hardware monitoring; advanced mobile power management; clock stop, PC98/99 compatibility, etc.

The VIA Apollo KT133 chipset consists of two chips: the VT8363 — North Bridge, and the VT82C686A — South Bridge.

Based on this chipset, the firm has developed an enhanced product named VIA Apollo KT133A (North Bridge — VT8363A). In contrast to its predecessor, this new chipset supports both 200 MHz frequency (100 MHz DDR) and 266 MHz (133 MHz DDR). In order to simplify the development process for products based on the VIA Apollo KT133A chipset, VIA created a reference design for the motherboard, which was taken as a basis by all vendors of products of this category.

The **VIA Apollo Pro266** chipset is oriented towards systems based on Celeron, Pentium II/III, and VIA Cyrix III processors for Socket 370 that support FSB frequencies of 66/100/133 MHz. North Bridge and South Bridge are connected using the V-Link bus (266 MB/sec). Supported memory: DDR200/266 (PC1600/2100) SDRAM or PC66/100/133 SDRAM — up to 4 GB. North Bridge — VT8633, South Bridge — VT 8233.

VIA Apollo KT266. Oriented towards systems based on AMD Athlon and AMD Duron Socket A processors with the following FSB frequencies: 100/133 MHz. North Bridge and South Bridge are connected using the V-Link bus (266 MB/sec). Supported memory: DDR200/266 (PC1600/2100) SDRAM or PC66/100/133 SDRAM — up to 4 GB. North Bridge — VT8366, South Bridge — VT 8233.

Based on this chipset, VIA has developed a more advanced product known as VIA Apollo KT266A, with North Bridge VT8366A, including a more advanced high-performance memory controller.

VIA P4X266. Oriented towards systems based on Pentium 4 processors for Socket 423 and Socket 478 with an FSB frequency of 100 MHz (400 MHz Data

Bus and 200 MHz Address Bus). North Bridge and South Bridge are connected by a V-Link bus (266 MB/sec). Supported memory: DDR200/266 (PC1600/2100) SDRAM or PC100/133 SDRAM — up to 4 GB. North Bridge — P4X266, South Bridge — VT 8233.

There is also an improved product known as VIA P4X266A. Support for Pentium 4 processors with 133 MHz FSB frequency (533 MHz Data Bus) was added.

It is necessary to mention that improved products based on chipsets oriented towards Intel Celeron and Pentium II/III have been released. These improved chipsets support the use of processors with the Tualatin core (0.13 µm). These improved variations are marked by adding the letter T to the traditional markings of the chipsets, for example: VIA Apollo Pro133T, VIA Apollo Pro266T, etc.

Chipsets from VIA allow you to create systems with a wide range of functional capabilities. When it comes to performance, however, systems based on the VIA Apollo ProPlus, the VIA Apollo Pro133, or the VIA Apollo Pro133A generally fall a little short of analogous systems built on the basis of i440BX and i440ZX chipsets — the VIA Apollo ProPlus and the VIA Apollo Pro133 by about 10—20%, and the VIA Apollo Pro133A by 5—10%.

Systems with i815E and i815 chipsets are no worse than analogous sets based on the i440 BX. However, the i815E and the i815 differ from their predecessors in that an FSB frequency of 133 MHz is one of the standard work modes. This is why these chipsets support a divisor for the AGP bus of not only 2/3 (of the FSB), but also 1/2, which makes it easier to choose the optimal overcloking mode for the video adapter.

Comparative Characteristics of the VIA and Intel Chipsets

Characteristics	VIA	VIA	Intel	Intel	Intel	Intel
	Apollo Pro133A	Apollo ProPlus	815E	815	440BX	440ZX
North Bridge	VT82C694X	VT82C693	82815	82815	82443BX	82443ZX
Processors	Celeron Pentium II/III	Celeron Pentium II/III	Celeron Pentium III	Celeron Pentium III	Celeron Pentium II/III	Celeron Pentium II/III
FSB type	GTL+	GTL+	AGTL+	AGTL+	GTL+	GTL+
Frequency of the FSB, MHz	66/100/133	66/100	66/100/133	66/100/133	66/100	66/100
Memory bus, MHz	66/100/133	66/100	100/133	100/133	66/100	66/100

continues

Continued

Characteristics	VIA	VIA	Intel	Intel	Intel	Intel
Maximum capacity, MB	2,048	1,024	512	512	1,024	256
Memory modules	PC66/100/133	PC66/100	PC100/133	PC100/133	PC66/100	PC66/100
Memory type	SDRAM VCM SDRAM EDO DRAM	SDRAM VCM SDRAM EDO DRAM	SDRAM	SDRAM	SDRAM EDO DRAM	SDRAM EDO DRAM
Max. DIMM	4	4	3	3	4	2
ECC	yes	yes	no	no	no	no
Asynchronous modes	yes	yes	yes	yes	no	no
AGP	1X/2X/4X	1X/2X	1X/2X/4X	1X/2X/4X	1X/2X	1X/2X
Integrated graphics	no	no	yes	yes	no	no
South Bridge	VT82C596B	VT82C596B	82801BA	82801AA	PXII4	PXII4
IDE	UltraDMA/66/33	UltraDMA/66/33	UltraDMA/100	UltraDMA/66	UltraDMA/33	UltraDMA/33

Chapter 18

Cooling Devices and Methods

I n order to guarantee the reliable and stable functioning of the elements and subsystems of the computer in normal and especially in overcloking modes, you must ensure that they are being properly cooled. This can be achieved using the following methods:

❑ Choosing and using an appropriate case

❑ Acquiring an effective heatsink

❑ Acquiring an effective cooling fan

❑ Using the appropriate software coolers

For the architecture of modern computers, the best choice of case is the standard ATX. Taking into consideration the high heat flux from the elements used in overcloking modes, it makes sense to direct your attention towards the mini ATX cases, or even the larger midi ATXs, which guarantee better temperature conditions for all components of the system.

It's advisable to supply the case you selected with an additional fan(s), which will lower the air temperature inside the given case. This will improve the efficiency of all local cooling devices.

Beginning with 486DX2/66 processors, heatsinks have become an integral attribute of all processors. Along with the growth of CPU processing power, the heat flux has also grown, and thus the size of the heatsinks also had to be increased. Starting with Pentium processors, heatsinks began coming with a cooling fan mounted onto them. These devices are also known simply as coolers.

In order to improve the heat contact between the body of the element to be cooled and the attached heatsink, it makes sense to buy and use special thermal grease, or thermal tape. These thermal compounds eliminate tiny air gaps between the body of the element and the heatsink attached to it. This improves heat transfer to the heatsink, and therefore provides more efficient cooling.

Heatsinks and Fans

Using heatsinks allows you to guarantee the best temperature conditions for the electronic components. Heatsinks intensify heat exchange between cooled elements, such as the CPU, the video chipset, etc. and their surrounding environments. This is achieved due to fact that the heatsink area is significantly larger than the area of the cooled element itself. The larger the heatsink surface area, the more intense will be the heat dissipation from the cooled element. There is a large variety of technologies used for heatsink manufacturing, which affect its quality. However, note that high-quality heatsinks are generally not only effective, but expensive as well. Usually, these high-priced heatsinks are the best choices for a cooling system.

Heatsinks are usually made from aluminum − an inexpensive material that has a high heat conductivity. Copper, of course, is better, but is much more expensive. Besides which, copper weighs much more, which would increase the weight of the heatsink and complicate the problem of mounting it.

You know from physics, of course, that darker objects radiate heat better than lighter ones. This is exactly why when choosing a heatsink, the preferred color is black. Note, however, that the black color is achieved by using special technology such as chemical treatments, dusting with special substances, etc. Of course, you couldn't just paint the heatsink black, as the paint is a heat insulator rather than a conductor.

The most important characteristics of a heatsink are its *thermal conductivity* and *thermal resistance*. Thermal resistance is a quantity, the opposite of thermal conductivity, that to a large extent depends on the material from which the heatsink is composed. Thermal resistance is measured in °C/W. You must keep in mind that the value of this parameter is affected not only by the material that the heatsink is made of, but also by its size, form, etc., as well as by the technology used, and the quality of manufacturing. Thermal resistance is the amount by which the temperature of the heatsink rises relative to the temperature of the immediate surroundings when the cooled element, for example, a processor, with the power capacity of 1 W, is dissipating heat. For example, at a thermal resistance level of 2°C/W, and dissipation from a processor that uses 15 W, the temperature will increase by 30°C. The value of this parameter is usually between 0.5 and 2°C/W. By the way, the design of the heatsink plays an important role, more important than even its size. This is why bigger is not necessarily better.

An example of a heatsink for processors that use socket is presented in Fig. 18.1.

The best cooling devices have a construction that consists of a heatsink and a fan. The fan is usually set over the heatsink, which is attached to the object to be cooled. The fan moves hot air away from the heatsink while simultaneously supplying it with cooler air.

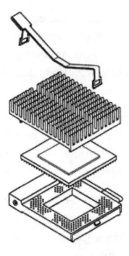

Fig. 18.1. An example of a heatsink for a processor

There are several types of fans; the most common ones used on CPU heatsinks are sleeve bearing fans and ball bearing fans. Fans with ball bearings are preferable. This is because sleeve bearings generally are less reliable and usually make more noise. Fans that use ball bearings work on the average two times as long as sleeve bearings. Note that most popular fans labeled as "ball bearing" actually have one ball bearing and one sleeve bearing. Most overclockers highly recommend buying only ball bearing fans, also known as a "double ball bearing" coolers. By using a double ball bearing cooler, the service life of the fan is at least 1.5 times longer than is estimated for one that uses both types of bearings.

The life of the fan is usually 2—3 years. However, you should clean the dust that collects on the fan no less than once a year. The dust accumulates with time, and this may significantly degrade the parameters of the cooling equipment, or even stop the fan completely. If the cooler fails, the cooled component (processor, video chip, etc.) will also fail very soon due to overheating. Note that in order to avoid the processor overheating due to a fan failure, modern hardware and software components, such as the processor itself, motherboard, BIOS, and system software, provide an entire system of preventive defense against overheating. Such a system includes various sensors that control both the temperature and the voltage. When buying hardware components, make sure that this function is present.

There are certain basic parameters that characterize the performance of the fan. These parameters are CFM, LFPM, and RPM.

❑ The CFM (Cubic Feet per Minute) parameter characterizes the volumetric flow rate, that is, it shows how many cubic feet of air the fan blows per minute. For most modern CPU fans this parameter is about 10—12 CFM.

❑ The LFPM (Linear Feet Per Minute) parameter characterizes the linear flow rate of the airflow (feet per minute). A typical value is 500—600. By multiplying the LFPM value by the cross-section area of the air flow from the fan, you get the CFM value.

❑ The RPM (Rotations Per Minute) parameter shows the fan speed (in rotations per minute). A typical value for this parameter is 4,000—6,000 RPM.

The larger the value of each of these parameters, the higher the performance of the fan, and thus the better it performs its functions as a cooling system element.

The dimensions of fans for modern processors are usually 50×50×10 mm.

The noise level, measured in decibels (dB), is another parameter that characterizes the quality of the fan. A high noise level affects your nerves and may annoy you. High-quality fans are those with a noise level about 20—25 dB (the lower the noise level, the better for you). Sometimes, a high noise level is due to the construction of the fan. Therefore, another sign of a high quality fan is the absence of significant vibration. If you feel the fan vibrating while holding it in your hand, then the fan is not of a very high quality, and you should direct your attention to a better one.

An example of a fan is presented in Fig. 18.2.

Fig. 18.2. An example of a fan for a processor

Usually, a cooling device consists of two parts: a heatsink and a fan, which together work as an efficient high-performance cooler. When selecting the best cooler you should pay attention to the brand name products of well-known manufacturers. Their products are generally highly reliable and have stable parameters.

And of course, the cooler of choice should perform well. As examples of such coolers, it is necessary to mention the products from companies like Intel, Titan, Thermaltake, Iwill, ASUSTeK, Sanyo, AVC, etc.

Fig. 18.3 presents a diagram of a cooler consisting of a fan with a heatsink attached to a processor that uses Socket 7.

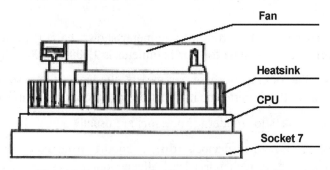

Fig. 18.3. An example of a processor's cooler

In Fig. 18.4, an external view of a popular cooler from Sanyo is presented.

Fig. 18.4. The external view of a cooler from Sanyo

The Intel cooler (Fig. 18.5) is supplied with a Pentium III 700 processor in the box version. This cooler is optimal for these processors, and can be used with them both in nominal modes and in moderate overcloking modes (10—20%). However, if you are using extreme overcloking modes characterized by high frequencies and voltage levels, it is recommended that you use either the Intel coolers supplied with more powerful models or implement more intense cooling. As an example, one can mention such cooler models as TTC-D2T (Fig. 18.6), TTC-D3T,

TTC-D3TB from Titan, and Chrome Orb (Fig. 18.7) or Super Orb from Thermaltake. The results of testing these coolers can be found at various Internet sites, for example at the iXBT site.

Fig. 18.5. The Intel cooler recommended for the Pentium III 700 processor

Fig. 18.6. The TTC-D2T cooler from Titan recommended for AMD Duron and AMD Athlon (Thunderbird) processors

Fig. 18.7. The Chrome Orb cooler from Thermaltake

Without covering the structural details of the above-listed popular coolers, it should be pointed out that their parameters are quite similar. This is especially true for products from Titan and Thermaltake. Tests have shown that the temperature modes of processors supported by coolers from these vendors differ by about 3—5°. Within the range from 50—60 degrees, this difference is not significant. Quite often, other factors, such as cable layout (which influences the air circulation within the system unit) and the positioning of supplementary fans, have a greater impact on the temperature modes of the processor.

Keep in mind that the processor is not the only component that requires intensive cooling. Quite often, intensive cooling is also required by ICs forming chipsets, by video adapters, and by certain types of memory chips as well. It is also strongly recommended that you cool high-performance, large-capacity hard drives, as their operation, too, is accompanied by significant heat release, especially in overcloking modes.

Examples of Coolers
Choosing a Cooler for Pentium I/III Processors

When selecting an efficient cooler for Intel Pentium II or Pentium III processors, you should pay attention to all of the basic principles of selecting a high-quality heatsink and fan. However, there are certain particular features that stem from the design of the processors under consideration conforming to the Slot 1 and Slot 2 standards. These particular features influence both the process and the result of selection.

First, make sure that the airflow through the heatsink will be powerful enough. You can ensure this by using heatsinks of the appropriate form.

Second, in relation to the fact that the processor chip is rectangular, you have to make sure that the airflow reaches the very ends of the given chip in order to ensure effective cooling. You can achieve this by using closed heatsinks. In such heatsinks, the side fins are unbroken, and sometimes special forms, etc. are even used.

Presented in Fig. 18.8 is a diagram of a relatively inexpensive but effective heatsink for processors with the standard Slot 1. This heatsink is made with its major parts positioned as indicated, thanks to which the air blast blows freely through the entire cooler, sufficiently cooling the heatsink, and therefore the processor.

This diagram of the cooler construction allows you to organize intensive cooling of the Pentium II or Pentium III processor chip. It is exactly this type of cooler that works well as cooling equipment for Intel Celeron processors with the standard Slot 1 that have been set to and are being used in overcloking modes.

Fig. 18.8. Example of a cooler for Pentium II/III

Coolers from Titan

Processor Cooling

Name	Processors (max. frequency, MHz)	RPM	CFM	Noise level, dB	Bearings type
MGF586M	P (200)	4,500	6.7	24	sleeve/1 ball/ 2 ball
MGFK615M	P (233), Cyrix (200), K6 (200)	4,800	10.5	24	sleeve/1 ball/ 2 ball
MGFK620M	P (233), Cyrix (233), K6 (266)	4,800	10.5	24	sleeve/1 ball/ 2 ball
TTC-588H	P (233), Cyrix (300), K6 (300)	4,600	9.5	24/25/25	sleeve/1 ball/ 2 ball
TTC-586S3	P (233), Cyrix (300), K6 (300)	4,600	9.5	25	sleeve/1 ball/ 2 ball
TIC-K2M	PII (266)	4,800	10.5	24	sleeve/1 ball/ 2 ball

continues

Continued

Name	Processors (max. frequency, MHz)	RPM	CFM	Noise level, dB	Bearings type
TIC-601H	PII (300)	4,800/5,000/ 5,200	6.0/6.1/6.3	23/24/25	sleeve/1 ball/ 2 ball
TIC-602H	PII (350)	3,900/4,100/ 4,300	8.0/8.6/9.0	21/22/22	sleeve/1 ball/ 2 ball
TIC-605H	PII (300)	4,800	10.5	22/24/24	sleeve/1 ball/ 2 ball

Cooling the System Unit

Name	RPM	CFM	Noise level, dB	Bearings type
TTC-001	3,400	6.0	30/31/32	sleeve/1 ball/2 ball
TTC-002	2,400	30.0	32/34/34	sleeve/1 ball/2 ball
TTC-HD12	2,400	30.0	32/34/34	sleeve/1 ball/2 ball
TTC-HD22	5,000	5.0	24/25/25	sleeve/1 ball/2 ball

Coolers from Global Win

Cooling for Processors with Socket 7

Name	Processors	Thermal resistance, $^\circ$C/W	Bearings type	RPM	CFM	Service life, hours	Noise level, dB
VBP04	AMD-K6-233 28.3 W	0.79	Ball bearing	4,000— 5,400	9.4	43,968 (45°C)	29.0
FK516	AMD-K6-233 28.3 W	0.77/0.67	Ball bearing	5,000/ 5,800	8.5/ 12.0	33,165/2 7083	27.2/27.0
VC502	AMD-K6-200	0.95	Ball bearing	4,000— 5,400	8.0	42,890 (45°C)	30.0
VB504	AMD-K6-166 12.7 W, Cyrix 200, Pentium 233	1.00	Ball bearing	4,000— 5,400	11.3	36,968	29.0

Cooling Intel Pentium II processors

Name	Processors	Thermal resistance, $°C/W$	Bearings type	RPM	CFM	Service life, hours	Noise level, dB
FHK20	iPII 300, 400	0.59	Ball bearing	4,500—5,500	11.0	32,000 (45°C)	25
VBK04	iPII 300, 400	0.61	Ball bearing	3,900—5,300	9.2	41,000 (45°C)	29
VAK16	iPII 300, 400	0.54	Ball bearing	4,500—5,500	8.1	37,646 (45°C)	29

Cooling Intel Celeron processors

Name	Processors	Thermal conductivity, $W/m \times K$	Bearings type	RPM	CFM	Service life, hours	Noise level, dB
FAB04	iCeleron 333	5.0—6.5	Ball bearing	3,900—5,300	11	4,100 (45°C)	30

SAN ACE MC Coolers from Sanyo

Performance of SAN ACE MC Coolers

Model	RPM	Thermal resistance, $°C/W$	Noise level, dB	Weight, g	Size, mm
109P4405H8026	5,000	1.70	27	48	45×18
109P4412H8026	5,000	1.70	27	48	45×18
109P5405H8026	5,400	1.40	29	57	54×18
109P5412H8026	5,400	1.40	29	57	54×18
109P5405H2026	4,000	0.97	28	78	50.8×30
109P5412H2026	4,000	0.97	28	78	50.8×30
109P6605H2026	3,600	0.79	29	126	66×62×30
109P6612H2026	3,600	0.79	29	126	66×62×30

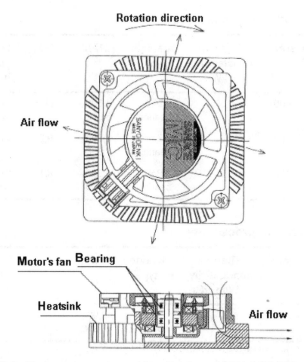

Fig. 18.9. The components and functioning of SAN ACE MC coolers

The following characteristics are common for Sanyo coolers:

❑ Operating temperature ranges from $-10°C$ to $+60°C$

❑ Every cooler has a defense system that prevents the fan from failures due to the wrong polarity being set when connecting the cooler

❑ The average time of trouble-free operation is 40,000 hours at the temperature of $60°C$

A diagram of the components and functioning of SAN ACE MC coolers is presented in Fig. 18.9.

Recommended Coolers for Certain Processors

Processor	Frequency, MHz	Recommended cooler model
Pentium II (SECC)	233, 266	109X1512H3016
	300	109X1512S3016

continues

Continued

Processor	Frequency, MHz	Recommended cooler model
Pentium II (SECC)	333—450	109X1512H3016
Pentium II (Slot 1, PLGA)	350	109X1512H2066
Pentium II (Slot 1, OLGA)	400, 450	109X1512H2076
Celeron (SEPP)	266—400	109X1512H2016
Celeron (PPGA)	366, 400	109X6512H2016
		109X6512H2026
Pentium	90—150	109P4412H8026
	166, 200	109P5412H2026
Pentium MMX	166—233	109P5412H2026
Pentium Pro	150—200	109P6612H2026

Fans and Coolers from AVC

Fans from AVC measuring 50×50 mm are relatively popular. They are used in many cooling systems.

Parameters of 5010 (12 V) Fans

Model	Bearings type	RPM	CFM	Noise level, dB
D5010S12E	sleeve	3,500	9.32	22.0
D5010T12E	sleeve and ball	3,500	9.32	22.0
D5010B12E	double-ball	3,500	9.32	22.0
D5010S12L	sleeve	4,000	10.48	24.0
D5010T12L	sleeve and ball	4,200	10.73	25.0
D5010B12L	double-ball	4,200	10.73	25.0

contunues

Continued

Model	Bearings type	RPM	CFM	Noise level, dB
D5010S12M	sleeve	5,000	12.14	30.0
D5010T12M	sleeve and ball	5,200	12.78	30.5
D5010B12M	double-ball	5,200	12.78	30.5
D5010T12H	sleeve and ball	6,200	14.79	34.5
D5010B12H	double-ball	6,200	14.79	34.5
B5010T12E	sleeve and ball	3,500	9.32	22.0
B5010B12E	double-ball	3,500	9.32	22.0
B5010T12L	sleeve and ball	4,200	10.73	25.0
B5010B12L	double-ball	4,200	10.73	25.0
B5010T12M	sleeve and ball	5,200	12.78	30.5
B5010B12M	double-ball	5,200	12.78	30.5
B5010T12H	sleeve and ball	6,200	14.79	34.5
B5010B12H	double-ball	6,200	14.79	34.5

Parameters of 5010 (12 V) Fans (with Sensor)

Model	Bearings type	RPM	CFM	Noise level, dB
C5010T12E	sleeve and ball	3,500	9.32	22.0
C5010B12E	double-ball	3,500	9.32	22.0
C5010T12L	sleeve and ball	4,200	10.73	25.0
C5010B12L	double-ball	4,200	10.73	25.0
C5010T12M	sleeve and ball	5,200	12.78	30.5
C5010B12M	double-ball	5,200	12.78	30.5
C5010T12H	sleeve and ball	6,200	14.79	34.5
C5010B12H	double-ball	6,200	14.79	34.5
C5010B12HK	double-ball	6,200	14.79	34.5

Certain other Coolers from AVC

Processor	Frequency, MHz	Cooler
Pentium II	266–450	P2-60B-B
Pentium II	233	P2-632-B
Pentium II	266	P2-639-B, P2-640-B
Pentium II	266–450	P2-652-B
Pentium/Cyrix 6x86/AMD K5	200/166/166	58603
Pentium/Cyrix M2/AMD K6	233/200/200	58605A(CH629)
Pentium/Cyrix M2/AMD K6	233/233/233	58605B(CH616), 58605C(CH644)

Coolers from Coolmaster

Coolers for processors with Socket 7

❏ **DP5-5021**

- Processors:

  AMD K6 166/200/233/266/300, K6-2 266/300/333/350, Cyrix 6x86 P120/P133/P150/P166/P200, 6x86MX PR166/PR200/PR233/PR266, MII 300/333/350, IBM 6x86MX PR166/PR200/PR233/PR266, IDT WinChip C6 150/180/200/225/240, WinChip 2 200/225/240/250/266, Intel Pentium 60/66/75/90/100/120/133/150/166/200, Pentium MMX 166/200/233/266

- Heatsink — 52×50×20 mm

- Fan — 50×50×10 mm, 5,500 RPM, 9.8 CFM, 29 dB

❏ **TP5-5020**

- Processors:

  AMD K6 166/200/233/266/300, K6-2 266/300/333/350/366/380/400, Cyrix 6x86 P120/P133, 6x86MX PR166/PR200, IBM 6x86MX PR166/PR200, IDT WinChip C6 150/180/200/225/240, WinChip 2 200/225/240/250/266, Intel Pentium 60/66/75/90/100/120/133/150/166/200, Pentium MMX 166/200/233/266

- Heatsink — 50×52×20 mm

- Fan — 50×50×10 mm, 5,000 RPM, 9.8 CFM, 28 dB

Coolers for processors with Slot 1:

❑ **DP2-5020**

- Processors:

  Intel Pentium II 233/266/300/333/350/400/450

- Heatsink — 120×52×20 mm

- Fan — 50×50×10 mm, 5,500 RPM, 9.8 CFM, 30 dB

❑ **TP2-5020**

- Processors:

  Intel Pentium II 233/333/350/400/450

- Heatsink — 120×52×20 mm

- Fan — 50×50×10 mm, 5,000 RPM, 9.8 CFM, 30 dB

Peltier Semiconductor Coolers

The operation of modern high-performance electronic components, upon which the whole architecture of a modern computer is based, is accompanied by significant heat release, especially in overcloking modes. Efficient operation of such components requires adequate cooling in order to ensure the required temperature conditions. It is a common practice to use special cooling devices or coolers to ensure optimum temperature conditions. Generally, these coolers are based on traditional heatsinks and fans.

The reliability and performance of such cooling devices are being constantly improved due to technological advances, improvements in their design, and implementation of several management facilities, including various sensors. This ensures the possibility of integrating such facilities with computer systems, providing diagnostic and management facilities for controlling temperature conditions. This most certainly will improve reliability and prolong the trouble-free operation of hardware components.

The parameters of traditional coolers are being constantly improved. Despite this fact, some specific cooling devices, like semiconductor Peltier coolers, have recently appeared on the market. These new cooling devices soon became very popular.

Peltier coolers contain special semiconductor thermoelectric modules. Their operating principles are based on the Peltier effect, discovered in 1834. These cooling devices have impressive perspectives. They have been successfully used for a long time in various branches of science and technology.

In the sixties and seventies there were multiple attempts at implementing small-sized household refrigerators based on the Peltier effect. Unfortunately, the insufficient level of technology and relatively high prices did not allow such a device to be created with the exception of a few experimental instances.

Fortunately, the Peltier effect and thermoelectric modules were never reduced to simply an interesting topic of scientific research. As technology improved, it became possible to reduce most of the negative effects. As a result of these efforts, efficient and reliable semiconductor coolers appeared.

Currently, these modules based on the Peltier effect are actively being used for cooling various electronic components of modern computers, such as processors.

The unique properties of Peltier modules allow you to achieve the required cooling of the computer components, while at the same time avoiding technical problems and significant financial investments. Peltier coolers are very promising, because they are space-saving, reliable, convenient, and very efficient.

The most promising semiconductor coolers are those used for overclocked systems, especially for ones operating in extremely overcloking modes. Extreme overclocking ensures a significant gain in performance, but the temperature conditions of elements in such modes often near the limits of modern hardware endurance.

Notice that high-performance processors are not the only components whose operation is accompanied by significant heat release. Modern video adapters and sometimes memory modules also require a sufficient cooling, even in normal operating modes, not to mention overcloking ones.

Peltier Modules

Peltier coolers are thermoelectric refrigerators, based on the Peltier effect — a phenomenon named after the French watchmaker and amateur physicist Jean C. A. Peltier (1785—1845), who made his discovery more than 150 years ago (in 1834).

The true idea behind this phenomenon was revealed several years later, in 1838, by the German physicist Heinrich F. E. Lenz (1804—1865). While experimenting with electrical current flowing through the junction of two dissimilar conductors, Lenz placed a drop of water into a small cavity at the junction of two bars made of bismuth (Bi) and antimony (Sb). When electric current was flowing in one direction, the drop of water froze. When the current was flowing in the opposite direction, the frozen water melted. This experiment has shown, that whenever electric current flows through the junction of two dissimilar conductors, the junction of two conductors will either absorb or release heat depending on the direction of the current flow. This phenomenon was then named the Peltier effect.

Actually, this effect is the reverse of the Seebeck phenomenon, which was discovered earlier. This phenomenon takes place in a closed electric circuit consisting of dissimilar metals or semiconductors. If there is a temperature difference at the two junction points of dissimilar metals or semiconductors, a voltage potential is induced in the circuit. This phenomenon was discovered in 1821 by the German physicist Thomas J. Seebeck (1770—1831).

According to the well-known Joule's law, a conductor carrying a current generates heat, which is proportional to the product of the resistance (R) of the conductor and the square of the current (I). Thus, Joule heat evolved during the time period (t) is calculated by the following formula:

$$Q_J = R I^2 t$$

In contrast to Joule heat, Peltier heat is proportional to the current, and the direction of heat transfer is reversed if the current is reversed. According to experimental research, Peltier heat can be expressed by the following formula:

$$Q_P = P q$$

where q is the electric charge ($q = It$), and P is the so-called Peltier factor, the value of which depends both on the properties of dissimilar materials carrying the current and on their temperature.

Peltier heat is considered to be positive if it is released, otherwise it is considered negative.

In the course of the experiment conducted according to the scheme represented in Fig. 18.10, the same Joule heat will be released in each calorimeter, if both wires have the same resistance R (Cu+Bi). This heat can be calculated according to the following formula: $Q = R I^2 t$. Peltier heat, on the other hand, will be positive in one calorimeter and negative in the other. This experiment allows us to measure Peltier heat and derive Peltier factor values for different pairs of conductors.

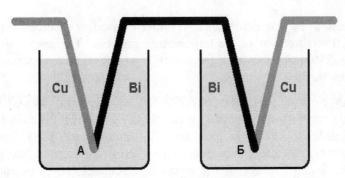

Fig. 18.10. Experimental arrangement for measuring Peltier heat
(Cu — copper, Bi — bismuth)

Note that the Peltier factor strongly depends on the temperature. Several values of Peltier factors for different combinations of metals and alloys at different absolute temperatures are provided in the following table.

Peltier Factors for Various Pairs of Conductors

Fe – constantan		Cu – Ni		Pb – constantan	
T, K	P, mV	T, K	P, mV	T, K	P, mV
273	13.0	292	8.0	293	8.7
299	15.0	328	9.0	383	11.8
403	19.0	478	10.3	508	16.0
513	26.0	563	8.6	578	18.7
593	34.0	613	8.0	633	20.6
833	52.0	718	10.0	713	23.4

The Peltier factor, which is an important technical characteristic of materials, can be calculated using the Thomson coefficient, rather than having to be measured experimentally:

$$P = \alpha T,$$

where P — Peltier factor, α — Thomson coefficient, T — absolute temperature.

This discovery had a huge effect on subsequent developments in physics, and later on in the area of engineering as well.

The idea of the discovered effect is this: when an electric current flows through the junction of two dissimilar materials, besides Joule heat (which is always evolved), additional heat, known as Peltier heat, is either evolved or absorbed depending the direction of the current or of the temperature gradient. The degree to which this effect is manifested depends to a large extent on the chosen conductors and the electric modes used.

Classic theory explains the Peltier effect as follows. Electrons, moved by the current from one conductor to another, speed up or slow down because of the internal potential difference at the junction point. In the first case, the kinetic energy of the electrons increases and is subsequently released in the form of heat. In the second case, the kinetic energy of the electrons decreases, and this energy loss is compensated by heat absorption. The second material, as a result, will be cooled.

The Peltier effect, like other thermoelectric phenomena, most strongly manifests itself in semiconductor circuits, composed of n- and p-type semiconductors.

Let us consider the thermoelectric processes that take place at the contact of such semiconductors. Suppose that the electric field direction causes electrons in the n-semiconductor and holes in p-semiconductor to move towards one another. After passing through the boundary, an electron enters the p-semiconductor zone and takes the place of a hole. This recombination results in heat release (Fig. 18.11).

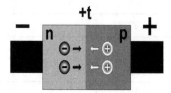

Fig. 18.11. Release of Peltier heat at the contact of n- and p-type semiconductors

If the direction of the electric field is reversed, electrons and holes will move in opposite directions. Holes moving away from the boundary will increase in number due to generation of new pairs that appear when electrons pass from the p-semiconductor to the n-semiconductor. The generation of such pairs consumes energy, and this energy loss is compensated for by the heat oscillations of the atomic lattice. Electrons and holes, generated as a result of appearing pairs, are driven in opposite directions by the electric fields. Therefore, new pairs will continue to appear as long as there is a current through the contact. This will result in heat absorption (Fig. 18.12).

Thus, depending on the direction of the electric current through the contact of semiconductors of different types — p-n- and n-p-junctions — heat will be either released or absorbed depending on the interactions between electrons (n) and holes

(p) and the recombination or generation of new pairs of charges. Usage of p- and n-semiconductors in thermoelectric refrigerators is illustrated in Fig. 18.13.

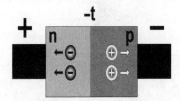

Fig. 18.12. Absorption of Peltier heat at the contact of n- and p-type semiconductors

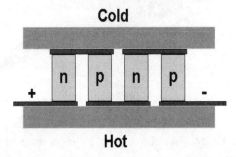

Fig. 18.13. Usage of p- and n-semiconductors in thermoelectric refrigerators

The joining large numbers of n- and p-semiconductor junctions allows the creation of cooling elements − Peltier modules of significant capacity. The structure of a semiconductor Peltier module is represented in Fig. 18.14.

The Peltier module is a thermoelectric refrigerator that consists of coupled p- and n-type semiconductors, which together constitute p-n- and n-p-junctions. Each one of these junctions has heat contact with one of two heatsinks. As a result of an electric current of a certain polarity passing through, there is a drop in temperature between the heatsinks in the Peltier module: one heatsink is working as a refrigerator, the other heats up and abstracts the heat.

Fig. 18.15 shows an external view of a typical Peltier module.

A typical module provides a significant temperature difference, which normally is several tens of degrees. If the hot side is adequately cooled, the other side will achieve negative temperatures. To increase the temperature difference, it is possible to cascade Peltier modules provided that they are properly cooled. This method provides a simple, reliable, and inexpensive way of obtaining a significant temperature difference, sufficient enough to provide efficient cooling for electronic components.

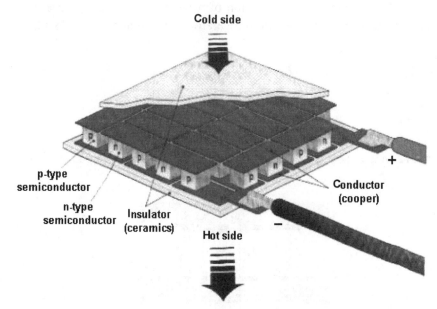

Fig. 18.14. The structure of a Peltier module

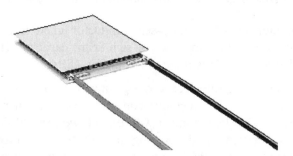

Fig. 18.15. External view of a typical Peltier module

Fig. 18.16 shows an example of cascaded Peltier modules.

A cooling component based on Peltier modules is often called an active Peltier cooler, or more simply, a Peltier cooler.

Using Peltier modules in coolers makes them more efficient in comparison to the standard type of cooler based on the traditional heatsink and fan combination. However, in the process of designing and using coolers that use Peltier modules, you must keep in mind certain specific traits. These specific features are due to the modules' construction, the principles of their operation, the architecture of the hardware of a modern computer, and the functional capabilities of the system and application software.

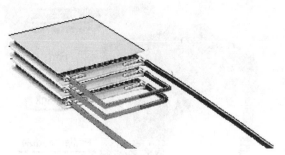

Fig. 18.16. Cascaded Peltier modules

A big role is played by the power of the Peltier module, which generally depends on its size. A not-very-powerful module will not be able to guarantee the level of cooling necessary, which may lead to the failure of the cooled electronic element — the processor for example — as a result of its overheating. However, using a Peltier module that is too powerful may lower the temperature of the cooling heatsink to such a level that the moisture in the air condenses, which is dangerous when dealing with electronic circuits. This is because the water that is constantly being formed as a result of condensation may cause the electronic circuits of the computer to short circuit. This is the time to recall that the distance between lead wires in modern circuit boards is often only a fraction of a millimeter. Nonetheless, and despite everything, it is exactly these powerful Peltier modules in high-performance coolers and in additional cooling systems that allowed KryoTech and AMD, in a combined research project, to overclock AMD processors created with the traditional technology to frequencies higher than 1 GHz. Notice that they managed to almost double the operating frequency. You should note, however, that the given performance level was reached under conditions that ensured the stability and reliability of the processors working in overcloking modes. The result of such an experimental overclocking was a performance record among 80x86 processors. Similar research was conducted with Intel Celeron, Pentium II and Pentium III processors, the result of which was also a significant rise in performance.

Note that Peltier modules, in the process of operating, give off a relatively large amount of heat. For this reason, you should not only have a powerful fan for your cooler, but a means of lowering the temperature of the inside of the computer's case in order to avoid the overheating of the rest of the components. To do this, you should use additional fans in the construction of the case.

An external view of an active cooler that uses semiconductor Peltier modules is presented in Fig. 18.17.

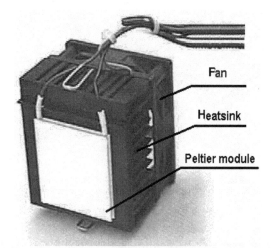

Fig. 18.17. An external view of a cooler with a Peltier module

Keep in mind that cooling systems based on Peltier modules are used not only in electronic systems such as computers. Similar modules are used to cool various high-precision devices. This primarily concerns experimental research in physics, chemistry, and biology.

Information on modules in Peltier coolers, including their features and results of their usage, can be found on the Internet at the following addresses:

❑ www.melcor.com

❑ www.kryotech.com

❑ www.computernerd.com

❑ www.tomshardware.com

❑ www.ixbt.com

Features of Operation

Peltier modules, when used for cooling electronic elements, are characterized by their relatively high reliability, and in contrast to refrigerators created using traditional technology, do not have moving parts. To increase the efficiency of their operation, these modules can be cascaded. Cascading allows cooling of the protected electronic components to temperatures below zero, even if there is significant power dissipation.

Besides the obvious advantages, Peltier modules have some specific properties that must be considered when using them in cooling equipment. Some of these properties have been mentioned, but in order to correctly use a Peltier module, you need to take a more detailed look at these specific characteristics. The following operating features are among the most important:

❑ Peltier modules release significant amount of heat in the course of operation. They require the presence of heatsinks and fans in the cooler that are able to efficiently deflect the surplus heat from the cooling modules. Thermoelectric modules are noted for their relatively low efficiency coefficient and, while they act as a heat pump, they themselves are powerful sources of heat. Using these modules in cooling devices, intended to protect the electronic components of the computer, leads to a significant increase of the temperature within the system unit. Sometimes this requires additional cooling devices within the computer case. If you don't use additional cooling, the high temperatures complicate the operating conditions for even the modules themselves, and naturally for the other components as well. Also note that using Peltier modules creates a relatively powerful extra load for the power supply to handle. This all points to the fact that it makes good sense to choose ATX motherboards and cases with a powerful power supply unit. Using this construct simplifies the task of organizing the optimum temperature conditions and electric modes for the components of the computer.

❑ If a Peltier module fails, the cooled element is isolated from the heatsink of the cooler. This leads to a speedy breakdown of the stable temperature conditions of the element, which is soon followed by the breakdown of the element itself from overheating.

❑ The low temperatures that are the result of the functioning of Peltier coolers that are too powerful can cause moisture from the air to condense. This is dangerous for the electric components, since the water can cause a short circuit between elements. In order to avoid such danger you should choose a Peltier cooler with the optimal amount of power for your needs. Whether or not there is condensation depends on a few parameters. The most important ones are: the temperature of the surrounding area (in this case, the temperature of the air inside the case), the temperature of the object being cooled, and the humidity of the air. The warmer the air inside the case and the more humid, the more likely it is that the moisture will condense, and thus that the electronic elements of the computer will break down. Below is a table that illustrates the dependence of the temperature at which moisture will condense on the amount of moisture in the air and the air temperature. Using this table, you can easily figure out whether or not there is a danger of condensation. For example, if the temperature inside the case is 25°C, and the humidity is 65%, then condensation of moisture on the cooled object will occur when its surface temperature goes lower than 18°C.

Temperatures at Which Moisture will Condense

Air temperature inside the case, °C	Humidity, %													
	30	35	40	45	50	55	60	65	70	75	80	85	90	95
30	10.5	12.9	14.9	16.8	18.4	20.0	21.4	22.7	23.9	25,1	26.2	27.2	28.2	29.1
29	9.7	12.0	14.0	15.9	17.5	19.0	20.4	21.7	23.0	24.1	25.2	26.2	27.2	28.1
28	8.8	11.1	13.1	15.0	16.6	18.1	19.5	20.8	22.0	23.2	24.2	25.2	26.2	27.1
27	8.0	10.2	12.2	14.1	15.7	17.2	18.6	19.9	21.1	22.2	23.3	24.3	25.2	26.1
26	7.1	9.4	11.4	13.2	14.8	16.3	17.6	18.9	20.1	21.2	22.3	23.3	24.2	25.1
25	6.2	8.5	10.5	12.2	13.9	15.3	16.7	18.0	19.1	20.3	21.3	22.3	23.2	24.1
24	5.4	7.6	9.6	11.3	12.9	14.4	15.8	17.0	18.2	19.3	20.3	21.3	22.3	23.1
23	4.5	6.7	8.7	10.4	12.0	13.5	14.8	16.1	17.2	18.3	19.4	20.3	21.3	22.2
22	3.6	5.9	7.8	9.5	11.1	12.5	13.9	15.1	16.3	17.4	18.4	19.4	20.3	21.2
21	2.8	5.0	6.9	8.6	10.2	11.6	12.9	14.2	15.3	16.4	17.4	18.4	19.3	20.2
20	1.9	4.1	6.0	7.7	9.3	10.7	12.0	13.2	14.4	15.4	16.4	17.4	18.3	19.2
19	1.0	3.2	5.1	6.8	8.3	9.8	11.1	12.3	13.4	14.5	15.5	16.4	17.3	18.2
18	0.2	2.3	4.2	5.9	7.4	8.8	10.1	11.3	12.5	13.5	14.5	15.4	16.3	17.2
17	-0.6	1.4	3.3	5.0	6.5	7.9	9.2	10.4	11.5	12.5	13.5	14.5	15.3	16.2
16	-1.4	0.5	2.4	4.1	5.6	7.0	8.2	9.4	10.5	11.6	12.6	13.5	14.4	15.2
15	-2.2	-0.3	1.5	3.2	4.7	6.1	7.3	8.5	9.6	10.6	11.6	12.5	13.4	14.2
14	-2.9	-1.0	0.6	2.3	3.7	5.1	6.4	7.5	8.6	9.6	10.6	11.5	12.4	13.2
13	-3.7	-1.9	-0.1	1.3	2.8	4.2	5.5	6.6	7.7	8.7	9.6	10.5	11.4	12.2
12	-4.5	-2.6	-1.0	0.4	1.9	3.2	4.5	5.7	6.7	7.7	8.7	9.6	10.4	11.2
11	-5.2	-3.4	-1.8	-0.4	1.0	2.3	3.5	4.7	5.8	6.7	7.7	8.6	9.4	10.2
10	-6.0	-4.2	-2.6	-1.2	0.1	1.4	2.6	3.7	4.8	5.8	6.7	7.6	8.4	9.2

Besides the features already mentioned, you must also take into consideration certain specific situations connected with using thermoelectric Peltier modules in your cooler in order to cool high-performance CPUs in powerful computers.

The architecture of modern processors and certain system programs provide for modification of the energy consumed, depending on the burden of the processor. This allows you to optimize the amount of energy used. By the way, this is also provided for by the energy saving standards supported by certain functions built into the hardware and software of modern computers. Under normal conditions, optimizing the functioning of the processor and its consumption energy, positively affects the thermal conditions of the processor, as well as the general thermal balance. However, you should note that modes with periodic fluctuations in the amount of power consumed might not harmonize well with cooling equipment that uses Peltier modules. This is due to the fact that existing Peltier coolers are intended for constant functioning. This is why, if the processor is changed to a mode in which the amount of power consumed, and therefore the heat flux, has been lowered, the temperature of the chip and crystal of the processor will also be significantly lowered. In certain cases, if the processor core is too cool, the processor may experience a temporary cessation of functioning, which as a result will cause the computer system to persistently freeze. You must keep in mind that the corresponding documentation from Intel states that the minimum temperature at which the proper functioning of Pentium II and Pentium III series processors is guaranteed is +5°C.

Certain problems may also arise as a result of the work of a series of built-in functions, for example, those that control the functioning of the fans in the cooler. In part, the mode that controls the energy consumption of the processor provides for changes in the rotation speed of the cooling fan using hardware built in to the motherboard. Under normal conditions, this significantly improves the heating rate of the computer processor. However, if you are using one of the simpler Peltier coolers, lowering the rotation speed of the fan may lead to an actual worsening of the heating rate, with fatal consequences for the processor (overheating) even if the Peltier module is still functioning.

Note that, as in the case of central processors, Peltier coolers may be a good alternative to the traditional means of cooling video chipsets used in modern, high-performance video adapters. The work of such video chipsets is accompanied by significant heat flux and usually not subject to sharp changes in its functional modes.

In order to avoid problems with modes that change the power consumption, which gives rise to condensation of the moisture in the air and possibly to overcooling, and in certain situations may even bring about the overheating of protected elements like the computer processor, you should not use such modes or built in functions. However, as an alternative, you can use a cooling system that provides for the intelligent control of Peltier coolers. This will control not only the work of the fan, but also be able to change the work modes of the thermoelectric modules used in active coolers. Many research laboratories are doing work investigating this, since such cooling systems are considered to be extremely promising.

Examples of Peltier Coolers

Active Peltier Coolers

Name	Producer/supplier	Fan parameters	Processor
PAX56B	ComputerNerd	ball-bearing	Pentium/MMX to 200 MHz, 25 W
PA6EXB	ComputerNerd	dual ball-bearing, tachometer	Pentium MMX to 40 W
DT-P54A	DesTech Solutions	dual ball bearing	Pentium
AC-P2	AOC Cooler	ball bearing	Pentium II
PAP2X3B	ComputerNerd	3 ball bearing	Pentium II
STEP-UP-53X2	Step Thermodynamics	2 ball bearing	Pentium II, Celeron
PAP2CX3B-10 BCool PC-Peltier	ComputerNerd	3 ball-bearing, tachometer	Pentium II, Celeron
PAP2CX3B-25 BCool-ER PC-Peltier	ComputerNerd	3 ball-bearing, tachometer	Pentium II, Celeron
PAP2CX3B-10S BCool-EST PC-Peltier	ComputerNerd	3 ball-bearing, tachometer	Pentium II, Celeron

PAX56B coolers were developed in order to cool Intel Pentium and Pentium MMX, Cyrix, and AMD processors that work at a frequency of 200 MHz. 30×30 thermoelectric modules allow the cooler to support a processor temperature of less than 63°C at the power dissipation of 25 W and the internal temperature of 25°C. In connection with the fact that the majority of processors dissipate less heat, this cooler allows the support of a much lower processor temperature than do many alternative means of cooling consisting of just heatsinks and fans. The power supply of the Peltier module included in the PAX56B cooler is from a source of 5 W and is able to support the maximum current of 1.5 A. This cooler's fan requires the voltage of 12 V and the maximum current of 0.1 A. The parameters of the PAX56B's fan: ball bearing, 47.5 mm, 65,000 hours, and 26 dB. The dimensions of the entire cooler are 25×25×28.7 mm. The approximate price of a PAX56B is $35. This price is from the company price-list from mid-2000.

The PA6EXB cooler is intended for cooling the more powerful Pentium MMX processors that dissipate a power of 40 W. This cooler is compatible with all processors from Intel, Cyrix, and AMD that use Socket 5 or Socket 7. The thermoelectric Peltier modules included in the PA6XB are 40×40 mm. The maximum current is 8 A (but usually 3 A) at the voltage of 5 V when connected through a standard power socket of the computer. The dimensions of the entire PA6EXB are 60×60×52.5 mm. In order to install the cooler correctly and ensure optimal heat exchange between the heatsink and its surroundings, you must make sure that there is at least 10 mm of space above it and 2.5 mm to the sides. The PA6EXB guarantees a processor temperature of 62.7°C at a dissipation power of 40 W and an internal temperature of 45°C. Taking into consideration the way the thermoelectric module inside the PA6EXB works, you must avoid using programs that have the processor in idle modes for long periods of time in order to prevent condensation and possible short circuits. The estimated price of a PA6EXB cooler, taken from the company mid-2000 price-list, is $65.

The DT-P54A (also known as the PA5B from Computernerd) was developed for Pentium processors. However, some companies that sell the cooler recommend it to users of Cyrix/IBM and AMD processors as well. The cooler heatsink is relatively small, 29×29 mm. There is a thermal sensor built into the cooler that will inform you in case of any danger of overheating. It also monitors the Peltier module. There is an external controlling device that is also included. This device keeps an eye on the voltage, the functioning of the Peltier element and the fan, and the temperature of the processor. The device will give off a warning signal if the Peltier element or the fan has broken down, if the fan is rotating at less than 70% of its normal speed (4,500 RPM), or if the temperature of the processor has climbed higher than 145°F (63°C). When the processor temperature goes higher than 100°F (38°C), the Peltier element automatically turns on. If the temperature is below this, the Peltier element is kept turned off. This last function eliminates the problems connected with moisture condensation. Unfortunately, the Peltier element is so securely attached to the heatsink that you won't be able to remove it without destroying the construction. This means that you don't have the ability to install it on another, more powerful heatsink. As for the fan: voltage — 12 V, rotating speed — 4,500 RPM, air supply speed — 6.0 CFM, power consumed — 1 W, noise level — 30 dB. This cooler performs fairly well and is useful for overclocking. In certain cases, however, overclocking the processor simply requires a bigger heatsink and a good fan. The price of the DTP54A, taken from the price lists of several companies in mid-2000, is approximately from $39 to $49.

The AC-P2 cooler was developed for Pentium II-type processors. Included are a 60 mm fan, a heatsink, and a 40 mm Peltier element. It does not work well with Pentium II processors of 400 MHz and higher, since the SRAM memory chips are not cooled at all. The estimated price in mid-2000 is $59.

The PAP2X3B cooler (Fig. 18.18) is similar to the AOC ACP2. It comes with two 60 mm fans. The problem of cooling the SRAM memory is not dealt with. Keep in mind that the cooler is not recommended for use with cooling programs such as, for example, CpuIdle, or with the Windows NT or Linux operating systems, since moisture condensation on the processor is much more likely. The estimated price in mid-2000 is $79.

The STEP-UP-53X2 cooler is equipped with two fans that blow through the heatsink. In mid-2000, the estimated price is $79 (Pentium II) and $69 (Celeron).

Fig. 18.18. External view of the PAP2X3B cooler

The BCool series coolers from Computernerd (PAP2CX3B-10 BCool PC-Peltier, PAP2CX3B-25 BCool-ER PC-Peltier, PAP2CX3B-10S, BCool-EST PC-Peltier) were developed for Pentium II and Celeron processors, and all have similar characteristics, which are presented in the following table.

BCool Coolers

Characteristics	PAP2CX3B-10	PAP2CX3B-25	PAP2CX3B-10S
Type of central fan	Ball-Bearing, tachometer (12 V, 120 mA)		
Size of the central fan	$60\times60\times10$ mm		
Type of external fan	Ball-Bearing	Ball-Bearing, tachometer	Ball-Bearing, thermistor
Size of external fan	$60\times60\times10$ mm	$60\times60\times25$ mm	
Voltage, current	12 V, 90 mA	12 V, 130 mA	12 V, 80—225 mA
Total area covered by the fans	84.9 cm^2		
Total current for the fans (power consumption)	300 mA (3.6 W)	380 mA (4.56 W)	280—570 mA (3.36—6.84 W)
Number of pins on the central heatsink	63 long and 72 short		
Number of pins on the left (right) heatsink	45 long and 18 short		
Total number of pins on the heatsink	153 long and 108 short		
Size of the central heatsink	$57\times59\times27$ mm (including the thermoelectric module)		
Size of the left (right) heatsink	$41\times59\times32$ mm		
Dimensions of the heatsink	$145\times59\times38$ mm (including the thermoelectric module)		
Dimensions of the cooler	$145\times60\times50$ mm	$145\times60\times65$ mm	
Weight of the cooler	357 grams	416 grams	422 grams
Warranty	5 years		
Estimated price (2000)	$74.95	$79.95	$84.95

Note that BCool coolers include devices that have similar characteristics but do not include Peltier elements. Such coolers are naturally cheaper, but are less effective as a means of cooling the computer components.

Cooling the Processor with Software

Additional protection of the central processor from overheating can be achieved by using special software, so-called cooling programs or program-coolers. The way these coolers work is based on inclusion of commands in the work cycle of the processor that order it to temporarily stop for a period of time during which the computer processor stops working. The idle processor uses less electrical power and therefore gives off less heat. Similar functions are included in such operating systems as Windows NT and Linux. These systems execute what is known as a halt cycle when performing low-priority tasks. The processor core is temporarily stalled while the other systems continue their work.

There are programs and drivers for Windows $9x$ as well that temporarily stall the central processor. Some examples are popular and widespread programs such as CpuIdle, Rain, Waterfall Pro, etc. Using such programs, you will be able to overclock your processor to high levels even with only the standard cooling equipment and to even higher levels using additional means.

Examples of the work of the CpuIdle 5.0 program is illustrated in Figs. 18.19 and 18.20.

Fig. 18.19. Dialog box of the CpuIdle program

Fig. 18.20. Working process of the CpuIdle program

The CpuIdle program supports the following types of processors:

❑ AMD — K5, K6, K6-2, K6-III, Athlon (K7)

❑ Intel — Pentium, Pentium-MMX, Pentium Pro, Pentium II/III, and Celeron

❑ Cyrix — Cx486S/S2/D/D2/DX/DX2/DX4, Cx5x86 (M1SC), Cyrix Cx6x86 (M1), Cx6x86MX (M2)

❑ IBM — BL486DX/DX2 (Blue Lightning), 5x86, 6x86

❑ Texas Instruments — TI486DX2, TI486DX4

❑ Other x86-compatible processors that support a Windows operating system. (It's possible that CpuIdle won't be able to correctly identify the type of processor, but the program will still function.)

A series of tests were conducted in order to determine the level of effectiveness with which the CpuIdle program functions as a means of optimizing the temperature condition of the processor. While the computer was functioning in an overcloking mode, its temperature was measured while using the CpuIdle program and without it.

Configurations of the System Tested

❑ Motherboard: Abit BE6-II (BIOS version — 05/2000).

❑ Processor: Intel Pentium III 550E (Coppermine core, 256 KB L2 cache memory that works at the full frequency of the core, Slot 1, in box).

❑ Hard drive: IBM DPTA-372050 (20 GB, 2 MB cache memory, 7,200 RPM, UltraDMA/66).

❑ RAM: 128 MB, PC100.

❑ Video adapter: Asus AGP-V3800 TV (TNT2 video chipset, 32 B SGRAM video memory).

❑ CD-ROM: ASUS CD-S400/A (40x).

❑ S: Windows 98 with installed UDMA/66 hard drive controller drivers.

Overclocking Mode

Frequency of the processor bus — 130 MHz, multiplier — x5.5, frequency of the processor — 715 MHz = 130 MHz×5.5.

Test Results

Motherboard Monitor v4.12 was chosen as the diagnostic program of the processor temperature. The temperature of the processor without using the software was 37°C (Sensor 1), which is 14 degrees higher than the temperature of the surrounding area — 23°C (Sensor 2). After loading the CpuIdle program, the temperature of the processor was 25°C (Sensor 1) which was only 2 degrees higher than the temperature of the surrounding area — 23°C (Sensor 2). In this manner, CpuIdle managed to cool the processor with software and lower its temperature by an entire 12°C, which allows for extreme overclocking. The amount that the temperature can be lowered by using the software depends on the level to which the processor is loaded with work: the less work, the more effective the software will be. The results of testing and controlling the temperature with the help of the Motherboard Monitor program are presented in Figs. 18.21 and 18.22.

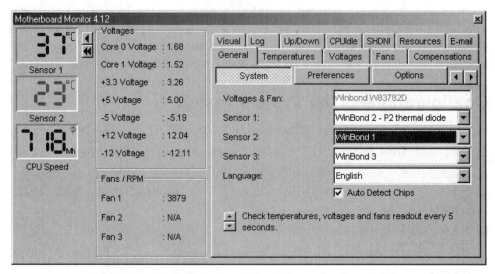

Fig. 18.21. Temperature values without using the software

Note that the CpuIdle program not only allows you to cool your processor with software, but in certain cases may even optimize its functioning. Modern processors have some additional functions that sometimes promote performance growth. If these functions are not enabled, the program is able to activate them, and with that, raise the performance of the system. For this, you have to check the **optimize functioning** checkbox when setting it up. Setting the parameters of CpuIdle 5.6 is illustrated in Fig. 18.23.

A series of tests from the WinBench 99 v1.1 package were executed with the aim of researching the optimizing ability of CpuIdle, first with the initialized CpuIdle program, and then without it. The configurations of the system used for this testing are the same as for the previous temperature monitoring test. The results of testing the optimizing abilities of the CpuIdle program are provided in the following table, and in graphic form in Fig. 18.24.

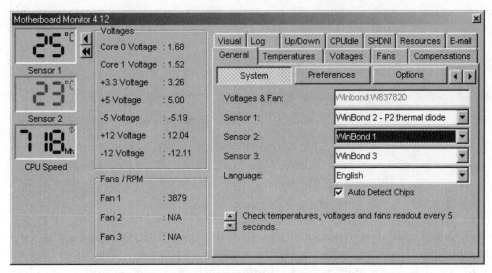

Fig. 18.22. Temperature values when using the software

Fig. 18.23. Setting up the working parameters of Cpuldle

Analysis of the Optimization Abilities of the Cpuldle Program

	With Cpuldle	Without Cpuldle
CPUmark 99	66.8	65.6
FPU WinMark	3850	3850

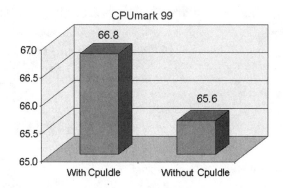

Fig. 18.24. CPUmark 99 test results

You should note that these results of the CPUmark99 test illustrates that as a means of optimizing the processor, the CpuIdle is not very effective; there was only less than a 2% improvement. However, there was some growth in perform-ance, and therefore it is possible to draw the conclusion that the CpuIdle program, as stated in its description, does indeed optimize the functioning of the CPU.

In the process of its functioning, the CpuIdle program analyzes the degree to which the processor is burdened with work and allows you to assess the results (see Fig. 18.20). It's also possible to indicate the form in which the test results and analysis will be displayed on the monitor's screen: indicator mode — graphic or numerical, parameter renewal interval, etc. An example of setting the parameters is shown in Fig. 18.25.

Fig. 18.25. Setting the indicator parameters for the CpuIdle program

The CpuIdle program also has the ability to control the temperature of the processor. If the temperature goes higher than a certain value predetermined by the user, CpuIdle can, for example, increase the priority of cooling the processor, or even initialize the shutting down of the computer. For this to work, the system must support parameter monitoring of the processor, including its temperature, and the monitoring program Motherboard Monitor must also be installed in the computer. Setting up control of the temperature of the processor in the CpuIdle program is illustrated in Fig. 18.26.

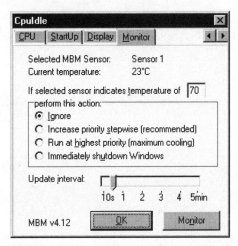

Fig. 18.26. Setting the temperature control parameters

In the set up, you can assign a temperature value which, when reached by the processor, will trigger the program to take the appropriate action when the corresponding functions are enabled. The following options are possible:

❑ Ignore

❑ Incremental increasing of the priority (recommended)

❑ Highest priority (maximum cooling)

❑ Immediately shut down Windows (this makes sense if the system supports automatic turning off of the computer power supply — advanced power management)

When solving the problem of cooling the components of the computer, it makes sense to become acquainted with the material on certain Internet sites whose addresses are given at the end of the book. The following sites are highly recommended:

❑ www.kryotech.com

❑ www.tomshardware.com

❑ ixbt.stack.net/~termoscope

Chapter 19

Examples
and Results
of Overclocking

As was mentioned earlier, there are many ways to increase system performance. The most popular method is replacing legacy components with newer and faster ones. But unfortunately, upgrading your computer can often be very expensive. There are other methods of increasing system performance, such as overclocking the computer, modifying certain values in BIOS Setup, etc.

However, once again it is necessary to mention that you should be very careful when overclocking. Never forget to take safety measures. You must also understand and keep in mind the possible consequences of overclocking, which can be very disappointing: your processor might burn out, the video card or hard drive might fail, etc. In brief, an unskilled overclocker may ruin the computer completely.

An overclocking plan can be quite extensive. There are, however, certain recommended actions that should be taken in any case. These recommendations are provided below:

1. Perform system diagnostics procedures, read the manuals, and analyze beforehand exactly how you are going to overclock and/or optimize your computer. Remove the case and check the computer configurations. It's also recommended that you make sure that everything is connected correctly, that there are no unnecessary wires, etc.

2. Perform a thorough testing of the computer. Make sure that in a regular mode all of the components are functioning normally. For this, you might want to use one of the popular tests, etc.

   - Run some tests (such as WinStone, WinBench, CheckIt, etc.). Notice that it is recommended to run each test more than once.

   - Run some popular resource-consuming applications (Microsoft Word/Excel, CorelDraw, PhotoShop, Xing, WinAmp).

   - Play some popular games (DOOM, Descent, Quake, etc.).

   It makes sense to write down the data produced by these tests for future reference and comparison. Only when you are absolutely sure that the computer is in good working order may you continue.

3. Using BIOS Setup or the appropriate jumpers on the motherboard, set the overclocking mode. It is recommended to proceed gradually, doing one step at a time. For example, you may increase the frequency of the host bus from 66 to 75 MHz (or to 68 MHz, if the motherboard supports this bus frequency).

It is not recommended, however, to jump over several levels at once. This means that it isn't wise to go straight from 66 to 83 MHz, or from 166 to 210 MHz, etc. Everything must be done gradually, making sure of every step. The best thing to do is write everything down (to the smallest details) on a piece of paper. You should also keep in mind that the system, and especially the processor, needs to be cooled. Often you will need a powerful heat sink and cooler for the processor, the video card, and other hardware components as well.

4. Test your computer in the overclocking mode. This time, the test conditions should be tougher, and the testing itself should continue for a longer time. Certain recommendations on testing the computer are given in the appropriate section of this book. If you find any instability, you must immediately take preventive measures. You can simply abandon the overclocking. When you are sure that the system is able to function properly, you can then take another step, etc.

5. Before, after, and maybe completely instead of overclocking, it might be useful to modify certain settings in the BIOS Setup. Most often, this relates to setting the memory timing options. Sometimes, you can significantly increase the operating speed of the memory just by changing a few values in BIOS Setup. But here as well it is necessary to take precautions. Be very careful, and always test the results.

Overclocking and Optimizing i486 Computers

Some i486 computers have a case design that complicates replacement of the motherboard. Quite often this is the case with brand name computers. For such computers, overclocking can be used to prolong the time period during which it is possible to efficiently use them.

As an example of such an approach, let us consider the overclocking of an Intel Champion (Champion Low Profile Platform), a widespread brand name computer. Included in the text are all the necessary data on setting the modes and testing the computer.

Using the test results provided here, you could trace performance growth for the processor, the hard drive, and the built-in video adapter.

Preliminary Testing of the Processor

An i486SX processor with an operating frequency of 25 MHz was used.

Below are the results of testing the processor (WinCheckIt 2.03) with its frequency at 25 MHz.

```
System performance

        CPU      45.84
        NPU      1.52

Hard Drive

        Composite            897.11
        Throughput KB/Sec    1052.27
        Avg Seek             0.27
        Track Seek           0.27

Video

        Composite        35.60
        BIOS CPS         5323.01
        Direct CPS       124745.11
```

Overclocking and Testing

Processor Settings (jumpers JC1–JC4)

Processor type	Packaging type	JC1	JC2	JC3	JC4
Intel486 SX	PGA	2–3	2–3	off	off
Intel486 SX	PQFP	2–3	2–3	off	off
Intel486 SX with Intel487 SX	PQFP PGA	1–2	1–2	off	off
Intel486 DX	PGA	1–2	1–2	on	on
IntelDX2	PGA	1–2	1–2	on	on

Frequency of the Processor (jumper set JK1)

Processor type	Clock frequency, MHz	1–2	3–4	5–6	7–8
Intel486 SX-25	25	off	off	on	off
Intel486 DX-25	25	off	off	on	off

continues

Continued

Processor type	Clock frequency, MHz	1–2	3–4	5–6	7–8
Intel486 SX-33	33.3	on	off	off	off
Intel486 DX-33	33.3	on	off	off	off
IntelDX2-50	25.0	off	off	on	off
IntelDX2-66	33.3	on	off	off	off

An i486Sx processor with a clock frequency of 25 MHz was used.

Presented below are the results of testing the processor (using WinCheckIt 2.03) at the frequency set to 33 MHz.

```
System Performance

        CPU     63.10
        NPU     1.84

Hard Drive

        Composite           958.98
        Throughput KB/Sec   1052.39
        Avg Seek            0.23
        Track Seek          0.23

Video

        Composite    47.09
        BIOS CPS     6772.13
        Direct CPS   167720.35
```

Comparison of the Test Results

The test results for this particular computer are presented in the following tables and in diagrams shown in Figs. 19.1—19.4.

```
System Performance

                  SX-25    SX-33     Growth, %
        CPU       45.84    63.10     38
        NPU       1.52     1.84      21

Hard Drive

                        SX-25     SX-33      Growth, %
        Composite       897.11    958.98     7
        Throughput KB/Sec 1052.27 1052.39    0
        Avg Seek        0.27      0.23       15
        Track Seek      0.27      0.23       15
```

```
Video
              SX-25        SX-33        Growth, %
Composite     35.60        47.09        32
BIOS CPS      5323.01      6772.13      27
Direct CPS    124745.11    167720.35    34
```

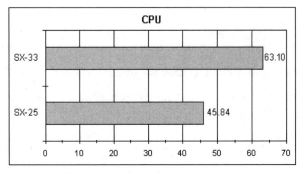

Fig. 19.1. Processor test results

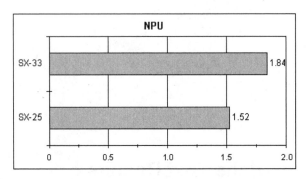

Fig. 19.2. Co-processor test results

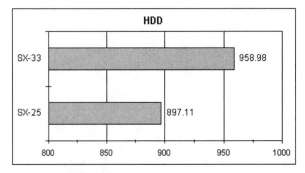

Fig. 19.3. Hard drive test results

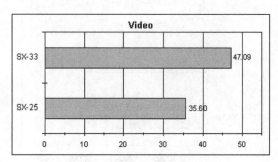

Fig. 19.4. Video system test results

Now let us consider an example that illustrates performance gain achieved as a result of overclocking individual hardware components. In this particular case, performance growth was achieved by increasing the host bus frequency of an AMD Am5×86-133 processor, also known as the Am486DX4-133.

This processor is intended to operate at a clock frequency of 133 MHz, which is obtained by multiplying the host bus frequency, 33 MHz, by the multiplier, which is 4. This multiplier value is locked within the architecture of the processor. Using the built-in capabilities of the motherboard, it is possible to increase the CPU frequency from 133 to 160 MHz. This results in an adequate performance growth for both the processor and the entire system. The results of testing the computer with an AMD5x86-133 processor using CheckIt 3.0 are presented in the following table.

Test Results from CheckIt 3.0

	$133 = 33.3 \times 4$	$160 = 40 \times 4$	**Growth**
Dhrystones	64,150	78,220	+22 %
Whetstones	23,910 K	29,260 K	+22 %

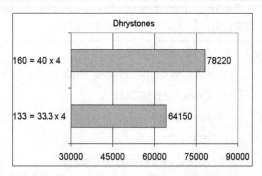

Fig. 19.5. Results of testing a computer with an AMD Am5×86-133 processor

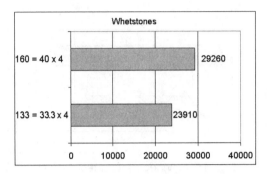

Fig. 19.6. Results of testing a computer with an AMD Am5x86-133 processor

Overclocking and Optimizing a Computer with an iPentium MMX 166 Processor

Setting the Overclocking Mode and Testing the System

This section contains a detailed description of the process of overclocking and optimizing a computer with an iPentium MMX-166 processor.

1. Careful study of the system.

   - Using the motherboard manual, it was discovered that this particular motherboard supports the SeePu standard. This means that CPU clock frequency and voltage, as well as the host bus frequency, are set using BIOS Setup rather than by switching the jumpers on the motherboard.

   - After opening the case, almost the entire configuration of the system was determined (all this information was also confirmed by the appropriate programs as well as by the data displayed at boot time).

Computer type	Pentium
Processor	Intel Pentium-166 MHz MMX (with a locked multiplier)
Motherboard	ChainTech 5TDM2
Co-processor	Integrated
Buses	ISA, PCI
BIOS	Award v4.51 (plug-and-play)

continues

Continued

Memory	32 MB SDRAM
Cache memory	512 KB pipelined burst on the board
Video	Matrox MGA Millennium (2 MB)
Hard drive	WDC AC21600H — 1622M (786 cyls, 64 heads, 63 sectors)
Floppy disk	1.44 MB (3.5)
Serial port	COM2: (2F8h)
Parallel port	LPT1: (378h)
Keyboard	101 keys
Mouse	Connected through a serial port (2 buttons)
CD-ROM	ATAPI (20x)
Sound card	Sound Blaster AWE32
OS	Windows 95 OSR2

- During a detailed analysis of the computer, two unreliable contacts were found. The voltage to the processor fan was poorly connected, which meant the processor overheating at any moment. The ribbon cable from the board to the hard drive was also in need of fixing. All loose wires were neatly tied.

2. System tests done before overclocking.

   - Loading the operating system (Windows 95).

   - All logical drives were thoroughly checked for errors using the ScanDisk program.

   - Defragmentation of the entire hard drive using the disk defragmentation program (Defrag).

   - Running the WinCheckIt (v.2.03) test program in custom-advanced mode. The data on the system performance was then recorded.

   - Running the Xing program (XingMPEG Player v3.0) and playing the MPEG video clip for 30—60 minutes. The clips were taken from a compact disk that came along with the video card. You can also use the test.mpg clip that is included in the Xing software package.

   - Running the Xing test (5—10 times). You should record the data obtained as a result of this test.

- Starting some popular games and playing each game for 10—15 minutes. The following games were used for testing: Descent 2, DOOM II, and Duke3D.

- Running several resource-consuming applications and working with files (for 5—10 minutes). For this test, popular software was used, including such applications as Microsoft Word 95/97, Microsoft Excel 95/97, Internet Explorer 4.01, Acrobat Reader 3.0, PhotoShop 4.0, etc.

- Rebooting the computer.

- Repeated running of the WinCheckIt test program (10 times). Performance data produced by these tests were averaged.

- Repeated disk defragmentation using the Defrag program.

- Shutting down the computer.

Data on the performance of the computer at a frequency of 166 MHz (66 MHz×2.5) obtained from WinCheckIt (v2.03):

```
System Performance
        CPU Rank          564.72
        NPU Rank          641.03
Hard Drive
        Throughput KB/Sec    2337.43
        Avg Seek             0.02
        Track Seek           0.02
        Composite            6686.22
Video
        BIOS Rank CPS     30210.91
        Direct Rank CPS   1753974.00
        Composite         411.22
```

Data from the test in the Xing video clip playing program (v3.0) (at a frequency of 66 MHz×2.5 = 166 MHz):

	FPS	Disk	CPU	Display/Bus
1x	54.5	29	963	673
Full screen	51.2	25	947	555

3. Setting the overclocking mode.

   - Go to BIOS Setup by pressing the <Delete> key almost immediately after the computer has been powered on. Set the necessary parameters:

1) Go to BIOS Setup by pressing the <Delete> key almost immediately after the computer has been powered on.

Display screen during booting

```
Award Modulator BIOS v4.51PG, An Energy Star Ally
Copyright (C) 1984-97, Award Software, Inc.


Pentium-MMX CPU at 166MHz
Memory Test : 32768K OK


Award Plug and Play BIOS Extension v1.0A
Copyright (C) 1997, Award Software, Inc.
Detecting HDD Primary Master ... WDC AC21600H
Detecting HDD Primary Slave ...
Detecting HDD Secondary Master... None
Detecting HDD Secondary Slave ... None


Press DEL to Enter SETUP
09/10/97-i430TX-8679-2A59IC3EC-00
```

BIOS Setup main menu
(accessed by pressing the <Delete> key while booting)

```
ROM PCI/ISA BIOS (2A59IC3E)
CMOS SETUP UTILITY
AWARD SOFTWARE, INC.
STANDART CMOS SETUP           INTERGRATED PERIPHERIALS
BIOS FEATURES SETUP           SUPERVISOR PASSWORD
SeePU & CHIPSET SETUP         USER PASSWORD
POWER MANAGEMENT SETUP        IDE HDD AUTO DETECTION
PNP/PCI CONFIGURATION         SAVE & EXIT SETUP
LOAD SETUP DEFAULTS           EXIT WITHOUT SAVING
```

2) Go into the **SeePU & Chipset SETUP** menu.

**The SeePU and Chipset SETUP menu
(before changing all default parameters)**

```
rom pci/isa bios (2a59ic3e)
SeePU & Chipset SETUP
AWARD SOFTWARE, INC.

AUTO Configuration          : Enabled      Spectrum Spread          : Disabled
DRAM Timing                 : 70ns         Power-Supply Type        : Auto
                                           Flash BIOS Protection    : Disabled
DRAM Leadoff Timing         : 10/6/4       Hardware Reset Protection : Disabled
DRAM Read Burst (EDO/FP)    : x333/x444    ***** CPU Setup ******
DRAM Write Burst Timing     : x333         CPU Type                 : Intel P55C
Fast EDO Lead Off           : Disabled     User's favorite          : Disabled
Refreash RAS# Assertion     : 5 Clks       CPU Speed                : 166 (66*2.5)2.8V
Fast RAS to CAS Delay       : 3
DRAM Page Idle Timer        : 2Clks
DRAM Enhanched Paging       : Enabled
Fast MA to RAS# Delay       : 2 Clks
SDRAM (CAS Lat/RAS-to-CAS)  : 3/3
SDRAM Speculative Read      : Disabled
System BIOS Cacheable       : Disabled
Video BIOS Cacheable        : Disabled
8 Bit I/O Recovery Time     : 1
16 Bit I/O Recovery Time    : 1
Memory Hole At 15M-16M      : Disabled
Specific PCI 2.1 Transfer   : Disabled
```

3) Change the **User's favorite** value from **Disabled** to **Enabled**.

In the menu that appears, change the value of the **CPU BUS Frequency** parameter from **66 MHz** to **75 MHz** so that you receive the following data:

```
***** CPU Setup ******
CPU Type                 : Intel P55C
User's favorite          : Enabled

CPU Vcore                : 2.8 V
CPU BUS Frequency        : 75 MHz
Frequency Ratio          : x2.5
```

4) Exit this menu by pressing the <Esc> key.

5) Save the changed data and exit. In the main menu, choose the **SAVE & EXIT SETUP** command by pressing the <y> key, and then hit <Enter>.

4. Testing the overclocked system.

   - Starting the computer:

   1) Boot the computer.

   2) The system should start normally, and the new processor frequency (in this case, $75 \times 2.5 = 187.5$ MHz) should be shown.

   Computer's display screen while starting

```
Award Modulator BIOS v4.51PG, An Energy Star Ally
Copyright (C) 1984-97, Award Software, Inc.

Pentium-MMX CPU at 188MHz
Memory Test : 32768K OK
Award Plug and Play BIOS Extension v1.0A
Copyright (C) 1997, Award Software, Inc.
Detecting HDD Primary Master ... WDC AC21600H
Detecting HDD Primary Slave ...
Detecting HDD Secondary Master... None
Detecting HDD Secondary Slave ... None


Press DEL to Enter SETUP
09/10/97-i430TX-8679-2A59IC3EC-00


CPU Type            : PENTIUM-MMX       Base Memory      : 640K
Co-Processor        : Installed         Extended Memory  : 31744K
CPU Clock           : 188MHz            Cache Memory     : 512K
Diskette Drive A    : 1.44M, 3.5 in.    Display Type     : EGA/VGA
Diskette Drive B    : None              Serial Port(s)   : 3F8 2F8
Pri. Master Disk    : LBA,Mode 4, 1624MB Parallel Port(s) : 378
Pri. Slave Disk     : CDROM,Mode 4      EDO DRAM at Row(s) : None
Sec. Master Disk    : None              SDRAM at Row(s)  : 2 3
Sec. Slave Desk     : None              L2 Cache Type    : Pipelined Burst
```

   - The operating system should boot (there shouldn't be any errors while the OS is booting).

   - You must test the entire system, using a complete set of tests, and then if possible compare the newly obtained performance data to the data produced by performance testing before overclocking. Do the following:

   1) Run the test program WinCheckIt (v2.03) in custom-advanced mode. Write down the data on the system performance.

   2) Run the Xing program (XingMPEG Player v3.0) and play the MPEG video clip for 2—3 hours. The clips were taken from a compact disk that

came along with the video card. You can also use the test.mpg clip that is included in the Xing software package.

3) Run the Xing test (5—10 times). You should record the data received somewhere.

4) Run and play the following games for 30—60 minutes: Descent 2, DOOM II, and Duke3D.

5) Run and work (for 5—10 minutes) in such application programs as Microsoft Word 95/97, Microsoft Excel 95/97, Internet Explorer 4.01, Acrobat Reader 3.0, PhotoShop 4.0, etc.

6) Reboot the computer.

7) Repeat point number 1 (10 times). Compare these tests' evaluation of the performance and take the average of the results.

8) Check all the logical sections of the hard drive using the ScanDisk program.

9) Data on the performance of the computer (at a frequency of $75 \times 2.5 = 187.5$ MHz) obtained from WinCheckIt (v2.03):

```
System Performance
      CPU Rank           643.04
      NPU Rank           718.69


Hard drive
      Throughput KB/Sec  2337.25
      Avg Seek           0.02
      Track Seek         0.02
      Composite          7395.15

Video
      BIOS Rank CPS      33877.63
      Direct Rank CPS    1970499.89
      Composite          461.86
```

Data from the test in the Xing (v.3.0) video playing program (at a frequency of $75 \times 2.5 = 187.5$ MHz):

	FPS	Disk	CPU	Display/Bus
1x	60.1	22	805	523
Full screen	57.3	23	827	642

- If all the tests were successful (as they were in this example), the system was successfully overclocked and remains stable. If any of the tests were not successful, you must either return to the original configuration or try to achieve system stability using other methods. (For example, consider improving the cooling of the processor and/or other components, replacing the component that caused the instability, etc.)

- Compare the test data.

Modifications, as Given by the WinCheckIt Test Program

	$166 = 66 \times 2.5$	$187.5 = 75 \times 2.5$	Growth
Processor	0564.72	0643.04	+13 %
Co-processor	0641.03	0718.69	+12 %
Hard drive	6686.22	7395.15	+10 %
Video	0411.22	0461.86	+12 %

Performance Comparison Using the Data from the Xing Test

	1x (FPS)	Full screen (FPS)
$166 = 66 \times 2.5$	54.5	51.2
$187.5 = 75 \times 2.5$	60.1	57.3
Growth	+10%	+12%

- The conclusion (from the given example) — the system is working well. We have achieved significant performance gain, and we may therefore proceed to the next level of overclocking.

5. Continuing the overclocking process.

   - Go to BIOS Setup by pressing the <Delete> key almost immediately after the computer has been powered on. Set the necessary parameters:

   1) Go into the **SeePU & Chipset SETUP** menu.

   2) In the **CPU Setup** menu, change the value of the **CPU BUS Frequency** parameter from **75 MHz** to **83 MHz**, so that you receive the following data:

```
***** CPU Setup ******
CPU Type              : Intel P55C
User's favorite       : Enabled
```

```
CPU Vcore              : 2.8 V
CPU BUS Frequency      : 83 MHz
Frequency Ratio        : x2.5
```

3) Leave the menu by pressing the <Esc> key.

4) Save the changed data and exit. In the main menu, choose the **SAVE & EXIT SETUP** command by pressing the <y> key, and then hit <Enter>.

6. Testing the overclocked system.

- Starting the computer:

  1) Boot the computer.

  2) Starting the system should proceed normally, and the new processor frequency (in this case, $83 \times 2.5 = 207.5$ MHz) should be shown.

Computer's display screen while starting

```
Award Modulator BIOS v4.51PG, An Energy Star Ally
Copyright (C) 1984-97, Award Software, Inc.


Pentium-MMX CPU at 210MHz
Memory Test : 32768K OK

Award Plug and Play BIOS Extension v1.0A
Copyright (C) 1997, Award Software, Inc.
Detecting HDD Primary Master ... WDC AC21600H
Detecting HDD Primary Slave ...
Detecting HDD Secondary Master... None
Detecting HDD Secondary Slave ... None


Press DEL to Enter SETUP
09/10/97-i430TX-8679-2A59IC3EC-00
```

```
CPU Type           : PENTIUM-MMX      Base Memory       : 640K
Co-Processor       : Installed        Extended Memory   : 31744K
CPU Clock          : 210MHz           Cache Memory      : 512K
Diskette Drive A   : 1.44M, 3.5 in.   Display Type      : EGA/VGA
Diskette Drive B   : None             Serial Port(s)    : 3F8 2F8
Pri. Master Disk   : LBA,Mode 4, 1624MB  Parallel Port(s) : 378
Pri. Slave Disk    : CDROM,Mode 4     EDO DRAM at Row(s) : None
Sec. Master Disk   : None             SDRAM at Row(s)   : 2 3
Sec. Slave Desk    : None             L2 Cache Type     : Pipelined Burst
```

- The operating system should start (there shouldn't be any errors during system startup).

- You must test the entire system, using a complete set of tests, and then, if possible, compare the newly obtained performance data with the data obtained before overclocking, as was done last time:

1) Run the test program WinCheckIt (v2.03) in custom-advanced mode and write down the data on the system performance.

2) Run the Xing program (XingMPEG Player v3.0) and play the MPEG video clip for 2—3 hours. The clips were taken from a compact disk that came along with the video card. You can also use the test.mpg clip that is included in the Xing software package.

3) Run the Xing test (5—10 times). You should record the data produced by this test.

4) Run and play the following games for 30—60 minutes: Descent 2, DOOM II, Duke3D.

5) Run and work (for 10—20 minutes) in such application programs as Microsoft Word 95/97, Microsoft Excel 95/97, Internet Explorer 4.01, Acrobat Reader 3.0, PhotoShop 4.0, etc.

6) Reboot the computer.

7) Repeat point number 1 (10 times). Compare results produced by these tests and calculate the average values.

8) Check all the logical disks using the ScanDisk program.

Data on the performance of the computer (at a frequency of $83 \times 2.5 = 207.5$ MHz) obtained from WinCheckIt (v2.03):

```
System Performance
        CPU Rank           711.16
        NPU Rank           795.50
Hard drive
        Throughput KB/Sec  2307.30
        Avg Seek           0.01
        Track Seek         0.01
        Composite          8140.68
Video
        BIOS Rank CPS      37671.52
        Direct Rank CPS    2189711.23
        Composite          513.29
```

Data from the test in the Xing (v.3.0) video clip playing program (at a frequency of 83 MHz$\times$2.5 = 207.5 MHz):

	FPS	Disk	CPU	Display/Bus
1x	70.0	23	744	441
Full screen	62.7	25	772	574

- In this case, not all of the tests went as well as last time. There was an error during the second step of testing — while playing the video clips the system froze. Since the system is not stable, it's necessary to either return to the earlier configuration, or improve the cooling of the processor and/or other components. You can also try to replace the unstable component. After a detailed analysis of all of the components it was decided that it was the video card that caused the instability. The video card's processor was heating intensely due to the fact that the frequency of the PCI had risen to 83 MHz/2 = 41.5 MHz. When the second series of tests was repeated, the system produced no errors.

- Compare the data from the tests (Figs. 19.7 and 19.8).

Modifications, as Given by the WinCheckIt Test Program

	187.5 = 75 × 2.5	207.5 = 83 × 2.5	Growth
Processor	643.04	711.16	+10%
Co-processor	718.69	795.50	+10%
Hard drive	7395.15	8140.68	+10%
Video	461.86	513.29	+11%

Performance Comparison Using the Data from the Xing Test

	1x (FPS)	Full screen (FPS)
187.5 = 75 x 2.5	60.1	57.3
207.5 = 83 x 2.5	70.0	62.7
Growth	+16%	+9%

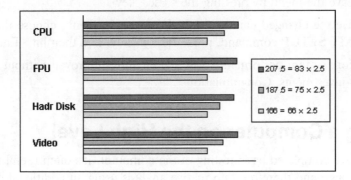

Fig. 19.7. Growth in performance from the data given by the WinCheckIt test program (v2.03)

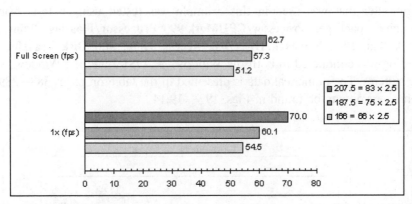

Fig. 19.8. Growth in performance from the data given by the Xing test (v3.0)

- Conclusion: since the system is not stable, and since there is also a good chance that the video card will fail, it makes sense to return to the previous configuration: 75 MHz×2.5 = 187.5 MHz by doing the following:

1) Go into the **SeePU & CHIPSET SETUP** menu.

2) In the CPU Setup menu, change the value of the **CPU BUS Frequency** from **83 MHz** to **75 MHz** so that you receive the following data:

```
***** CPU Setup ******
CPU Type                   : Intel P55C
User's favorite            : Enabled

CPU Vcore                  : 2.8 V
CPU BUS Frequency          : 75 MHz
Frequency Ratio            : x2.5
```

1) Leave the menu by pressing the <Esc> key.

2) Save the changed data and exit. In the main menu, choose the **SAVE & EXIT SETUP** command, press the <y> key, and then hit <Enter>.

7. Conclusion: system performance was significantly improved without significant financial investments. Congratulations!

Testing a Computer on the High Level

After you have completed basic testing of the computer, it's often useful to perform a more thorough and therefore informative analysis using an additional set of tests. You might want to use, for example, the popular WinBench test.

The computer that was used in this example was tested using 6 tests from the WinBench99 package: **Processor/CPUMark 99**, **Processor/Floating Point**, **Disk Playback/Bus**, **Disk Playback/HE**, **Disk Access Time**, and **Disk Transfer Rate**. The testing was conducted in both the Windows 95 OSR2 and the Windows 98 operating systems. The numerical data is presented in the table on pages 388—389, and a graphic version can be found in Figs. 19.9—19.14.

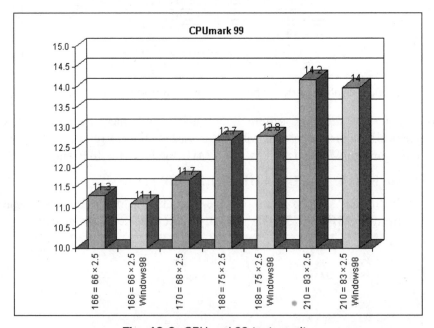

Fig. 19.9. CPUmark99 test results

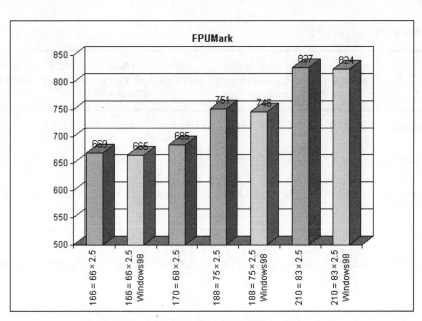

Fig. 19.10. FPU WinMark test results

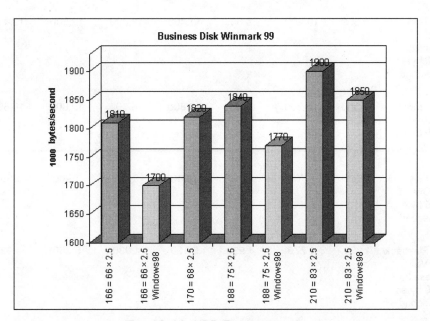

Fig. 19.11. HDD/Bus test results

Test Results

	$166 =$ $= 66 \times 2.5$	$166 =$ $= 66 \times 2.5$ Windows 98	$170 =$ $= 68 \times 2.5$	$188 =$ $= 75 \times 2.5$	$188 =$ $= 75 \times 2.5$ Windows 98	$210 =$ $= 83 \times 2.5$	$210 =$ $= 83 \times 2.5$ Windows 98
CPUmark 99	11.3	11.1	11.7	12.7	12.8	14.2	14.0
FPU WinMark	669	665	685	751	746	827	824
Business Disk WinMark 99 (1000 bytes per second)	1,810	1,700	1,820	1,840	1,770	1,900	1,850
High-End Disk WinMark 99 (1000 bytes per second)	6,430	6,250	6,560	6,700	6,490	7,040	6,690
Disk Access Time (msec)	13.0	13.1	13.0	12.9	13.0	12.9	12.8
Disk Transfer Rate: Beginning (1000 bytes per second)	10,500	10,200	10,600	11,400	11,300	12,500	12,400
Disk Transfer Rate:End (1000 bytes per second)	10,300	10,200	10,500	10,800	10,700	10,800	10,800
Disk Playback/ Bus:Overall (1000 bytes per second)	1,810	1,700	1,820	1,840	1,770	1,900	1,850
Disk Playback/ HE:AVS/ Express 3.4 (1000 bytes per second)	4,930	4,770	4,960	5,100	4,930	5,360	4,930

continues

Continued

	$166 =$ $= 66 \times 2.5$	$166 =$ $= 66 \times 2.5$ Windows 98	$170 =$ $= 68 \times 2.5$	$188 =$ $= 75 \times 2.5$	$188 =$ $= 75 \times 2.5$ Windows 98	$210 =$ $= 83 \times 2.5$	$210 =$ $= 83 \times 2.5$ Windows 98
Disk Playback/ HE:FrontPage 98 (1000 bytes per second)	22,900	21,500	22,900	25,000	23,900	27,600	25,600
Disk Playback/ HE:MicroStation SE (1000 bytes per second)	6,920	6,850	7,000	7,380	7,150	7,720	7,370
Disk Playback/ HE:Overall (1000 bytes per second)	6,430	6,250	6,560	6,700	6,490	7,040	6,690
Disk Playback/ HE:Photoshop 4.0 (1000 bytes per second)	4,780	4,720	4,790	4,810	4,800	4,860	4,830
Disk Playback/ HE:Premiere 4.2 (1000 bytes per second)	5,160	5,600	5,500	5,520	5,810	5,760	6,080
Disk Playback/ HE:Sound Forge 4.0 (1000 bytes per second)	6,760	6,140	6,920	6,920	6,360	7,710	6,720
Disk Playback/ HE:Visual C++ 5.0 (1000 bytes per second)	6,810	6,090	6,920	7,140	6,420	7,530	6,760

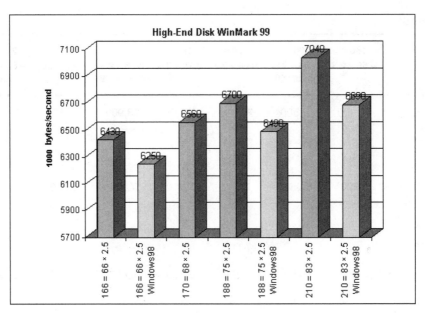

Fig. 19.12. HDD/HE test results

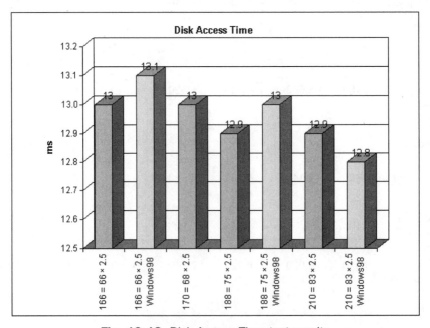

Fig. 19.13. Disk Access Time test results

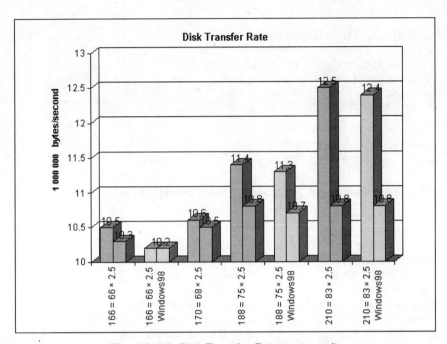

Fig. 19.14. Disk Transfer Rate test results

Optimizing the Memory and Video Subsystem Using BIOS Setup

After overclocking the computer and the subsequent performance improvement, the next step was performed — memory and video subsystem optimization. This was achieved by changing certain settings in BIOS Setup.

First, the video system will be optimized, and then the memory will be dealt with. For this, you must:

1. Go into BIOS Setup by pressing the <Delete> key while the computer is booting.

Display screen while the computer is booting

```
Award Modulator BIOS v4.51PG, An Energy Star Ally
Copyright (C) 1984-97, Award Software, Inc.


Pentium-MMX CPU at 188MHz
Memory Test : 32768K OK
```

```
Award Plug and Play BIOS Extension v1.0A
Copyright (C) 1997, Award Software, Inc.
Detecting HDD Primary Master ... WDC AC21600H
Detecting HDD Primary Slave ...
Detecting HDD Secondary Master... None
Detecting HDD Secondary Slave ... None


Press DEL to Enter SETUP
09/10/97-i430TX-8679-2A59IC3EC-00
```

BIOS Setup main menu (after hitting the <Delete> key)

```
ROM PCI/ISA BIOS (2A59IC3E)
CMOS SETUP UTILITY
AWARD SOFTWARE, INC.
STANDART CMOS SETUP            INTERGRATED PERIPHERIALS
BIOS FEATURES SETUP           SUPERVISOR PASSWORD
See & CHIPSET SETUP           USER PASSWORD
POWER MANAGEMENT SETUP        IDE HDD AUTO DETECTION
PNP/PCI CONFIGURATION         SAVE & EXIT SETUP
LOAD SETUP DEFAULTS           EXIT WITHOUT SAVING
```

2. Go into the **BIOS FEATURES SETUP** menu.

All parameters in the **BIOS FEATURES SETUP** menu are set to the default. The items on the menu that will be changed in the process of optimization are in bold italics.

```
ROM PCI/ISA BIOS (2A59IC3E)
BIOS FEATURES SETUP
AWARD SOFTWARE, INC.
Virus Warning              : Disabled    Video BIOS Shadow   : Enabled
CPU Internal Cache         : Enabled     C8000-CBFFF Shadow  : Disabled
External Cache             : Enabled     CC000-CFFFF Shadow  : Disabled
Quick Power On Self Test   : Enabled     D0000-D3FFF Shadow  : Disabled
Boot Sequence              : A,C,SCSI    D4000-D7FFF Shadow  : Disabled
Swap Floppy Drive          : Disabled    D8000-DBFFF Shadow  : Disabled
Boot Up Floppy Seek        : Enabled     DC000-DFFFF Shadow  : Disabled
Boot Up NumLock Status     : On
Boot Up System Speed       : High
Typematic Rate Setting     : Disabled
Typematic Rate (Chars/sec) : 6
Typematic Delay (Msec)     : 250
Security Option            : Setup
PCI/ISA Palette Snoop      : Disabled
OS Select (For DRAM > 64MB) : Non-OS2
```

3. Change all of the **Disabled** values in bold italics to **Enabled**.

Below is the **BIOS FEATURES SETUP** menu after optimization. The menu items that have been changed are in bold italics.

```
ROM PCI/ISA BIOS (2A59IC3E)
BIOS FEATURES SETUP
AWARD SOFTWARE, INC.
Virus Warning                : Enabled    Video BIOS Shadow    : Enabled
CPU Internal Cache           : Enabled    C8000-CBFFF Shadow   : Enabled
External Cache               : Enabled    CC000-CFFFF Shadow   : Enabled
Quick Power On Self Test     : Enabled    D0000-D3FFF Shadow   : Enabled
Boot Sequence                : A,C,SCSI   D4000-D7FFF Shadow   : Enabled
Swap Floppy Drive            : Disabled   D8000-DBFFF Shadow   : Enabled
Boot Up Floppy Seek          : Enabled    DC000-DFFFF Shadow   : Enabled
Boot Up NumLock Status       : On
Boot Up System Speed         : High
Typematic Rate Setting       : Disabled
Typematic Rate (Chars/sec)   : 6
Typematic Delay (Msec)       : 250
Security Option              : Setup
PCI/ISA Palette Snoop        : Disabled
OS Select (For DRAM > 64MB)  : Non-OS2
```

4. Exit the **BIOS FEATURES SETUP** menu to the main menu (<Esc> key).

5. Go into the **SeePU & CHIPSET SETUP** menu.

Below is the **SeePU & CHIPSET SETUP** menu (before the values have been changed, all are set to their default settings). The items on the menu that have been changed in the process of optimization are in bold italics.

```
ROM PCI/ISA BIOS (2A59IC3E)
SeePU & CHIPSET SETUP
AWARD SOFTWARE, INC
AUTO Configuration           : Enabled    Spectrum Spread           : Disabled
DRAM Timing                  : 70ns       Power-Supply Type         : Auto
                                          Flash BIOS Protection     : Disabled
DRAM Leadoff Timing          : 10/6/4     Hardware Reset Protection : Disabled
DRAM Read Burst (EDO/FP)     : x333/x444  ***** CPU Setup ******
DRAM Write Burst Timing      : x333       CPU Type                  : Intel P55C
Fast EDO Lead Off            : Disabled   User's favorite           : Enabled
Refreash RAS# Assertion      : 5 Clks
Fast RAS to CAS Delay        : 3          CPU Vcore                 : 2.8 V
DRAM Page Idle Timer         : 2Clks      CPU BUS Frequency         : 75 MHz
DRAM Enhanched Paging        : Enabled    Frequency Ratio           : x2.5
Fast MA to RAS# Delay        : 2 Clks
```

```
SDRAM (CAS Lat/RAS-to-CAS)     : 3/3
SDRAM Speculative Read         : Disabled
System BIOS Cacheable          : Disabled
Video BIOS Cacheable           : Disabled
8 Bit I/O Recovery Time        : 1
16 Bit I/O Recovery Time       : 1
Memory Hole At 15M-16M         : Disabled
Specific PCI 2.1 Transfer      : Disabled
```

6. Change the value of the appropriate parameters to the values shown below in bold italics in the **SeePU & CHIPSET SETUP** menu (after optimization).

```
ROM PCI/ISA BIOS (2A59IC3E)
SeePU & CHIPSET SETUP
AWARD SOFTWARE, INC
AUTO Configuration          : Enabled      Spectrum Spread           : Disabled
DRAM Timing                 : 70ns         Power-Supply Type         : Auto
                                           Flash BIOS Protection     : Disabled
DRAM Leadoff Timing         : 10/6/4       Hardware Reset Protection : Disabled
DRAM Read Burst (EDO/FP)    : x333/x444    ***** CPU Setup ******
DRAM Write Burst Timing     : x333         CPU Type                  : Intel P55C
Fast EDO Lead Off           : Disabled     User's favorite           : Enabled
Refreash RAS# Assertion     : 5 Clks
Fast RAS to CAS Delay       : 3            CPU Vcore                 : 2.8 V
DRAM Page Idle Timer        : 2Clks        CPU BUS Frequency         : 75 MHz
DRAM Enhanched Paging       : Enabled      Frequency Ratio           : x2.5
Fast MA to RAS# Delay       : 2 Clks
SDRAM (CAS Lat/RAS-to-CAS)  : 3/3
SDRAM Speculative Read      : Disabled
System BIOS Cacheable       : Disabled
Video BIOS Cacheable        : Disabled
8 Bit I/O Recovery Time     : 1
16 Bit I/O Recovery Time    : 1
Memory Hole At 15M-16M      : Disabled
Specific PCI 2.1 Transfer   : Disabled
```

7. Return from the **SeePU & CHIPSET SETUP** menu to the main menu (<Esc> key).

8. Save the changed data and exit. In the main menu, choose the **SAVE & EXIT SETUP** command, press the <y> key, and then hit <Enter>.

9. Conduct testing of the optimized system.

   • Start the computer:

     1) Boot up the computer.

     2) Starting the system should proceed normally, and the new processor frequency (in this case, $75 \times 2.5 = 187.5$ MHz) should be shown.

Computer's display screen while starting

```
Award Modulator BIOS v4.51PG, An Energy Star Ally
Copyright (C) 1984-97, Award Software, Inc.


Pentium-MMX CPU at 188MHz
Memory Test : 32768K OK


Award Plug and Play BIOS Extension v1.0A
Copyright (C) 1997, Award Software, Inc.
Detecting HDD Primary Master ... WDC AC21600H
Detecting HDD Primary Slave ...
Detecting HDD Secondary Master... None
Detecting HDD Secondary Slave ... None


Press DEL to Enter SETUP
09/10/97-i430TX-8679-2A59IC3EC-00
```

CPU Type	: PENTIUM-MMX	Base Memory	: 640K
Co-Processor	: Installed	Extended Memory	: 31744K
CPU Clock	: 188MHz	Cache Memory	: 512K
Diskette Drive A	: 1.44M, 3.5 in.	Display Type	: EGA/VGA
Diskette Drive B	: None	Serial Port(s)	: 3F8 2F8
Pri. Master Disk	: LBA,Mode 4, 1624MB	Parallel Port(s)	: 378
Pri. Slave Disk	: CDROM,Mode 4	EDO DRAM at Row(s)	: None
Sec. Master Disk	: None	SDRAM at Row(s)	: 2 3
Sec. Slave Desk	: None	L2 Cache Type	: Pipelined Burst

- The operating system should start (there shouldn't be any errors while the OS is booting).

- You must test the entire system, using a complete set of tests, and then if possible compare the newly obtained performance data with the averaged data obtained before optimization took place. The set of tests is similar to the one used to test the overclocked system.

1) Run the test program WinCheckIt (v2.03) in custom-advanced mode. Write down the data on the system performance.

2) Run the Xing program (XingMPEG Player v3.0) and play the MPEG video clip for 2—3 hours. The clips were taken from a compact disk that came along with the video card. You can also use the test.mpg clip that is included in the Xing software package.

3) Run the Xing test (5—10 times). You should record somewhere the data received.

4) Run and play the following games for 30–60 minutes: Descent 2, DOOM II, and Duke3D.

5) Run and work (for 10–20 minutes) in such application programs as Microsoft Word 95/97, Microsoft Excel 95/97, Internet Explorer 4.01, Acrobat Reader 3.0, PhotoShop 4.0, etc.

6) Reboot the computer.

7) Repeat point number 1 (10 times). Compare these tests' evaluations of the performance and take the average of the results.

8) Check all the logical sections of the hard drive using the ScanDisk program.

Data on the performance of the optimized computer obtained from Win-CheckIt (v2.03):

```
System Performance

      CPU Rank            664.26
      NPU Rank            717.40

Hard Drive

      Throughput KB/Sec   2337.37
      Avg Seek            0.02
      Track Seek          0.02
      Composite           7419.07

Video

      BIOS Rank CPS       52671.54
      Direct Rank CPS     1974182.30
      Composite           500.18
```

Data from the test in the Xing (v.3.0) clip playing program.

	FPS	Disk	CPU	Display/Bus
Full screen	60.8	22	796	596

- In this case, all of the tests were successful; the system is stable. (Otherwise, it would be necessary to return to the previous configurations by going into BIOS Setup, and, in the **SETUP DEFAULTS** menu, pressing <y>, then <Enter>. Note that you will also have to reset the overclocking parameters if they were set in the first place.)

- Compare the test results.

Modifications, as Given by the WinCheckIt Test Program (v2.03)

	Before optimization	After optimization	Growth
Processor	643.04	664.26	+3 %
Co-processor	718.69	717.40	+0 %
Hard drive	7,395.15	7,419.07	+0 %
Video	461.86	500.18	+8 %

Details of the Changes in the Performance of the Video (WinCheckIt v2.03)

	Before optimization	After optimization	Growth
BIOS Rank CPS	33,877.63	52,671.54	+55.5%
Direct Rank CPS	1,970,499.89	1,974,182.30	+0.2%
Composite	461.86	500.18	+8.3%

Performance Comparison Data from the Xing Test

	Full screen (FPS)
Before optimization	57.3
After optimization	60.8
Growth	+6.1%

- The system is working normally, and has achieved, as a result, a fair amount of performance growth.

10. Conclusion: the performance of the computer has been increased without significant financial investment. You should congratulate yourself.

Results of Overclocking an AMD-K6-2 Computer

Processors from AMD deserve their popularity because of their high performance and low price. The table below presents the results of testing a computer with a K6-2 processor in various overclocking modes.

Test Results (3DMark 99 Max Test Package)

K6-2 350 MHz	3DMark	CPU 3DMark
450 MHz (100 MHz FSB), 2.9 V	2,923	5,634
428.5 MHz (95 MHz FSB), 2.6 V	2,758	5,212
400 MHz (100 MHz FSB), 2.4 V	2,789	5,296

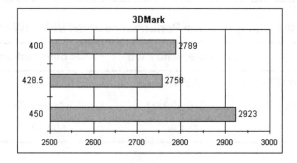

Fig. 19.15. 3D Mark test results

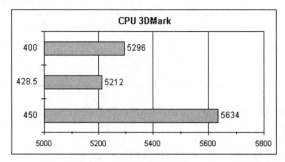

Fig. 19.16. CPU 3Dmark test results

System configuration

❑ Motherboard — M577 PCChips

❑ Processor — AMD-K6-2 350 MHz

❑ Memory — 98 MB PC100 8 nsec

❑ Cooling — a large heatsink and a high quality fan

At a frequency of 450 MHz, the system became unstable and therefore an optimum system configuration at a frequency of 400 MHz was chosen (100 MHz FSB).

Overclocking Computers with iCeleron Processors

Computers with iCeleron 266/300 Processors

The table presented below lists some data obtained in the course of testing a computer with a Celeron 266 and a Celeron 300 processor in overclocking modes. The programs Winstone 98, WinBench 98, and Quake2 (640×480) were used as the tests.

Results of Testing the Computer

Processor/ test	Winstone 98	CPU Mark32	FPU Mark	Quake2, fpu
Celeron 266 (266)	16.5	400	1300	12
Celeron 300 (300)	17.5	420	1400	13
Celeron 266 (300)	18.0	450	1450	14
Celeron 300 (337)	19.0	470	1600	15
Celeron 266 (333)	19.5	500	1600	15
Celeron 300 (374)	20.0	525	1750	16
Celeron 266 (400)	22.0	600	1950	19

From these results, it can be concluded that using the Celeron 266 and Celeron 300 processors in overclocking modes allows you to significantly increase the performance of the computer.

For computers with Celeron 266 processors, the most promising mode is one where the frequency of the processor bus is set to 100 MHz, which allows you to raise the working frequency of the processor to 400 MHz.

Further growth in performance is possible by setting higher values for the host bus frequency, as long as it is not accompanied by a decrease in the stability of the processor and other subsystems.

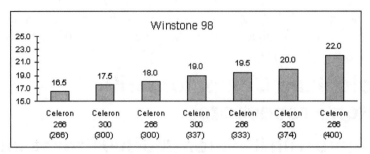

Fig. 19.17. Winstone test results

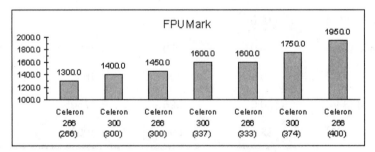

Fig. 19.18. CPU Mark32 test results

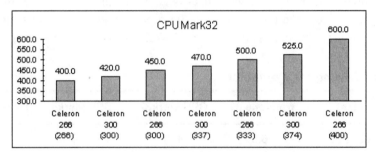

Fig. 19.19. FPU Mark test results

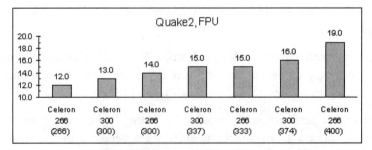

Fig. 19.20. Quake2 test results

Computers with iCeleron 300A/333 Processors

Presented below are certain test results obtained from testing overclocked Celeron 300A and Celeron 333 processors in comparison with Pentium II, Celeron 266, and Celeron 300 processors (Figs. 19.21—19.25).

The tests used are: Winstone 98, WinBench 98, Quake2 (640×480 with OpenGL), and Unreal (640×480).

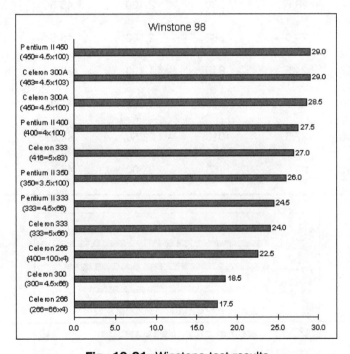

Fig. 19.21. Winstone test results

Results of Comparative Testing of the Processors

	Winstone 98	CPU Mark32	FPU Mark	Quake2, FPS	Unreal, FPS
Celeron 266 266 (66×4)	17.5	400	1,250	27.0	15.5
Celeron 266 400 (100×4)	22.5	600	1,900	39.0	23.5

continues

Continued

	Winstone 98	CPU Mark32	FPU Mark	Quake2, FPS	Unreal, FPS
Celeron 300 300 (4.5×66)	18.5	420	1,400	29.0	17.0
Celeron 333 333 (5×66)	24.0	660	1,750	39.0	22.0
Celeron 333 416 (5×83)	27.0	890	2,200	44.0	27.0
Celeron 300A 450 (4.5×100)	28.5	930	2,400	45.5	30.5
Celeron 300A 463 (4.5×103)	29.0	960	2,450	45.5	30.5
Pentium II 333 333 (4.5×66)	24.5	840	1,700	39.5	21.5
Pentium II 350 350 (3.5×100)	26.0	920	1,800	42.0	25.0
Pentium II 400 400 (4×100)	27.5	1010	2,050	44.0	26.5
Pentium II 450 450 (4.5×100)	29.0	1160	2,300	45.5	28.5

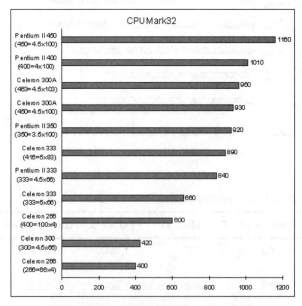

Fig. 19.22. CPU Mark32 test results

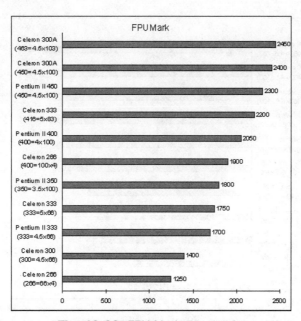

Fig. 19.23. FPU Mark test results

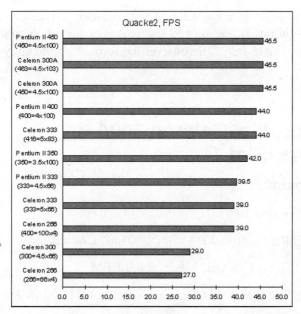

Fig. 19.24. Test results from Quake2, FPS

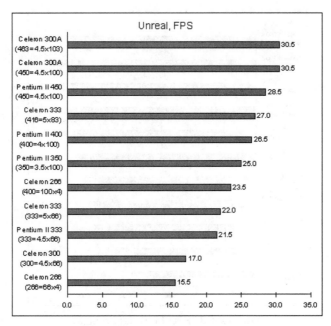

Fig. 19.25. Unreal test results, FPS

From all of these figures, it can be said that overclocked Celeron processors are not inferior to Pentium II 450 processors. This goes for office applications as well as games. In the Unreal test, Celeron even performed significantly better than the Pentium II 450.

Computers with iCeleron 300A Processors (Slot 1)

System Configuration

❑ Motherboard — Abit BH-6

❑ Processor — Intel Celeron 300A, Slot 1, OEM, Costa Rica

❑ Hard drive — IBM, 10.1 GB, 16GP, 5,400 RPM

❑ Memory — 128 MB Mushkin/Samsung-G8 125 MHz (CAS 2)

❑ Cooling — ComputerNerd BCool-ER 3-fan/heatsink combo

❑ Overclocking parameters:

- Bus frequency — 103 MHz
- Frequency of the processor — 103 MHz × 4.5 = 464 MHz
- Voltage — 2.20 V

The WinBench 99 test package was used to test the system. The test results are provided in Figs. 19.26—19.29.

Test Results

	300 MHz = 66 MHz × 4.5	464 MHz = 103 MHz × 4.5
CPU	25	38.7
FPU	1,600	2,470
Business Disk WinMark 99 (1,000 bytes/sec)	2,350	2,520
High-End Disk WinMark 99 (1,000 bytes/sec)	8,060	8,600

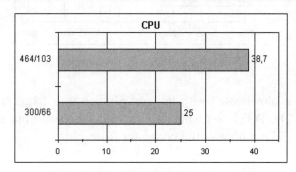

Fig. 19.26. CPU Mark99 test results

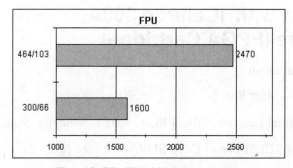

Fig. 19.27. FPU Mark test results

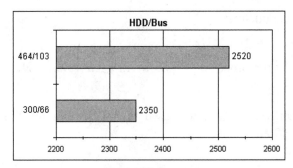

Fig. 19.28. HDD/Bus test results

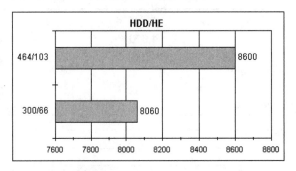

Fig. 19.29. HDD/HE test results

The computer was also booted with its configuration at a frequency of 504 MHz (112 MHz×4.5). The POST test while booting was successful, but the Windows 95 operating system did not boot — the computer froze.

Computers with iCeleron 300A Processors (PPGA Cartridge)

System configuration

❑ Motherboard — Abit BM-6

❑ Processor — Intel Celeron 300A, PPGA, Retail, Malaysia, Sspec# — SL35Q

❑ Memory — 64 MB Micron PC100 SDRAM 8 nsec (CAS 2)

❑ Cooling — ComputerNerd facrx2b twin cooler

❑ Overclocking parameters:

- Bus frequency — 66, 75, 83, 100, 103, 105, 110, 112 MHz
- Frequency of the processor — 300, 338, 374, 450, 464, 472, 495, 504 MHz
- Voltage — 2.00 V

The SiSoft Sandra test was used for testing.

Test Results

Frequency of the processor/bus, MHz	CPU	FPU
300/66	817	400
338/75	918	450
374/83	1,020	500
450/100	1,227	603
464/103	1,262	621
472/105	1,286	633
495/110	1,347	664
504/112	1,374	677

The computer was also booted with a configuration of 115 MHz×4.5. The POST procedure while booting went successfully, but the Windows 95 operating system did not load. In order to compare the Intel Pentium II 450 MHz and the Intel Pentium III 500 MHz, the following results are presented:

Testing Other Processors

Processor	CPU	FPU
Pentium III 500 MHz	1,350	670
Pentium II 450 MHz	1,220	590

It's clear that the Intel Celeron processor in an overclocking mode gives better results than the Pentium II and Pentium III processors with almost exactly the same core frequency (Figs. 19.30 and 19.31). You should note that the processor was cooled very intensely. A large heat sink and a double fan with an external voltage source were used.

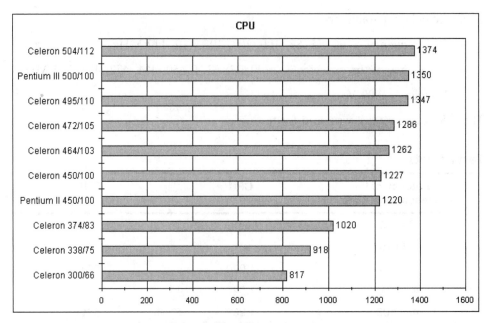

Fig. 19.30. CPU test results

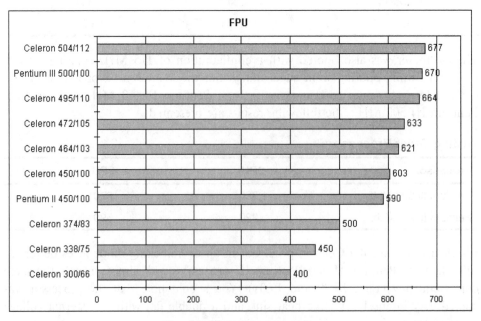

Fig. 19.31. FPU test results

Computers with iCeleron 333 Processors (Slot 1)

System configuration

❑ Motherboard — Abit BH-6

❑ Processor — Intel Celeron 333, Slot 1, Retail, Costa Rica, Sspec# — SL2WN

❑ Memory — 64 MB Micron PC100 SDRAM (CAS 2)

❑ Video — Creative Labs TNT, 16 MB, AGP

❑ Hard drive — IBM, 10 GB

❑ Cooling — Dual CPU fan, 486 fan on the video card (TNT)

❑ Overclocking parameters:

  • Bus frequency — 75 MHz

  • Frequency of the processor — 375 MHz

  • Voltage — 1.80 V

The WinBench 99 v1.1 test package and the Quake 1.03 program (with the parameters glquake, timedemo, demo1.dem, and 640×480×16) were used for testing. The test results are presented in Figs. 19.32—19.34.

Test Results

Frequency of the processor/bus, MHz	CPUMark99	FPUMark	Quake, fps
333/66	25.8	1,740	92.9
375/75	28.9	1,960	98.4
416/83	31.4	2,170	104.3

At 416 MHz (83 MHz×5) the computer booted normally, but after 5—10 minutes, the operating system (Windows 95 OSR 2.1b) began producing errors. Therefore, an optimal configuration was chosen with the bus frequency of 75 MHz. Note that a double fan was used for the processor, and a fan was also used for the 80486 processor (for the video card).

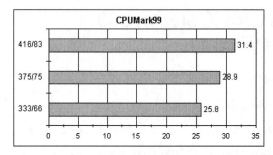

Fig. 19.32. CPUMark99 test results

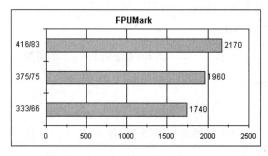

Fig. 19.33. FPUMark test results

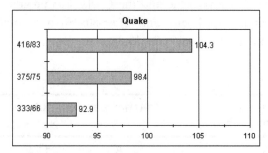

Fig. 19.34. Quake test results

Computers with iCeleron 366 Processors (PPGA Cartridge)

System configuration

❑ Motherboard — Epox BXA

❑ Processor — Intel Celeron 366, PPGA, Retail, Costa Rica

❑ Memory — 128 MB PC100 SDRAM

❑ Cooling — usual

❑ Overclocking parameters:

- Bus frequency — 83 MHz

- Frequency of the processor — 458 MHz

- Voltage — 2.00 V

The Quake2 test (timedemo) with a resolution of 1024×768 was used for testing (Fig. 19.35).

Test Results

Frequency of the processor/bus, MHz	Quake2, FPS
366/66	33
458/83	46

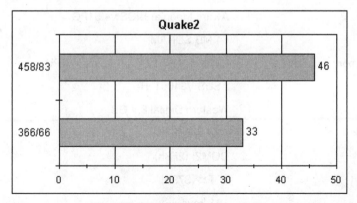

Fig. 19.35. Quake2 test results

You should note that the system works excellently without additional cooling, that is, using only the cooling equipment that normally comes with the Celeron 366 processor. However, it is recommended even in this case, that you use additional equipment for cooling the processor and/or other computer components.

Overclocking Computers with iPentium II Processors

Computers with iPentium II 300 Processors

As you probably know, Pentium II processors with a working frequency of 300 MHz work well in overclocking modes. This is especially true for those with motherboards specially developed with built-in means of overclocking. Some of the best of these are motherboards from Abit, for example, the Abit BX6. This board allows you to reach a very high performance level.

Presented below are the results of overclocking and testing a computer with an Intel Pentium II processor that uses an Abit BX6 motherboard.

Computer type	Pentium II
Processor	Intel Pentium II 300 MHz
Motherboard	Abit BX6
Co-processor	Integrated
Buses	ISA, PCI
BIOS	Award Modular BIOS v4.51PG
Memory	64 MB SDRAM
Cache memory	32 KB (L1), 512 KB (L2) in the CPU
Video	ASUS V3400TNT
Hard drive	Western Digital 8.4 GB
Floppy disk	1.44 MB (3.5")
Serial port	COM2: (2F8h)
Parallel port	LPT1: (378h)
Keyboard	101 keys
Mouse	Through a serial port (2 buttons)
CD-ROM	ATAPI (40x)
Sound card	Sound Blaster AWE32
OS	Windows 98 (4.10.1998)

Setting the overclocking mode was done in BIOS Setup in **!! CPU SOFT MENU !!**

Starting configuration

```
CPU Name Is:            Intel Pentium II MMX
CPU Operating Speed:    300(66)
-Turbo Frequency:       Disabled
CPU Power Supply:       Default
-Core Voltage:          2.00v
```

Setting the overclocking mode

```
CPU Name Is:            Intel Pentium II MMX
CPU Operating Speed:    User Define
-Turbo Frequency:       Disabled
-External Clock:        100MHz
-Multiplier Clock:      x4.5
AGPCLK/CPUCLK:          2/3
-Speed Error Hold:      Enabled
CPU Power Supply:       User Define
-Core Voltage:          2.10v
```

In the process of overclocking, the frequency of the system bus was raised from 66 to 100 MHz. As a result, the frequency of the processor increased by 1.5 times: from 300 to 450 MHz. To ensure the processor stability, the core processor voltage was raised to 2.10 from 2.00 V. Just in case, the system temperature was monitored (the **System Temperature** parameter in the **CHIPSET Features Setup** menu): before overclocking –41°C, after overclocking –42°C.

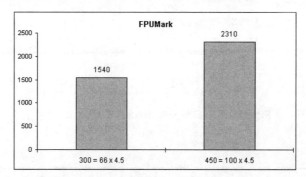

Fig. 19.36. Performance of the processor

The WinBench 99 package was used for testing. The FPUMark test (Fig. 19.36), the Disk Playback/Bus test, and the Disk Playback/HE test (Figs. 19.37, 19.38) were conducted. Unfortunately, the CPUMark 99 test did not load, which was probably connected to the unstable functioning of the operating system version used (Windows 98).

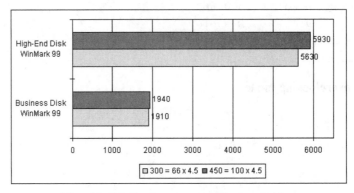

Fig. 19.37. Performance of the hard drive

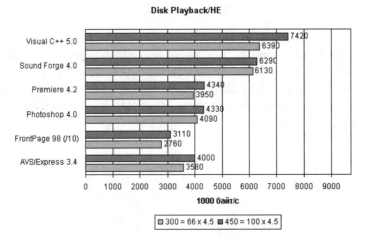

Fig. 19.38. Disk/Playback/HE test results

Test Results

	300 MHz = 66 MHz × 4.5	450 MHz = 100 MHz × 4.5
Business Disk WinMark 99 (1,000 bytes/sec)	1,910	1,940

continues

Continued

	300 MHz = 66 MHz × 4.5	450 MHz = 100 MHz × 4.5
High-End Disk WinMark 99 (1,000 bytes/sec)	5,630	5,930
FPU Mark	1,540	2,310

Disk Playback/HE Test Results (1000 bytes/sec)

	300 MHz= 66 MHz × 4.5	450 MHz = 100 MHz × 4.5
AVS/Express 3.4	3,580	4,000
FrontPage 98	27,600	31,100
Photoshop 4.0	4,090	4,330
Premiere 4.2	3,950	4,340
Sound Forge 4.0	6,130	6,290
Visual C++ 5.0	6,390	7,420

Computers with iPentium II 333 Processors

The Intel Pentium II 333 MHz processor is relatively popular among users. This processor shows fairly good results when tested and is a worthy representative of Pentium II processors.

As for an overclocked Intel Pentium 333 MHz, its processor shows fairly good results. It seems that it can be overclocked to 416 MHz (5×83).

In certain motherboards that support a high host bus frequency (92 or 95 MHz, for example), you will sometimes be able to overclock the processor to 460 MHz. But if you do decide to go through with this, you absolutely must use additional cooling equipment for the processor and the other components of the computer.

Overclocking the processor was done by increasing the frequency of the host bus from 66 to 95 MHz. When using such high frequencies as 83, 92, and 95 MHz the computer was not stable. At frequencies of 92 and 95 MHz the system often produced errors during testing, even with the additional cooling. The stability of the processor was attained by increasing the voltage to the processor by 0.1 V.

WinBench 98 was used for testing.

Results of Overclocking a Pentium II 333 Processor

Overclocking parameters	CPUMark32	FPUMark
$333 = 5 \times 66$	850	1,700
$375 = 5 \times 75$	950	1,950
$416 = 5 \times 83$	1,050	2,150
$460 = 5 \times 92$	1,200	2,400
$475 = 5 \times 95$	1,250	2,500

The test results show considerable system performance growth as a result of overclocking the processor. However, as was mentioned above, the system was not stable at frequencies of 83, 92, and 95 MHz (416, 460, and 475 MHz, respectively).

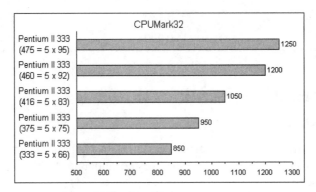

Fig. 19.39. CPUMark 32 test results

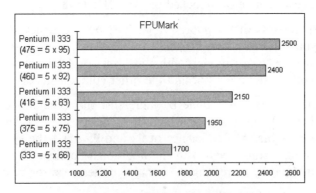

Fig. 19.40. FPUMark test results

The optimal and recommended configuration is 375 MHz = 5×75 MHz without increasing the voltage to the processor, and 416 MHz = 5×83 MHz if the voltage is increased.

As when overclocking any processor, you must make sure the processor is sufficiently and effectively cooled.

Results of Overclocking a Computer with the iPentium III 500 Processor

The CT-6BTM motherboard supports standard frequencies of 66/100 MHz. When overclocking, the following frequencies are possible: 68/75/83/103/112/113 MHz. The WinBench 99 v1.1, Norton Utilities, and Quake2 test packages were used in testing. The test results are illustrated in the appropriate graphs (Figs. 19.41—19.43).

Results of Overclocking a Pentium III 500 Processor

Overclocking parameters	CPUMark99	SI Norton Utilities 4.0	Quake2
500 = 5 × 100	38.3	230	64.5
515 = 5 × 103	39.5	236	64.7
560 = 5 × 112	42.9	260	65.2

The processor has proven itself to be stable in all of the overclocking modes shown without having to raise the voltage to the processor.

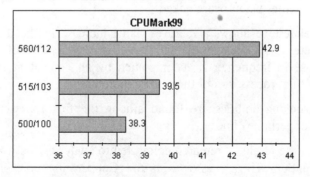

Fig. 19.41. CPUMark99 test results

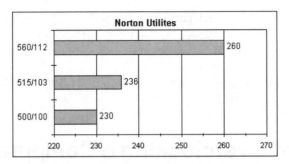

Fig. 19.42. SI Norton Utilities 4.0 test results

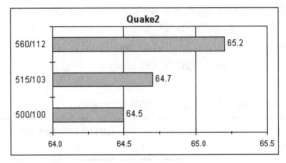

Fig. 19.43. Quake 2 test results

Overclocking Computers with Pentium III (Coppermine) Processors

Pentium III 500 processors with the Coppermine core use 0.18-micron technology and are characterized by not only their relatively high performance, but also by their extensive abilities when overclocked.

Its technological reserve allows a relatively large increase in the frequency of the FSB, which determines the external and internal frequencies of the processor. Such an increase in frequency is accompanied by an equivalent increase in the performance of the processor, and thus, the computer.

The best overclocking abilities are found among the first representatives of the Pentium III (Coppermine) line.

Found below are the results of research connected to analyzing the work of the high-performance Pentium III processor with the Coppermine core in overclocking modes.

Computers with Pentium III 500E Processors

Configuration of the System Used in Testing

❑ Motherboard: Abit BE6-II (i440BX AGPset chipset).

❑ Processor: Intel Pentium III 500E (Coppermine core, 256 KB L2 cache memory that works at the processor frequency, recommended frequency for the processor bus — 100 MHz, voltage to the core — 1.6 V, FC-PGA, the processor is connected to the motherboard through a Slot 1 — Socket 370 adapter).

❑ Hard drive: IBM DPTA-372050 (20 GB, 2 MB cache memory, UltraDMA/66).

❑ RAM: 128 MB, PC100.

❑ Video adapter: ASUS AGP-V3800 TV (TNT2 video chipset, 32 MB video memory).

❑ CD-ROM: ASUS CD-S400/A (40x).

❑ OS: Windows 98 with UDMA/66 hard drive controller drivers installed.

Overclocking

Setting the overclocking mode is done in BIOS Setup by increasing the frequency of the processor bus. The standard core voltage at all frequencies is 1.6 V. The order of changing the settings and the choice of parameters is illustrated in Figs. 19.44—19.46.

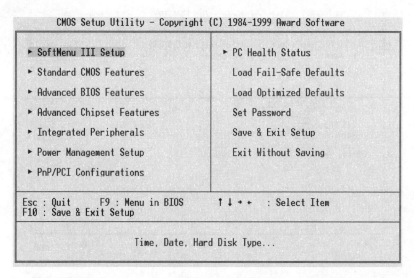

Fig. 19.44. Items on the BIOS Setup's SoftMenu III Setup menu

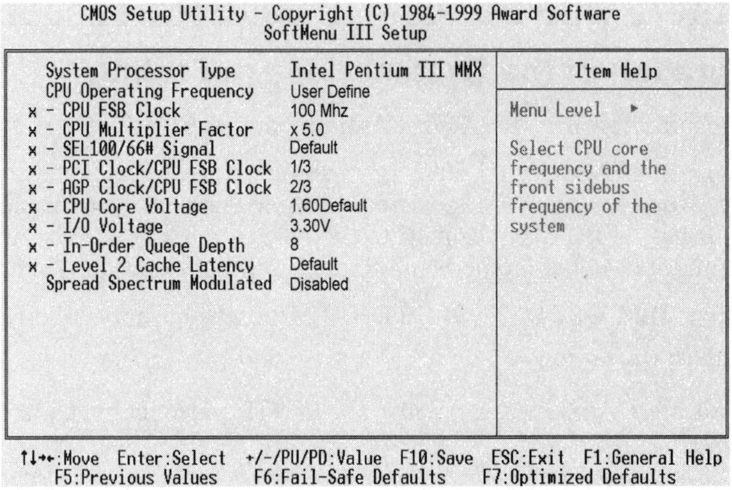

Fig. 19.45. Setting the recommended parameters in SoftMenu III Setup

Testing

Testing programs from the WinBench 99 (v1.1) test package were used, more specifically, CPUMark99 and FPU WinMark. The test results are shown in the table and in Figs. 19.47 and 19.48.

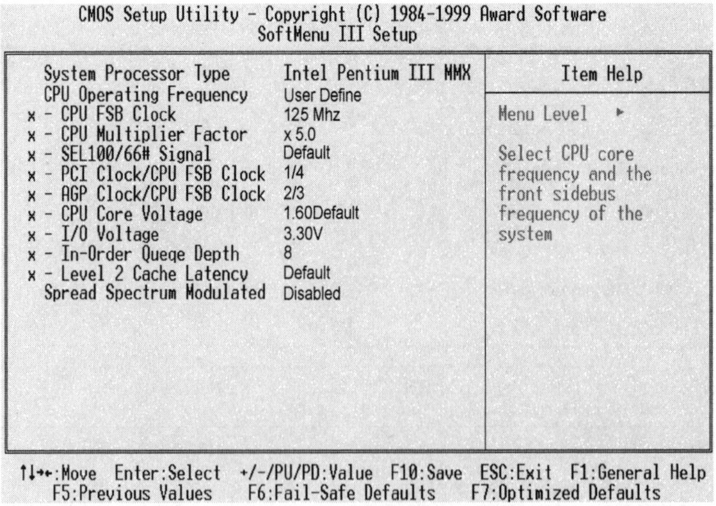

Fig. 19.46. An example of setting the overclocking parameters in SoftMenu III Setup

Test Results

Processor	Frequency of the FSB, MHz	Frequency of the CPU, MHz	CPUmark 99	FPU WinMark
Pentium III 500E	100	$500 = 100 \times 5.0$	41.9	2,700
Pentium III 500E	120	$600 = 120 \times 5.0$	50.2	3,255
Pentium III 500E	125	$625 = 125 \times 5.0$	52.1	3,373
Pentium III 500E	135	$675 = 135 \times 5.0$	56.1	3,636
Pentium III 500E	140	$700 = 140 \times 5.0$	58.5	3,781

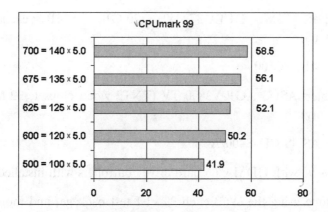

Fig. 19.47. Test results

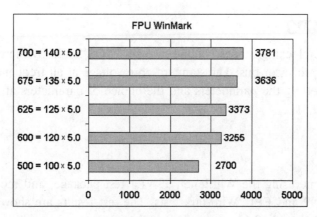

Fig. 19.48. Test results

Computers with Pentium III 550E Processors

Configuration of the System Used in Testing

❑ Motherboard: Abit BE6-II (i440BX AGPset chipset).

❑ Processor: Intel Pentium III 550E (Coppermine core, L2 — 256 KB cache memory that works at the frequency of the processor, recommended processor bus frequency — 100 Hz, voltage to the core — 1.65 V, in box, pack date 01/28/2000, version A13433-001, made in Malaysia, S-Spec — SL3V5).

❑ Hard drive: IBM DPTA-372050 (20 GB, 2 MB cache memory, UltraDMA/66).

❑ RAM: 128 MB, PC100.

❑ Video adapter: ASUS AGP-V3800 TV (TNT2 video chipset, 32 MB SGRAM video memory).

❑ CD-ROM: ASUS CD-S400/A (40x).

❑ S: Windows 98 with UDMA/66 hard drive controllers with installed drivers.

Testing was done using the WinBench 99 v1.1 test package, and more specifically the CPUMark99 and FPU WinMark tests.

Overclocking

Setting the overclocking modes is done through BIOS Setup by increasing the frequency of the processor bus. The standard core voltage at all frequencies is 1.65 V. The order of setting the parameters and the choice of parameters are illustrated in Figs. 19.49—19.51.

Testing

Testing was done using the WinBench 99 v1.1 test package, and more specifically the CPUMark99 and FPU WinMark tests. The test results are shown in the table and in Figs. 19.52 and 19.53.

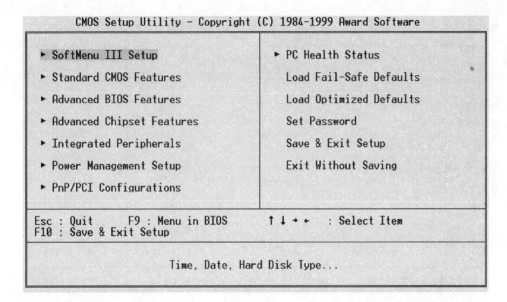

Fig. 19.49. Items on the BIOS Setup SoftMenu III Setup menu

```
CMOS Setup Utility - Copyright (C) 1984-1999 Award Software
                    SoftMenu III Setup
┌───────────────────────────────────────────────────────┬─────────────────┐
│ System Processor Type        Intel Pentium III MMX     │   Item Help     │
│ CPU Operating Frequency      User Define               │                 │
│ x - CPU FSB Clock            100 Mhz                    │ Menu Level   ▶  │
│ x - CPU Multiplier Factor    x 5.5                      │                 │
│ x - SEL100/66# Signal        Default                   │ Select CPU core │
│ x - PCI Clock/CPU FSB Clock  1/3                        │ frequency and the│
│ x - AGP Clock/CPU FSB Clock  2/3                        │ front sidebus   │
│ x - CPU Core Voltage         1.65Default               │ frequency of the│
│ x - I/O Voltage              3.30V                      │ system          │
│ x - In-Order Quege Depth     8                          │                 │
│ x - Level 2 Cache Latency    Default                   │                 │
│ Spread Spectrum Modulated    Disabled                  │                 │
└───────────────────────────────────────────────────────┴─────────────────┘
↑↓→←:Move  Enter:Select  +/-/PU/PD:Value  F10:Save  ESC:Exit  F1:General Help
       F5:Previous Values      F6:Fail-Safe Defaults    F7:Optimized Defaults
```

Fig. 19.50. Setting the recommended parameters in SoftMenu III Setup

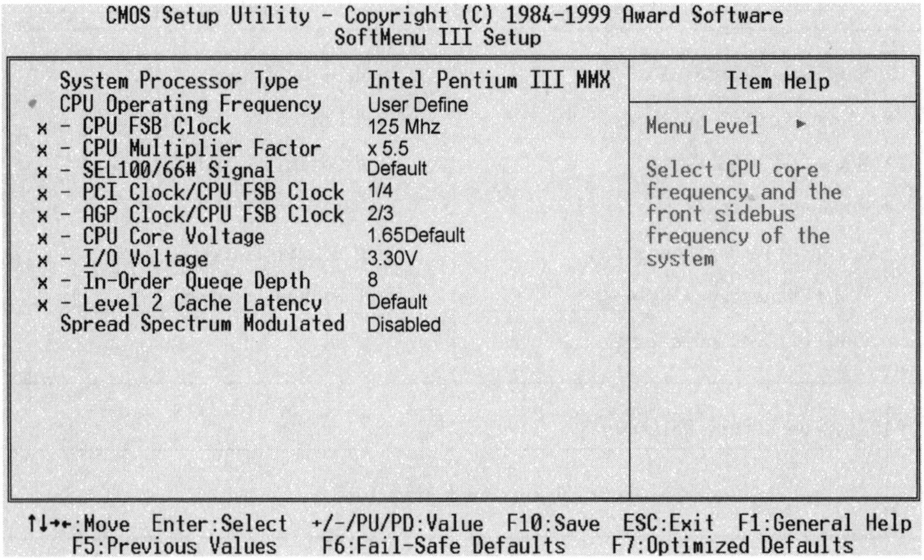

```
         CMOS Setup Utility - Copyright (C) 1984-1999 Award Software
                           SoftMenu III Setup
   ┌────────────────────────────────────────────────┬──────────────────────┐
   │   System Processor Type    Intel Pentium III MMX │      Item Help       │
 • │   CPU Operating Frequency  User Define           │                      │
   │ x - CPU FSB Clock          125 Mhz               │ Menu Level    ►      │
   │ x - CPU Multiplier Factor  x 5.5                 │                      │
   │ x - SEL100/66# Signal      Default               │ Select CPU core      │
   │ x - PCI Clock/CPU FSB Clock 1/4                  │ frequency and the    │
   │ x - AGP Clock/CPU FSB Clock 2/3                  │ front sidebus        │
   │ x - CPU Core Voltage       1.65Default           │ frequency of the     │
   │ x - I/O Voltage            3.30V                 │ system               │
   │ x - In-Order Queqe Depth   8                     │                      │
   │ x - Level 2 Cache Latency  Default               │                      │
   │   Spread Spectrum Modulated Disabled             │                      │
   │                                                  │                      │
   └────────────────────────────────────────────────┴──────────────────────┘
   ↑↓→←:Move  Enter:Select  +/-/PU/PD:Value  F10:Save  ESC:Exit  F1:General Help
       F5:Previous Values      F6:Fail-Safe Defaults    F7:Optimized Defaults
```

Fig. 19.51. An example of setting the overclocking parameters in SoftMenu III Setup

Test Results

Processor	Frequency of the FSB, MHz	Frequency of the CPU, MHz	CPUmark 99	FPU WinMark
Pentium III 550E	100	$550 = 100 \times 5.5$	46.1	2,970
Pentium III 550E	120	$660 = 120 \times 5.5$	55.2	3,580
Pentium III 550E	125	$688 = 125 \times 5.5$	57.3	3,710
Pentium III 550E	135	$743 = 135 \times 5.5$	61.7	4,000
Pentium III 550E	140	$770 = 140 \times 5.5$	64.3	4,160

The test results presented show the existence of a significant technological reserve in the Intel Pentium 500E and Intel Pentium 550E processors, the architecture of which is based on the use of the new Coppermine core and of a cache memory that works at the full frequency of the processor core and is characterized by a perfected work algorithm (256-bit Advanced Transfer Cache).

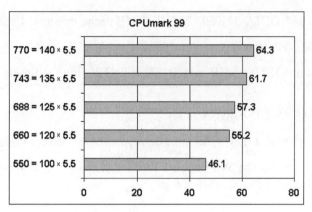

Fig. 19.52. Test results

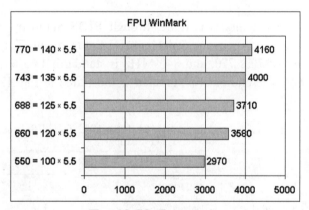

Fig. 19.53. Test results

Computers with Pentium III 700E Processors

Configuration of the System Used in Testing

❑ Motherboard: Abit BE6-II (i440BX AGPset chipset).

❑ Processor: Intel Pentium III 700E (Coppermine core, 256 KB L2 cache memory that works at the frequency of the processor, recommended frequency of the processor bus — 100 MHz, core voltage — 1.65 V, in box, FC-PGA (connected through an adapter), pack date 04/27/2000, version A15753-001, S-Spec — SL45Y).

❑ Hard drive: IBM DPTA-372050 (20 GB, 2 MB cache memory, UltraDMA/66).

❑ RAM: 128 MB, PC100.

❑ Video adapter: ASUS AGP-V3800 TV (TNT2 video chipset, 32 MB video memory).

❑ CD-ROM: ASUS CD-S400/A (40x).

❑ S: Windows 98 with UDMA/66 hard drive controller drivers installed.

Testing was done using the WinBench 99 v1.1 test package, and more specifically the CPUMark99 and FPU WinMark tests.

Overclocking

Setting the overclocking modes is done through BIOS Setup by raising the frequency of the processor bus in the SoftMenu III Setup menu. The voltage of the core at frequencies of 700, 770, and 840 MHz is standard, 1.65 V; at a frequency of 910 MHz, 1.7 V. The choice of parameters is illustrated in Fig. 19.54.

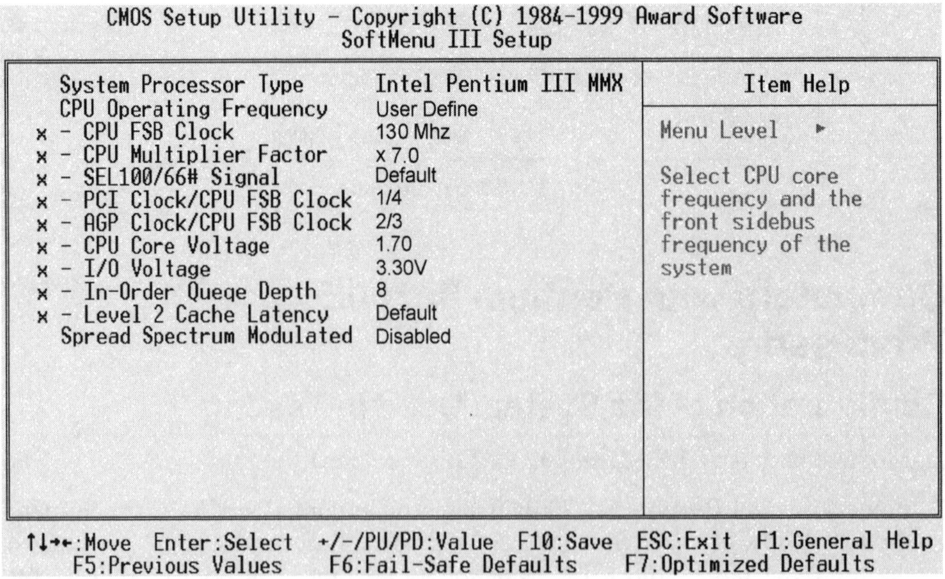

```
        CMOS Setup Utility - Copyright (C) 1984-1999 Award Software
                        SoftMenu III Setup
   ┌─────────────────────────────────────────────────┬──────────────────┐
   │  System Processor Type   Intel Pentium III MMX   │    Item Help     │
   │  CPU Operating Frequency  User Define             ├──────────────────┤
   │  x - CPU FSB Clock        130 Mhz                 │  Menu Level  ►   │
   │  x - CPU Multiplier Factor x 7.0                  │                  │
   │  x - SEL100/66# Signal    Default                 │  Select CPU core │
   │  x - PCI Clock/CPU FSB Clock 1/4                  │  frequency and the│
   │  x - AGP Clock/CPU FSB Clock 2/3                  │  front sidebus   │
   │  x - CPU Core Voltage     1.70                    │  frequency of the│
   │  x - I/O Voltage          3.30V                   │  system          │
   │  x - In-Order Queqe Depth 8                       │                  │
   │  x - Level 2 Cache Latency Default                │                  │
   │  Spread Spectrum Modulated Disabled               │                  │
   │                                                   │                  │
   └─────────────────────────────────────────────────┴──────────────────┘
   ↑↓→←:Move  Enter:Select  +/-/PU/PD:Value  F10:Save  ESC:Exit  F1:General Help
        F5:Previous Values   F6:Fail-Safe Defaults   F7:Optimized Defaults
```

Fig. 19.54. An example of setting the overclocking parameters in SoftMenu III Setup

Testing

Testing was done using the WinBench 99 v1.1 test package, and more specifically the CPUMark99 and FPU WinMark tests. The test results are shown in the table and in Figs. 19.55 and 19.56.

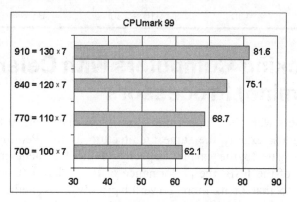

Fig. 19.55. Test results

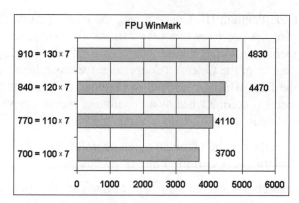

Fig. 19.56. Test results

Test Results

Processor	Frequency of the FSB, MHz	Frequency of the CPU, MHz	CPUmark 99	FPU WinMark
Pentium III 700	100	$700 = 100 \times 7$	62.1	3,700
Pentium III 770	110	$770 = 110 \times 7$	68.7	4,110

continues

Continued

Processor	Frequency of the FSB, MHz	Frequency of the CPU, MHz	CPUmark 99	FPU WinMark
Pentium III 770	120	$840 = 12 \times 7$	75.1	4,470
Pentium III 770	130	$910 = 130 \times 7$	81.6	4,830

Overclocking Computers with Celeron (Coppermine) Processors

Celeron processors with the Coppermine core, developed with 0.18-micron technology, have almost exactly the same architecture as the Pentium III (Coppermine). However, due to the smaller capacity of the L2 cache memory and the lower frequency of the FSB, the performance of the Celeron (Coppermine) processor is inferior to that of its more powerful prototype. Nonetheless, as with the Pentium III (Coppermine) processors, it does have a relatively high performance level and many functional abilities in overclocking modes.

As is the case with the Pentium III (Coppermine), the multiplier that gives the internal, working frequency of the processor using the external frequency, has a fixed value in the Celeron (Coppermine). Changing the multiplier is impossible. However, the existing technological reserve of the Celeron (Coppermine) allows a high value to be set for the frequency of the FSB, which determines the external and internal frequency of the processor. This process is accompanied by an equivalent rise in the performance of the processor, and therefore in the performance of the entire system.

Particularly good results can be obtained when overclocking one of the first representatives of the Celeron (Coppermine) line of processors.

The results of research connected with the analysis of the functioning of high-performance Celeron (Coppermine) processors in overclocking modes are presented below.

Computers with Celeron 533 Processors

Configuration of the System Used in Testing

❑ Motherboard: Abit BE6-II (i440BX AGPset chipset).

❑ Processor: Intel Celeron 533 (Coppermine core, L2 cache memory — 128 KB that works at the frequency of the processor, standard frequency of the FSB — 66 MHz,

SL46S, made in Malaysia, the processor is connected to the motherboard through the Slot 1 — Socket 370 adapter).

❏ Means of supporting necessary temperature conditions: a powerful heatsink and fan were used to cool the processor.

❏ RAM: 128 MB DIMM PC133 SDRAM.

❏ Hard drive: Western Digital 6.4 GB.

❏ Video adapter: MSI MS-8809 GeForce.

❏ CD-ROM: ASUS CD-S400/A (40x).

❏ S: Windows 98.

The programs used in testing are: SiSoft Sandra 2000 Professional, 3Dmark 2000, and Quake 3 (demol).

Overclocking

In the process of overclocking, the frequency of the system bus was raised from 66 to 100 MHz. Thanks to the standard abilities of the motherboard created on the basis of the i440BX chipset, the work of the hard drive, the video adapter, and other components was able to be performed in a normal mode where the multiplier for the AGP bus is 2/3, and the multiplier for the PCI bus is 1/3.

In accordance with the set parameters, the working frequency of the processor is 800 MHz, for the video adapter — 66 MHz, for the hard drive and the other PCI devices — 33 MHz.

The frequency of the FSB was later increased to 104 MHz, and the frequency of the processor thus became 832 MHz.

SiSoft Sandra Test Results

Processor	Frequency of the FSB, MHz	Frequency of the CPU, MHz	CPU	FPU	MMX Integer	MMX FPU
Celeron 533	66	533	1,389	658	1,547	2,131
Celeron 533	100	800	2,093	1,023	2,419	3,269
Celeron 533	104	832	2,227	1,069	2,522	3,407

3DMark 2000 Test Results

Processor	Frequency of the FSB, MHz	Frequency of the CPU, MHz	3DMark
Celeron 533	66	533	3,166
Celeron 533	100	800	3,987
Celeron 533	104	832	4,037

The test results are presented in the tables and in Figs. 19.57—19.60.

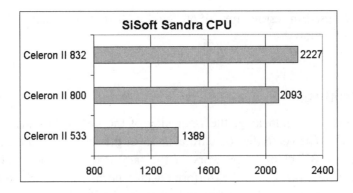

Fig. 19.57. SiSoft Sandra CPU test results

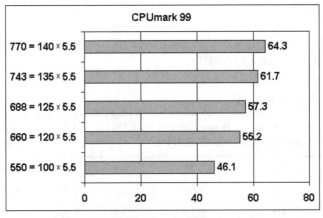

Fig. 19.58. CPUmark 99 test results

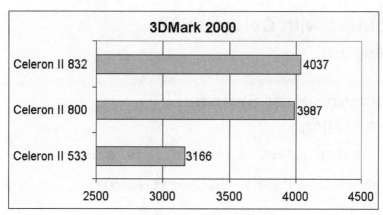

Fig. 19.59. 3D Mark 2000 test results

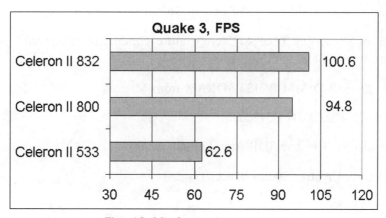

Fig. 19.60. Quake 3 test results

Quake 3 Test Results

Processor	Frequency of the FSB, MHz	Frequency of the CPU, MHz	FPS
Celeron 533	66	533	62.6
Celeron 533	100	800	94.8
Celeron 533	104	832	100.6

Computers with Celeron 667 Processors

Configuration of the System Used in Testing

From the material at and with the permission of **www.ixbt.com**.

❑ Motherboard: ASUS P3B-F (i440BX AGPset chipset).

❑ Processor: Intel Celeron 667 (Coppermine core, L2 cache memory — 128 KB that works at the frequency of the processor, standard frequency of the FSB — 66 MHz, core voltage — 1.65 V, the processor is connected to the motherboard through an ASUS S370 — 133 Slot 1 — Socket 370 adapter).

❑ Means of supporting necessary temperature conditions: a powerful heat sink and fan from Golden Orb was used.

❑ RAM: 256 MB DIMM PC133 SDRAM from Micron.

❑ Hard drive: IBM DJNA 372200.

❑ Video adapter: Creative 3DBlaster Annihilator Pro.

❑ Sound card: Creative Sound Blaster Live!.

❑ S: Windows 98.

Overclocking

In the process of overclocking, the frequency of the processor bus was increased from 66 to 100 MHz.

In accordance with the parameters set, the working frequency of the processor is 1000 MHz, for the video adapter — 66 MHz, and for the hard drive and the other PCI components — 33 MHz.

Results of testing are shown in the table on page 435 and in Figs. 19.61—19.64.

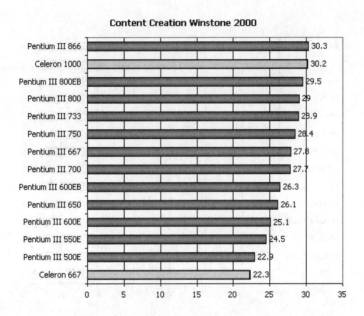

Fig. 19.61. Content Creation Winstone 2000 test results

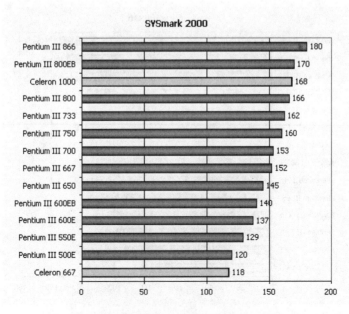

Fig. 19.62. SYSmark 2000 test results

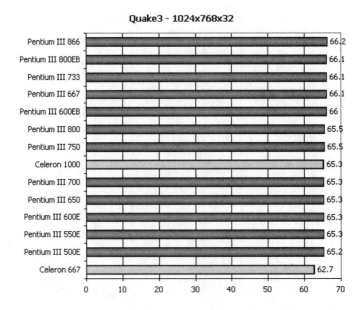

Fig. 19.63. Quake3 (1024x768x32) test results

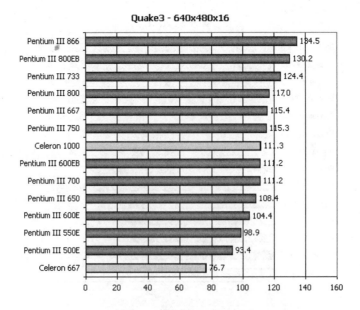

Fig. 19.64. Quake3 (640x480x16) test results

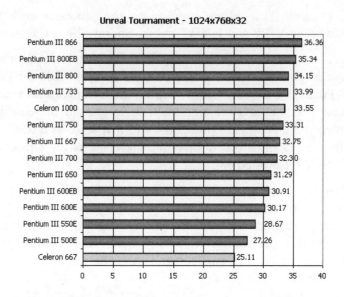

Fig. 19.65. Unreal Tournament (1024x768x32) test results

Test Results

Proces-sor	Frequency of the FSB, MHz	Frequency of the CPU, MHz	Content Creation Winstone 2000	SYSmark 2000	Quake3 1024×768×32	Quake3 640×468×16	Unreal Tournament 1024×768×32
Celeron 667	66	667	22.3	118	62.7	76.7	25.11
Celeron 667	100	1,000	30.2	168	65.3	111.3	33.55

Oveclocking Computers with iPentium 4 (Willamette) Processors

Pentium 4 processors based on the Willamette core are manufactured using 0.18 μm technology. They are based on the Intel NetBurst micro-architecture using the Quad Pumped Bus as the processor's FSB.

Pentium 4 processors with the Willamette core are supplied in two FCPGA (Flip Chip Pin Grid Array) constructive variants, providing for the usage of Socket 423 and Socket 478 slots. The voltage supplied to the processor core (Vcore) for Socket 423 processors is 1.7 and 1.75 V, and for Socket 478 processors is 1.75 V.

Improved core architecture and technology, optimized while developing the previous generation of products with the Coppermine core, provide for the high performance of Pentium 4 processors. The significant technological reserve of these processors can in many cases be implemented by careful overclocking. Special chipsets developed for Pentium 4 processors and that serve as a basis for their respective motherboards allow you to take full advantage of the new core architecture and high technological potential.

However, when planning overclocking (considering both the advantages and drawbacks of such an approach), it is necessary to take into account the fact that, like their predecessors, Pentium 4 processors are supplied with fixed frequency multipliers. Because of this, processor overclocking is performed exclusively by increasing the FSB clock frequency, and, consequently, the frequency modes of other hardware components.

For successful overclocking, it is advisable to use the appropriate motherboards. Such motherboards must provide built-in overclocking tools, including hardware monitoring, and be compatible withthe slot of the selected processors (Socket 423 and Socket 478). High-quality motherboards allow you to significantly increase the Pentium 4's performance. For example, for models intended to run at 1.7 GHz (Socket 478), correct overclocking allows you to increase the processor's performance by 20%. Quite often, some models intended for running at 1.4 GHz (Socket 478) can be overclocked by even 25—30%. However, you should always remember that the overclocking potential depends not only on the working modes and the processor model, but also on the specific instance of the product.

The tables provided below list the results of overclocking several instances of Pentium 4 1.4 GHz and Pentium 4 1.7 GHz.

Pentium 4 1.4 GHz

Processor marking	Maximum stable frequency
SL59U-MALAY-L130A673-0772	1,679
SL59U-MALAY-L130A673-1037	1,679
SL59U-MALAY-L130A673-1056	1,917

continues

Continued

Processor marking	Maximum stable frequency
SL59U-MALAY-L130A673-0774	1,750
SL59U-MALAY-L130A673-0780	1,680
SL59U-MALAY-L130A673-1034	1,610
SL59U-MALAY-L130A673-0840	1,792
SL59U-MALAY-L130A673-0771	1,680
SL59U-MALAY-L130A673-0777	1,750
SLSTG-L129B272-0226 Malay	2,100
SLSTG-L129B272-0223 Malay	2,100
SLSTG-L129B272-0222 Malay	2,100

Pentium 4 1.7 GHz

Processor marking	Maximum stable frequency
SL59X-MALAY-L132A473-0683	2,090
SL59X-MALAY-L132A473-0105	1,955
SL59X-MALAY-L132A473-0686	1,955
SL5TK-CostaR-3141A265-1341	2,040
SL5TK-CostaR-3141A265-1344	2,041

Computers with Pentium 4 1.7 GHz Processors

Configuration of the System Used in Testing

❑ Motherboard: ASUS P4T (i850 chipset, BIOS 1004 Final from 30.03.2001)

❑ Processor: Intel Pentium 4 1.7 GHz (Willamette core, L1 — 8 KB, L2 — 256 KB cache memory that works at the frequency of the processor, recommended processor bus frequency — 100 MHz and 400 MHz Data Bus, voltage to the core — 1.75 V, Socket 423).

❑ Hard drive: IBM Deskstar 75GXP (45 GB, 2 MB cache memory, 7200 RPM, Ultra ATA/100.

❑ RAM: Buffalo PC800 2x128 MB ECC RDRAM.

❑ Video adapter: NVIDIA GeForce3 64 MB (core: 200 MHz; memory: 230 MHz DDR).

❑ CD-ROM: ASUS CD-S400/A (40x).

❑ S: Windows 2000 Professional (SP1).

Overclocking

Setting the overclocking modes is done by increasing the frequency of the processor bus.

Testing

Testing was done using the 3DMark 2001, Business Winstone 2001, and SYSmark 2000 test packages. The test results are shown in the following tables and in Figs. 19.66—19.68.

FSB frequency, MHz	Processor frequency, GHz	Business Winstone 2001
100	1.700 = 100 x 17	48.3
120	2.040 = 120 x 17	51.1

FSB frequency, MHz	Processor frequency, GHz	SYSmark 2000 Windows Media Encoder 4
100	1.700 = 100 x 17	361
120	2.040 = 120 x 17	393

FSB frequency, MHz	Processor frequency, GHz	3DMark 2001
100	1.700 = 100 x 17	5,696
120	2.040 = 120 x 17	5,757

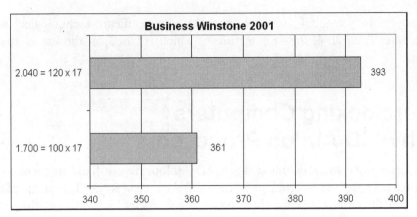

Fig. 19.66. The Business Winstone 2001 test results

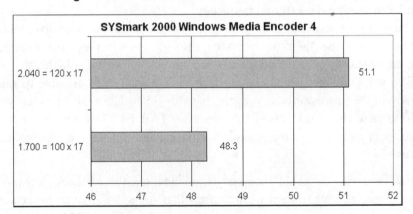

Fig. 19.67. The SYSmark 2000 test results

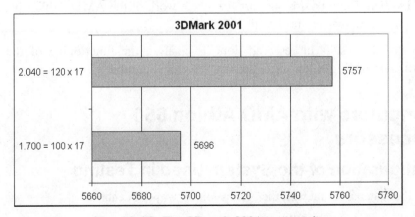

Fig. 19.68. The 3Dmark 2001 test results

The test results presented show the existence of a significant technological reserve in the Intel Pentium 4, the architecture of which is based on the use of the Willamette.

Overclocking Computers with AMD Athlon Processors

All modern processors, including the AMD Athlon, have a fixed frequency multiplier that connects the internal and external frequencies. Regardless of the fact that it can actually be changed for these types of processors by modifying the resistors or by using the technological socket, overclocking modes are reached for the AMD Athlon by increasing the external frequency.

AMD Athlon processors have a significantly large technological reserve, which allows you to increase their performance through overclocking, for example, by raising the frequency of the FSB EV6 processor bus. However, a high value for the FSB EV6 will limit the overclocking possibilities. Usually you are able to raise the frequency of the processor bus no more than 10—15%. The limit to which you will be able to raise the frequency of the processor FSB EV6 bus and, of course, the subsequent growth in the computer performance, depend on the type of motherboard used.

In accordance with the peculiarities of its architecture, the AMD Athlon processor requires a special motherboard with chipsets that support the given processor. Examples are the following motherboards: ASUS K7V, ASUS K7M, and the Gigabyte GA-7IX. These boards support the stable work of the AMD Athlon processor if the voltage sources are no less than 235 W.

Below are the results of research done to analyze the functioning of the high-performance AMD Athlon processors in overclocking modes.

Computers with AMD Athlon 650 Processors

Configuration of the System Used in Testing

From the material at and with the permission of **www.ixbt.com**.

❑ Motherboard: ASUS K7M (AMD 751+VT82C686A).

❏ Processor: AMD Athlon 650 (L1 cache memory — 128 KB, 512 KB L2 cache memory on the processor's chip that works at the frequency of the processor's core, standard FSB EV6 clock frequency — 100 MHz and data transfer at 200 MHz, core voltage — 1.6 V, Slot A).

❏ RAM: 128 MB PC100 SDRAM from SEC (CAS2).

❏ Hard drive: IBM DJNA 372200.

❏ Video adapter: Chaintech Desperado AGP-RI40 (NVIDIA Riva TNT2, 16 MB SDRAM).

❏ Sound card: Creative Sound Blaster Live!.

❏ S: Windows 98.

Overclocking

In the process of overclocking, the frequency of the system bus was increased from 100 to 110 MHz. The subsequently increased clock frequency led to the system working unstably, which was probably connected to the particular features of the architecture of the EV6 processor bus and the AMD 751 chip.

The test results are shown in the table (p. 442) and in Fig. 19.69.

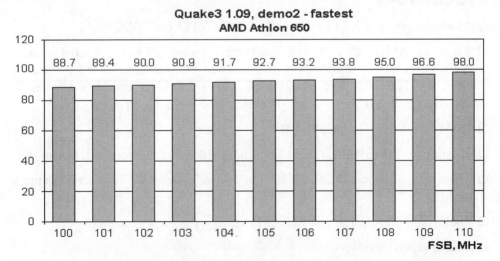

Fig. 19.69. Quake3 1.09, demo2-fastest test results for the AMD Athlon 650

Test Results

Processor	Frequency of the FSB, MHz	Frequency of the CPU, MHz	Quake3 1.09, demo2-fastest	Winstone 99
AMD Athlon 650	100	650	88.7	28.7
AMD Athlon 650	101	657	89.4	—
AMD Athlon 650	102	663	90	—
AMD Athlon 650	103	670	90.9	—
AMD Athlon 650	104	676	91.7	—
AMD Athlon 650	105	683	92.7	—
AMD Athlon 650	106	689	93.2	—
AMD Athlon 650	107	696	93.8	—
AMD Athlon 650	108	702	95	—
AMD Athlon 650	109	709	96.6	—
AMD Athlon 650	110	715	98	—

Computers with AMD Athlon 700 (Thunderbird) Processors

❑ Motherboard: Abit KT7 (VIA Apollo KT133, VT8363+VT82C686A).

❑ Processor: AMD Athlon 700 (L1 cache memory — 128 KB, 256 KB L2 cache memory on the processor's chip that works at the frequency of the processor's core, standard FSB EV6 clock frequency — 100 MHz and data transfer at 200 MHz, core voltage — 1.7 V, Socket A (462 pins).

❑ RAM: 128 MB, SDRAM, PC100.

❑ Hard drive: IBM DPTA-372050 (20 GB, 2 MB cache memory, UDMA/66).

❑ Video adapter: Asus AGP-V3800 TV (video chipset TNT2, video memory 32 MB).

❑ Sound card: Creative Sound Blaster Live!.

❑ Source power: 250 W.

❑ S: Windows 98 Second Edition.

Processor

The tested processor is shown in Fig. 19.70.

Fig. 19.70. The tested AMD Athlon (Thunderbird) processor

Main Parameters of the Abit KT7 Motherboard Important for Overclocking

The Abit KT7 motherboard used in testing is shown in Fig. 19.71.

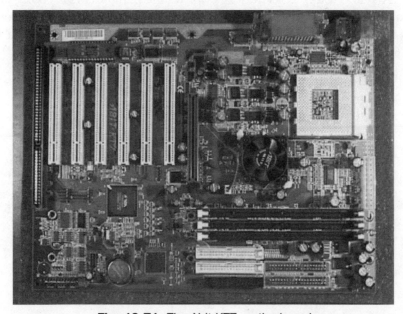

Fig. 19.71. The Abit KT7 motherboard

The main parameters of this motherboard are listed below:

❏ Processors: AMD Athlon (Thunderbird) and AMD Duron. Processor slot: Socket A (462). Standard FSB frequency — 100 MHz.

❏ Overclocking: via BIOS Setup — 100, 101, 103, 105, 107, 110, 112, 115, 117, 120, 122, 124, 127, 133, 136, 140, 145, 150, 155 MHz.

❏ Core voltage: 1.1—1.85 V with an increment of 0.25 V.

❏ Changing the multiplier: via BIOS Setup.

❏ Chipset: VIA Apollo KT133 (VT8363+VT82C686A).

❏ RAM: up to 1.5 GB in 3 DIMM (168 pins, 3.3 V) PC100/133 SDRAM, frequency — 100/133 MHz.

❏ BIOS: Award Plug and Play BIOS.

Testing Facilities

Tests: WinBench 99 (CPUmark 99 and FPU WinMark).

Cooling Facilities

The TITAN TTC-D2T cooler was used for testing purposes. This cooler provides efficient cooling for AMD Athlon (Thunderbird) and AMD Duron processors. Fan control was performed by built-in hardware monitoring facilities provided by the VT82C686A chip.

Fig. 19.72. The Titan TTC-D2T cooler

Control over the processor temperature is maintained using the solid-state temperature sensor at the motherboard and built-in hardware monitoring facilities.

Fig. 19.73. The solid-state temperature sensor at the motherboard

Overclocking Processors via Increasing the FSB Frequency

Selection of the clock frequency of the FSB is performed using BIOS Setup. In the course of tests, the FSB frequency was increased up to 115 MHz. Listed below are testing results for the processors overclocked by increasing the FSB frequency.

AMD Athlon Overclocking Results (Abit KT7 Motherboard)

Processor frequency = bus frequency x multiplier	CPUmark 99	FPU WinMark
700 = 100 x 7	64.7	3,810
770 = 110 x 7	71.2	4,190
784 = 112 x 7	72.5	4,270

Overclocking Processors by Changing Multipliers

As a matter of fact, Athlon (Thunderbird) processors are supplied with a fixed frequency multiplier. The Abit KT7 motherboard used in the testing process, however, provides the ability to change this multiplier. Despite the fact that for some time AMD has been limiting this capability by cutting the L1 bridges at the surface of the processor case, these bridges were not cut in the processor instance used in testing.

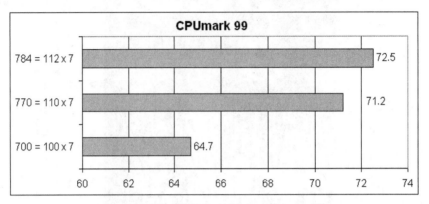

Fig. 19.74. CPUmark 99 testing results
(overclocking by increasing the FSB frequency)

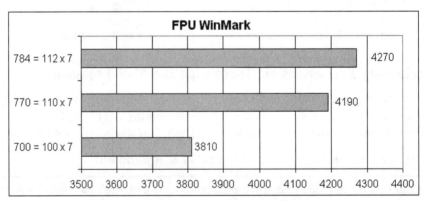

Fig. 19.75. FPU WinMark testing results
(overclocking by increasing the FSB frequency)

Thus, the instance of the AMD Athlon (Thunderbird) processor did not require the procedure of restoring these bridges, as you can see from the photo (Fig. 19.76).

Notice that selection of the overclocking parameters is performed by the built-in BIOS Setup functionality via SoftMenu. The results of overclocking and the modes selected are presented in the tables and diagrams below.

Fig. 19.76. Intact L1 bridges at the surface of the Athlon processor case

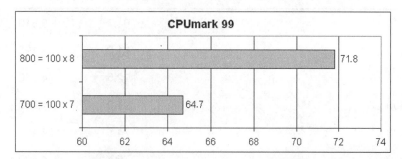

Fig. 19.77. CPUmark 99 testing results (overclocking via multiplier)

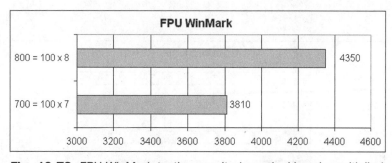

Fig. 19.78. FPU WinMark testing results (overclocking via multiplier)

Overclocking of the Athlon Processor (Abit KT7 Motherboard)

Processor frequency = bus frequency x multiplier	CPUmark 99	FPU WinMark
700 = 100 x 7	64.7	3,810
800 = 100 x 8	71.8	4,350

Overclocking via the Bus and Multiplier

It should be mentioned that maximum performance levels can be achieved by selecting optimal frequencies for the FSB at appropriate values of the frequency multiplier.

The results of AMD Athlon overclocking are presented below. Despite the fact that the AMD Athlon processor was overclocked only up to 825 MHz, the overall performance of the system was improved significantly.

Overclocking of AMD (Abit KT7 Motherboard)

Processor frequency = bus frequency x multiplier	CPUmark 99	FPU WinMark
700 = 100 x 7	64.7	3,810
770 = 110 x 7	71.2	4,190
784 = 112 x 7	72.5	4,270
800 = 100 x 8	71.8	4,350
824 = 103 x 8	74.5	4,490
825 = 110 x 7.5	75.4	4,490

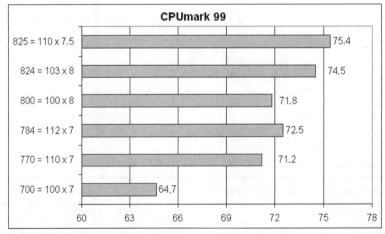

Fig. 19.79. CPUmark 99 testing results (overclocking via the bus and multiplier)

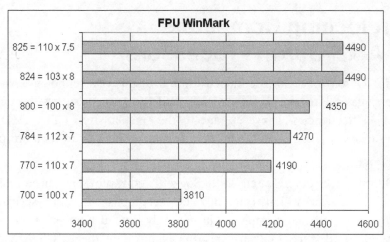

Fig. 19.80. FPU WinMark testing results (overclocking via the bus and multiplier)

Voltages and Temperatures in the Course of AMD Athlon Overclocking (Abit KT7 Motherboard)

Processor frequency = bus frequency x multiplier	Voltage, V	Temperature, °C
700 = 100 x 7	1.7	44
800 = 100 x 8	1.75	45
824 = 103 x 8	1.8	49
825 = 110 x 7.5	1.8	49

AMD Athlon Overclocking (Abit KT7 Motherboard)

Parameters	Voltage, V	POST procedure	Windows	Winbench
800 = 100 x 8	1.7	Ok	Halt	
	1.725	Ok	Ok	Halt
	1.75	Ok	Ok	Ok
840 = 105 x 8	1.8	No		
840 = 112 x 7.5	1.8	No		

Overclocking Computers with AMD Duron Processors

The AMD Duron processor, developed using 0.18-micron technology, has practically the same architecture as the AMD Thunderbird, and also has the same EV6 bus working frequencies. However, due to the smaller size of the AMD Duron L2 cache memory, the AMD Duron performance is inferior to its more powerful prototype.

AMD Duron processors, released in the Socket A construct, have fixed multipliers, the modification of which can only be accomplished using special hardware/software means that support a still relatively limited number of motherboard types. As expected, this ability will also be included in the ASUS A7V and the QDI K7T motherboards. For this reason, overclocking AMD processors is done, generally, by increasing the clock frequency of the processor bus.

The peculiar features of the EV6 bus and the architecture of the existing motherboards, regardless of the technological reserve within the AMD Duron processors, do not allow you to reach a significantly higher clock frequency. Usually you won't be able to increase it by more than 10% of the standard frequency. This process is accompanied by an equivalent growth in the performance of the processor, and thus, of the entire computer.

Presented below are the results of research connected with analyzing the abilities of the functioning of high-performance AMD Duron processors in overclocking modes.

Computers with AMD Duron-650 Processors

Configuration of the System Used in Testing

❏ Motherboard: Gigabyte GA-7ZM (VIA Apollo KT133 chipset).

❏ Processor: AMD Duron 650 (L1 cache memory — 128 KB, L1 cache memory — 64 KB that works at the full frequency of the processor, Standard FSB clock frequency— 100 MHz, core voltage — 1.5 V, Socket A).

❏ RAM: 128 MB DIMM PC133 SDRAM.

❏ Hard drive: IBM DJNA 372200.

❏ Video adapter: Creative 3DBlaster Annihilator Pro.

❏ Sound card Creative Sound Blaster Live!.

❏ S: Windows 98.

Overclocking

In the process of overclocking, the frequency of the system bus was gradually increased from 100 to 110 MHz. Further raising of the clock frequency of the bus led to the system working unstably, probably mostly connected to the particular features of the architecture of the EV6 processor bus and the VIA Apollo KT133 chipset, the basis around which the motherboard used was created.

The test results are presented in the table and in Figs. 19.81 and 19.82.

Test Results

Processor	Frequency of the FSB, MHz	Frequency of the CPU, MHz	CPUmark 99	FPU WinMark
AMD Duron 650	100	650	55	3,520
AMD Duron 650	105	683	58	3,695
AMD Duron 650	110	715	61	3,870

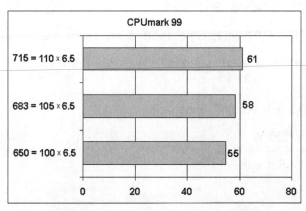

Fig. 19.81. CPUmark 99 test results

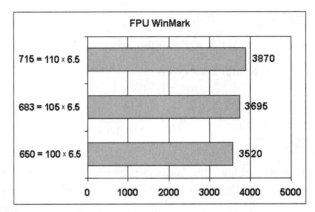

Fig. 19.82. FPU WinMark test results

Computers with AMD Duron 600 Processors

❏ Motherboard 1: Abit KT7 (VIA Apollo KT133, VT8363+VT82C686A)

❏ Motherboard 2: Soltek SL-75KV+ (VIA Apollo KT133, VT8363+VT82C686A)

❏ Processor: AMD Duron 600 (L1 cache memory — 128 KB, 64 KB L2 cache memory on the processor's chip that works at the frequency of the processor's core, standard FSB EV6 clock frequency — 100 MHz and data transfer at 200 Hz, core voltage — 1.5 V, Socket A (462 pins).

❏ RAM: 128 MB, SDRAM, PC100.

❏ Hard drive: IBM DPTA-372050 (20 GB, 2 MB cache memory, UDMA/66).

❏ Video adapter: Asus AGP-V3800 TV (TNT2 video chipset, video memory 32 MB).

❏ Sound card: Creative Sound Blaster Live!.

❏ Source power: 250 W.

❏ S: Windows 98 Second Edition.

Processor

The AMD Duron 600 processor used in testing is shown in Fig. 19.83.

Fig. 19.83. The AMD Duron 600 processor

Main Parameters of the Motherboard Important for Overclocking

Soltek SL-75KV+

The Soltek SL-75KV+ motherboard used in the testing procedure is shown in Fig. 19.84.

Fig. 19.84. Photo of the Soltek SL-75KV+ motherboard

❏ Processors: AMD Athlon (Thunderbird) and AMD Duron. Processor slot: Socket A (462 pins). Nominal value of the FSB frequency — 100 MHz.

❏ Overclocking: via DIP switches — 100, 103, 105, 110, 112, 115, 120, 124, 133.3, 140, 150 MHz, via BIOS Setup — 100, 103, 105, 112, 115, 120, 124 MHz.

❏ Core voltage: 1.5–1.85 V with an increment of 0.25 V.

❏ Multiplier settings: via DIP switches.

❏ Chipset: VIA Apollo KT133 (VT8363+VT82C686A).

❏ RAM: up to 768 MB in 3 DIMM (168 pins, 3.3 V), frequency — 100/133 MHz.

❏ BIOS: Award Plug and Play BIOS.

Abit KT7

The Abit KT7 motherboard used in testing is shown in Fig. 19.85.

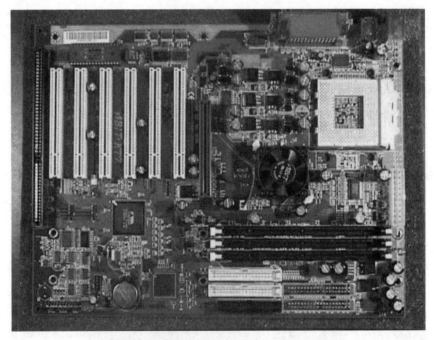

Fig. 19.85. The Abit KT7 motherboard

❏ Processors: AMD Athlon (Thunderbird) and AMD Duron. Processor slot: Socket A (462 pins). Nominal FSB frequency — 100 MHz.

❏ Overclocking: via BIOS Setup — 100, 101, 103, 105, 107, 110, 112, 115, 117, 120, 122, 124, 127, 133, 136, 140, 145, 150, 155 MHz.

❏ Core voltage: 1.1−1.85 V with an increment of 0.25 V.

❏ Multiplier setting: via BIOS Setup.

❏ Chipset: VIA Apollo KT133 (VT8363+VT82C686A).

❏ RAM: up to 1.5 GB in 3 DIMM (168 pins, 3.3 V) PC100/133 SDRAM, frequency — 100/133 MHz.

❏ BIOS: Award Plug and Play BIOS.

Testing Facilities

Test: WinBench 99 (CPUmark 99 and FPU WinMark).

Cooling Facilities

The TITAN TTC-D2T cooler (Fig. 19.86) was used as a cooling facility. This cooler provides efficient cooling for the AMD Athlon (Thunderbird) and AMD Duron processors. Control over the cooler was maintained using the built-in hardware monitoring tools and the VT82C686A chip.

Fig. 19.86. The TITAN TTC-D2T cooler

Control over the processor temperature was maintained using temperature sensors (a flexible one for SL-75KV+, and a solid state sensor for Abit KT7) and built-in hardware monitoring tools.

Fig. 19.87. Flexible temperature sensor on the SL-75KV+ motherboard

Fig. 19.88. The solid-state temperature sensor on the Abit KT7 motherboard

Overclocking the Processor by Increasing the FSB Frequency

When using the Soltek SL-75KV+ motherboard, the FSB frequency is selected using one of the two DIP switches (SW1), which is highlighted in the SL-75KV+ motherboard photo (Fig. 19.89), or via BIOS Setup.

Fig. 19.89. DIP switches on the SL-75KV+ motherboard (SW1 is highlighted)

For Abit KT7, frequency selection is performed via SoftMenu in BIOS Setup. Better overclocking results were obtained for the Abit KT7 motherboard: we were able to raise the bus frequency up to 115 MHz.

The Results of Duron Overclocking (Abit KT7 Motherboard)

Processor frequency = bus frequency x multiplier	CPUmark 99	FPU WinMark
600 = 100 x 6	51.4	3,260
672 = 112 x 6	57.8	3,660
690 = 115 x 6	59.4	3,760

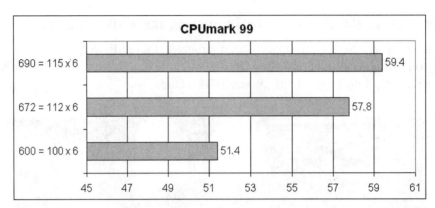

Fig. 19.90. CPUmark 99 testing results (overclocking via the bus, Abit KT7)

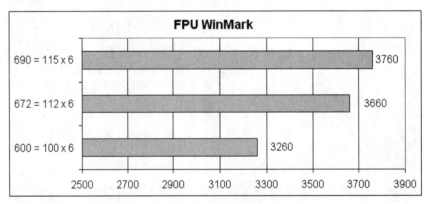

Fig. 19.91. FPU WinMark testing results (overclocking via the bus, Abit KT7)

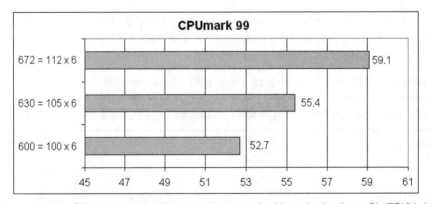

Fig. 19.92. CPUmark 99 testing results (overclocking via the bus, SL-75KV+)

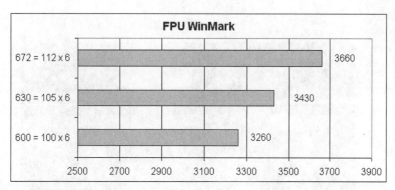

Fig. 19.93. FPU WinMark testing results (overclocking via the bus, SL-75KV+)

AMD Duron Overclocking (SL-75KV+ Motherboard)

Processor frequency = bus frequency x multiplier	CPUmark 99	FPU WinMark
600 = 100 x 6	52.7	3,260
630 = 105 x 6	55.4	3,430
672 = 112 x 6	59.1	3,660

Overclocking Processors via Changing Multipliers

It is well-known that practically all modern processors are supplied with fixed frequency multipliers. Despite this fact, when dealing with AMD processors, some motherboards, such as Soltek SL-75KV+ or Abit KT7, still provide the capability of changing these multipliers. However, this is only true for processors with uninterrupted L1 bridges (which can be found at the surface of the processor case).

You can restore the capabilities of changing the frequency multiplier by restoring the L1 bridges cut by the vendor. This operation can be easily performed using a sharp soft pencil (as a matter of fact, graphite is quite a good conductor). Take the pencil rub the grapgite between the interrupted contacts, trying to press the graphite particles into the gaps to produce small bulges. When doing so, avoid connecting the neighboring bridges. To provide better visual control, use a strong magnifying glass, and make sure that your working place is well lighted. Also, take care to provide for the electrostatic safety of the processor.

The results of restoring the conductivity of the L1 bridges are shown in the photographs provided below. These illustrations show fragments of the AMD Duron surface.

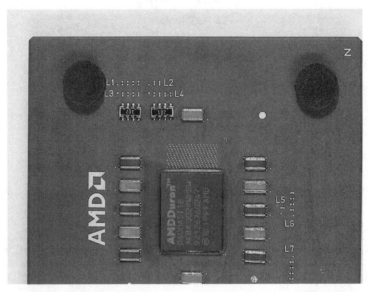

Fig. 19.94. Initial state of the L1 bridges at the surface of the AMD Duron processor

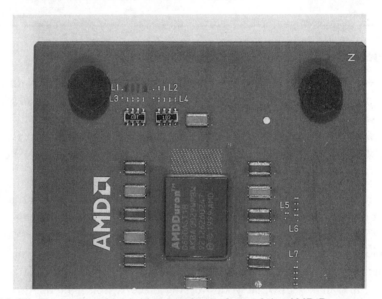

Fig. 19.95. The restored L1 bridges at the surface of the AMD Duron processor

After restoring the cut bridges on the AMD Duron, you'll be able to change the frequency multiplier using built-in hardware facilities and software tools provided by certain motherboards.

Selection of the frequency multiplier value when using the Soltek SL-75KV+ motherboard is performed using the appropriate DIP switch, highlighted in the Soltek SL-75KV+ motherboard photo (Fig. 19.96).

Fig. 19.96. DIP switches on the SL-75KV+ motherboard (SW2 highlighted)

Overclocking results and selected modes are presented in the tables and diagrams provided below.

AMD Duron Overclocking Results (Abit KT7 Motherboard)

Processor frequency = bus frequency x multiplier	CPUmark 99	FPU WinMark
600 = 100 x 6	51.4	3,260
650 = 100 x 6.5	55	3,550
700 = 100 x 7	57.6	3,810
800 = 100 x 8	63.2	4,350
850 = 100 x 8.5	65.8	4,640
900 = 100 x 9	68.3	4,900

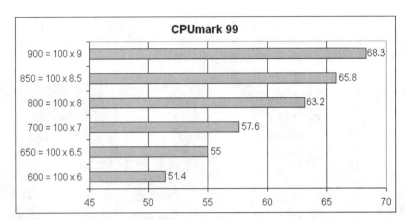

Fig. 19.97. CPUmark 99 testing results (overclocking via the multiplier, Abit KT7)

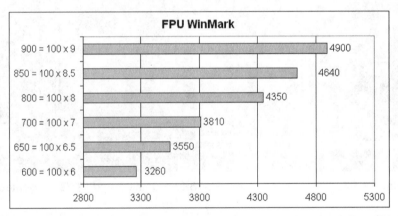

Fig. 19.98. FPU WinMark testing results (overclocking via the multiplier, Abit KT7)

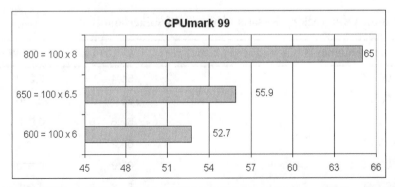

Fig. 19.99. CPUmark 99 testing results (overclocking via the multiplier, SL-75KV+)

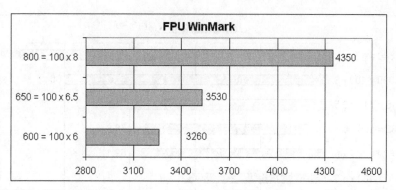

Fig. 19.100. FPU WinMark testing results (overclocking via the multiplier, SL-75KV+)

AMD Duron Overclocking (the SL-75KV+ Motherboard)

Processor frequency = bus frequency x Multiplier	CPUmark 99	FPU WinMark
600 = 100 x 6	52.7	3,260
650 = 100 x 6.5	55.9	3,530
800 = 100 x 8	65	4,350

Overclocking via Both the Bus and the Multiplier

It is necessary to point out that maximum performance levels can be achieved by selecting optimal bus frequencies for the appropriate multiplier values.

The results of overclocking using this combined method for both motherboards used in testing are shown below.

AMD Duron Overclocking (Soltek SL-75KV+)

Processor frequency = bus frequency x multiplier	CPUmark 99	FPU WinMark
600 = 100 x 6	52.7	3,260
630 = 105 x 6	55.4	3,430
650 = 100 x 6.5	55.9	3,530
672 = 112 x 6	59.1	3,660
683 = 105 x 6.5	58.8	3,720
715 = 110 x 6.5	61.6	3,890
800 = 100 x 8	65	4,350
840 = 105 x 8	68.4	4,580

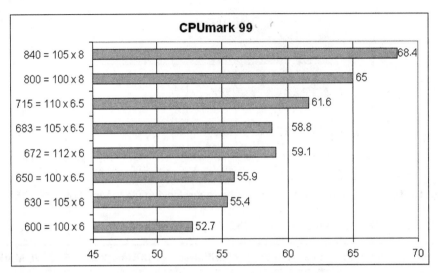

Fig. 19.101. CPUmark 99 testing results
(overclocking using both the bus and the multiplier, SL-75KV+)

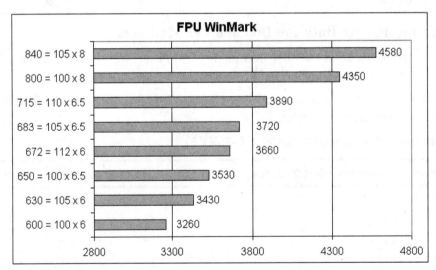

Fig. 19.102. FPU WinMark testing results
(overclocking via the bus and the multiplier, SL-75KV+)

Here, maximum performance is achieved at the maximum value of the multiplier and the maximum bus frequency.

AMD Duron Overclocking (Abit KT7 Motherboard)

Processor frequency = bus frequency x multiplier	CPUmark 99	FPU WinMark
600 = 100 x 6	51.4	3,260
650 = 100 x 6.5	55	3,550
672 = 112 x 6	57.8	3,660
683 = 105 x 6.5	57.4	3,720
690 = 115 x 6	59.4	3,760
700 = 100 x 7	57.6	3,810
715 = 110 x 6.5	60.2	3,890
748 = 115 x 6.5	63.2	4,080
770 = 110 x 7	63.5	4,190
800 = 100 x 8	63.2	4,350
840 = 105 x 8	66.7	4,580
850 = 100 x 8.5	65.8	4,640
880 = 110 x 8	69.9	4,790
893 = 105 x 8.5	69.4	4,860
896 = 112 x 8	71.2	4,880
900 = 100 x 9	68.3	4,900
910 = 107 x 8.5	70.9	4,980

For the Abit KT7, we were able to achieve better results — the processor frequency has increased by more than 1.5 times. Maximum performance of operations with integer numbers is achieved when using the 896 MHz = 112 MHz x 8 mode. The highest performance with floating-point calculations was achieved at a frequency of 910 MHz.

It must be emphasized that it was impossible to achieve high frequency values without increasing the voltage supplied to the processor core and input/output circuits. The following table summarizes the voltage and temperature modes during overclocking.

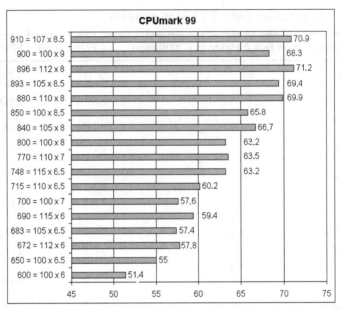

Fig. 19.103. CPUmark 99 testing results
(overclocking via the bus and the multiplier, Abit KT7)

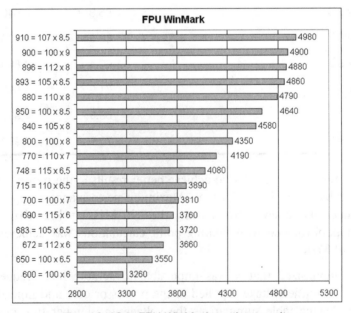

Fig. 19.104. FPU WinMark testing results
(overclocking both the bus and the multiplier, Abit KT7)

Voltage and Temperature Modes During AMD Duron Overclocking (Abit KT7)

Processor frequency = bus frequency x multiplier	Core voltage / I/O, V	Temperature, °C
600 = 100 x 6	1.5 / 3.3	37
770 = 110 x 7	1.6 / 3.4	41
850 = 100 x 8.5	1.65 / 3.4	44
880 = 110 x 8	1.7 / 3.4	47
893 = 105 x 8.5	1.7 / 3.4	48
900 = 100 x 9	1.75 / 3.4	50
910 = 107 x 8.5	1.75 / 3.4	50

Voltage and Temperature Modes During AMD Duron Overclocking (Soltek SL-75KV+)

Processor frequency = bus frequency x multiplier	Core voltage / I/O, V	Temperature, °C
600 = 100 x 6	1.5 / 3.3	37
840 = 105 x 8	1.6 / 3.4	43

Some overclocking attempts failed: the Power-On Self Test (POST) routine could not complete successfully — either the operating system could not load or the system froze during the test. All modes in which at least the POST routine completed successfully are listed in the table provided below. According to the data presented in this table, it follows that in most cases, the instability problem could be solved by increasing the voltage supplied to the processor. Obviously, further increase of the processor core voltage could allow us to achieve even higher processor clock frequencies. However, this also increases the risk of processor failure.

AMD Duron Overclocking (Abit KT7 Motherboard)

Parameters	Voltage, V	POST	Windows	Winbench
893 = 110 x 8.5	1.65	Ok	Halt - IOS error	
	1.675	Ok	Halt	
	1.7	Ok	Ok	Ok
800 = 100 x 9	1.7	Ok	Ok	Halt
	1.75	Ok	Ok	Ok
927 = 103 x 9	1.75	Ok	Halt	
935 = 110 x 8.5	1.75	Ok	Halt	

Chapter 20

Web Addresses

When tuning and optimizing your computer, and especially when planning and executing the overclocking process, consult the manuals supplied with the computer, the motherboard, and other elements and subsystems. It's also useful to acquaint yourself with certain Internet sites listed below.

❑ **Optimization and overclocking**

www.tomshardware.com   www.anandtech.com

www.sysopt.com   www.award.com

www.kryotech.com   www.chaintech.com.tw

www.hwupgrade.com   www.sysdoc.pair.com

www.gamers.com   www.ixbt.com

ixbt.stack.net   www.digit-life.com

www.xbitlabs.com

❑ **Cooling methods and devices**

ixbt.stack.net/~termoscope   www.kryotech.com

www.heatsink-guide.com   www.tomshardware.com

www.aptekus.com   www.avc.com.tw

www.bergquistcompany.com   www.computernerd.com

www.coolermaster.com   www.dynatron-corp.com

www.etrinet.com   www.globalwin.com.tw

www.iercdya.com   www.indek.com

www.isjm.com/tst/heatsink   www.melcor.com

www.sanyodenki.co.jp   www.sunon.com

www.tennmax.com   www.thermalloy.com

www.thermalnet.com   www.titan-cd.com

www.wakefield.com   www.ixbt.com

www.xbitlabs.com   www.digit-life.com

❑ **Web addresses: technical data on elements**

Processors and chipsets

www.intel.com   www.cyrix.com

developer.intel.com   www.chips.ibm.com

www.amd.com   www.ixbt.com

www.ibm.com   www.tomshardware.com

www.idt.com

www.winchip.com

www.ali.com.tw

www.viatech.com

www.xbitlabs.com

Motherboards

www.abit.com.tw

www.asus.com

www.acer.com

www.airwebs.com

www.chaintech.com.tw

www.ixbt.com

users.deltanet.com

www.aopen.com.tw

www.bcmcom.com

www.computersources.com.hk

www.dfiusa.com

www.dfi.com

www.ecs.com.tw

www.epox.com

www.fic.com.tw

www.fugu.com.tw

www.giga-byte.com

www.intel.com

www.iwillusa.com

www.jbond.com

www.lucky-star.com.tw

www.micronics.com

www.mpl.ch

www.mtiusa.com

www.nexgen.com

www.opti.com

www.pcpartner.com.hk

www.pinegroup.com

www.premiopc.com

www.qdi.nl

www.via.com.tw

www.opti.com

www.sis.com.tw

www.anandtech.com

www.digit-life.com

www.asus.com.tw

www.acorp.com.tw

www.achme.com

www.anandtech.com

www.tomshardware.com

josstech.com

www.atrend.com.tw

www.arvida.ca

www.biostar.com.tw

www.dataexpert.com

www.dtk.com

www.dfiusa.com

www.ecsusa.com

www.fica.com

www.freetech.com

www.genoasys.com

www.gigabyte.com.tw

www.iwill.com.tw

www.j-mark.com

www.jetway.com.tw

www.mei.micron.com

www.mitac.com.tw

www.msi.com.tw

www.mycomp-tmc.com

www.ocean-usa.com

www.pcchips.com

www.pcware.com

www.premiopc.com

www.qdigrp.com

www.san-li.com.tw

```
www.soyo.com
www.soyo.com.tw
www.shuttlegroup.com
www.taken.com.tw
www.tyan.com
www.zida.com
www.xbitlabs.com
```

```
www.spacewalker.com
www.supermicro.com
www.ttitech.com
www.vextrec.com
www1.magic-pro.com.hk
www.digit-life.com
```

Video adapters and video chipsets

```
www.3dfx.com
www.asus.com
www.atrend.com.tw
www.aceshardware.com
www.cirrus.com
www.diamondmm.com
www.intel.com
www.matrox.com
www.s3.com
www.tomshardware.com
www.tseng.com
```

```
www.asus.com.tw
www.atitech.ca
www.anandtech.com
www.chaintech.com.tw
www.diamond.com
www.hercules.com
www.ixbt.com
www.orchid.com
www.stb.com
www.tridentmicro.com
www.digit-life.com
```

Hard drives

```
www.storage.ibm.com
www.fujitsu-europe.com
www.maxtor.com
www.wdc.com
www.xbitlabs.com
```

```
www.fujitsu.com
www.quantum.com
www.seagate.com
www.ixbt.com
www.digit-life.com
```

INDEX

3

3D WinBench, 90
3DNow!, 218
3D WinBench 98, 284

8

82430HX, 292

A

Abit, 80, 107, 171, 305
  BE6, 171, 308
  BE6-II, 83, 103, 171, 172, 308
  BF6, 309
  BH6, 171, 171, 309
  BX6, 171
  KT7, 240, 309
  KT7A, 311
  KT7-RAID, 309
Acorp, 108
ACPI, 309, 319
Advanced Chipset Setup, 9, 163
Advanced Dynamic Execution
  Engine technology, 205
Advanced transfer cache, 200, 205
AGB Aperture Size, 11, 67
AGP, 11, 152, 280
  bus speed, 201

bus, 153
  modes, 66
AGP/CLK, 11
AGP2x mode, 66
AGTL+, 280
  bus, 219
Ali, 322
Alpha EV6, 280
  bus, 219, 235
Am486DX4/100, 215
AMD Athlon, 6, 101, 158, 218
  alternative overclocking methods,
    220
  modifying resistors, 221
  overclocking device, 227
  overclocking results, 440
AMD Duron, 101, 159, 233, 327
  overclocking results, 450
AMD K5, 157
AMD K6, 157, 217
AMD Thunderbird, 159, 233, 235,
  327
AMD, 2, 169, 215, 39, 90
Amdcpuid utility, 255
AMD K6-2, 218
AMD K6-III, 218
AOpen, 108
APM, 309
Archive, self-extracting, 82
Arithmetic Logic Unit, 205
ASUS CUSL2, 313

Live Music on Your PC

E. Medvedev, V. Trusova

At present, more and more musicians are looking for tools and ways to create computer music similar to "live" music. This comprehensive reference meets their needs. Written for both professional and home-hobbyist musicians, this book contains professional notes, tips, and tricks explaining how to turn your personal computer into a virtual studio with the ability to create an entire musical project (up to AUDIO CD). This in-depth reference focuses on multitrack recording and mastering music and sound on your PC. It shows you how to use the rapidly developing technologies making live MIDIs. The chapters progress throughout the book and cover the following topics: live recording with SAWPro in virtual studio; Cool Edit Pro — the universal tool for a home studio; Samplitude 2496 — the high-tech virtual studio; creating live MIDI sound with Cubase VST 24; using Cubase VST 24 and Samplitude 2496 together; mastering with WaveLab 3.0; and tube mastering with T-RackS. This book teaches users about the software's major features, placing emphasis on the realization of non-destructive editing (keeping original music). The methods outlined in this book allow one to store every obtained result, up to the final stage, without losing the quality of the sound.

CD-ROM: A CD-ROM with samples, plug-ins, and complete projects is included.

ISBN: 1-931769-06-0
PRICE: $49.95
PUB DATE: May 2002
PAGES: 704pp
SOFTCOVER: 7.375 x 9.25

Windows .NET Domains & Active Directory

A. Tchekmarev

The book is intended for system administrators who have general knowledge of Windows 2000 or Windows XP/.NET. It opens with basic information vitally important for understanding the Active Directory™ service architecture, as well as for the proper use of this service and many system utilities: the fundamentals of LDAP protocol, Active Directory and DNS interoperation, and Active Directory concepts. The book proceeds with the issues that are the most difficult when deploying Windows .NET domains, including upgrading from Windows NT 4.0 and Windows 2000 domains; planning Active Directory; installing Active Directory and adding domain clients; and monitoring and tuning Active Directory. It describes methods of performing common administrative tasks, as well as how to use various instruments for this purpose: administrative snap-ins, system tools, and scripts. Some of these tasks are: creating directory objects; publishing network resources; searching the directory for various object types; delegating administration; audit; managing user environment; triggering replication; and backing up and restoring Active Directory.

This book focuses on troubleshooting problems that occur *after* deploying Windows .NET domains (i.e. while maintaining Active Directory), as well as system tools that should be used for solving such problems. (Many tools from the *Windows Support Tools* and *Windows Resource Kit* packs are covered.) These topics are highly valuable for administrators, but relatively rarely discussed in computer books. The general characteristics given for system tools help administrators to easily choose the proper instrument for a specific task. The most useful tools' commands are discussed in examples. The following tasks are covered, among many others: verifying domain controllers, directory partitions, and group policy objects; exporting and importing Active Directory objects; reconstructing domains and forests; managing domain trusts; and tuning security.

ISBN: 1-931769-00-1
PRICE: $39.95
PUB DATE: August 2002
PAGES: 560pp
SOFTCOVER: 7.375 x 9.25

The last chapters cover the *Active Directory Service Interfaces* (ADSI), a flexible and powerful instrument for performing various administrative tasks. The chosen narration style helps the non-programmer to learn the main ADSI concepts and to begin to write his/her own scripts. These chapters contain annotated listings of ready-to-use scripts that illustrate programming principles or methods of solving specific administrative tasks. These principles and tasks vary, ranging from simple ones, such as creating users, to complex ones, such as extending the Active Directory schema or managing security descriptors for directories, files, and other system objects.

The book contains a reference on registry keys related to Active Directory, as well as Active Directory objects and attributes that have no user interface, but can be valuable for administrators. The list of frequently asked questions ("How to…?"), placed at the end of the book, helps a reader quickly locate answers to specific tasks. The book also contains a glossary and index.

Web Services Development with Delphi

P. Darakhvelidze, E. Markov

This book focuses on the latest technological standards for creating distributed applications with Delphi and for adding various creations of the individual user. These are rather complex, and capable of radically changing the entire outlook of the average developer. It also discusses the development of data processing using the XML language and creating web services based on it.

In the beginning of the book the reader will find the basics of the Delphi object model, as well as the basic classes and components. Special attention is given to the principles of working with exceptional situations. The next sections deal with working with databases, from A to Z. The authors look at all aspects of working with data — presenting data; local, client-server, and distributed systems; and technologies of accessing data, from BDE to dbExpress and dbGo. Part 6 is dedicated to working with COM objects and interfaces. Here, the reader will find information on how to use ShellAPI and ready ActiveX controls, how to create your own controls,and how to work with Microsoft Transaction Server. Finally, the last two parts of the book concentrate on developing exclusively for the Internet. Part 7 looks at all the hierarchical levels of programming for the World Wide Web — from sockets to high-level protocols like HTTP. A separate chapter is dedicated to the line of Indy components that are used as a basis for the portability of Internet applications between Delphi and Kylix. Part 8 takes a look at technology for e-business applications realized in Delphi 6. The basics of the XML language and the SOAP protocol, and creating web services with its help, are looked at in detail.

In light of this, this book is not a Delphi textbook for beginners: it does not contain the ABCs of programming in a Delphi environment. What it does do is look at modern database technology and inter-program and network interaction in detail. The book is generally intended for an audience of professional developers working in Delphi who are looking for a way to move into the sphere of new programming technology for e-business.

Each chapter of the book is illustrated by at least one or two independent examples of ready applications, and includes material intended for practicing.

CD-ROM: CD-ROM contains client/server applications for Web Services creating with Delphi, SOAP Toolkit, and IBM WebServices Toolkit

ISBN: 1-931769-08-7
PRICE: $49.95
PUB DATE: July 2002
PAGES: 704pp
SOFTCOVER: 7.375 x 9.25